Latin
Made Simple

Rhoda A. Hendricks, M.A.

Revised by **Lisa Padol, M.A.**

Edited and prepared for publication by The Stonesong Press, Inc.

MADE
SIMPLE
BOOKS

A MADE SIMPLE BOOK

DOUBLEDAY

NEW YORK   LONDON   TORONTO   SYDNEY   AUCKLAND

Edited and prepared for publication by The Stonesong Press, Inc.

Executive Editor: Sheree Bykofsky

Series Editor: Sarah Gold

Editor: Peter F. Skinner

Editorial Consultant: Rob Schleifer

Production Consultant: *RECAP:* Publications, Inc.

A MADE SIMPLE BOOK
PUBLISHED BY DOUBLEDAY
a division of Bantam Doubleday Dell Publishing Group, Inc.
1540 Broadway, New York, New York 10036

MADE SIMPLE and DOUBLEDAY are trademarks of Doubleday,
a division of Bantam Doubleday Dell Publishing Group, Inc.

10   9   8   7

Library of Congress Cataloging-in-Publication Data
Hendricks, Rhoda.
     Latin made simple/Rhoda Hendricks; revised by Lisa Padol.
       p.   cm.
     A MADE SIMPLE BOOK
      1. Latin language — Grammar — 1976–   I. Padol, Lisa   II. Title.
PA2087.5.H46   1992
1st ed.
478.2'421 — dc20   91-36614
ISBN 0-385-41339-4   CIP

CONTENTS

About This Book

Although a "classical" language, Latin is vital and living — a pillar of our language, our culture, and our civilization. Latin is a thread that connects us with our own history; if it were to snap, we would lose our relationship to that past.

Fortunately, more and more people are discovering the importance and rewards of learning Latin. We are witnessing a major revival — one which seems likely to continue. As Latin is no longer a spoken language, today's students are primarily interested in being able to *read* Latin, for pleasure and profit, with reasonable facility and comprehension. *Latin Made Simple* was conceived, organized, and written to help others achieve this objective.

The book presents Latin grammar with economy and clarity — and this alone makes it valuable to the reader and student. Of even greater value is the book's focus on the practical *reading* requirements of the non-specialist. We have tried to anticipate your questions, divine your needs, and respond to your most likely interests and concerns.

Latin Made Simple is for the readers and students who want to read the rich treasury of Latin literature, history, law, and religion in the original — since all translations have their failings. The rewards are many and include understanding of innumerable ways in which Latin has nourished and enriched English and become woven into contemporary life. Our coins and bills, the legend on school diplomas, the language of medical prescriptions, and the scores of words and phrases we unconsciously use every day all reflect the continuing vitality of Latin. *Latin Made Simple* is intended for the lively minded and curious, in school or no longer in school, who want to know more about a language and a culture that have done much to shape our own.

Introduction to a Living Language

A BRIEF HISTORY OF LATIN

Latin was one of the many languages spoken in Italy before 200 B.C. Over the next century, it became the common dialect of the peninsula, and developed into a literary language as well as being a spoken one. This we call Classical Latin.

As the Roman Empire expanded, dialects of Latin developed, some giving rise to the Romance languages — Romanian, Italian, Spanish, French, and Portuguese.

One dialect, known as Medieval Latin, was used in the Middle Ages both as a spoken trade language and as a written language. Though extremely similar to Classical Latin, Medieval Latin dispensed with some of the more complex constructions of the latter. Thus, if you learn Classical Latin, you can read Medieval Latin as well.

Until quite recently, the Catholic liturgy used spoken Latin, and today, many churches are attempting to revive its use.

Written Latin never died. Renaissance scholars used it, and today scientists draw new words from it — many of the chemical elements have Latin names. Lawyers and doctors also draw on Latin, and in this book you will learn some of the phrases that they have borrowed.

Latin and English

English is not derived from Latin in the same way as the Romance languages named above, but comes from Anglo-Saxon, a Germanic language.

Nevertheless, Latin has greatly influenced English. When the Normans invaded Britain in A.D. 1066, they brought with them the French language, derived from a Latin dialect. French had an indirect influence on the development of English during the Middle Ages, the period when Chaucer wrote *The Canterbury Tales* and other works.

The Normans also brought Latin to Britain. Latin was Europe's trade language and was also used in church and in official documents. Needed new words were often taken from Latin. Thus, Latin directly influenced the development of English; as borrowing still occurs, Latin continues to influence the development of English.

The Parts of Speech

Latin has the same parts of speech as English, and a clear understanding of them will make it much easier to learn Latin. However, Latin has no articles (*the, a, an*), and we must supply them when translating into English.

Noun — the name of a person, place, or thing, e.g., *Caesar, Rome, town, book.*

Pronoun — a word used instead of a noun, e.g., *he, it.* In the sentence *Caesar wrote a book about the victories he won,* the word *he* is used instead of repeating the word *Caesar; he* replaces *Caesar.*

Adjective — a word that describes a noun or a pronoun, e.g., *good*. In the sentence *I read a good book*, the word *good* describes, or modifies, the noun *book*. An article is a kind of adjective. As mentioned above, Latin does not have articles. A strictly literal translation of **Habeo librum** is *I have book*. For grammatically correct English, you would translate **Habeo librum** as *I have a book*, or as *I have the book*, depending on the context.

Verb — a word that shows action or state of being, e.g., *run, is*.

Adverb — a word that modifies, or describes, a verb, adjective, or adverb, e.g., *quickly, very*. In the sentence *I ran quickly*, the word *quickly* modifies the verb *ran*. In the sentence *The book is very good*, the word *very* modifies the adjective *good*. In the sentence *I ran very quickly*, the word *very* modifies the adverb *quickly*.

Preposition — a word that shows relationship between a noun or pronoun and another word or words, e.g., *in, by, with*. In the sentence *The shirt is in the closet*, the word *in* shows the relationship between the words *shirt* and *closet*.

Conjunction — a word that joins words, phrases, clauses, or sentences, e.g., *and*. In the sentence *He bought milk and bread*, the word *and* joins the words *milk* and *bread*.

Interjection — an exclamation showing emotion, e.g., *oh!*

Inflection

In English, the order of the words in a sentence indicates the meaning of the sentence; in Latin, the spelling of the words (not their order) indicates the meaning.

The man bites the dog. (subject - verb - object)
The dog bites the man. (subject - verb - object)

In both sentences, the word order makes it clear who is doing the biting (the subject) and who is being bitten (the object). However, in Latin, the use of a word as subject or object is indicated by its spelling.

Homo canem mordet.	**Mordet canem homo.**	**Canem mordet homo.**
Canem homo mordet.	**Mordet homo canem.**	**Homo mordet canem.**

All of these sentences mean: *The man bites the dog.*

Hominem canis mordet.	**Mordet canis hominem**	**Canis mordet hominem.**
Canis hominem mordet.	**Mordet hominem canis.**	**Hominem mordet canis.**

All of these sentences mean: *The dog bites the man.*

Homo and **hominem** both mean *man*. **Canis** and **canem** both mean *dog*. The difference in spelling indicates the use of the word as subject or object. Thus:

Homo is used if *man* is the subject of the sentence; **hominem** if *man* is the object; similarly **canis** is used if *dog* is the subject and **canem** if *dog* is the object of the sentence.

The terms *subject* and *object* define nouns in relation to verbs. The verb in this sentence is **mordet**, meaning *bites*. Clearly, the subject is the person or animal doing the biting, and the object is the person or animal being bitten.

In English, the subject usually comes before the verb, and the object usually comes after it. The word order *The man bites the dog* indicates that *man* is the subject and *dog* is the object. The man is doing the biting; the dog is being bitten.

However, in Latin, the word order *The man bites the dog* could mean either that the man is biting the dog or that the dog is biting the man. The spelling (inflection) confirms the meaning. If the sentence reads: **Homo mordet canem**, then the man is biting the dog; if it reads: **Hominem mordet canis**, then the dog is biting the man.

Furthermore, Latin can use word orders not allowed in English. In English, you would never write: *The man the dog bites* or *Bites the dog the man* as these sentences are meaningless; they give no clear indication of who is biting whom. In Latin, this is not a problem. You could write: *Bites the dog the man* with one of two different spellings:

Mordet canis hominem.	This means: *The dog bites the man.*
Mordet canem homo.	This means: *The man bites the dog.*

The change in the spelling of **canis** to **canem** changes the dog from subject to object, and changing **hominem** to **homo** changes man from object to subject, changing the meaning of the sentences. This process of change is called *inflection*. Inflection occurs in English as well as in Latin:

singular:	boy	subject:	I	present:	does
plural:	boys	object:	me	past:	did

You will notice that the Latin spelling change can take place anywhere within the word, and that verbs can be inflected as well as nouns. In the English verb, the change in spelling from *does* to *did* indicates a change in when the action takes place.

In Latin, nouns, pronouns, adjectives, and verbs are inflected. This change in the form or ending of a noun, pronoun, or adjective is called a declension and shows case, number, and gender.

Case indicates whether a word is used as a subject (**homo, canis**), object (**hominem, canem**), or in a different way. The cases have names; e.g., if a noun is used as the subject, it is said to be in the nominative case. Case names will be explained later, in greater detail.

Number shows whether a word is singular (*man*) or plural (*men*). **Homo** and **canem** are both singular.

Gender can be masculine, feminine, or neuter. In Latin, gender can be natural (male or female) or grammatical (based not on sex, but on classification of the word or the spelling of the nominative case). **Homo** is masculine; **femina**, a feminine noun, means *woman;* **canis** may be either masculine or feminine, depending on the sex of the dog.

The change in a verb is called conjugation and shows tense, mood, person, voice, and number. Tense refers to time (past, present, or future); mood to the manner in which a sentence is expressed (statement, question, command); person to the subject (I, you, he, etc.); voice to whether the subject is acting or being acted upon (active or passive); and number to one or more than one (singular or plural).

In **Homo canem mordet**, *The man bites the dog,* the verb is **mordet** or *bites.* It is in the present tense, because the man is biting the dog now. The sentence is a statement, not a command or a question, so is in the indicative mood. The subject is in the third person; therefore, the verb is also in the third person. The man is acting (doing the biting), so the verb is in the active voice. If the sentence was: *The man is bitten by the dog, man* would still be the subject, but the verb, *is bitten,* would be in the passive voice. Finally, since there is only one man, the verb must be singular. **Mordet** is a verb in the third person singular present active indicative. Later, all of these terms will be more fully described and explained.

Latin is a highly inflected language, so the ending of a word is of primary importance and must be considered as carefully as the base of the word, which shows only the basic vocabulary meaning. Inflection will be clearly explained throughout this book and ample practice will be given.

The Alphabet

The Latin and English alphabets are identical, except for lack of **j** and **w** in Latin. Latin uses **i** for both **i** and **j**, and **v** for both **v** and **w**. The letter **k** is used, but rarely and only at the beginning of a word, and **y** and **z** were introduced later, appearing almost exclusively in words taken from Greek.

Pronunciation

Pronunciation is not necessary for reading Latin, but is helpful in comparing Latin words with those of English and other languages. The consonants are pronounced as they are in English, except:

c and **ch** are always like *k*, as in *coop*.

t is always like *t*, as in *tie*, not like *sh*.

g is always hard, as in *go*.

v is always like *w*, as in *woman*.

i-consonant is like *y*, as in *you*.

x is like *x*, as in *xerography, xenophobia*.

s is always *s*, as in *so*, not like *z*.

gu, qu are like *gw, qw*, as in *queen*.

Vowels are either long or short, with a long vowel taking longer to pronounce than a short vowel. There are no fixed rules for the length of vowels and the proper pronunciation can be learned best by paying close attention to the phonetic pronunciation given in the practice below and by listening to a practiced Latin speaker.

The diphthongs (two vowels pronounced as one) are as follows:

ae, pronounced like *ai*, as in *aisle*.

oe, pronounced like *oi*, as in *soil*.

au, pronounced like *ou*, as in *ouch*.

ui, pronounced like *we*.

ei, pronounced like *ei*, as in *eight*.

Syllables

A Latin word contains as many syllables as it has vowels and diphthongs. When dividing a word into syllables:
1. A single consonant (t) is placed with the following vowel: **pa - ter.**
2. Double consonants (tt) are separated: **di - mit - te.**
3. If there are two or more consonants, the first is generally placed with the preceding vowel: **nos - trum.**

Accent

Latin words are accented as follows:
1. On the next-to-last syllable (the penultimate syllable), if it is long:
di - m̄it - te.
2. On the third-to-last syllable (the antepenult), if the next-to-last is short:
ad - v̄e - ni - at.
3. On the first syllable of a two-syllable word:
n̄os - ter.

In general, the accent goes as far back as possible.

Practice In Pronunciation

Practice reading this passage aloud, following the English sound guide, until you can read it clearly and without hesitation. Remember that in Latin every consonant and vowel is pronounced.

Pater noster qui es in caelis
    Pah-*tehr* naws-*tehr quee ehs in* kai-*lees*

Our father who art in heaven,

sanctificetur nomen tuum.
    sahnk-*tih-fih-*kay-*toor* noh-*mehn* too-*uhm.*

hallowed be thy name.

Adveniat regnum tuum.
    *Ahd-*weh-*nee-aht* reg-*nuhm* too-*uhm.*

Thy kingdom come.

Fiat voluntas tua
    Fee-*aht woh-*luhn-*tahs* too-*ah*

Thy will be done

sicut in caelo et terra.
    seek-*uht in* kai-*loh eht in* tehr-*rah.*

on earth as it is in heaven.

Panem nostrum cotidianum
    Pah-*nehm* nohs-*trum* koh-*tee-dee-*ah-*um*

[our daily bread]⌐

da nobis hodie.
    dah noh-*bees* hoh-*dee-ay.*

Give us this day [our daily bread].

Et dimitte nobis debita nostra
    *Eht dee-*miht-*eh* noh-*bees* deh-*biht-ah* naws-*trah*

And forgive us our debts

sicut et nos dimittimus
    seek-*uht eht nohs dee-*miht-*tih-muhs*

as we forgive

debitoribus nostris. Et
    *deh-bih-*taw-*rih-buhs* naws-*trees. Eht*

our debtors. And

nos ne inducas in tentationem
    *nay nohs in-*doo-*kahs in* ten-*tah-tee-*oh-*nehm*

lead us not into temptation,

sed libera nos a malo.
    sehd lee-*beh-rah nohs ah* mah-*loh.*

but deliver us from evil.

Amen.
    ah-*mehn.*

Amen.

First Declension Nouns and First Conjugation Verbs

Word Derivation

1. Many of our English words come directly from Latin, with little or no change in spelling.

animal	**labor**	**captivus**	**fortuna**	**multitudo**	**natio**
animal	labor	captive	fortune	multitude	nation

2. Other words derived from Latin are familiar to us because of their frequent use in the Romance (Roman-based) languages.

LATIN	ITALIAN	FRENCH	SPANISH	PORTUGUESE	ENGLISH
filia	**la figlia**	**la fille**	**la hija**	**a filha**	daughter
vos	**voi**	**vous**	**vosotros**	**vos**	you
bonus	**buono**	**bon**	**bueno**	**bom**	good
terra	**la terra**	**la terre**	**la tierra**	**a terra**	earth

3. A third group of English words comes from Latin in the form of derivatives.

LATIN	ENGLISH	ENGLISH DERIVATIVE
agricola	farmer	agriculture
stella	star	constellation
terra	earth	terrace
filia	daughter	filial

You will find that you are familiar with more Latin than you realized. Watch for Latin words that have come directly or indirectly into English, for English derivatives, and for Latin phrases and expressions in everyday use. These will be brought to your attention throughout the book.

Some Women's Names of Latin Origin and Their Meanings

Rosa	rose	**Regina**	queen	**Flora**	flowers
Victoria	victory	**Gloria**	glory	**Augusta**	majestic
Barbara	foreign	**Viola, Violet**	violet	**Alma**	cherishing
Amabel	lovable	**Clara**	bright	**Letitia**	happiness
Amy	beloved	**Laura**	laurel	**Sylvia**	of the forest
Amanda	worthy of love	**Stella, Estelle**	star	**Gratia, Grace**	grace, gratitude
Beatrice	making happiness	**Celestine**	heavenly	**Miranda**	worthy of admiration

As you study the Reading Grammar in this section, you will see that most of these names end in **-a** because they are feminine and come from the **a-declension**.

Reading Vocabulary

Conjunctions

et (eht), and

Verbs

amo (ah-*moh*), **amare** (*ah*-mah-reh), like, love (amateur)
porto (por-*toh*), **portare** (*por*-tah-*reh*), carry (portage, deportment)
laudo (lou-*doh*), **laudare** (*lou*-dah-*reh*), praise (laudable)
laboro (*lah*-bor-*oh*), **laborare** (*lah-bor-ah-reh*), work (laboratory)
voco (woh-*koh*), **vocare** (*woh*-kah-*reh*), call (vocation, vocative)

THE SIGNS OF THE ZODIAC

The names of the signs of the zodiac are all Latin words, and we can easily remember them by associating their meanings with their pictorial representations.

Aries: the Ram	**Leo**: the Lion	**Sagittarius**: the Archer
Taurus: the Bull	**Virgo**: the Maiden	**Capricorn[us]**: the Goat
Gemini: the Twins	**Libra**: the Scales	**Aquarius**: the Water Bearer
Cancer: the Crab	**Scorpio**: the Scorpion	**Pisces**: the Fishes

THE PLANETS

Many of the planets are named for the Roman deities, such as:

Jupiter from **Iuppiter**	King of the gods	**Mars**	god of War
Saturn from **Saturnus**	god of Sowing	**Neptune** from **Neptunus**	god of the Sea
Mercury from **Mercurius**	the Messenger god	**Pluto**	god of the Lower World
Venus	goddess of Love		

Remember that the names of the signs of the zodiac and the names of the planets are nouns and are declined according to their use in a sentence.

The first form of each verb given is the first person singular of the present active indicative tense. For example, **amo**, I like, I am liking, I do like. The second form is the present active infinitive. For example, **amare**, to like. This infinitive furnishes the base on which the present tenses are formed. Base: **ama-, porta-, lauda-, labora-, voca-.**

In a Latin dictionary, verbs are usually listed under the first person singular of the present tense. This form is followed by the present infinitive (as above) and then by one, or, more often, two other forms. These forms are called the principal parts of the verb.

The principal parts are those forms of the verb from which all other forms are derived. In other words, if you know the four prinicpal parts of a verb in Latin, you can figure out all the other forms of that verb from them.

Nouns

stella (steh-*lah*), **stellae** (steh-*lai*), **f.**, star (stellar, constellation)
puella (*poo*-eh-*lah*), **puellae** (*poo*-eh-*lai*), **f.**, girl

casa (kah-*sah*), casae (kah-*sai*), f., cottage, house
femina (fay-*mih-nah*), feminae (fay-*mih-nai*), f., woman (feminine)
aqua (ah-*kwah*), aquae (ah-*quai*), f., water (aquarium)
terra (tehr-*rah*), terrae (tehr-*rai*), f., land, earth (terrace, territory)
agricola (*ah*-grih-koh-*lah*), agricolae (*ah*-grih-koh-*lai*), m., farmer (agriculture)

In the vocabulary above, two forms of each noun are given, followed by its gender, feminine (f.), masculine (m.), or neuter (n.). This is how nouns are listed in Latin dictionaries. The first form is the subject case, called the nominative case. The second form is the possessive case, called the genitive case. This case furnishes the base to which the rest of the case endings are added. Base: **stell-, puell-, cas-, femin-, aqu-, terr-, agricol-.**

Reading Grammar

Nouns

1. The different forms of a noun, which are indicated by the endings, are known as cases. A case can be singular or plural. The most important case to know while learning Latin is the genitive singular. This is the case that supplies the base of the noun. All other cases, except for the nominative singular, are formed by adding the case endings onto the base. The nominative singular may be formed that way, as it is in the nouns you have seen so far, but it may also be formed differently. Thus, a Latin dictionary will supply the genitive singular, along with the nominative singular. This will give you enough information to form the other cases of the noun.

2. When you list the different cases of a noun, you are declining that noun. Latin has five different declensions, and each noun belongs to one of these declensions. In this chapter, you are learning the first declension, also known as the **a-declension.**

3. Nouns that have -ae as the ending of the genitive singular are of the first declension or **a-declension.**

4. **a-declension** nouns have -a- in most of the case endings.

5. **a-declension** nouns are all feminine, unless the word indicates a male, as in the case of **agricola,** which means *farmer.*

Consider the declension of the **a-declension** noun **stella:**

CASE NAME	USE	SINGULAR	PLURAL	EXAMPLE
Nominative	subject	stella the star	stellae the stars	The star shines brightly.
Genitive	possession	stellae of the star	stellarum of the stars	The light of the star is bright.
Dative	indirect object	stellae to, for the star	stellis to, for the stars	The rocket flies to the stars.
Accusative	direct object	stellam the star	stellas the stars	I like the stars.
Ablative	prepositional phrases	stella from, by, with, in the star	stellis from, by, with, in the stars	The light came from the stars.
Vocative	direct address	stella O star	stellae O stars	O stars, shine brightly!

The base, or root, of **stella, stellae** is **stell-.** This is obtained by dropping the genitive singular ending, -ae. The other endings can be added directly on to the base. The endings are:

CASE	SINGULAR	PLURAL
Nominative	-a	-ae
Genitive	-ae	-arum
Dative	-ae	-is
Accusative	-am	-as
Ablative	-a	-is
Vocative	-a	-ae

This is true of all **a-declension** nouns.

You will notice that some cases have the same endings. For example, the genitive and dative singular, as well as the nominative and vocative plural, all end in -ae. However, when you encounter the word **stellae,** you will be able to figure out which case it is in from the words around it. For the purpose of clarity, the vocative will not be used in the exercises, except where specifically indicated.

Later lessons will explore the use and meanings of the various cases in greater detail. For now, all you have to do is practice what you have learned so far.

Grammar Practice No. 1

Decline **puella, casa, femina, terra, aqua,** and **agricola** in the same way **stella** is declined, giving the Latin form and its English meaning, and then check your answers below. Do this until you can give all the forms, including the vocative, easily and quickly.

Example: puella, the girl; **puellae,** of the girl; **puellae,** to, for the girl; **puellam,** the girl; etc.

Verbs

1. The ending of a verb changes to show tense (time), person (the subject of the verb), and number (singular or plural). These endings are added to one of the four principal parts, depending on the tense. You already know the first two principal parts of the verbs listed in the vocabulary for this chapter: the first person singular of the present active indicative and the present active infinitive.

2. When you list the different forms of a verb, you are conjugating that verb. Latin has four different conjugations. Each verb belongs to one of the four conjugations and is conjugated in only one way. A few verbs are irregular and do not belong to any of the four conjugations. The first of these will be examined in the next chapter. In this chapter, you are learning the first or **a-conjugation.**

3. Verbs that have -a- in the present active infinitive are **a-conjugation verbs.** This infinitive supplies the base onto which the endings for the present active indicative are added.

4. **a-conjugation** verbs have -a-in most of the forms.

5. A verb must be in the same person and number as its subject. For example:

> **agricola laborat,** the farmer works (third person singular)
> **agricolae laborant,** the farmers work (third person plural)

Present Active Indicative Tense of a-conjugation Verbs

You will notice that verbs in this tense can be translated in three ways. Although all three translations are listed only for the first person singular, they are understood to be present for all three persons, singular and plural, in this tense.

PERSON	SINGULAR	PLURAL	EXAMPLE
1st	**amo** I like, am liking, do like	**amamus** we like	**Amamus aquam.** We like water.
2nd	**amas** you like	**amatis** you like	**Amas aquam.** You like water.
3rd	**amat** he, she, it likes	**amant** they like	**Amant aquam.** They like water.

These are the present active indicative forms of **amo**. Present because the action is taking place in the present; active because the subject of the verb is doing, not receiving, the action. Consider the following sentences:

> The girl likes the farmer.
> The girl is liked by the farmer.

The subject of both sentences is *The girl*. However, the verb is active in the first sentence, in which *The girl* is doing the liking, and passive in the second, in which she is receiving the liking. *The farmer* is doing the liking, but is not the subject of the sentence. Later chapters will explain the use of the passive in greater detail. For now, unless otherwise indicated, you will be dealing with the active voice.

The forms of **amo** given above are also indicative. The indicative mood is used when dealing with concrete situations. There are two other moods in Latin, the imperative, for giving orders, and the subjunctive, used to express hoped-for or possible actions. These will be considered much later. For now, unless otherwise indicated, you will be dealing only with the indicative mood.

There is one other form of **amo** that you already know. This is **amare**, the present active infinitive. **Amare** means *to love*.

Amare supplies the base for the present active indicative forms. Most present active infinitives end in **-vowel-re**. The vowel provides a good indication of which conjugation the verb belongs to. In this case, the second **-a-** shows that **amare** is an **a-conjugation verb**. The letters before the vowel provide the base for the present active indicative. In the **a-conjugation**, the **-a-** is also part of the base. The endings of the present tense are added to the base. The one exception to this is the first person of the present tense. As you can see, **amo** does not have the **-a-** before the tense ending. This is true of the first person singular of all **a-conjugation** verbs.

The endings for the present active indicative are as follows:

	SINGULAR		PLURAL	
1st person	I	**-o**	we	**-mus**
2nd person	you	**-s**	you	**-tis**
3rd person	he, she, it	**-t**	they	**-nt**

Remember:

1. If the subject of the verb is a pronoun (I, you, he, she, it, we, they), you do not need to use a separate word to express the pronoun. The verb itself will tell you what the subject is. For example, **amo** means *I like*. You do not need a separate word for *I* (although such a word does exist in Latin), because *I* is part of the verb.

2. Latin distinguishes between the singular and plural *you*. This distinction is lost in English, except in some literary and biblical expressions that use *ye* or *thou*.

3. The first person ending of the **a-conjugation** does not have **-a-** before it. All other endings in the present tense do have **-a-**.

4. The present active infinitive of **a-conjugation** verbs ends in **-are**.

Grammar Practice No. 2

Conjugate the present tense of **porto, laudo, laboro,** and **voco** in the same way as **amo**, giving the Latin form and its English meaning, and then check your answers below. Do this until you can give all the forms easily and quickly. The ability to read Latin depends on the rapid recognition of the meanings of the endings and of the vocabulary, so it is essential that you master these.

Example: **porto,** I carry, I do carry, I am carrying; **portas,** you carry; **portat,** he, she, it carries, etc.

Practice Exercises

No. 1. For each of these singular forms, give the corresponding plural.

Example: **stellam,** the star   **stellas,** the stars
           vocas, you call   **vocatis,** you call

1. **aquam,** the water   3. **terra,** the land   5. **stella,** by the star   7. **laboras,** you work
2. **puellae,** of the girl   4. **agricolae,** for the farmer   6. **vocat,** he calls   8. **porto,** I carry

No. 2. Supply the English to complete the translation.

Example: **puellarum,** _____ girls   <u>of the</u> girls

1. **agricolarum,** _____ farmers   4. **feminae,** for the _____   7. **vocatis,** _____ call
2. **puellam,** _____ girl   5. **terris,** by the _____   8. **laborant,** _____ working
3. **casae,** _____ cottages   6. **laudat,** _____ praising   9. **amamus,** _____ like

No. 3. What is the English pronoun shown by each of the following?

   1. **-mus**   2. **-t**   3. **-o**   4. **-tis**   5. **-nt**

No. 4. What case uses each pair of endings? How is this case used in a sentence?

   1. **am, as**   2. **a, is**   3. **a, ae**   4. **ae, is**   5. **ae, arum**

No. 5. Change the following to the singular or plural.

Example: **portat   portant**
   1. **porto**   3. **portamus**   5. **vocat**   7. **portant**   9. **amo**
   2. **amant**   4. **laudo**   6. **laboras**   8. **vocatis**   10. **laudas**

Introduction to Adjectives

Reading Vocabulary

Nouns

nauta (nou-*tah*), **nautae** (nou-*tai*), m., sailor (nautical)
filia (fee-*lee-ah*), **filiae** (fee-*lee-ai*), f., daughter (filial)

Adjectives

magna (mahg-*nah*), large, great (magnanimous)
parva (pahr-*wah*), small

mea (may-*ah*), my, mine
tua (too-*ah*), your, yours

bona (**boh**-*nah*), good (bonanza)
mala (**mah**-*lah*), bad, evil (malice)

Romana (*roh*-**mah**-*nah*), Roman
pulchra (**puhl**-*krah*), pretty, beautiful

Verbs

sum (*suhm*), esse (**ehs**-*seh*), be

nato (**nah**-*toh*), natare (*nah*-**tah**-*reh*), swim

Adverbs

non (*nohn*), not (non-stop)
male (**mah**-*leh*), badly (malformed)

bene (**beh**-*neh*), well (benefactor)

Sign of a question

-ne (*neh*)

Reading Grammar

Adjectives

1. An adjective describes or tells something about a noun.

filia	filia pulchra	filia bona
daughter	pretty daughter	good daughter

You will notice that although the adjective generally comes before the noun it describes in English, in Latin it can come after the noun it describes.

2. An adjective must be in the same gender (masculine, feminine, or neuter), and number (singular or plural), and have the same use in the sentence (be in the same case), as the noun it modifies.

CASE	SINGULAR	PLURAL
Nominative	casa magna large cottage	casae magnae large cottages
Genitive	casae magnae of the large cottage	casarum magnarum of the large cottages
Dative	casae magnae to, for the large cottage	casis magnis to, for the large cottages
Accusative	casam magnam the large cottage	casas magnas the large cottages
Ablative	casa magna from, with, by, in the large cottage	casis magnis from, with, by, in the large cottages
Vocative	casa magna O large cottage	casae magnae O large cottages

Adjectives have masculine and neuter forms as well as feminine forms. These will be introduced later.

Adverbs

An adverb tells something about the verb, and usually precedes it.

Agricola non natat.	The farmer does not swim.
Agricola bene natat.	The farmer swims well.
Agricola male natat.	The farmer swims badly.

The adverbs **bene, male,** and **non** all tell something about the verb **natat.** They answer the question: *How does the farmer swim?* In the first sentence, the answer is *not:* The farmer does not swim at all. In the second sentence, the answer is *well,* while in the third sentence, the answer is *badly.*

Questions

-ne on the end of the first word of a sentence indicates that the sentence is a question.

Natane agricola?	Does the farmer swim?

The Verb *sum,* to be

As mentioned earlier, Latin has a few irregular verbs. Their conjugations must be learned separately. The first irregular verb you are going to learn is the verb **sum,** meaning *to be.*
Its present tense is as follows:

SINGULAR	PLURAL
sum I am	**sumus** we are
es you are	**estis** you are
est he, she, it is; there is	**sunt** they are; there are

Present Active Infinitive: **esse,** to be

FAMILIAR PHRASES

Many Latin phrases are in everyday use and can be recognized and used easily, with a little practice.

nota bene, note well, is used in writing and speaking to draw attention to something that should be noticed especially. It is often abbreviated: **N.B.**

bona fide, with good faith or honesty. For example: It is a **bona fide** certificate. The opposite is **mala fide,** in bad faith.

adsum, I am present, is used often in answering a roll call.

meum et tuum, mine and thine, is used frequently in place of the English phrase.

terra firma, firm land. For example: They were glad to step on **terra firma.**

aqua occurs frequently in English. Examples include: **aqua pura,** pure water; **aqua vitae,** water of life (brandy or alcohol); **aqua fortis** (literally, strong water), nitric acid; and **aqueous humor,** the watery fluid between the cornea and lens of the eye.

As you can see, although the endings are the same as the regular present tense endings, the base is not always derived from the infinitive **esse**. In addition, **esse** is itself irregular. As the term irregular suggests, there is no set pattern to describe the conjugation of **esse** and the other irregular verbs. You will have to memorize the way these verbs are conjugated.

You will notice that in the third person of **esse**, the verb can mean *there is,* or *there are*. For example:

Est aqua means: *There is water.*
Sunt nautae means: *There are sailors.*

This is the impersonal use of **sum**, because the subject is not a person.

Practice Exercises

No. 6. Supply the correct ending for each adjective.
   Example: aquam mal_____, bad water   aquam malam
1. casam parv_____, small cottage
2. me_____ filiarum, of my daughters
3. pulchr_____ stellas, pretty stars
4. tu_____ terra, your land
5. filiae mal_____, to the bad girl
6. casis Roman_____, for Roman cottages
7. puellas parv_____, small girls
8. aquam bon_____, good water
9. feminae parv_____, to the small woman
10. casarum pulchr_____, of pretty cottages

No. 7. What is the English for each of the following?
   1. estis   3. sunt   5. es
   2. est   4. sum   6. sumus

No. 8. Make questions of the following and then translate the questions.
   Example: natat   natatne? Does he (she, it) swim?
   1. natant   6. sunt   11. laudat
   2. portas   7. natamus   12. vocant
   3. amamus   8. portat   13. est
   4. laborat   9. estis   14. natas
   5. vocatis   10. laudas   15. amant

No. 9. Give three translations for each of the following:
   1. amas   3. vocas   5. amant   7. natat   9. laboras
   2. laudamus   4. laboro   6. vocatis 8. portamus 10. laudat

Noun Cases

Roman Numerals

The basic Roman numerals and the corresponding Arabic numerals are:
I, 1   V, 5   X, 10   L, 50   C, 100   D, 500   M, 1000
   These Roman numerals are used in various combinations to express any desired number:

1. A smaller numeral placed in front subtracts from the larger. For example,

    IV, 4   **IX**, 9   **XC**, 90   **CM**, 900.

Note that this is actually a modern rule, created for convenience. The Romans would have written the above numbers as follows:

    IIII, 4   **VIIII**, 9   **LXXXX**, 90   **DCCCC**, 900.

2. A smaller numeral placed after adds to the larger. For example,

    VI, 6   **XI**, 11   **CX**, 110   **MC**, 1100.

3. Repeated numerals double, triple a number, and so on. For example,

    XX, 20   **XXX**, 30   **CC**, 200   **CCC**, 300.

4. When a line is drawn over a numeral, it multiplies that numeral by 1000. For example,

    $\overline{V}$, 5000 $\overline{X}$, 10,000 $\overline{C}$, 100,000 $\overline{D}$,500,000.

A Guide to Roman Numerals

For the sake of simplicity, only the later shorter forms of large numbers are given here.

I	1	XV	15	LXI	61	CDI	401
II	2	XVI	16	LXX	70	D	500
III	3	XVII	17	LXXI	71	DI	501
IV	4	XVIII	18	XXC	80	DC	600
V	5	XIX	19	XXCI	81	DCI	601
VI	6	XX	20	XC	90	DCC	700
VII	7	XXI	21	XCI	91	DCCI	701
VIII	8	XXX	30	C	100	DCCC	800
IX	9	XXXI	31	CI	101	CCMI	801
X	10	XL	40	CC	200	CM	900
XI	11	XLI	41	CCI	201	CMI	901
XII	12	L	50	CCC	300	M	1000
XIII	13	LI	51	CCCI	301	MI	1001
XIV	14	LX	60	CD	400	MM	2000
						MMI	2001

Roman Numeral Practice No. 1

Give the corresponding Arabic numerals for the following. Note that the later forms of the Roman numerals are used (IV instead of IIII, CCM instead of DCCCC).

XIII	MC	XLIII	DII	$\underline{C}XX$
CCC	XXV	DCX	CDXX	$\overline{X}CCC$
IX	CM	XXXVI	XCV	LXXIV

Roman Numeral Practice No. 2

Give the corresponding Roman numerals for the following. You may use the later forms of the Roman numerals (IX instead of VIIII, XIX instead of XVIIII).

59	42	65	2222	818
304	5040	1066	26	271
85	1492	753	960	101

Reading Vocabulary

Nouns

insula (**een**-*soo-lah*), **insulae** (**een**-*soo-lai*), **f.**, island (insular, insulate)
patria (pah-*tree-ah*), **patriae** (pah-*tree-ai*), **f.**, native country (patriot)
paeninsula (*pai*-neen-*soo-lah*), **paeninsulae** (*pai*-neen-*soo-lai*), **f.**, peninsula
copia (koh-*pee-ah*), **copiae** (koh-*pee-ai*), **f.**, supply, abundance (copious, cornucopia).
copiae (plural), forces, troops
silva (sihl-*wah*), **silvae** (sihl-*wai*) **f.**, forest, woods (sylvan)
Germania (*gehr*-mah-*nee-ah*), **Germaniae** (*gehr*-mah-*nee-ai*), **f.**, Germany
Britannia (*brih*-tah-*nee-ah*), **Britanniae** (*brih*-tah-*nee-ai*), **f.**, Britain
Italia (*ih*-tah-*lee-ah*), **Italiae** (*ih*-tah-*lee-ai*), **f.**, Italy
Iulia (yoo-*lee-ah*), **Iuliae** (yoo-*lee-ai*), **f.**, Julia

Adjectives

multa (muhl-*tah*), much. In the plural, **multae** means many (multicolored)
clara (klah-*rah*), clear, famous, bright (clarity)
antiqua (*ahn*-tee-*kwah*), ancient, old (antique)

Verbs

pugno (puhg-*noh*), **pugnare** (*puhg-nah-reh*), fight (pugnacious)
oppugno (*ohp*-puhg-*noh*), **oppugnare** (*ohp-puhg*-nah-*reh*), attack
iuvo (yoo-*woh*), **iuvare** (*yoo*-wah-*reh*), help, aid

Adverbs

cur (*kuhr*), why

Conjunctions

quod (*kwohd*), because

Reading Grammar

A. The nominative case shows:

1. The subject of the verb. The subject is the person or thing which the sentence is primarily about. If the verb is in the active voice, the subject initiates the action of the verb. If the verb is in the passive, the subject receives the action of the verb.

Nauta pugnat.	*The sailor* fights. (Passive: The sailor is being fought.)
Nautae pugnant.	*The sailors* fight. (Passive: The sailors are being fought.)

Nauta is the subject of **pugnat; nautae** is the subject of **pugnant.** Both are in the nominative case.

2. The predicate noun. This is also known as the predicate nominative.

  Britannia insula est.   Britain is *an island.*

Insula is a noun in the predicate and tells something about the subject, **Britannia**. The predicate is usually used with the verb **esse,** *to be.*

You will notice that there is no action in this sentence. Instead, a state of being is described. Consider the following sentences:

  I call the doctor.   *I am a doctor.*

The first sentence describes an action. Thus, *doctor* is the direct object. However, in the second sentence, there is no action. The verb, *to be*, functions somewhat like an equals sign in math (=). The subject on one side of the verb is equal to the predicate on the other side:

  I am a doctor.   I = a doctor.   Britain is an island. Britain = an island.

If you can replace the verb with an equals sign, you are dealing with the predicate noun. You cannot do this with the sentence *I call a doctor.*

This is true of Latin as well. However, you will recall that word order is not as important to the meaning of a sentence in Latin as it is in English. Thus, you could say **Britannia insula est** or **Britannia est insula.** Both mean *Britain is an island.* In both sentences, **Britannia** is the subject and **insula** is the predicate nominative.

  3. The predicate adjective. This is another kind of predicate nominative; however, the predicate is an adjective in this case.

  Britannia est pulchra.   Britain is *pretty.*

Pulchra is an adjective in the predicate and describes the subject, **Britannia**. Predicate adjectives, like predicate nouns, can precede or follow the verb. Thus, **Britannia pulchra est** also means *Britain is pretty.* Note, however, that you would be unlikely to find the sentence **Pulchra Britannia est,** and that the sentence **Insula Britannia est** means something slightly different from **Britannia est insula.** The first sentence means *The island is Britain.* The second sentence means *Britain is an island.* In the first sentence, **Insula** is the subject and **Britannia** is the predicate. In the second sentence, this is reversed. Thus, while word order is less important in Latin than in English, it is not by any means unimportant. Later lessons will cover the rules for traditional word order in Latin in greater detail.

  4. The **a-declension** nouns and adjectives end in -a (*ah*) in the nominative singular and -ae (*ai*) in the nominative plural.

  B. The genitive case shows possession.

    terra agricolae, the land *of the farmer* — *the farmer's* land

    terra agricolarum, the land *of the farmers* — *the farmers'* land

Agricolae (of the farmer) and **agricolarum** (of the farmers) tell something about **terra**. Compare this to the use of an adjective:

    terra pulchra, *the pretty land*

Pulchra, *pretty,* tells something about **terra**. However, an adjective must have the same case, number, and gender as the noun it modifies. This is not true of the genitive; **agricolarum** is a masculine genitive plural, whereas **terra** is a feminine nominative singular. As we learned earlier, the a-declension nouns and adjectives end in -ae (*ai*) in the genitive singular and -arum (*ah-ruhm*) in the genitive plural.

Practice Exercises

No. 10. Give the English for each of the following:
  Example: filiae nautarum, the daughters of the sailors

1. casa puellae	4. casae feminarum	7. filia agricolae
2. copia aquae	5. patria nautae	8. casae nautarum
3. terra agricolarum	6. insula nautae	9. copia stellarum

No. 11. Pick out and translate the subjects:

Example: Femina laborat. Femina, the woman

1. Feminae laborant.
2. Puella portat.
3. Agricolae amant.
4. Nauta oppugnat.
5. Agricola amat.
6. Filiae laudant.
7. Patria est.
8. Insulae sunt.
9. Filia laborat.

No. 12. Pick out and translate the predicate adjectives:

Example: Insula est pulchra. pulchra, pretty

1. Insula est magna.
2. Silvae sunt pulchrae.
3. Filiae sunt bonae.
4. Copiae sunt Romanae.
5. Terra est mala.
6. Paeninsula est tua.
7. Casae sunt parvae.
8. Silva est pulchra.
9. Femina est bona.

No. 13. Pick out and translate the predicate nouns:

Example: Sunt agricolae. agricolae, farmers.

1. Est agricola.
2. Sunt nautae.
3. Germania est patria mea.
4. Sunt casae.
5. Sum nauta.
6. Estis feminae.
7. Es puella.
8. Sumus agricolae.
9. Non est silva.

FAMILIAR QUOTATIONS

Many quotations from Latin authors are in use today, either in Latin or in translation. If you become so familiar with these quotations and their meanings that you know them by heart, you will have acquired some of the real flavor of the Latin language and thought.

Roma aeterna, Eternal Rome. Tibullus.
Errare humanum est, To err is human. Seneca.
Dira necessitas, Dire necessity. Horace.
Aurea mediocritas, The golden mean. Horace.
Rara avis, A rare bird. Horace.
Ars longa, vita brevis, Art is long, life is short. Seneca.
Fortuna caeca est, Fortune is blind. Cicero.
Laborare est orare, To labor is to pray. Motto of the Benedictine Order.

Noun Cases Concluded

Reading Vocabulary

Nouns

fabula (fah-*buh-lah*), fabulae (fah-*buh-lai*), **f.**, story (fable, fabulous)
via (wee-*ah*), viae (wee-*ai*), **f.**, road, way, street (via, viaduct)
incola (ihn-*koh-lah*), incolae (ihn-*koh-lai*) **m.** or **f.**, inhabitant
fama (fah-*mah*), famae (fah-*mai*) **f.**, rumor, renown, report (fame)
Europa (*yoo*-roh-*pah*), Europae (*yoo*-roh-*pai*) **f.**, Europe

Adjectives

longa (lawn-*gah*), long (longitude)   lata (lah-*tah*), wide (latitude)

Verbs

do (*doh*), dare (dah-*reh*), give (dative)
ambulo (ahm-*buh-loh*), ambulare (*ahm-buh*-lah-*reh*), walk (ambulance, perambulator)
narro (nah-*roh*), narrare (*nah*-rah-*reh*), tell, relate (narrate)
monstro (mawn-*stroh*), monstrare (*mawn*-strah-*reh*), point out, show (monstrance, demonstrate)
habito (hah-*bih-toh*), habitare (*hah-bih*-tah-*reh*), dwell, live (habitat)
navigo (nah-*wih-goh*), navigare (*nah-wih*-gah-*reh*), sail, cruise (navigate)

Prepositions

ad (*ahd*), to, toward (administer)   cum (*kuhm*), with
a (*ah*) or ab (*ahb*), from, away from (abdicate)   in (*ihn*), in, on, into, onto (inhabit, induce)
e (*ay*) or ex (*ehks*), from, out from (emit, exceed)

Reading Grammar

A. The accusative case shows the direct object of the verb.
   1. The direct object shows the person or thing that receives the action of the verb.

Fabulam narro.	I tell *a story*.
Fabulas narro.	I tell *stories*.

Fabulam, *story,* and **Fabulas**, *stories,* are the direct objects of **narro**, *I tell*. Both are in the accusative **case**.
   2. All **a-declension** nouns and adjectives end in **-am** (*ahm*) in the accusative singular and **-as** (*ahs*) in the accusative plural.

B. The dative case shows the indirect object of the verb.
    1. The indirect object shows to whom or what something is given, said, or directed.

Puellae aquam do.	I give the water *to the girl.*
Puellis aquam do.	I give the water *to the girls.*

Puella, *to the girl* and **Puellis,** *to the girls,* are the indirect objects of **do,** *I give.* Both are in the dative case. *Water,* the direct object, is in the accusative case.

In English, if a word is being used as the direct object, it usually comes immediately after the verb, with no words in between. The indirect object will often, although not always, have prepositions such as *to* or *for* between it and the verb. Hence, in the sentence, *I give the water to the girls, water* is the direct object. You would not say *I give to the water* in this case (although you could say *I give the girls water. the girls* would still be the indirect object). In Latin, the case endings of a word will make it immediately obvious whether you are dealing with a direct or an indirect object.

    2. The **a-declension** nouns and adjectives end in -ae (*ai*) in the dative singular and -is (*ees*) in the dative plural.

C. The ablative case is used with prepositional phrases. In this chapter, you will begin to learn how to use this case.
The **a-declension** nouns and adjectives end in -a (*ah*) in the ablative singular and -is (*ees*) in the ablative plural.

D. The vocative case is used when addressing someone, or something, directly. There may be no obvious relation between the word in the vocative case and the verb.

Navigo, femina.	I am sailing, *O woman.*
Navigo, feminae.	I am sailing, *O women.*

Femina, *woman,* and **feminae,** *women,* are being spoken to directly, although they have no obvious connection with the verb, **Navigo,** *I am sailing.* Both are in the vocative case.
The a-declension nouns and adjectives end in -a (*ah*) in the vocative singular and -ae (*ai*) in the vocative plural.

E. Prepositional phrases in Latin are in either the accusative or ablative case. A prepositional phrase is merely one in which a preposition is used. Some prepositions are used only with one case; others may be used with either case. If a preposition can be used with both the accusative and the ablative case, you will be able to tell which case is being used, or which case you should use, from the context of the preposition.

    1. Accusative prepositional phrases are used with these prepositions:

ad, to, toward	**in,** into
Ad casam ambulo. I walk *toward the cottage.*	**In casam ambulo.** I walk *into the cottage.*
Ad casas ambulo. I walk *toward the cottages.*	**In casas ambulo.** I walk *into the cottages.*

    2. Ablative prepositional phrases are used with these prepositions.

cum, with
Cum puella ambulo. I walk *with the girl.*
Cum puellis ambulo. I walk *with the girls.*

Cum is used only with nouns or pronouns indicating people.

in, in, on

In casa sum. I am *in the cottage.*   In terra sum. I am *on land.*

In casis sunt. They are *in the cottages.*   In viis sunt. They are *on the streets.*

e or **ex,** from, out from

ex via *out of the street*   ex viis *out of the streets*

a or **ab,** from, away from

a silva *away from* the forest   a silvis *away from* the forests

    a or **e** is not used before a vowel or before h; **ab** or **ex** are substituted.

Reading

To see how much of the Latin you can translate on your own, cover the English below.

Italia

1. Italia est paeninsula in Europa.
2. Paeninsula longa est et non lata.
3. Incolae multae sunt agricolae et nautae.
4. Italia est clara et antiqua.
5. Magna est fama Italiae.
6. In Italia sunt viae multae et pulchrae et longae.
7. Sicilia et Sardinia et Corsica sunt magnae et pulchrae insulae.
8. Incolae patriam amant et bene laborant.

Italy

1. Italy is a peninsula in Europe.
2. The peninsula is long and not wide.
3. Many inhabitants are farmers and sailors.
4. Italy is famous and old.
5. The fame of Italy is great.
6. In Italy, there are many beautiful and long roads.
7. Sicily and Sardinia and Corsica are large and pretty islands.
8. The inhabitants love their country and work hard.

WORD DERIVATION

Derivatives are words that come from the same origin or source. Thus, many English words have the same basic meaning as their Latin sources, even though there may have been some changes in spelling and general meaning during the course of time. For example, **terra**, *earth, land.* From this Latin word are derived: 1) *terrestrial,* having to do with the earth or land; 2) *territory,* a tract of land or earth; 3) *terrace,* a flat raised area of earth or land.

Remember that similarity of sound and appearance alone are not enough to make a derivative; they must be combined with similarity of meaning. Continue to notice the English derivatives given in the Reading Vocabularies and see if you can add to them.

Practice Exercises

No. 14. Give the English for the following:
    Example: **in vias,** into the roads

1. ad viam	5. ex casis	9. in insulas	13. in aqua	17. ex terra
2. in casa	6. ab terra	10. ad vias	14. ad aquam	18. cum agricola
3. cum femina	7. a casis	11. in silvas	15. ab puellis	19. in patria
4. in silvam	8. e silvis	12. cum puella	16. ad insulam	20. cum puellis.

No. 15. Pick out and translate the direct objects in the following:
    Example: Puellam amat. **Puellam,** the girl

1. Puellis aquam do.	4. Nautam monstro.	7. Nautae viam monstro.
2. Puellae fabulam narro.	5. Agricolas iuvat.	8. Terram amant.
3. Puellae aquam do.	6. Nautis fabulam narrat.	9. Nautae terram amant.

No. 16. Pick out and translate the indirect objects in the following:
    Example: Nautis aquam do. **Nautis,** to the sailors

1. Feminae silvas monstramus.	4. Puellae viam monstrat.	7. Agricolis terram dant.
2. Nautae aquam do.	5. Puellis fabulam narrat.	8. Feminae casam das.
3. Nautis fabulas narrant.	6. Feminis casas monstratis.	9. Puellis silvas monstrat.

No. 17. Give three English meanings for each of the following, except 13 and 14, which have one English meaning each:

1. ambulatis	5. navigamus	9. laboras	13. estis	17. pugnat
2. narrat	6. das	10. portamus	14. sumus	18. pugnamus
3. ambulant	7. dat	11. laudatis	15. natant	19. oppugno
4. habito	8. vocant	12. amant	16. natas	20. oppugnant

Chapter One Review

Vocabulary Review

Nouns

1. agricola	5. copia	9. fama	13. incola	17. nauta	21. silva
2. aqua	6. copiae	10. femina	14. insula	18. paeninsula	22. stella
3. Britannia	7. Europa	11. filia	15. Italia	19. patria	23. terra
4. casa	8. fabula	12. Germania	16. Iulia	20. puella	24. via

Adjectives

1. antiqua	4. lata	7. mala	10. multae	13. Romana
2. bona	5. longa	8. mea	11. parva	14. tua
3. clara	6. magna	9. multa	12. pulchra	

Verbs

1. ambulo	5. iuvo	9. narro	13. porto
2. amo	6. laboro	10. nato	14. pugno
3. do	7. laudo	11. navigo	15. sum
4. habito	8. monstro	12. oppugno	16. voco

Adverbs

1. bene	2. cur	3. male	4. non

Prepositions

1. a, ab	2. ad	3. cum	4. e, ex	5. in

Conjunctions

1. et	2. quod

Practice Exercises

No. 18 Give the correct form of these adjectives, with their nouns:
Example: aquam (pulchra), aquam pulchram

1. Europam (antiqua)	5. insularum (multa)	8. famam (mala)
2. aquae (pulchra)	6. terra (Romana)	9. puellarum (pulchra)
3. silvis (parva)	7. filias (bona)	10. incolis (multa)
4. stellas (clara)		

No. 19. Give the genitive and gender of these nouns:
Example: casa, casae, f.

1. casa	5. fabula	9. filia	13. fama	17. incola
2. femina	6. insula	10. nauta	14. Italia	18. Europa
3. stella	7. puella	11. terra	15. silva	19. agricola
4. aqua	8. copia	12. Britannia	16. patria	20. via

No. 20. Give the infinitive for each of these verbs:
Example: amo, amare

1. amo	4. sum	7. monstro	10. porto	13. nato
2. laudo	5. voco	8. do	11. narro	14. pugno
3. navigo	6. oppugno	9. habito	12. laboro	15. ambulo

No. 21.

1. Make a list of all six Latin cases and give the use of each.

2. Give the complete declension of these phrases, with the English meaning of each form, including the vocative case:

insula lata, the wide island	**via longa,** the long road
insulae latae, of the wide island	**viae longae,** of the long road

3. Give the complete present tense of these verbs, with the English meaning of each form.

laboro, I work; I am working; I do work
laudo, I praise; I am praising; I do praise
sum, I am

Reading

The author of this hymn is unknown, but it was composed in the seventeenth century and translated by Frederick Oakley in the nineteenth century.

Adeste, Fideles	Oh Come All Ye Faithful
Adeste, fideles, laeti triumphantes,	Oh come, all ye faithful, joyful and triumphant,
Venite, venite in Bethlehem;	Oh come ye, oh come ye to Bethlehem;
Natum videte regem Angelorum;	Come and behold him, born the King of Angels;
Venite adoremus Dominum.	Oh come, let us adore him, Christ the Lord.
Deum de Deo, Lumen de Lumine,	God of God, Light of Light,
Gestant puellae viscera;	Lo! he abhors not the Virgin's womb;
Deum verum, genitum non factum;	Very God, begotten, not created;
Venite adoremus Dominum.	Oh come, let us adore him, Christ the Lord.
Cantet nunc hymnos, Chorus Angelorum;	Sing, choirs of angels, sing in exultation,
Cantet nunc aula caelestium,	Sing, all ye citizens of heaven above:
Gloria in excelsis Deo!	"Glory to God in the highest!"
Venite adoremus Dominum.	Oh come, let us adore him, Christ the King.
Ergo, Qui natus die hodierna,	Yea, Lord, we greet thee, born in this happy morning,
Iesu, tibi sit gloria;	Jesu, to thee be glory given,
Patris aeterni verbum caro factum;	Word of the Father, now in flesh appearing;
Venite adoremus Dominum.	Oh come, let us adore him, Christ the Lord.

Making Latin Sentences

FAMILIAR QUOTATIONS

Many of the nouns in these quotations belong to the **a-declension**.

Sed non culpa mea est. But the blame is not mine. Ovid.
Licentia poetica. Poetic license. Seneca.
Summa summarum. The total of totals. Plautus.
Periculum in mora. Peril in delay. Livy.
Si qua via est. If there is any way. Virgil.
Tanta potentia formae est. So great is the power of beauty. Ovid.
Sollicitae tu causa, pecunia, vitae. You, money, are the cause of an anxious life. Propertius.

Reading Vocabulary

Nouns

provincia, provinciae, f., province (provincial)
victoria, victoriae, f., victory (victorious)
Hispania, Hispaniae, f., Spain (Hispanic)
praeda, praedae, f., booty, plunder (predatory)

gloria, gloriae, f., glory (glorious)
Graecia, Graeciae, f., Greece (Grecian)
fossa, fossae, f., ditch (foss)

Adjectives

alta, high, deep (alto, altitude)

Verbs

supero, superare, surpass, overcome, conquer (superable)
aedifico, aedificare, build (edify)
exspecto, exspectare, to await, expect, wait for (expectant)
sto, stare, stand (station)

Adverbs

saepe, often
ibi, there, in that place

ubi, where, when (ubiquitous)
hic, here, in this place

Prepositions

ante, before, in front of (antedate, antecedent). With the accusative case.
post, behind, in back of (postdate, postpone). With the accusative case.

Reading Grammar

A. Review of Latin Sentence Construction.

In an English sentence, the meaning is shown by the position of the words, and any changes in position change the meaning. For example, *The farmer calls the girl* means something completely different than *The girl calls the farmer.* In Latin, the inflection or form of the endings of words shows their use in the sentence, and a change in the position of the words does not change the meaning of the sentence. For example, **Agricola puellam vocat** and **Puellam agricola vocat** both mean the same thing: *The farmer calls the girl.* You can tell by the endings that **agricola** is in the nominative case and **puellam** is in the accusative case in both sentences.

B. Latin Word Order.

1. Even though word order does not change the meaning of a sentence, there is a normal word order in a Latin sentence.

    a. The subject or question word stands first.

Puella fabulas narrat.	The girl (subject) tells stories.
Narratne puella fabulas?	Does (question) the girl tell stories?

    b. Adjectives and genitives stand next to their nouns.

filia pulchra -or- **pulchra filia**	pretty daughter
filia agricolae -or- **agricolae filia**	the farmer's daughter

    c. Adverbs precede the word they modify.

non narrat	she does not tell
non multae puellae	not many girls
non saepe	not often

    d. An indirect object usually precedes the direct object.

Puella agricolae fabulas narrat.	The girl tells stories to the farmer.

    e. Verbs stand at the end of their clauses. The verb *to be,* however, usually has the same position as in English.

Puella fabulas narrat.	The girl tells stories.
Puella est pulchra.	The girl is pretty.

2. Any change in the normal word order of a Latin sentence is usually for emphasis or a special effect.

Puellam femina amat quod bona est.	The woman likes the girl because she is good.

C. The word *there.* Be careful to distinguish between the two uses of the word *there.*

    1. With the third person of the verb "to be," *there is* or *there are.*

Est femina in casa.	There is a woman in the cottage.
Sunt feminae in casa.	There are women in the cottage.

    2. The adverb **ibi,** *there* or **in that place.**

Ibi pugnant.	They are fighting there.
Ibi sunt feminae.	There are the women.

Reading

Proserpina	Proserpina
1. Dea agricolarum est Ceres.	1. The goddess of the farmers is Ceres.
2. Filia sua est Proserpina et Ceres filiam pulchram amat.	2. Her daughter is Proserpina and Ceres loves her beautiful daughter.
3. Ceres et Proserpina terram et silvas amant et agricolas iuvant.	3. Ceres and Proserpina love the land and woods and help the farmers.
4. Proserpina est clara et incolae terrarum multarum Proserpinam bene amant et laudant.	4. Proserpina is famous and the inhabitants of many lands love Proserpina well and praise her.
5. Pluto Proserpina ad terram infernam[1] portat quod puellam amat.	5. Pluto carries Proserpina to the lower world because he loves the girl.
6. Dea Ceres filiam vocat quod misera est et agricolae non laborant et terra non bona est.	6. The goddess, Ceres, calls her daughter because she is unhappy and the farmers do not work and the land is not good.
7. Pluto agricolis Proserpinam dat et terra est pulchra et bona quod bene laborant.	7. Pluto gives Proserpina to the farmers and the earth is pretty and good because they work hard.
8. Aestate[2] Proserpina est hic cum agricolis et hieme[3] est ibi in terra inferna et non cum agricolis.	8. In summer Proserpina is here with the farmers and in winter she is there in the lower world and not with the farmers.

NOTES: (1) **infernam**, lower. (2) **aestate**, in summer. (3) **hieme**, in winter.

Practice Exercises

No. 22. Give the English meanings for these forms:

1. sumus	4. est	7. sunt	10. navigant	13. aedificamus
2. superant	5. exspectatis	8. natamus	11. datis	14. ambulant
3. stat	6. aedificat	9. superat	12. vocas	15. statis

No. 23. Translate these prepositional phrases:

1. in Italia	4. ad Italiam	7. in paeninsula	10. cum puella
2. ad Britanniam	5. in provincia	8. ante casas	11. in silvis
3. cum feminis	6. cum copiis	9. post casas	12. ad viam

No. 24. Give the English translations for the following:

1. incolae	10. ex casa	19. ad vias
2. Cur laborant?	11. ab via	20. Ibi est provincia.
3. Patriam tuam iuvas.	12. Ubi est?	21. Ibi sunt feminae.
4. Praedam portat.	13. Hic sum.	22. Est gloria.
5. Bene pugnat.	14. ante insulam	23. Sunt multae puellae.
6. Sunt pulchrae.	15. post victoriam	24. Ubi sunt?
7. multarum victoriarum	16. cum copiis	25. Hic sunt.
8. patria clara	17. ex provinciis	
9. fabulam longam	18. Sunt copiae hic.	

Second Declension Nouns

Reading Vocabulary

Nouns

amicus, amici, m., friend (amicable)
inimicus, inimici, m., (personal) enemy (inimical)
arma, armorum, n. pl., arms, weapons (armory)
auxilium, auxilii or auxili, n., help, aid (auxiliary)
socius, socii or soci, m., ally, comrade (social)
gladius, gladii or gladi, m., sword (gladiatorial)
nuntius, nuntii or nunti, m., messenger, message
      (nuncio, announcement)

puer, pueri, m., boy (puerile)
vir, viri, m., man (virile)
ager, agri, m., field (agriculture)
proelium, proelii or proeli, n., battle
periculum, periculi, n., danger (peril)
oppidum, oppidi, n., town (oppidan)
bellum, belli, n., war (bellicose)
castra, castrorum, n. pl., camp (castle)

Adjectives

angusta, narrow (anguish)

Verbs

aro, arare, plow (arable)
nuntio, nuntiare, announce, report (pronounce)
occupo, occupare, seize, take possession of (occupy)

neco, necare, kill
armo, armare, arm (army)

Prepositions

per, through (persevere, permeate). With the accusative case.
de, about, concerning, down from (descend). With the ablative case.

Adverbs

etiam, even, also

Conjunctions

sed, but

SOME MEN'S NAMES OF LATIN ORIGIN AND THEIR MEANINGS

Rex, king, ruler
Claude, lame
Constant, firm, true
Patrick, patrician
Octavius, the eighth child
Dexter, on the right, fortunate
Pius, devoted, faithful
Leo, Leon, lion

Sylvester, of the woods
Augustus, majestic, august
Valentine, healthy, strong
Dominic, of the Lord
Martin, of Mars
Vincent, conquering
Rufus, red
Clarence, Clare, bright

Victor, conqueror
Lucius, light
Felix, happy, lucky
Septimus, the seventh child
Aurelius, golden
Benedict, blessed
Clement, kind, mild
Paul, small

Reading Grammar

A. Introduction to **o-declension** nouns.

1. Nouns that have **-i** as the ending of the second, or genitive singular form, are considered to be **o-declension** or second declension nouns.

2. **o-declension** nouns that end in **-us** or **-er** or **-ir** in the nominative singular case, or first form, are masculine.

3. **o-declension** nouns that end in **-um** in the nominative singular case are neuter.

B. **o-declension** nouns fall into two main groups—the masculine and the neuter.

1. Masculine **o-declension** Nouns.

Although the nominative singular and the vocative singular and plural sometimes vary, there is one basic pattern for all masculine **o-declension** nouns:

CASE	SINGULAR	PLURAL
Nominative	**-us**	**-i**
Genitive	**-i**	**-orum**
Dative	**-o**	**-is**
Accusative	**-um**	**-os**
Ablative	**-o**	**-is**
Vocative	**-e**	**-i**

Consider **amicus,** a typical masculine second declension noun:

CASE	SINGULAR		PLURAL	
Nom.	**amicus**	the friend	**amici**	the friends
Gen.	**amici**	of the friend	**amicorum**	of the friends
Dat.	**amico**	to, for the friend	**amicis**	to, for the friends
Acc.	**amicum**	the friend	**amicos**	the friends
Abl.	**amico**	from/with/by/in the friend	**amicis**	from/with/by/in the friends
Voc.	**amice**	O friend	**amici**	O friends

PREFIXES

Prefixes are syllables which occur at the beginning of a word. In both Latin and English, they are used to modify the basic meaning of a word. For example, if you add the prefix "im-" to the word "moral" in English, you have the word "immoral," which means "not moral." If you add "re-" to the word "do," you have "redo," which means "do again."

In Latin, the prefixes are usually prepositions. An understanding of the meaning of the prefix makes the meaning of the Latin or English compound word clearer. Prefixes occur most frequently in verb forms. These are some of the most common Latin prepositions and their meanings as prefixes:

a, ab, abs, away	**absum,** be away, be absent
ante, before, in front	**antecedo,** go before
post, after, behind	**postpono,** put after, put behind
de, down, from, away	**depono,** put down, put away
ad, to, toward	**advoco,** call to

The endings of the **o-declension** nouns are added on to the base, or stem, just as the endings of **a-declension** nouns are. In both cases, the base is identified by dropping the genitive singular ending, in this declension, **-i.** Thus, the stem of **amicus** is **amic-.**

Some masculine **o-declension** nouns are spelled with an -i- in the stem. Compare **socius** with **amicus:**

CASE	SINGULAR		PLURAL	
Nom.	socius	the ally	socii	the allies
Gen.	socii or soci	of the ally	sociorum	of the allies
Dat.	socio	to, for the ally	sociis	to, for the allies
Acc.	socium	the ally	socios	the allies
Abl.	socio	from/with/by/in the ally	sociis	from/with/by/in the allies
Voc.	soci	O ally	socii	O allies

Note that the vocative singular of **filius** is **fili.** The vocative singular of a proper noun (a name) also ends in -i. Thus, the vocative singular of Mercury is **Mercuri.**

Some masculine **o-declension** nouns end in -er. Of these, some keep the -e- in all forms and others drop the -e- after the nominative singular. Notice the declension of the nouns **puer** and **ager** and compare them with **amicus** and **socius** above.

a. Nouns which keep the -e.

CASE	SINGULAR		PLURAL	
Nom.	puer	the boy	pueri	the boys
Gen.	pueri	of the boy	puerorum	of the boys
Dat.	puero	to, for the boy	pueris	to, for the boys
Acc.	puerum	the boy	pueros	the boys
Abl.	puero	from/with/by/in the boy	pueris	from/with/by/in the boys
Voc.	puer	O boy	pueri	O boys

b. Nouns which drop the -e.

CASE	SINGULAR		PLURAL	
Nom.	**ager**	the field	**agri**	the fields
Gen.	**agri**	of the field	**agrorum**	of the fields
Dat.	**agro**	to, for the field	**agris**	to, for the fields
Acc.	**agrum**	the field	**agros**	the fields
Abl.	**agro**	from/with/by/in the field	**agris**	from/with/by/in the fields
Voc.	**ager**	O field	**agri**	O fields

2. Neuter **o-declension** nouns.

CASE	SINGULAR		PLURAL	
Nom.	**bellum**	the war	**bella**	the wars
Gen.	**belli**	of the war	**bellorum**	of the wars
Dat.	**bello**	to, for the war	**bellis**	to, for the wars
Acc.	**bellum**	the war	**bella**	the wars
Abl.	**bello**	from, with, by, in the war	**bellis**	from/with/by/in the wars
Voc.	**bellum**	O war	**bella**	O wars

Some neuter **o-declension** nouns are spelled with an -i- in the stem. Compare **proelium** with **bellum**:

CASE	SINGULAR		PLURAL	
Nom.	**proelium**	the battle	**proelia**	the battles
Gen.	**proelii/proeli**	of the battle	**proeliorum**	of the battles
Dat.	**proelio**	to, for the battle	**proeliis**	to, for the battles
Acc.	**proelium**	the battle	**proelia**	the battles
Abl.	**proelio**	from/with/by/in the battle	**proeliis**	from/with/by/in the battles
Voc.	**proelium**	O battle	**proelia**	O battles

Regardless of the peculiarities of individual nouns, the case endings for **o-declension** neuter nouns are:

CASE	SINGULAR	PLURAL
Nom.	-um	-a
Gen.	-i	-orum
Dat.	-o	-is
Acc.	-um	-a
Abl.	-o	-is
Voc.	-um	-a

Practice Exercises

No. 25. Give the English for these forms:

1. agro	4. pueri	7. castra	10. nuntio	13. oppidi
2. bellis	5. socium	8. gladios	11. pericula	14. virum
3. proeliorum	6. amicos	9. auxilium	12. armorum	15. inimicos

No. 26. Change each of these forms to the plural, and give the English:

1. amicus	4. belli	7. periculum	10. auxilio	13. periculo
2. pueri	5. oppidum	8. gladi	11. nuntio	14. ager
3. agro	6. vir	9. nuntium	12. viro	15. bellum

No. 27. Fill in the blanks with the correct English:

1. castrorum, _____ camps
2. socius, _____ ally
3. gladium, _____ sword
4. de bello, _____ the war
5. per periculum, _____ danger
6. oppidi, _____ town
7. viri, _____ the man
8. inimici, _____ enemies
9. agros, _____ fields
10. pueri, _____ the boy

No. 28. Give the English translation for the following:

1. ex agro
2. Armantne?
3. angusta via
4. amicos
5. cum puero
6. Ibi arat.
7. post castra
8. amicorum
9. cum viro
10. Bellum pugnant.
11. Oppida monstrant.
12. Viro arma dant.
13. Fabulas de bello narramus.
14. Pericula amat.
15. Castra sunt in agro.

First and Second Declension Adjectives

Reading Vocabulary

Nouns

equus, equi, m., horse (equestrian)
servus, servi, m., slave, servant (servitude)
dominus, domini, m., master (dominion)
frumentum, frumenti, n., grain (frumentaceous)

domina, dominae, f., mistress
filius, filii or fili, m., son (filial)
cura, curae, f., care (curate)

Adjectives

miser, misera, miserum, wretched, unhappy (miser)
laetus, laeta, laetum, happy

liber, libera, liberum, free (liberal)
aeger, aegra, aegrum, sick, ill

Verbs

libero, liberare, free, set free (liberate)
curo, curare, care for, cure (curator)

erat, he, she, it was; there was
erant, they were; there were

Adverbs

hodie, today

Reading Grammar

A. **a-declension** and **o-declension** Adjectives.

1. You have already studied **a-declension** adjectives. These same adjectives also belong to the **o-declension**. **a-declension** and **o-declension** adjectives are also known as first and second declension adjectives. An adjective must agree with (or match) the noun it modifies in gender, as well as in case and number. Therefore, an adjective has different endings when it modifies a feminine noun, a masculine noun, or neuter noun. The adjectives have the same cases as the nouns of these declensions.

The basic endings for **a-declension** and **o-declension** adjectives are:

	CASE	MASCULINE	FEMININE	NEUTER
Singular:	Nominative	-us	-a	-um
	Genitive	-i	-ae	-i
	Dative	-o	-ae	-o
	Accusative	-um	-am	-um
	Ablative	-o	-a	-o
	Vocative	-e	-a	-um

	CASE	MASCULINE	FEMININE	NEUTER
Plural:	Nominative	-i	-ae	-a
	Genitive	-orum	-arum	-orum
	Dative	-is	-is	-is
	Accusative	-os	-as	-os
	Ablative	-is	-is	-is
	Vocative	-i	-ae	-a

The feminine endings are placed first here, to show you the first and second declension adjectives more clearly. The usual order is masculine, feminine, neuter.

Consider the declension of **bonus**, a typical first and second declension adjective:

	CASE	MASCULINE	FEMININE	NEUTER
Singular:	Nominative	bonus	bona	bonum
	Genitive	boni	bonae	boni
	Dative	bono	bonae	bono
	Accusative	bonum	bonam	bonum
	Ablative	bono	bona	bono
	Vocative	bone	bona	bonum
Plural:	Nominative	boni	bonae	bona
	Genitive	bonorum	bonarum	bonorum
	Dative	bonis	bonis	bonis
	Accusative	bonos	bonas	bona
	Ablative	bonis	bonis	bonis
	Vocative	boni	bonae	bona

2. Adjectives which end in **-er** in the masculine nominative singular may either keep or drop the **-e-** in all other forms.

a. Adjectives which keep the **-e-**.

CASE	MASCULINE	FEMININE	NEUTER
Nominative	miser	misera	miserum
Genitive	miseri	miserae	miseri
Dative	misero, etc.	miserae, etc	misero, etc.

b. Adjectives which drop the -e-.

CASE	MASCULINE	FEMININE	NEUTER
Nominative	pulcher	pulchra	pulchrum
Genitive	pulchri	pulchrae	pulchrum
Dative	pulchro, etc.	pulchrae, etc.	pulchro, etc.

A Latin dictionary will list first and second declension adjectives under the masculine nominative singular form, followed by the feminine and neuter endings. Thus, **bonus** would be listed as **bonus, -a, -um**. If the adjective ends in -er in the masculine nominative singular, the dictionary will indicate whether the adjective keeps or drops the -e-. Thus, **miser** would be listed as **miser, -ra, -rum**, but **pulcher** would be listed as **pulcher, -chra, -chrum**.

The vocabulary at the back of this book gives the complete forms (rather than just the endings) of the feminine and neuter nominative singular nouns for first and second declension adjectives.

B. Agreement of Adjectives.

Adjectives must agree with the nouns they modify in gender, number, and case. Note that they do not necessarily agree in declension or spelling. For example, **nauta bonus** below is a masculine **a-declension** noun modified by a masculine **o-declension** adjective.

cura bona, good care (f.)
nauta bonus, good sailor (m.)
equus bonus, good horse (m.)
puer bonus, good boy (m.)
servus miser, wretched slave (m.)

equus pulcher, pretty horse (m.)
frumentum bonum, good grain (n.)
bellum miserum, wretched war (n.)
oppidum pulchrum, pretty town (n.)

C. Omission of the Noun with the Adjective.

The masculine nominative and accusative plural of adjectives are commonly used to mean *men* (or *people*). The neuter nominative and accusative plural of adjectives are commonly used to mean *things*. Because the gender makes it clear, the noun may be omitted.

boni, good people (subject)
bonos, good people, (direct object)
bona, good things or goods (subject, direct object)

multi, many people (subject)
multos, many people, (direct object)
multa, many things (subject, direct object)

Sometimes the noun is omitted with other cases in the plural.

multorum, of many people; of many things (possession)
multis, to, for many people; to, for many things (indirect object)

Reading

Servi

1. Romani servos multos in bello occupant.
2. Ex oppidis Graeciae ad Italiam servos portant.
3. Servi erant boni, sed in Italia saepe non erant laeti.
4. Servi erant praeda belli et multi servos bene curant, sed multi servos mali curant.
5. Servi in agris et in casis et in viis laborant.
6. Saepe aegri erant, sed multi servos aegros bene curant.
7. Romani servis multa dant et curam bonam dant.
8. Servi dominos bonos et dominas bonas amant.
9. Multi servi erant clari et filios dominorum bene iuvant.
10. Multi domini servos liberant et multi servi liberi erant viri clari.

Slaves

1. The Romans seized many slaves in war.
2. They carried the slaves to Italy from the towns of Greece.
3. The slaves were good, but in Italy they were often not happy.
4. Slaves were the booty of war and many people cared for their slaves well, but many cared for them badly.
5. The slaves worked in the fields and in the houses and on the roads.
6. They were often sick, but many people took good care of the sick slaves.
7. The Romans gave many things to the slaves and gave them good care.
8. The slaves liked good masters and good mistresses.
9. Many slaves were famous and aided the sons of their masters very much.
10. Many masters freed their slaves and many free slaves were famous men.

LATIN ON TOMBSTONES AND MONUMENTS

Latin often appears on tombstones and monuments. The following are some of the abbreviations and phrases frequently used.

c., standing for **circa** or **circum,** about, is used with dates.
in aeternum, forever
in perpetuum, forever
ae., aet., aetat., stands for **aetatis,** of age
anno aetatis suae, in the year of his (her) age
ob., standing for **obiit,** he (she) died
hic iacet, here lies
R.I.P., standing for **requiescat in pace,** may he (she) rest in peace
in memoriam, in memory, to the memory of
A.D., standing for **Anno Domini,** in the year of (our) Lord

Practice Exercises

No. 29. Give the English for the following:

1. Amicus meus ibi est.
2. ad casas tuas
3. ex fossis altis
4. cum viris claris
5. ante castra Romana
6. post agros meos
7. de aqua bona
8. per silvam magnam
9. mali amici

No. 30. Add the correct ending to the adjectives:

1. virorum mult_____
2. filiae me_____
3. frumento bon_____
4. me_____ filiis
5. pueros aegr_____
6. puellae miser_____
7. soci liber_____
8. feminam miser_____
9. agris pulchr_____

No. 31. Match the Latin adjective in Column II with the English adjective in Column I:

Column I

1. many **viros**
2. sick **pueri**
3. pretty **oppidum**
4. many **servorum**
5. happy **puellam**
6. good **fili**
7. bad **famam**
8. wretched **equis**
9. Roman **terrae**
10. happy **agricola**

Column II

1. pulchrum
2. multorum
3. multos
4. laetam
5. aegri
6. boni
7. laetus
8. malam
9. miseris
10. Romanae

No. 32. Complete the verbs with the correct endings:

1. cura_____ (we)
2. libera_____ (you s.)
3. labora_____ (you pl.)
4. porta_____ (he)
5. ar_____ (I)
6. neca_____ (they)
7. nuntia_____ (she)
8. occupa_____ (we)
9. sta_____ (you pl.)

No. 33. Give the English for the following:

1. Sunt liberi.
2. dominarum laetarum
3. in aquam altam
4. de curis magnis
5. in agris latis
6. de dominis bonis
7. Cur estis laeti?
8. Sunt multi.
9. Sumus aegri.
10. cum amicis bonis
11. in terris liberis
12. Est pulchra.
13. Suntne pulchrae?
14. Est miser.
15. multa

Second Conjugation Verbs

Reading Vocabulary

Nouns

deus, dei, m., god (deity)
oceanus, oceani, m., ocean (oceanic)

dea, deae, f., goddess
caelum, caeli, n., sky, heaven (celestial)

sapientia, sapientiae, f., wisdom (sapience)
templum, templi, n., temple (templar)
fortuna, fortunae, f., fortune, fate, luck (fortunate)
    Note: The dative and ablative plural of **dea** is **deabus,** to distinguish it from **deis.**

regina, reginae, f., queen
luna, lunae, f., moon (lunar)

Adjectives

suus, sua, suum, his, her, its, their (own)
noster, nostra, nostrum, our, ours (nostrum)

vester, vestra, vestrum, your, yours (pl.)

Verbs

adoro, adorare, worship, adore (adorable)
timeo, timere, fear, be afraid of (timid)
regno, regnare, rule (regnant)

habeo, habere, have, hold (habit)
video, videre, see (vision, video)

Prepositions

trans, across. With the accusative case (trans-Atlantic).

Reading Grammar

A. Possessive adjectives are used when the subject of the verb is the possessor, as in the sentence *I lost my book*. Thus, the word *own* may always be added for clarity.
    The possessive adjectives are:

Singular:	1st person	meus, mea, meum, my (own), mine
	2nd person	tuus, tua, tuum, your (own), yours
	3rd person	suus, sua, suum, his (own), her (own), its (own)

Plural:	1st person	noster, nostra, nostrum, our (own), her (own), its (own)
	2nd person	vester, vestra, vestrum, your (own), yours
	3rd person	suus, sua, suum, their (own), theirs

These adjectives are declined just like other adjectives of the first and second declension, except for the masculine vocative singular of **meus,** which is **mi.** Thus,

mea puella, O my girl   meae puellae, O my girls
mi puer, O my boy   mei pueri, O my boys

Remember that the possessive adjectives are indeed adjectives. Therefore, they must agree with the nouns they modify in case, number, and gender. For example, you would say **suam casam** regardless of whether the owner of the house is male or female; **suam** must be feminine because **casam** is feminine. The context will tell you whether a man or a woman owns the house.
    Similarly, you would say **Amas tuas filias,** your daughters. **filias** is plural; so **tuas** must also be plural, even though it refers to a single person. **tuas** is also accusative, because **filias** is accusative. This is true even though

you is the subject of the sentence. The ending of an adjective is determined by the noun it modifies, **not** by the subject of the sentence, unless the two are the same.

B. **e-conjugation** or second conjugation verbs have an -e- in the present infinitive.

hab-e-re, to have   **tim-e-re,** to fear   **vid-e-re,** to see

e-conjugation verbs form the present tense in the same way as the **a-conjugation** verbs, but there is an -e- in each form, not an -a-.

Singular:		Plural:	
habeo	I have, do have, am having	**habemus**	we have
habes	you have	**habetis**	you have
habet	he, she, it has	**habent**	they have

You will notice that in **e-conjugation** verbs, even the first person singular has an -e-.

Reading

Dei Antiqui

1. Romani deos multos et deas multas adorant et fabulas antiquas de deis suis narrant.
2. Iuppiter in caelo habitat et erat bonus et magnus.
3. Mercurius erat nuntius deorum et trans terram et aquam viris et deis famas portat.
4. Nautae Neptunum adorant quod deus oceani erat.
5. In aqua habitat et amicus nautarum erat.
6. Mars viros in proeliis et in bellis curat.
7. Vulcanus erat deus et deis arma dat.
8. In patria nostra et in vestra deas et deos non adoramus, sed in Italia antiqua deae et dei erant amici virorum et feminarum.
9. Hodie in Italia deos multos non adorant.

The Ancient Gods

1. The Romans worshipped many gods and many goddesses and told old stories about their gods.
2. Jupiter lived in the sky and was good and great.
3. Mercury was the messenger of the gods and carried reports to men and gods across land and water.
4. The sailors worshipped Neptune because he was the god of the ocean.
5. He lived in the water and was the sailors' friend.
6. Mars took care of men in battles and in wars.
7. Vulcan was a god and he gave weapons to the gods.
8. In our native country and in yours, we do not worship goddesses and gods, but in ancient Italy, goddesses and gods were the friends of the men and women.
9. Today in Italy, they do not worship many gods.

Deae Antiquae

1. Multas fabulas de deabus Romanis narrant.
2. Feminae Romanae deas in templis et in casis suis saepe adorant.
3. Iuno regina dearum erat.
4. Clara et bona erat et deas regnat.
5. Vesta curam casarum habet.

The Ancient Goddesses

1. They tell many stories about the Roman goddesses.
2. Roman women often worshipped the goddesses in the temples and in their homes.
3. Juno was the queen of the goddesses.
4. She was famous and good and she ruled the goddesses.
5. Vesta had the care of houses.

6. Diana puellas curat et nautae non timent quod nautis in oceano fortunam bonam et auxilium dat.

7. Dea lunae etiam erat et silvas bene amat.

8. Venus pulchra erat et erant feminae multae in templo.

9. Agricolae bene arant quod Ceres agricolas iuvat et frumentum curat.

10. Etiam hodie magna est fama dearum Romanarum.

6. Diana cared for girls, and sailors were not afraid because she gave good fortune and help to sailors on the ocean.

7. She was also the goddess of the moon and liked the forests very much.

8. Venus was beautiful and there were many women in her temple.

9. Farmers plowed well because Ceres helped farmers and cared for the grain.

10. Even today the fame of the Roman goddesses is great.

Practice Exercises

No. 34. Fill in the correct possessive adjective:
1. our **reginam**
2. your (sing.) **deas**
3. his own **fortuna**
4. their own **templa**
5. your (pl.) **reginae**
6. our own **patriam**
7. its own **oceani**
8. their own **filiarum**
9. my **sapientiam**

No. 35. Give the English for the following:
1. timeo
2. videt
3. timetis
4. adorat
5. regnant
6. vides
7. timent
8. habemus
9. regnamus
10. habent
11. timet
12. videtis
13. habeo
14. regnas
15. adoratis

No. 36. Give the English for the following:
1. antiquos deos
2. deae Romanae
3. meorum amicorum
4. tuam praedam
5. filias nostras
6. suus dominus
7. suum filium
8. sua sapientia
9. gloriam nostram

No. 37. Translate the following sentences into English:
1. Gloria vestra non est magna.
2. Cur inimicum tuum necas?
3. Nuntiusne multa narrat?
4. Viri trans agros suos ambulant.
5. Feminae in casis suis sunt.
6. Filiae tuae hodie sunt aegrae.
7. Multi trans oceanum navigant.
8. Sunt deae nostrae.
9. Sunt dei nostri.
10. Femina suas filias curat.
11. Ante casas sto.
12. Non multa habet.
13. De luna narramus.
14. Fortuna vestra est bona.
15. Servi dominos timent.
16. Cur non timetis?
17. Templa pulchra videmus.
18. Castra ibi habet.
19. Pueros post fossam videmus.
20. Sapientiam magnam habetis.

Chapter Two Review

Vocabulary Review

Nouns

1. ager	8. cura	15. fortuna	22. inimicus	29. proelium
2. amicus	9. dea	16. fossa	23. luna	30. provincia
3. arma	10. deus	17. frumentum	24. nuntius	31. puer
4. auxilium	11. domina	18. gladius	25. oceanus	32. regina
5. bellum	12. dominus	19. gloria	26. oppidum	33. sapientia
6. caelum	13. equus	20. Graecia	27. periculum	34. servus
7. castra	14. filius	21. Hispania	28. praeda	35. socius

Adjectives

1. aeger	4. laetus	7. noster
2. altus	5. liber	8. suus
3. angustus	6. miser	9. vester

Verbs

1. adoro	4. aro	7. habeo	10. nuntio	13. sto
2. aedifico	5. curo	8. libero	11. occupo	14. supero
3. armo	6. exspecto	9. neco	12. regno	15. timeo

Adverbs

1. etiam	3. hodie	5. saepe
2. hic	4. ibi	6. ubi

Prepositions

1. ante	3. per	5. trans
2. de	4. post	

Conjunctions

1. sed

Practice Exercises

No. 38. Give the infinitive of each of these verbs:

1. aedifico	4. supero	7. regno	10. curo	13. timeo
2. nuncio	5. video	8. aro	11. neco	14. habeo
3. exspecto	6. libero	9. sto	12. adoro	15. occupo

No. 39. Give the genitive and gender of these nouns:

1. dea	5. oceanus	9. inimicus	13. castra	17. gladius
2. proelium	6. socius	10. regina	14. periculum	18. cura
3. provincia	7. fortuna	11. puer	15. victoria	19. praeda
4. bellum	8. amicus	12. ager	16. vir	20. equus

No. 40.
1. Rearrange these sentences in the usual Latin order:

    a. **Frumentum cur datis non viris?**   b. **Curam dat insularum bonamne incolis?**

2. Give the present tense with English meanings of **sto** and **timeo**.

No. 41. Put into English:

1. agricolas nostros	6. suos filios	11. multi
2. filiarum laetarum	7. miseros	12. parvus puer
3. caelum altum	8. vias angustas	13. agrorum latorum
4. patriae liberae	9. tuus nuntius	14. cura bona
5. vester servus	10. fortuna mea	15. gladi longi

No. 42. Translate these vocatives:

1. amici	4. deus	7. fili	10. mi serve	13. multi amici
2. bella	5. domine	8. gloria	11. bone vir	14. bone agricola
3. deae	6. domina	9. nuntii	12. bona puella	15. amici noster

Reading

Gaius Valerius Catullus

Catullus was born about 84 B.C. at Verona, in northeastern Italy, but spent most of his life in Rome. He was a master of lyric poetry, especially love poems, and made use of many of the best features of Greek verse. Catullus died in 54 B.C. (From now on, the translations of the Chapter Review Readings will be found in the Answers section.)

Da mi basia mille, deinde centum,
dein mille altera, dein secunda centum,
deinde usque altera mille, deinde centum.
Dein, cum milia multa fecerimus,
conturbabimus illa, ne sciamus,
aut ne quis malus invidere possit,
cum tantum sciat esse basiorum.
                Catullus V

Odi et amo. Quare id faciam, fortasse requiris.
Nescio, sed fieri sentio et excrucior.
Catallus LXXXV

The Vulgate Bible

Toward the end of the fourth century, the Bible was translated into Latin by St. Jerome and others. This Latin version is called the Vulgate, meaning the Bible for the common people.

In principio erat Verbum et
Verbum erat apud Deum, et Deus erat
Verbum. Hoc erat in principio
apud Deum. Omnia, per ipsum facta
sunt, et sine ipso factum est nihil,
quod factum est; in ipso vita erat,
et vita erat lux hominum; et lux in
tenebris lucet, et tenebrae eam non
comprehenderunt. Fuit homo missus
a Deo, cui nomen erat Ioannes. Hic
venit in testimonium, ut testimonium
perhiberet de lumine, ut omnes crederent
per illum. Non erat ille lux, sed ut
testimonium perhiberet de lumine. Erat lux
vera, quae illuminat omnem hominem
venientem in hunc mundum: in mundo
erat, et mundus per ipsum factus
est et mundus eum non cognovit.
Evangelium Secundum Ioannem, I, i–x

CHAPTER THREE

Verbs and Tenses: *Possum* and *Eo*

FAMILIAR PHRASES

persona grata, an acceptable (or welcome) person.
persona non grata, an unacceptable (or unwelcome) person.
verbatim ac litteratim, word for word and letter for letter.
pro bono publico, for the public good.
ad infinitum, to infinity; with no limit.
sine dubio, without doubt.
vice versa, changed and turned; turned about.
addenda et corrigenda, things added and corrected; a supplement, especially to a book.

Reading Vocabulary

Nouns

populus, populi, m., people (popular)
lingua, linguae, f., language (linguist)
aedificium, aedificii or **aedifici, n.,** building (edifice)

Troia, Troiae, f., Troy
Latium, Latii or **Lati, n.,** Latin

Adjectives

latinus, latina, latinum, Latin

Verbs

paro, parare, prepare, get ready (preparation)
maneo, manere, remain, stay (manor, mansion)
debeo, debere, owe, ought (debit)

possum, posse, be able, can
eo, ire, go
propero, properare, hurry, hasten

Adverbs

nonne, expects the answer "yes"
minime, by no means, not at all (minimum)
certe, certainly, surely, indeed (certes)

num, expects the answer "no"
ita, yes; thus, so
vero, truly, in truth (verity)

When **populus** is a collective noun (when it represents a group), it is in the singular and its verb is also singular. In the plural, it means *peoples*.

populus est, the people are   **populi terrae sunt,** the peoples of the earth are

Reading Grammar

A. The verb **possum, posse,** meaning *can, be able,* is irregular. It is conjugated like **sum, esse:**

Singular:		Plural:	
possum	I am able, can	**possumus**	we are able, can
potes	you are able, can	**potestis**	you are able, can
potest	he, she, it is able, can	**possunt**	they are able, can

Present Infinitive   **possum**   to be able

The endings for the present tense of **possum** are the various forms of the verb **sum.** When the form begins with **s-,** it is attatched to the prefix **pos-.** When the form begins with **e-,** it is attatched to the prefix **pot-.** The change from **pos-** to **pot-** before the vowel **e-**is made so that it will be easier to pronounce the word clearly.

B. The verb **eo, ire,** meaning *go,* is irregular. In the present tense, it is conjugated as follows:

Singular:		Plural:	
eo	I go, am going, do go	**imus**	we go, are going, do go
is	you go, are going, do go	**itis**	you go, are going, do go
it	he, she, it goes, is going, does go	**eunt**	they go, are going, do go

Present Infinitive   **ire**   to go

C. Questions and Answers.

 1. Questions.

Although many Latin books today have modern punctuation added for clarity, Latin had no question mark. Thus, certain words had to be used in sentences to show that a question was being asked.

    a. A question word like **cur,** *why?* asks a direct question.

        Cur manes   Why do you stay?

    b. A simple question is indicated by **-ne** on the end of the first word.

        Suntne boni   Are they good?

    c. **Nonne** at the beginning of a sentence asks a question expecting the answer *yes.*

        Nonne sunt boni   They are good, aren't they?

    d. **Num** at the beginning of a sentence asks a question expecting the answer *no.*

        Num sunt boni   They are not good, are they?

 2. Answers.

Answers to questions may be expressed in various ways.

    a. By a statement, either positive or negative.

        Sunt boni   They are good.   **Non sunt boni**   They are not good.

    b. By a positive or affirmative word.

        Ita   Yes.   **Vero**   Yes, truly.   **Certe**   Certainly.

    c. By a negative word.

        Non   No.   **Minime**   By no means. Not at all.

D. Some verbs, such as **paro** (*prepare*), **debeo** (*ought*), **propero** (*hasten*), or **possum** (*be able, can*), are not complete unless another verb is used with them to complete their meaning. The completing verb is always an infinitive. This is often true of the corresponding verbs in English as well.

Manere debeo   I ought to stay.   Manere parat   He prepares to stay.
Navigare properas   You hasten to sail.   Navigare possumus   We are able to (can) sail.

Reading

Populus Romanus

1. Populus Romanus certe clarus est.
2. Nonne populum Romanum amas? Ita.
3. Populos terrarum multarum superant et viri Romani in provinciis Romanis habitant.
4. Multae copiae in provinciis manent et incolas bene regnant.
5. Vias bonas et aedificia magna et templa pulchra ibi aedeficant.
6. Incolis fortunam bonam portant.
7. Incolae provinciarum saepe erant socii et populus Romanus erat dominus bonus.
8. Socii populo Romano auxilium vero dant.

The Roman People

1. The Roman people were indeed famous.
2. You like the Roman people, don't you? Yes.
3. They conquered the peoples of many lands and the Roman men lived in the Roman provinces.
4. Many troops stayed in the provinces and ruled the inhabitants well.
5. They built good roads and large buildings and beautiful temples there.
6. They brought good fortune to the inhabitants.
7. The inhabitants of the provinces often were allies and the Roman people were good masters.
8. The allies truly gave aid to the Roman people.

Alba Longa

1. Alba Longa erat oppidum in Italia antiqua.
2. In Latio erat et agros latos et bonos habet.
3. Vergilius de Alba Longa in fabula sua narrat.
4. Quod populus Graeciae Troiam superat, multi viri erant clari.
5. Aeneas est vero clarus.
6. In Troia non manet, sed ad Latium navigat.
7. Latinus in Latio regnat.
8. Aeneas Latinum oppugnare parat et castra ibi aedificat.
9. Castra erant Alba Longa.
10. Aeneas Latinum superat et Latium occupat.
11. Populus Lati erat Latinus et lingua erat Latina.

Alba Longa

1. Alba Longa was a town in ancient Italy.
2. It was in Latium and had wide and good fields.
3. Virgil told about Alba Longa in his story.
4. Because the people of Greece conquered Troy, many men were famous.
5. Aeneas is truly famous.
6. He did not stay in Troy, but sailed to Latium.
7. Latinus ruled in Latium.
8. Aeneas prepared to attack Latinus and built a camp there.
9. The camp was Alba Longa.
10. Aeneas conquered Latinus and seized Latium.
11. The people of Latium were Latin and the language was Latin.

Practice Exercises

No. 43. Give the English for these questions and answers:
1. Nonne amicos habetis? Certe.
2. Aedificantne casas? Ita. Casas aedificant.
3. Nonne vero times? Vero timeo.
4. Num populus pugnat? Populus non pugnat.
5. Num viae sunt longae? Viae minime sunt longae.

6. Cur ad oppidum ambulant?
7. Manetne vir in aedificio? Vir in aedificio manet.
8. Estne provincia libera? Provincia vero est libera.
9. Num in oceano navigat? In oceano non navigat.

No. 44. Complete these verbs by filling in the correct vowel:

1. vid____tis
2. pot____st
3. hab____o
4. ador____s
5. vid____o
6. e____nt

7. iuv____t
8. man____nt
9. hab____s
10. st____tis
11. par____nt
12. deb____mus

13. poss____nt
14. aedific____s
15. oppugn____nt
16. ambul____tis
17. tim____t
18. proper____t

No. 45. Fill in the correct completing infinitive:

1. (To walk) debeo.
2. (To fight) parat.
3. (To kill) non debent.
4. (To conquer) paratis.
5. (To call) debemus.
6. (To swim) non parant.

7. (To help) properatis.
8. (To work) non debetis.
9. (To attack) parat.
10. (To stay) debes.
11. (To sail) possum.
12. (To go) non potest.

No. 46. Translate these into English:

1. Cur frumentum ibi parat?
2. Nonne linguam latinam amatis?
3. Ubi aedificia vestra stant?
4. Pueris gladios dare non debetis.
5. Dei arma sua etiam habent.

6. De bello longo Troiae fabulam narrant.
7. Aeneas cum viris suis ad Italiam navigat.
8. Deus populum Graeciae iuvat.
9. Cur Romani socios suos timent?
10. In caelo lunam claram videt.

Using the Imperfect Tense

Reading Vocabulary

Nouns

avunculus, avunculi, m., uncle (avuncular)
ripa, ripae, f., bank (of a river) (riparious)
ludus, ludi, m., game (ludicrous)
forum, fori, n., forum, market place (forensic)
Sabini, Sabinorum, m. pl., the Sabines
praemium, praemii or praemi, n., reward (premium)

arca, arcae, f., chest, box (ark)
vita, vitae, f., life (vital)
lupa, lupae, f., wolf (lupine)
Roma, Romae, f., Rome
Romanus, Romani, m., a Roman

Verbs

servo, servare, save, preserve (preservation)

loco, locare, place, put

Adverbs

nunc, now   **tum,** then

Prepositions

sine, without. With the ablative case (sinecure).

Conjunctions

cum, when, while

Reading Grammar

A. The imperfect tense shows action going on in the past over a period of time, as in the sentence *He was walking*. Thus, it deals with continuous action in the past, rather than with an action done once and completed.

1. In the indicative mood (the only mood you have learned so far), the imperfect tense of a regular verb is formed by adding -ba- between the base and the ending which indicates person, or who is performing the action. Thus, in the present active tense, the imperfect endings are:

Singular:		Plural:	
	-bam		**-bamus**
	-bas		**-batis**
	-bat		**-bant**

The -ba- in the verb may be translated as *was, used to,* or *did*.

You will notice that the first person singular ends in -m, not -o. -m is actually the normal ending for the first person singular in the active voice. The present active tense uses the -o, as do a couple of other tenses, but this is the exception, not the rule.

STATE MOTTOES

Ditat Deus, God enriches. Arizona.
Regnant populi, The people rule. Arkansas.
Esto perpetua, May it be everlasting. Idaho.
Ad astra per aspera, To the stars through hardships. Kansas.
Dirigo, I direct. Maine.
Virtute et armis, By courage and weapons. Mississipi.
Excelsior, Loftier. New York.
Imperium in imperio, An empire in an empire. Ohio.
Montani semper liberi, Mountaineers are always free. West Virginia.
Cedant arma togae, Let weapons yield to the toga. Wyoming.

---

2. Imperfect tense of **a-conjugation** verbs.

Singular:		Plural:	
amabam	I was loving/used to love/did love/loved	amabamus	we were loving
amabas	you were loving	amabatis	you were loving
amabat	he, she, it was loving	amabant	they were loving

Note that in the first person singular, the -a- which indicates a first conjugation verb does appear.

Thus, **amabam** is made up of four separate elements. **am-** is the base of the verb; **-a-** shows which conjunction the verb is from; **-ba-** shows that the verb is in the imperfect tense; and **-m** shows that it verb is both active and in the first person singular. The other forms of the imperfect can also be broken down in this way.

3. Imperfect tense of **e-conjugation** verbs.

Singular:		Plural:	
habebam	I was having/used to have/did have/had	habebamus	we were having
habebas	you were having	habebatis	you were having
habebat	he, she, it was having	habebant	they were having

These forms can be broken down in the same way as the forms for **a-conjugation** verbs. Thus, in **habebam**, **hab-** is the root; **-e-** shows that the verb is from the second, or **e-conjugation**; **-ba-** shows that it is imperfect; **-m** shows that it is active and first person singular.

4. The imperfect tense of the irregular verbs **sum, possum,** and **eo.**

a. The imperfect tense of **sum** may be recognized easily by the stem, **era-**. All the endings of the imperfect are added on to this stem.

Singular:		Plural:	
eram	I was/used to be	eramus	we were
eras	you were	eratis	you were
erat	he, she, it was; there was	erant	they were; there was

b. To make the imperfect tense of **possum**, add the forms of the imperfect tense of **sum** to the base. Since all forms of **sum** begin with the vowel **e** in this tense, the stem is always **pot-**.

Singular:		Plural:	
poteram	I was able/used to be able/could	poteramus	we were able
poteras	you were able	poteratis	you were able
poterat	he, she, it was able	poterant	they were able

c. The imperfect tense of **eo** is formed by adding the imperfect endings on to the stem, **i-**. (**i-** is usually used as the stem of this verb; however, since **eo** is irregular, **e-** is sometimes used instead.)

Singular:		Plural:	
ibam	I was going/used to go/did go/went	ibamus	we were going
ibas	you were going	ibatis	you were going
ibat	he, she, it was going	ibant	they were going

B. Cum is used as both a conjunction and a preposition.

1. **Cum,** as a conjunction, means *when* or *while* and introduces a clause showing time.

Cum puerum videbat, ambulabat.	When he saw the boy, he was walking.
Cum ambulabat, puerum videbat.	While he was walking, he saw the boy.

2. **Cum,** as a preposition, means *with* and is used with the ablative case.

Cum puero ambulabat.	He was walking with the boy.
Cum pueris ambulabat.	He was walking with the boys.

Cum is also used with the subjunctive mood. You will learn about this use of **cum** in later lessons.

Reading

Romulus et Remus

1. Quod Romulus et Remus filii erant dei armorum et belli, populus Romanus proelia amabat.
2. Erant etiam filii Rheae Silviae.
3. Amulius erat avunculus Rheae Silviae et Albam Longam regnabat, sed pueros non amabat.
4. Pueros amare debebat.
5. Amulius filios Rheae Silviae necare parabat, sed servus in aqua in arca pueros locabat et vitas puerorum servabat.
6. Mars filios suos ad ripam Tiberis portabat.
7. Lupa pueros ibi curabat et agricola bonus ad casam suam Romulum et Remum portabat.

Romulus and Remus

1. Because Romulus and Remus were the sons of the god of weapons and of war, the Roman people liked battles.
2. They were also the sons of Rhea Silvia.
3. Amulius was the uncle of Rhea Silvia and ruled Alba Longa, but he did not love the boys.
4. He ought to have loved the boys.
5. Amulius prepared to kill the sons of Rhea Silvia, but a slave placed the boys in a chest and saved the lives of the boys.
6. Mars carried his sons to the banks of the Tiber.
7. A wolf took care of the boys there and a good farmer carried Romulus and Remus to his cottage.

Sabini

1. Romulus et Remus cum amicis suis Romam aedificant, sed oppidum erat parvum et viri erant miseri quod sine feminis tum ibi erant.
2. Romulus ad ludos magnos Sabinos vocat et Sabini ad ludos feminas et filias suas portant.
3. Viri Romani ad casas suas puellas portant et Sabini pugnare properant.
4. In Foro Romano tum pugnabant, sed feminae erant miserae quod Sabini multos necabant.
5. Sabini vitas virorum suorum servabant, sed Romani praemium victoriae habebant.
6. Feminae et filiae Sabinorum cum Romanis nunc habitabant.

The Sabines

1. Romulus and Remus were building Rome with their friends, but the town was small and the men were unhappy because then they were there without women.
2. Romulus calls the Sabines to great games and the Sabines bring their women and daughters to the games.
3. The Roman men carry the girls to their cottages and the Sabines hasten to fight.
4. They fought then in the Roman Forum, but the women were unhappy because the Sabines were killing many people.
5. The Sabines saved the lives of their men, but the Romans had the reward of victory.
6. The women and daughters of the Sabines now lived with the Romans.

LEGAL TERMS

ius civile, civil law, referring to the laws of legal systems modeled after Roman law.

ius gentium, the law of nations, referring to International Law.

lex scripta, written law. Written laws are those passed and put into effect by a legislative body or corporation.

lex non scripta, unwritten law. Unwritten law develops out of common practice, custom, and usage. It is sometimes called common law.

sub iudice, before the judge, referring to a case under consideration by the judge, or court, but not yet decided.

corpus iuris, the body of law, comprised of all the laws of a sovereign power or legislative body collectively.

subpoena, under penalty or punishment. A **subpoena** is a writ naming a person and ordering him or her to appear in court, under penalty for failure to do so.

corpus delicti, the body of the crime or offense. The **corpus delicti** refers to the circumstances necessary to a crime. In murder, the **corpus delicti** is the fact of a criminal agent or of the death of the victim. It does not refer to the victim's body.

onus probandi, the burden of proof. The burden of proving its case rests with the side that makes the affirmation in a suit.

prima facie, on or at first appearance. **Prima facie** evidence is evidence that, at first presentation, is adequate enough to establish a fact.

Practice Exercises

No. 47. Fill in the blanks with the correct letters to complete the imperfect tense:

1. deb_____mus	6. vid_____s	11. hab_____tis	16. hab_____s
2. par_____m	7. cur_____m	12. st_____t	17. port_____tis
3. proper_____nt	8. ador_____mus	13. laud_____m	18. iuv_____t
4. man_____nt	9. loc_____s	14. man_____s	19. voc_____t
5. tim_____t	10. d_____tis	15. vid_____mus	20. tim_____mus

No. 48. Give the English for the following:

1. monstrabat	7. erat	13. ibamus	19. habebatis
2. voco	8. pugnatis	14. poteram	20. eratis
3. paramus	9. properabam	15. manemus	21. poterat
4. regnabatis	10. videbant	16. servabat	22. ibant
5. debebas	11. laudabatis	17. locabam	23. superabatis
6. timetis	12. portatis	18. oppugnabas	24. narrant

No. 49. Translate these phrases and clauses:

1. cum stabat	6. cum superat	11. cum puella
2. cum filia	7. cum lupa	12. cum erant
3. cum laboramus	8. cum videtis	13. cum avunculo meo
4. cum exspecto	9. cum erat	14. cum Romanis
5. cum amicis	10. cum pugnabatis	15. cum feminis multis

No. 50. Translate the following into English:
1. Num viros in castris habet?
2. Ibi esse hodie parabamus.
3. Amicus tuus in oppido nostro famam bonam habet.
4. Cum puellis manere parabam.
5. Nonne in silvis multas lupas saepe necat?
6. Romani gladios Sabinorum timere non debent.
7. Cum oppidum aedificant, templa et aedificia ibi locant.
8. Cur servis suis praemia dant?
9. Agricola cum amico suo in agro erat.
10. Nonne sine aqua estis?

Using the Future Tense

Reading Vocabulary

Nouns

barbarus, barbari, m., barbarian (barbarous)

finitimus, finitimi, m., neighbor

Adjectives

finitimus, finitima, finitimum, neighboring
amicus, amica, amicum, friendly (amicable)
inimicus, inimica, inimicum, unfriendly (inimical)
barbarus, barbara, barbarum, savage, uncivilized,
    barbarian (barbarous)

idoneus, idonea, idoneum, fit, suitable
gratus, grata, gratum, pleasing (grateful)
propinquus, propinqua, propinquum,
    near (propinquity)

Verbs

moneo, monere, warn, advise (admonition, monitor)
incito, incitare, arouse, stir up, incite (incitement)

Adverbs

cras, tomorrow (procrastinate)

Prepositions

ob, on account of, because of. With the accusative case.

Conjunctions

atque or **ac,** and also, also. **ac** is used only before consonants.

Reading Grammar

A. Some adjectives are followed by the dative case. They translate into English with the preposition *to* or *for*. They include **propinquus** (*near*), **idoneus** (*fit*), **amicus** (*friendly*), **inimicus** (*unfriendly*), **gratus** (*pleasing*), and **finitimus** (*neighboring*).

Est propinquus agro.	He is near to the field.
Est idoneum bello.	He is fit for war.
Est amicus puero.	He is friendly to the boy.
Est inimicus populo.	He is unfriendly to the people.
Est gratus viris.	He is pleasing to the men.
Est finitimum oppido.	It is neighboring to the town.

B. The future tense shows action going on in the future, as in the sentence *We will go.* It is translated with either *shall* or *will.*

1. In **first** and **second conjugation** verbs, all but the first person singular and third person plural add -**bi**- before the basic endings to show the future tense. These add -**bo** and -**bu**- for the future tense. Thus, the basic endings are:

Singular:		Plural:	
	-bo		-bimus
	-bis		-bitis
	-bit		-bunt

Remember, these are the endings only for the first and second conjugation verbs. The third and fourth conjugation verbs, which you will learn about in later chapters, form the future tense differently.

2. Future Tense of **a-conjugation** Verbs.

Singular:			Plural:		
	amabo	I shall love/like		**amabimus**	we shall love
	amabis	you will love		**amabitis**	you will love
	amabit	he, she, it will love		**amabunt**	they will love

These forms can be broken down, just like the forms of the imperfect. Thus, when you see the word **amabitis**, am- is the stem; -a- shows that the verb is of the **a-conjugation**; -bi- shows that it is in the future tense; and -**tis** shows that it is the active second person plural.

3. Future Tense of **e-conjugation** Verbs.

Singular:			Plural:		
	habebo	I shall have/hold		**habebimus**	we shall have
	habebis	you will have		**habebitis**	you will have
	habebit	he, she, it will have		**habebunt**	they will have

These forms can be broken down like the **a-declension** forms above. Of course, they will have an -e- instead of an -a- before the endings.

4. Future Tense of the irregular verbs **sum, possum,** and **eo.**

a. The future tense of **sum** is recognized by the stem, **eri-,** to which the basic endings are added. Note that the first person singular is **ero** and the third person plural is **erunt.**

Singular:	ero	I shall be	Plural:	erimus	we shall be
	eris	you will be		eritis	you will be
	erit	he/she/it will be; there will be		erunt	they will be/there will be

b. The future tense of **possum** is formed by adding the future tense of **sum** to the stem **pot-**. **pot-** is used because all the forms of **sum** in the future tense begin with the letter **e**.

Singular:	potero	I shall be able	Plural:	poterimus	we shall be able
	poteris	you will be able		poteritis	you will be able
	poterit	he, she, it will be able		poterunt	they will be able

c. The future tense of **eo** is formed by adding the normal future tense endings of the first and second conjugation verbs to the stem of **eo, i-**.

Singular:	ibo	I shall go	Plural:	ibimus	we shall go
	ibas	you will go		ibitis	you will go
	ibat	he, she, it will go		ibunt	they will go

Reading

Graecia

1. Gloria Graeciae et fama incolarum suarum sunt clarae.

2. Graecia est paeninsula et agri et silvae populo bonam fortunam et vitam laetam dabant.

3. Nautae trans oceanum ad terras multas navigabant et multa ad fora oppidorum Graeciae portabant.

4. Graecia est propinqua Italiae, sed non est finitima.

5. Proelia et bella non erant grata incolis, sed cum populis finitimis pugnare saepe parabant.

6. Populus multis amicis erat et bellum populo non idoneum erat.

7. Italia erat inimica Graeciae et terram occupabat.

8. Tum populus Graeciae erat socius populi Italiae, sed populus Romanus linguam et templa aedificia Graeciae laudabat.

Barbari

1. Romani multos finitimos barbaros habebant.

2. Barbari ob praedam bella et proelia saepe incitabant.

Greece

1. The glory of Greece and the fame of her inhabitants are well-known.

2. Greece is a peninsula and the fields and forests gave good fortune and a happy life to the people.

3. The sailors sailed across the ocean to many lands and brought many things to the market places of the towns of Greece.

4. Greece is near to Italy, but it is not neighboring.

5. Battles and wars were not pleasing to the inhabitants, but they often got ready to fight with the neighboring peoples.

6. The people were friendly to many and war was not suitable for the people.

7. Italy was unfriendly to Greece and seized the land.

8. Then the people of Greece were allies of the people of Italy, but the Roman people praised the language and temples and buildings of Greece.

The Barbarians

1. The Romans had many uncivilized neighbors.

2. The barbarians often stirred up wars and battles on account of booty.

3. Nonne nuntii de periculo monebant?

3. The messengers warned about the danger, didn't they?

4. Cum nuntium portabant, socii auxilium portare atque copias suas armare debebant.

4. When they brought the message, the allies had to bring aid and arm their troops.

5. Romani non timebant, sed in terris barbaris pugnabant.

5. The Romans were not afraid, but they fought in barbarian lands.

6. Oppida multa ibi oppugnabant et superabant.

6. They used to attack many towns there and conquer them.

7. Populus Germanus non erat amicus Romanis.

7. The German people were not friendly to the Romans.

8. Erat barbarus et patriae Romanorum finitimus.

8. They were uncivilized and neighboring to the native country of the Romans.

9. Victoriae copiarum Romanarum erant clarae et magnae.

9. The victories of the Roman troops were famous and great.

10. Copiis praemia dabant, cum nuntii famas bonas de gloria in provinciis narrabant.

10. They gave the troops rewards, when the messengers related good reports about their glory in the provinces.

Practice Exercises

No. 51. Give the English for these verb forms:

1. oppugnat	9. habebitis	17. pugnabis	25. oppugnabamus
2. liberabant	10. pugnabas	18. superabimus	26. incitabit
3. videbo	11. dabant	19. parabamus	27. natabant
4. manebit	12. erit	20. erunt	28. locabatis
5. erant	13. incitabunt	21. narrabunt	29. servabis
6. sunt	14. monebit	22. incitabat	30. iuvabitis
7. debent	15. portare	23. monebatis	31. ibitis
8. amare	16. timebit	24. sumus	32. potero

No. 52. Give the English for these phrases:

1. de caelo claro	6. in fossis latis	11. inimici reginae
2. finitimus patriae meae	7. gratus socio suo	12. de victoria tua
3. propinquum insulis	8. ante agros	13. per proelia multa
4. cum amico nostro	9. amicus servis	14. idoneus viro
5. ad aedificia alta	10. post bellum	15. sine praeda

No. 53. Give the tense of the following verbs:

1. sum	6. dabat	11. iuvabis	16. liberabam
2. monebunt	7. narrabit	12. natabas	17. debebit
3. manebat	8. oppugnant	13. amabunt	18. narrabant
4. debet	9. pugnabis	14. timebat	19. pugnabamus
5. erat	10. erit	15. incitabis	20. erunt

No. 54. Translate the following into English:

1. Ad vias angustas ambulabit.
2. Ante templa stabant.
3. Ex oceano natabatis.
4. In aqua pugnabunt.
5. Femina grata est.
6. Patriam liberam habere debebunt.
7. Puellae natabunt.
8. Finitimos suos amabat.
9. Avunculos tuos servabis.
10. Reginam laudabunt.
11. Ubi esse debetis?
12. Puerum vocabas.
13. Erit inimicus nuntio.
14. Non est provinciae propinquum.
15. Gladios tuos non timebimus.
16. Servi vestri iuvant.
17. Vir ibi manebit.
18. Fossam altam parabamus.
19. Dominus fabulam narrabit.
20. Agrum arabimus.

The Imperative Mood

Reading Vocabulary

Nouns

memoria, memoriae, f., memory (memorial)
Germanus, Germani, m., a German (person)
  (Germanic)

legatus, legati, m., lieutenant, legate (legion)
Gallia, Galliae, f., Gaul (the country) (Gallic)
Gallus, Galli, m., a Gaul (person)

Verbs

teneo, tenere, hold, keep, have (tenable)
memoria tenere, to remember. Literally, to keep by memory

Prepositions

contra, against. With the accusative case (contradict).
pro, for, in behalf of, on behalf of (procurator)

Reading Grammar

A. In the sentence *John, the doctor, is going home, the doctor* is in apposition to *John.* In *The doctor, John, is going home, John* is in apposition to *the doctor.* The two nouns are used in the same way, as the subject of the sentence; one could replace the other. In Latin, a noun in apposition to another noun must be in the same case, number, and, if possible, gender as well.

      Puella, filia legati, ibi est.   The girl, the daughter of the lieutenant, is there.

Filia is in apposition to **puella.** Therefore, **filia,** like **puella,** is in the nominative case and is singular. **Filia** is also of the same gender as **puella,** feminine. This will usually be the case with nouns in apposition, but not always.

FAMILIAR QUOTATIONS

Virginibus puerisque. For boys and girls. Horace.
Non scholae sed vitae discimus. We learn not for school, but for life. Seneca.
Parvum parva decent. Small things become the small. Horace.
Eheu fugaces anni. Alas, the fleeting years. Horace.
Vera amicitia est inter bonos. There is true friendship only among good men. Cicero.
Ave atque vale. Hail and farewell. Catullus.
Da dextram misero. Give your right hand to the wretched. Virgil.

B. To give direct commands, such as *Put that down!*, Latin uses the imperative mood of a verb. This mood uses only the second person singular and plural (the word *you*, whether singular or plural, is not expressed).

    1. The Imperative of **a-conjugation** Verbs.

The imperative singular is formed by dropping the -re from the infinitive. What remains is the stem of the verb plus -a. The imperative plural is formed by adding -te to the imperative singular.

Singular: **ama**   love! like!   Plural: **amate**   love! like!

    2. The Imperative of **e-conjugation** Verbs.

This is formed in the same way as the imperative of **a-conjugation** verbs, except that there is an -e- instead of an -a-.

Singular: **habe**   have! hold!   Plural: **habete**   have! hold!

    3. Imperative of the Irregular Verbs **sum, possum,** and **eo.**
    a. **sum** forms the imperative as follows:

Singular: **es**   be!   Plural: **este**   be!

    b. **possum** does not have the imperative mood.
    c. **eo** forms the imperative as follows:

Singular: **i**   go!   Plural: **ite**   go!

Reading

Gallia	Gaul
1. **Patria Gallorum erat Germaniae et Hispaniae finitima.**	1. The native country of the Gauls was neighboring to Germany and Spain.
2. **Galli proelia et bella non amabant, sed bellum non timebant.**	2. The Gauls did not like battles and wars, but they did not fear war.

3. Romani contra Gallos saepe pugnabant et Galli pro patria sua tum bene pugnabant.

4. Romani in Gallia legatos habebant quod Galli Romanis amici non erant.

5. Legati bellum cum Gallia pugnare saepe parabant.

6. Caesar ob victorias suas in Gallia gloriam magnam habebat.

7. Oppida in Gallia erant clara.

8. Ibi erant oppida multa et pulchra ac silvae multae et agri boni.

9. Ob periculum belli Romani in multis terris finitimis legatos habebat.

10. Romani pro patria etiam sine praemiis magnis et praeda pugnabant.

11. Erant in Gallia multi agri lati atque agricolis idonea erat.

12. Cum in Gallia habitabant, Romani linguam Latinam tenebant.

3. The Romans often fought against the Gauls, and the Gauls then fought hard for their native country.

4. The Romans had lieutenants in Gaul because the Gauls were not friendly to the Romans.

5. The lieutenants often got ready to fight with the Gauls.

6. Caesar had great glory because of his victories in Gaul.

7. The towns in Gaul were famous.

8. There were many and beautiful towns there, and also many forests and good fields.

9. On account of the danger of war, the Romans had legates in many neighboring lands.

10. The Romans fought for their country even without large rewards and booty.

11. There were many wide fields in Gaul, and it was suitable for farmers.

12. When they were living in Gaul, the Romans kept the Latin language.

Practice Exercises

No. 55. Translate these imperatives and indicate whether they are singular or plural:

1. ambula	5. laudate	9. timete	13. tene	17. sta
2. amate	6. navigate	10. vide	14. regna	18. iuvate
3. natate	7. date	11. state	15. tenete	19. monete
4. pugna	8. habita	12. habete	16. superate	20. mane

No. 56. Translate the nouns which are in apposition:

1. vir, agricola
2. viri, nautae
3. patria, Britannia
4. regina, puella
5. Galli, socii nostri
6. nuntius, puer
7. Gallos, inimicos
8. dominum, amicum
9. filiorum, puerorum

No. 57. Translate the following into English. Note: the vocative case is used in some of the sentences:

1. Puer aeger, filius tuus, in oppido manebit.
2. In proelio, amice, socios habere debes.
3. Contra bellum, popule Romane, viros tuos incita.
4. Incolas Galliae, nuntii, monete.
5. Sabinos, finitimos nostros, ad ludos vocabo.
6. Templa, puellae, aedificia pulchra, videte.
7. Roma, oppidum in Italia, clara erit.
8. Galliam, fili mi, memoria tene.
9. Habebimusne, amici, forum magnum?
10. Avunculos meos, nuntios, exspectabo.

Chapter Three Review

Vocabulary Review

Nouns

1. aedificium
2. arca
3. avunculus
4. barbarus
5. finitimus
6. forum
7. Gallia
8. Gallus
9. Germanus
10. Latinus
11. Latium
12. legatus
13. lingua
14. ludus
15. lupa
16. memoria
17. populus
18. praemium
19. ripa
20. Roma
21. Romanus
22. Sabini
23. Troia
24. vita

Adjectives

1. amicus
2. barbarus
3. finitimus
4. gratus
5. idoneus
6. inimicus
7. latinus
8. propinquus

Verbs

1. debeo
2. incito
3. loco
4. maneo
5. moneo
6. paro
7. propero
8. servo
9. teneo
10. memoria tenere
11. eo
12. possum

Adverbs

1. certe
2. cras
3. ita
4. minime
5. nonne
6. num
7. nunc
8. tum
9. vero

Prepositions

1. contra
2. ob
3. pro
4. sine

Conjunctions

1. atque, ac

Practice Exercises

No. 58. Tell whether each of the following is a simple question, expects the answer "yes," or expects the answer "no."

1. Estne aeger?
2. Ubi est puer?
3. Cur times?
4. Num manebat?
5. Nonne amici sunt?
6. Num manetis?
7. Properatne?
8. Cur debent?
9. Ubi arcam locat?

No. 59. Change these verbs to the imperfect tense:

1. debeo
2. locas
3. incitat
4. paratis
5. tenemus
6. servas
7. teneo
8. manemus
9. monet

No. 60. Change these verbs to the future tense:

1. videbam
2. stabant
3. timebas
4. necabatis
5. habebamus
6. aedificabam
7. superabas
8. curabamus
9. nuntiabant

No. 61. Give both the singular and plural imperatives of these infinitives:

1. servare
2. monere
3. incitare
4. navigare
5. parare
6. tenere
7. properare
8. necare
9. pugnare

No. 62. Give both the singular and plural vocative of these nouns:

1. populus
2. memoria
3. legatus
4. amicus
5. femina
6. bellum
7. avunculus
8. vir
9. filius
10. agricola

Reading

Gaius Iulius Caesar

Caesar was born of a noble family, in Rome, in 100 B.C. He was educated as an orator and lawyer, but soon turned to politics and became consul in 59 B.C. For the next seven years, he was proconsul in Gaul, where he was successful in subduing and conquering the Gallic tribes. His *Commentaries on the Gallic War* are a military history of this period. Caesar's refusal to surrender the command of his army led to Civil War, with his long dictatorship and political turmoil resulting in his assassination in 44 B.C.

Natio est omnis Gallorum admodum dedita religionibus . . . Deum maxime Mercurium colunt. Huius sunt plurima simulacra; hunc omnium inventorem artium ferunt, hunc viarum atque itinerum ducem, hunc ad quaestus pecuniae mercaturasque habere vim maximam arbitrantur. Post hunc Apollinem et Martem et Iovem et Minervam. De his eandum fere, quam reliquae gentes, habent opinionem: Apollinem morbos depellere, Minervam operum atque artificiorum initia tradere, Iovem imperium caelestium tenere, Martem bella regere.

Commentarii de Bello Gallico, VI, xvi, xvii

The Bible

In principio creavit Deus caelum et terram. Terra autem erat inanis et vacua, et tenebrae erant super faciem abyssi, et spiritus Dei ferebatur super aquas.

Dixitque Deus: Fiat lux. Et facta est lux. Et vidit Deus lucem quod esset bona et divisit lucem a tenebris. Appellavitque lucem diem et tenebras noctem. Factumque est vespere et mane, dies unus.

Dixit quoque Deus: Fiat firmamentum in medio aquarum et dividit aquas ab aquis. Et fecit Deus firmamentum divisitque aquas, quae erant sub firmamento, ab his quae erant super firmamentum. Et factum est ita. Vocavitque Deus firmamentum caelum. Et factum est vespere et mane, dies secundus.

Dixit vero Deus: Congregentur aquae, quae sub caelo sunt, in locum unum, et appareat arida. Et factum est ita. Et vocavit Deus aridam terram congregationesque aquarum appellavit maria. Et vidit Deus quod esset bonum. Et ait: Germinet terra herbam virentem et facientem semen et lignum pomiferum faciens fructum iuxta genus suum, cuius semen in semetipso sit super terram. Et factum est its. Et protulit terra herbam virentem et facientem semen iuxta genus suum lignumque faciens fructum et habens unumquoque sementem secundum speciem suam. Et vidit Deus quod esset bonum. Et factum est vespere et mane, dies tertius.

Liber Genesis I, i-xiii

CHAPTER FOUR

Passives; Prepositions; Principal Parts

FAMILIAR PHRASES

vi et armis, by force and arms.

pax vobiscum, peace be with you.

tempus fugit, time flies.

agenda, things that have to be done.

sic passim, thus everywhere.

multum in parvo, much in little.

senatus populusque Romanus, the Senate and the Roman people. Abbr. to S.P.Q.R.

res gestae, things done; acts or deeds.

alter idem, another self, referring to a close friend.

apparatus criticus, critical apparatus or material; reference material used in the critical study of a piece of literature.

Reading Vocabulary

Nouns

sagittarius, sagittarii or **sagittari, m.,** archer (Sagittarius)

pecunia, pecuniae, f., money (pecuniary)

littera, litterae, f., letter (of the alphabet) In the plural, a letter or epistle (literal, literature)

sagitta, sagittae, f., arrow (sagittal)

donum, doni, n., gift, present (donation)

Vandalii, Vandaliorum, m. pl., Vandals, a German tribe known for fierceness in battle (vandalism)

Adjectives

robustus, robusta, robustum, strong, robust

Verbs

castra movere, to break (move) camp

terreo, terrere, frighten, scare, terrify (terrorize)

moveo, movere, move (movable)

doleo, dolere, grieve, be sorry (dolorous)

Adverbs

mox, soon, presently

Prepositions

a or **ab,** by, away from, from (absent). With the ablative case.
inter, between, among (interlinear). With the accusative case.

Conjunctions

aut, or

Reading Grammar

A. The passive voice of a verb shows the subject as the receiver of the action.

> **Puer amatur,** The boy is loved.

The passive voice of the present, imperfect, and future tenses is formed in the same way as the active voice, except that the personal endings are passive instead of active. These endings are:

Singular:	1st person	-r	Plural:	-mur
	2nd person	-ris		-mini
	3rd person	-tur		-ntur

First and second conjugation verbs add passive endings directly to the stem plus the **-a** or **-e-,** or, in the case of the first person singular, on to the stem plus **-o-** or **-eo-.** In the imperfect, the endings are added after **-ba-,** which indicates the use of that tense. Similarly, in the future tense, the endings are added on to **-bo-,** **-be-,** **-bi-,** or **-bu-.** The only irregularity is that **-be-** is used for the second person singular.

1. Present Passive Tense.

A-CONJUGATION		E-CONJUGATION	
amor	I am loved/being loved	habebor	I am held/being held
amaris	you are loved	haberis	you are held
amatur	he, she, it is loved	habetur	he, she, it is held
amamur	we are loved	habemur	we are held
amamini	you are loved	habemini	you are held
amantur	they are loved	habentur	they are held

2. Imperfect Passive Tense.

A-CONJUGATION		E-CONJUGATION	
amabar	I was loved/being loved	habebar	I was held/being held
amabaris	you were loved	habebaris	you were held
amabatur	he, she, it was loved	habetur	he, she, it was held
amabamur	we were loved	habemur	we were held
amabamini	you were loved	habebamini	you were held
amabantur	they were loved	habebantur	they were held

3. Future Passive Tense.

A-CONJUGATION		E-CONJUGATION	
amabor	I shall be loved	habebor	I shall be held
amaberis	you will be loved	habeberis	you will be held
amabitur	he, she, it will be loved	habebitur	he, she, it will be held
amabimur	we shall be loved	habebimur	we shall be held
amabimini	you will be loved	habebimini	you will be loved
amabuntur	they will be loved	habebuntur	they will be held

Remember the irregularity in the second person singular: **amaberis, habeberis.**

4. **Video** often means *seem* when it is in the passive voice.

5. **Sum** and **possum** do not have passive forms. **Eo** does not generally use the passive voice either.

B. In the passive voice, the subject receives the action of the verb. However, someone or something is doing the action.

1. If the doer is a person, he of she is called the *agent* of the action. The agent of a passive verb is expressed in the ablative case, with the preposition **a**, or **ab** when a vowel follows.

Puer ab agricola amatur.   The boy is loved by the farmer.

Puer, *The boy* is the subject of the verb, **amatur,** *is loved. The boy* does not do the loving but receives it; therefore, the verb is in the passive voice. **agricola,** *the farmer* does the loving; therefore, he is the agent. **Puer,** the subject of the sentence, is in the nominative case, and **agricola** follows **ab,** and as agent is in the ablative case.

2. If the doer is a thing, it is called the *instrument* by means of which the action is performed and it is expressed in the ablative case, without any preposition.

Puer sagitta necatur.   The boy is killed by an arrow.

Both active and passive verbs can have instruments. If an active verb has an instrument, the ablative case it uses is often referred to as an *ablative of means.*

Puer sagitta lupam necat.   The boy kills the wolf with an arrow.

Puer, *the boy,* is the subject in both sentences. However, in the first example, the verb, **necatur,** *is killed,* is passive. *The boy* receives the action of *an arrow.* In the second example, **necat,** *kills,* is active. *The boy* is doing the killing. He kills *the wolf,* **lupam,** which is the direct object. In both sentences, **sagitta,** *an arrow,* is the instrument by means of which the killing is done.

Reading

Germani

1. **Germania Galliae finitima erat et Italiae propinqua.**

2. **Incolae Germaniae, terrae magnae, non in oppidis magnis et pulchris, sed in silvis aut in casis parvis habitabant, quod barbari erant.**

The Germans

1. Germany was neighboring to Gaul and near Italy.

2. The inhabitants of Germany, a big country, did not live in large and beautiful towns, but in forests or in small cottages, because they were uncivilized.

3. Inter Germanos erant multi sagittarii boni et in silvis lupae multae sagittis Germanorum necebantur.

3. Among the Germans, there were many good archers, and in the forest, many wolves were killed by the arrows of the Germans.

4. Multae terrae et patriae a Vandaliis oppugnabantur atque superabantur.

4. Many lands and native countries were attacked by the Vandals and conquered.

5. Germani populis Galliae et Italiae non erant amici.

5. The Germans were not friendly to the peoples of Gaul and Italy.

6. Vandalii robusti Italiam oppugnabant et populus certe terrebatur quod pro vita sua timebat.

6. The strong Vandals attacked Italy and the people were indeed frightened, because they feared for their lives.

7. Ubi Vandalii populum superabant, multi vero erant miseri.

7. When the Vandals conquered the people, many were truly wretched.

Practice Exercises

No. 63. Give the English for the following:

1. timeberis	6. stabo	11. necabat	16. monstrabar
2. laudabam	7. armabatur	12. aedificabuntur	17. ambulabant
3. curor	8. aras	13. superabo	18. dabitur
4. laudantur	9. occupabitur	14. navigabit	19. iuvamini
5. narrabuntur	10. stabitis	15. habitabam	20. vocabor

No. 64. Change these verbs to the passive voice:

1. exspectabam	6. habet	11. laudabant	16. monebas
2. tenent	7. videbatis	12. locatis	17. servas
3. monebit	8. portabit	13. properabunt	18. debebat
4. videbat	9. movebitis	14. timemus	19. vident
5. amabit	10. parant	15. incito	20. monebant

No. 65. Give the English for these phrases in the ablative case:

1. cum legato	6. a nuntio	11. equis	16. sapientia
2. gladio	7. cum avunculis	12. sagittis	17. a populo
3. a pueris	8. bellis	13. a sagittario	18. cum inimicis
4. fossis	9. ab dominis	14. a dea	19. aqua
5. ab amicis	10. cum socio	15. cum servo	20. ab viro

No. 66. Translate the following into English:
1. Pecunia viro atque puellae dabitur quod puer aeger est.
2. Memoria tenebar cum ad oppidum finitimum movebam.
3. Dolere videntur sed donum portabitur.
4. Ob pericula viri litteras timebant.
5. Pro Britannia, patria vestra, bene pugnate.
6. Multi ad templa deorum ambulabant.
7. Ubi ludus ab amico vestro dabitur?
8. In casa ubi puellas videtis habitabamus.
9. Num vir gladio oppugnabitur?
10. Nonne populus castra movere parabat?

SUFFIXES

Latin adds suffixes to nouns and adjectives to modify their basic meaning; they may also be used to form one part of speech from another. For example, if you add the suffix *-able* to the noun *miser,* the adjective *miserable* is formed. Some of the common suffixes in Latin and their effects are given below.

-tor (m.), **-trix** (f.) denote the doer or agent. In English, these suffixes become -er or -or.

victor, conqueror	**genitor,** father	**genetrix,** mother

-or denotes an action or state. In English, this remains -or.

terror, fear, terror	**pallor,** pallor	**horror,** horror

-tio denotes status or activity. In English, this becomes -tion.

natio, nation	**oratio,** oration	**statio,** station

-ia, -tia, -tudo, -tas denote quality or state.

-ia becomes -y in English

miseria, misery	**iniuria,** injury	**victoria,** victory

-tia becomes -ce, -ship, or -ness in English.

influentia, influence	**amicitia,** friendship	**laetitia,** happiness

-tudo becomes -tude in English.

longitudo, longitude	**latitido,** latitude	**altitudo,** altitude

-tas becomes -ty in English.

gravitas, gravity	**dignitas,** dignity	**suavitas,** suavity

Third Declension Nouns

Reading Vocabulary

Nouns

dictator, dictatoris, m., dictator (dictatorial)
Cincinnatus, Cincinnati, m., Cincinnatus
pars, partis, f., part (**partium**) (partake, particle)
caedes, caedis, f., slaughter, murder (**caedium,**)
hostis, hostis, m., enemy (**hostium**) (hostile), in the singular, an individual enemy in war; in the plural, a collective noun, "the enemy," taking a plural verb.

homo, hominis, m., man (homicide)
urbs, urbis, f., city (**urbium**) (suburb)
Horatius, Horati, m., Horatius
pons, pontis, m., bridge (**pontium**)
mare, maris, n. sea (**marium**) (marine)
miles, militis, m., soldier (military)
pax, pacis, f., peace (pacific)
caput, capitis, n., head (capital)

Adverbs

semper, always, ever (sempiternal)

Reading Grammar

A. Introduction to **i-declension** nouns.

1. More nouns belong to the **i-declension,** or third declension, than to any other declension. Thus, in learning Latin, it is important to master this declension.

2. **i-declension** nouns may be of any gender — masculine, feminine, or neuter.

a. The masculine and feminine nouns have the same basic endings.

CASE	SINGULAR	PLURAL
Nom.	**varies**	**-es**
Gen.	**-is**	**-ium or -um**
Dat.	**-i**	**-ibus**
Acc.	**-em**	**-es**
Abl.	**-e or -i**	**-ibus**
Voc.	**same as nominative**	**-es**

b. The endings for neuter third declension nouns are as follows:

CASE	SINGULAR	PLURAL
Nom.	**varies -is**	**-ia or -a**
Gen.	**-is**	**-ium or -um**
Dat.	**-i**	**-ibus**
Acc.	**same as nominative**	**-ia or a**
Abl.	**-i or -e**	**-ibus**
Voc.	**same as nominative**	**-ia or -a**

c. As indicated in the tables above, **i-declension** nouns have a variety of spellings in the nominative singular case, which have little similarity to the way the stem of the noun is spelled in the rest of the cases. Thus, you will have to look at the genitive singular case. When you drop the genitive case ending **-is,** you will have the stem for the rest of the cases. All case endings except the nominative singular, vocative singular, and accusative singular for neuter nouns are added onto this stem. This is why a Latin dictionary always gives you the genitive singular case after the nominative singular case.

d. The first two cases give no clues as to whether a noun is masculine, feminine, or neuter. Thus, a Latin dictionary always gives the gender of a noun, which you will have to memorize along with the meaning of the noun.

B. **i-declension** nouns are divided into two groups — those that have **-ium** for the genitive plural ending and those that have **-um.** The vocabulary in this book indicates the genitive plural in **-ium** for those nouns that have this form. Masculine and feminine nouns of this type may have **-i** as an alternative ending to the more usual **-e** in the ablative singular. Neuter nouns of this type almost always end in **-i** in the ablative singular. However, a very few neuter nouns, such as **mare,** may also end in **-e** in that case. Neuter nouns with **-ium** in the genitive singular end in **-ia** in the nominative, accusative, and vocative plural.

1. **i-declension** nouns with **-ium** in the genitive plural.

MASCULINE AND FEMININE NOUNS

CASE	SINGULAR		PLURAL	
Nom.	**urbs**	the city	**urbes**	the cities
Gen.	**urbis**	of the city	**urbium**	of the cities
Dat.	**urbi**	to, for the city	**urbibus**	to, for the cities
Acc.	**urbem**	the city	**urbes**	the city
Abl.	**urbe, urbi**	from/with/by/in the city	**urbibus**	from/with/by/in the cities
Voc.	**urbs**	O city	**urbes**	O cities

NEUTER

CASE	SINGULAR		PLURAL	
Nom.	mare	the sea	maria	the seas
Gen.	maris	of the sea	marium	of the seas
Dat.	mari	to, for the sea	maribus	to, for the seas
Acc.	mare	the sea	maria	the seas
Abl.	mari, mare	from/with/by/in the sea	maribus	from/with/by/in the seas
Voc.	mare	O sea	maria	O seas

The stem of **urbs** is **urb-** and the stem of **mare** is **mar-**. Both are derived by dropping the **-is** from the genitive singular.

    2. **i-declension** nouns with **-um** in the genitive plural.

MASCULINE AND FEMININE

CASE	SINGULAR		PLURAL	
Nom.	homo	the man	homines	the men
Gen.	hominis	of the man	hominum	of the men
Dat.	homini	to, for the man	hominibus	to, for the men
Acc.	hominem	the man	homines	the men
Abl.	homine	from/with/by/in the man	hominibus	from/with/by/in the men
Voc.	homo	O man	homines	O men

NEUTER

CASE	SINGULAR		PLURAL	
Nom.	caput	the head	capita	the heads
Gen.	capitis	of the head	capitum	of the heads
Dat.	capiti	to, for the head	capitibus	to, for the heads
Acc.	capitem	the head	capita	the heads
Abl.	capite	from/with/by/in the head	capitibus	from/with/by/in the heads
Voc.	caput	O head	capita	O heads

The stem of **homo** is **homin-** and the stem of **caput** is **capit-**.

    C. You will learn about **i-declension** adjectives in a later lesson. Adjectives will not always be of the same declension as the nouns they modify, but they must be of the same case, number and gender.

ponti longo	to, for the long bridge	maris inimicis	of the unfriendly sea
pontibus longis	to, for the long bridges	urbs bona	the good city
marium inimicorum	of the unfriendly seas	urbes bonae	the good cities

Reading

Cincinnatus	Cincinnatus
1. Roma pacem saepe non habebat, sed in periculo erat et contra finitimos suos pugnabat.	1. Often, Rome did not have peace, but was in danger and fought against her neighbors.
2. Roma copias bonas atque arma habebat, sed oppugnabatur et populus caput habere debebat quod terrebatur.	2. Rome had good troops and weapons, but she was being attacked and the people needed to have a leader because they were frightened.

3. Nuntii ad Cincinnatum properant et ubi Cincinnatum, agricolam Romanum, in agro vident, de bello et magno periculo narrant.

3. Messengers hurried to Cincinnatus and when they see Cincinnatus, a Roman farmer, in the field, they tell him about the war and great danger.

4. Cincinnatus agros suos bene amabat et bellum gratum non erat, sed Romam bene amabat et ab nuntiis movebatur.

4. Cincinnatus loved his fields well and war was not pleasing, but he loved Rome very much and was moved by the messengers.

5. Populo Romano magnum auxilium portabat quod dictator erat et Romam servabat.

5. He brought great help to the Roman people because he was dictator and he saved Rome.

6. Copiae Romanae a periculo patriam suam liberabant et Cincinnatus a Romanis semper memoria tenebatur.

6. The Roman troops freed their country from danger and Cincinnatus was always remembered by the Romans.

Horatius

1. Magnae copiae hostium Romam oppugnabant.

1. Large forces of the enemy were attacking Rome.

2. Pars urbis Romae erat in periculo quod hostes pontem ibi occupare parabant.

2. Part of the city of Rome was in danger because the enemy was preparing to seize the bridge there.

3. Homines Romae ab Horatio, milite bono, contra hostes incitabantur, sed pontem non tenbant.

3. The men of Rome were being stirred up against the enemy by Horatius, a good soldier, but they did not hold the bridge.

4. Tum Horatius in ponte sine auxilio stat. Pro vita sua non timet.

4. Then Horatius stood on the bridge without aid. He did not fear for his life.

5. Gladio suo multos milites hostium mox necat et hostes ab ponte tenet. Magna erat caedes.

5. Soon he killed many of the enemy's soldiers with his sword and held the enemy away from the bridge. The slaughter was great.

6. Post Horatium milites Romani laborabant et mox pons non stabat.

6. In back of Horatius, the Roman soldiers were working and soon the bridge was not standing.

7. Romani victoriam habent et Roma servatur quod aqua inter Romam et hostes stat.

7. The Romans had the victory and Rome was saved because the water stood between Rome and the enemy.

8. Horatius trans aquam ad ripam ubi erant socii natat.

8. Horatius swam across the water to the river bank where his comrades were.

9. Horatius inter Romanos laudabatur et multi agri Horatio dabantur.

9. Horatius was praised among the Romans and many fields were given to Horatius.

Practice Exercises

No. 67. Give the English for the following phrases:

1. pacis longae	6. dictatoribus suis	11. maris nostri	16. contra dictatores
2. pro milite	7. caput tuum	12. milites robustos	17. cum hominibus
3. milites clari	8. ab hominibus laetis	13. homines boni	18. sine militibus tuis
4. pax Romana	9. pars idonea	14. pacem longam	19. de pace grata
5. capita vestra	10. in urbe antiqua	15. in capitibus suis	20. homo amicus

No. 68. Fill in the blanks with the correct English:

1. militum, _____ the soldiers
2. pacis, _____ peace
3. caput, _____ head
4. partem, _____ part
5. in urbibus, _____ the cities
6. maria, _____ seas
7. cum milite, _____ the soldier
8. pontium, _____ the bridges
9. hostes, _____ enemy
10. de caede, _____ slaughter

No. 69. Change each of the following to the plural, and give the English:

1. pax
2. milite
3. capiti
4. partem
5. hosti
6. urbis
7. caedem
8. pons
9. homo
10. caput
11. militis
12. partis
13. hominem
14. pacis
15. dictatorem
16. ponti
17. maris
18. pontis
19. hostem
20. urbe

No. 70. Translate the following into English. Note that the vocative is used in some of the sentences:

1. Cincinnatus ex agro suo vocabitur et auxilium dabat.
2. Homines in terra regnant sed dei caelum atque terram regnant.
3. Praemia homini magno ab populo Romano dabuntur.
4. Lingua Latina semper servabitur.
5. Cras non arabit sed patriam nostram nox servabit.
6. Ad ripam natabat quod pons non stabat.
7. Gladio pro patria tua, Horati, bene pugna.
8. Milites, filii mei, gladiis armabuntur.
9. Ob pericula tuam aquam servare debes.
10. Natua mare amat sed agricola agros suos amat.

The Preposition *in*; -*que*; Gender

Reading Vocabulary

Nouns

labor, laboris, m., work, toil, labor (laboratory)
magnitudo, magnitudinis, f., size, great size (magnitude)
celeritas, celeritatis, f., speed, swiftness (celerity, accelerator)
virtus, virtutis, f., courage, valor (virtue)
natio, nationis, f., nation (national)
consilium, consilii or consili, n., plan, advice (council)
vis, vis, f., force; in the plural, strength

sol, solis, m., sun (solar)
cera, cerae, f., wax
ala, alae, f., wing
pater, patris, m., father (paternal)
Daedalus, Daedali, m., Daedalus
Creta, Cretae, f., Crete
Icarus, Icari, m., Icarus

Adjectives

medius, media, medium, middle, middle of (medium)
summus, summa, summum, greatest, highest, top of
     (summit, sum)

Verbs

volo, volare, fly (volatile)

Adverbs

diu, long, for a long time

Conjunctions

-que, and   **et . . . et,** both . . . and

Prepositions

circum, around, about (circumnavigate)

Reading Grammar

A. **Vis,** a third declension noun meaning *force,* is one of the very few irregular nouns in the Latin language. It is declined as follows:

CASE	SINGULAR		PLURAL	
Nom.	**vis**	the force	**vires**	the strength
Gen.	**vis**	of the force (rarely used)	**virium**	of the strength
Dat.	**vi**	to, for the force (rarely used)	**viribus**	to, for the strength
Acc.	**vim**	the force	**vires**	the strength
Abl.	**vi**	from/with/by/in the force	**viribus**	from/with/by/in the strength
Voc.	**vis**	O force	**vires**	O strength

You will notice that the irregularities are in the singular forms. The plural forms of **vis** are regular.

CHEMICAL ELEMENTS

The following are common chemical elements, with their Latin derivations.
Calcium, Ca, from **calx, calcis,** lime.
Carbon, C, from **carbo,** coal.
Copper, Cu, from **cuprum,** derived from the island Cyprus, anciently renowned for its copper mines.
Gold, Au, from **aurum,** gold.
Iron, Fe, from **ferum,** iron.
Lead, Pb, from **plumbum,** lead.
Radium, Ra, from **radius,** ray, because of alpha, beta, and gamma rays.
Silicon, Si, from **silex, silicis,** flint.
Silver, Ag, from **argentum,** silver.
Tellurium, Te, from **tellus, telluris,** earth.

B. As you will notice in the reading below, the preposition **in** (*in, on*) may stand after the adjective and before the noun.

parva in insula	on a small island	**medio in caelo**	in the middle of the sky

C. The conjunction **-que** (and) never stands alone, but is added to the second of two similarly used words or phrases. **-que** at the end of a word has the same meaning as **et** preceding a word.

vir feminaque	the man and the woman	**pueris puellisque**	to the boys and girls
vir et femina	the man and the woman	**pueris et puellis**	to the boys and girls

D. The *of* in *in the middle of* (**medius, media, medium**) or *top of* (**summus, summa, summum**) is part of the adjective and, therefore, does not affect the case of the noun it modifies. The noun has the case its use in the sentence requires, and the adjective simply agrees with it.

in caelo	in the sky	**medio in caelo**	in the middle of the sky
in terra	on land	**in summa terra**	on top of the land.

E. The following rules are helpful for remembering the gender of some **i-declension** nouns.
1. Nouns ending in **-or** are usually masculine, e.g., **labor**
2. Nouns ending in **-io** are usually feminine, e.g., **natio**
3. Nouns ending in **-tudo, -tus,** or **-tas** are feminine, e.g., **magnitudo, virtus, celeritas**

Reading

Daedalus et Icarus	Daedalus and Icarus
1. **Daedalus hominem necat et cum filio suo, Icaro, ex Graecia ad Cretam, insulam in mari, properat.**	1. Daedalus killed a man and with his son, Icarus, hurried from Greece to Crete, an island in the sea.
2. **Parva in insula diu manebant et tum pater filiusque ad Graeciam volare parant.**	2. They stayed for a long time on the small island and then the father and son prepared to fly toward Greece.
3. **Bene laborant et alas parant.**	3. They work hard and get wings ready.
4. **Pater puerum monet: "Per caelum, sed non ad solem volabimus."**	4. The father warns the boy: "We shall fly through the sky, but not toward the sun."
5. **Sol erat clarus et Icarus ob alas suas erat laetus.**	5. The sun was bright and Icarus was happy because of his wings.
6. **Consilium patris sui non diu memoria tenebat.**	6. He did not remember the advice of his father for long.
7. **Cum patre suo non manebat, sed summo in caelo ante solem volebat.**	7. He did not stay with his father, but flew very high in the sky in front of the sun.
8. **Cera in alis pueri non manebat.**	8. The wax did not stay on the boy's wings.
9. **Pater filium suum medio in mari mox videt.**	9. The father soon sees his son in the middle of the sea.
10. **Icarus non servatur et Daedalus vero dolebat quod puer consilio patris non bene monebatur.**	10. Icarus was not saved and Daedalus was truly grieved because the boy was not well warned by his father's advice.

Practice Exercises

No. 71. Give the English for the following:
1. dei et deae
2. deus deaque
3. tenemus et damus
4. tenebat dabatque
5. hominem et feminas
6. hominum feminarumque
7. ad solem et lunam
8. ad solem lunamque
9. ex mare et terra
10. ex terra mareque
11. cum vi et armibus
12. cum vi armibusque

No. 72. Translate these phrases:
1. in mediis viis
2. multis in oppidis
3. bello in magno
4. in summis aedificiis
5. parte in bona
6. in oceanis latis
7. multis in terris
8. medio in caelo
9. summo in mare

No. 73. Translate these phrases:
1. ad mare
2. ex urbibus
3. cum patribus suis
4. ante forum
5. post templum
6. de arca
7. sine consilio
8. trans oceanum
9. per maria
10. ob alas
11. pro regina tua
12. contra populum
13. inter hostes
14. ab viris
15. ab oppidis
16. ante castra
17. per pericula
18. ad dominum
19. trans agrum
20. de pace

No. 74. Give the English for these verbs:
1. erit
2. terrebitur
3. volabat
4. natabit
5. dolent
6. portamur
7. tenebatur
8. amabimur
9. movebo
10. laudabantur
11. pugnabat
12. locabis
13. vocabor
14. monebamur
15. laborabunt
16. incitantur
17. debebit
18. parant
19. curabantur
20. liberaberis

No. 75. Translate these vocatives and appositives:
1. Homo, avunculus meus
2. Amici boni
3. Fili bone
4. Nationum, Italiae Germaniaeque
5. Ob pecuniam, praemium
6. Feminarum, reginarum
7. Vir clare
8. Puer, servus
9. Puellis, filiis meis
10. Pater noster

The Principal Parts of the Verb

Reading Vocabulary

Nouns

Pluto, Plutonis, m., Pluto (plutonium)
captivus, captivi, m., captive (captivity)
gladiator, gladiatoris, m., gladiator (gladitorial)
Colosseum, Colossei, n., the Colosseum (colossal)

animal, animalis, n., animal (animalium)
annus, anni, m., year (annual)
Ceres, Cereris, f., Ceres (cereal)
Proserpina, Proserpinae, f., Proserpina

amphitheatrum, amphitheatri, n., amphitheater
(amphitheatrical)
Inferi, Inferorum, m. pl., Those Below, the
shades or ghosts of Hades

mater, matris, f., mother (maternal)
Iuppiter, Iovis, m., Jupiter (jovial)
Mercurius, Mercuri, m., Mercury

Verbs

specto, spectare, spectavi, spectatus, look at, watch (spectacle)
obtineo, obtinere, obtinui, obtentus, secure, obtain (obtainable)

Prepositions

sub, under, below, at the foot of (subordinate)
1. With the accusative case after verbs showing motion (transitive verbs), as in the sentence *I walk under the stars.*
2. With the ablative case after verbs showing rest (intransitive verbs), as in the sentence *I sit under the tree.*

Reading Grammar

Introduction to the Principal Parts of Verbs

A. You have already studied two of the principal parts of verbs:

1. **amo, habeo**	First Person Singular Present Active Tense.
2. **amare, habere**	Present Active Infinitive.

B. The first two principal parts are used to form the tenses you have learned so far:

1. Present Tense, Active and Passive
2. Imperfect Tense, Active and Passive
3. Future Tense, Active and Passive

C. The first two principal parts also show the conjugation to which the verb belongs:

1. **amo, amare** (a-conjugation)
2. **habeo, habere** (e-conjugation)

It is sometimes possible to determine a verb's conjugation from only one of these parts, but often, you will need both of them. This is especially true of second, third and fourth conjugation verbs. (These last two will be introduced in later lessons.)

D. The third principal part is the first person singular, perfect active tense.

1. **amavi** (a-conjugation)	I have loved; I have liked
2. **habui** (e-conjugation)	I have had; I have held

The third principal part for most of the **a-conjugation** verbs is formed by adding **-avi** to the stem. The exact spelling of this principal part will vary for the other conjugations. Thus, you will have to memorize this part for each individual verb. However, it will always end in **-i.**

PREFIXES

These Latin prepositions are commonly used as prefixes:
e, ex, out. **exspecto,** look out for, wait for, expect.
per, through; thorough, very. **perduco,** lead through. **pervenio,** arrive.
inter, between. **interpono,** put between.
in, in, on; into; not. **invenio,** discover (come on). **infirmus,** weak (not strong).
trans, across. **transmitto,** send across.
sub, under. **subligo,** drive under.

From the third principal part, the following tenses can be formed:

1. Perfect Active Tense   e.g., *I have loved.*
2. Pluperfect Active Tense   e.g., *I had loved.*
3. Future Perfect Active Tense   e.g., *I shall have loved.*

These tenses will be introduced in the next chapter.

E. The fourth principal part is the masculine nominative singular of the perfect passive participle.

1. **amatus** (a-conjugation)   having been loved; having been liked.
2. **habitus** (e-conjugation)   having been had; having been held.

From the fourth principal part, the following tenses can be formed:

1. Perfect Passive Tense   e.g., *I have been* or *was loved.*
2. Pluperfect Passive Tense   e.g., *I had been loved.*
3. Future Perfect Passive Tense   e.g., *I shall have been loved.*

F. Since all tenses are formed from one of the principal parts, if you know all four principal parts of a verb, you can derive all the different forms of that verb.

G. Most of the **a-conjugation** verbs form their principal parts like **amo:**

    amo, amare, amavi, amatus

Those that do not are:

do, dare, dedi, datus	give
iuvo, iuvare, iuvi, iutus	help, aid
sto, stare, steti, status	stand

H. Many of the **e-conjugation** verbs form their principal parts like **habeo.**

    habeo, habere, habui, habitus

Of those you have met so far, these do not:

maneo, manere, mansi, mansus	remain, stay
moveo, movere, movi, motus	move
video, videre, vidi, visus	see

I. Principal parts of **sum, possum,** and **eo.**

    1. **sum:** sum, esse, fui, futurus

Note that **futurus** is the future active participle, *about to be.* **Sum** does not have a perfect passive participle.

    2. **possum:**   possum, posse, potui

possum does not have either the fourth principal part or the perfect passive participle. All forms of **possum** can be derived from the three principal parts which it does have.

    3. **eo:**   eo, ire, ii or ivi, itus

Reading

Proserpina

1. Ceres, dea frumenti, filiam Proserpinam, habebat.
2. Pluto, deus Inferorum, Proserpinam in agro videt et ad Inferos Proserpinam portat.
3. Quod filiam suam non videbat, Ceres, mater, dolebat.
4. Quod Ceres misera erat, frumentum in agris agricolarum non erat.
5. Tum Iuppiter vitam populi in terra servat quod Mercurium vocat et Mercurius pro Iove ad Plutonem nuntiam portat.
6. Iuppiter movebatur et agricolis auxilium dabat.
7. Tum Proserpina cum Iove non semper manebat, sed in terra partem anni habebat.
8. Cum Proserpina in terra erat, Ceres laeta erat et agricolis copiam magnam frumenti dabat, sed cum Proserpina sub terra erat Ceres misera erat et frumentum non erat.

Proserpina

1. Ceres, the goddess of grain, had a daughter, Proserpina.
2. Pluto, god of Those Below, saw Proserpina in a field and carried Proserpina to Those Below.
3. Because she did not see her daughter, Ceres, the mother, grieved.
4. Because Ceres was unhappy, there was not grain in the farmers' fields.
5. Then Jupiter saved the lives of the people on earth because he called Mercury and Mercury carried a message for Jupiter to Pluto.
6. Jupiter was moved and gave help to the farmers.
7. Then Proserpina did not always stay with Jupiter, but had part of the year on earth.
8. When Proserpina was on earth, Ceres was happy and gave a great plenty of grain to the farmers, but when Proserpina was under the earth, Ceres was unhappy and there was not grain.

Colosseum

1. Romani in urbe sua aedificia multa habebant.
2. Colosseum bene amabant quod ludos ibi spectabant.
3. Colosseum erat magnum amphitheatrum et etiam nunc stat.
4. Milites Romani bello servos captivosque obtinebant.
5. Captivi, gladitores, gladiis suis contra homines aut contra animalia ibi pugnabant.
6. Multi captivi virtutem magnam habebant et liberabantur quod bene pugnabant.

The Colosseum

1. The Romans had many buildings in their city.
2. They liked the Colosseum very much because they watched the games there.
3. The Colosseum was a large amphitheatre and is standing even now.
4. The Roman soldiers secured slaves and captives in war.
5. The captives, as gladiators, fought there with their swords against men or against animals.
6. Many captives had great courage and were freed because they fought well.

Practice Exercises

No. 76. Give the present active infinitive of these verbs and the English translation:

1. voco	6. moneo	11. nuntio	16. paro
2. debeo	7. timeo	12. volo	17. servo
3. ambulo	8. narro	13. terreo	18. laudo
4. eo	9. curo	14. adoro	19. do
5. sum	10. doleo	15. moveo	20. video

No. 77. Give the third principal part, the first person singular active tense, and the translation for:

1. paro	6. eo	11. propero	16. monstro
2. incito	7. terreo	12. habeo	17. timeo
3. aro	8. aedifico	13. do	18. nato
4. debeo	9. habito	14. teneo	19. moveo
5. libero	10. moneo	15. servo	20. maneo

No. 78. Give the fourth principal part, the perfect passive participle, and the translation:

1. amo	6. exspecto	11. do	16. adoro
2. habeo	7. narro	12. moneo	17. moveo
3. libero	8. terreo	13. servo	18. specto
4. neco	9. occupo	14. iuvo	19. obtineo
5. moneo	10. porto	15. video	20. loco

No. 79. Translate the following into English:
1. Et mater tua et pater vester de virtute consilium dabant.
2. Medio in oppido erant aedificia multa.
3. Fama de natione mea ab nuntiis portabitur.
4. Puella puerque sub aqua natant.
5. Circum urbem ambulare et multa videre debemus.
6. Nonne multa mala memoria tenes?
7. Sol summa in aqua esse videbatur.
8. Nationes Europae non semper pugnabunt.
9. Nautae in maribus oceanisque navigant.
10. Milites Romani virtutem magnam habent.

Chapter Four Review

Vocabulary Review

Nouns

1. ala	10. Ceres	19. homo	28. mare	37. Pluto
2. amphitheatrum	11. Cincinnatus	20. Horatius	29. mater	38. pons
3. animal	12. Colosseum	21. hostis	30. Mercurius	39. Proserpina
4. annus	13. consilium	22. Icarus	31. miles	40. sagitta
5. caedes	14. Creta	23. Inferi	32. natio	41. sagittarius
6. captivus	15. Daedalus	24. Iuppiter	33. pars	42. sol
7. caput	16. dictator	25. labor	34. pater	43. stella
8. celeritas	17. donum	26. littera	35. pax	44. urbs
9. cera	18. gladiator	27. magnitudo	36. pecunia	45. virtus

Adjectives

1. medius	2. robustus	3. summus

Verbs

| 1. doleo | 2. moveo | 3. obtineo | 4. specto | 5. terreo |

Adverbs

| 1. diu | 2. mox | 3. semper |

Prepositions

| 1. a, ab | 2. circum | 3. inter | 4. sub |

Conjunctions

| 1. aut | 2. et . . . et | 3. -que |

Practice Exercises

No. 80. Complete these infinitives by filling in the correct vowel:

1. dol_____re	6. d_____re	11. deb_____re	16. par_____re
2. terr_____re	7. spect_____re	12. tim_____re	17. occup_____re
3. mov_____re	8. vol_____re	13. hab_____re	18. st_____re
4. voc_____re	9. laud_____re	14. vid_____re	19. iuv_____re
5. obtin_____re	10. man_____re	15. nec_____re	20. mon_____re

No. 81. Fill in the missing principal part:

1. specto, spectare, _____, spectatus	6. paro, parare, _____, paratus
2. curo, _____, curavi, curatus	7. servo, servare, servavi, _____
3. _____, monere, monui, monitus	8. terreo, terrere, terrui, _____
4. do, dare, _____, datus	9. _____, habitare, habitavi, habitatus
5. moveo, movere, movi, _____	10. laudo, _____, laudavi, laudatus

No. 82. Translate these phrases:

1. animalium hominumque	6. celeritatis magnitudinisque
2. ab patre	7. a Mercurio
3. a matribus	8. ab militibus
4. mare stellamque	9. a Plutone
5. patres matresque	10. bellum paxque

No. 83. Translate these verb forms:

1. laudabatur	7. obtinebimus	13. occupantur	19. parabamur
2. dolebant	8. videris	14. timebantur	20. debebitur
3. monebamur	9. iuvabatis	15. parabitur	21. curabaris
4. necantur	10. habebo	16. dabis	22. spectabamur
5. vocamini	11. moveberis	17. servaris	23. terrebunt
6. erunt	12. potes	18. ibant	24. eram

Reading

Eutropius

Very little is known about Eutropius, except that he held official positions in Rome and in the provinces, and that he may have been a secretary to the Emperor Constantine. Of his works, the only one extant is the **Brevarium,** a brief history of Rome from the founding of the city in 753 B.C. to A.D. 364

Hic quoque ingens bellum civile commovit cogente uxore Cleopatra, regina Aegypti, dum cupiditate muliebri optat etiam in urbe regnare. Victus est ab Augusto navali pugna clara et inlustri apud Actium, qui locus in Epiro est, ex qua fugit in Aegyptum et desperatis rebus, cum omnes ad Augustum transirent, ipse se interemit. Cleopatra sibi aspidem admisit et veneno eius exstincta est. Aegyptus per Octavianum Augustum imperio Romano adiecta est praepositusque ei C. Cornelius Gallus. Hunc primum Aegyptus Romanum iudicem habuit.

   Breviarii, Liber VII, vii

The Bible

   Psalmus David, cum fugeret a facie Absalom filii sui
Domine, quid multiplicati sunt qui tribulant me!
Multi insurgunt adversum me;
multi dicunt animae meae:
Non est salus ipsi in Deo eius.
Tu autem, Domine, susceptor meus es,
gloria mea et exaltans caput meum.
Voce mea ad Dominum clamavi,
et exaudivit me de monte sancto suo.
Ergo dormivi et soporatus sum
et exsurrexi, quia Dominus suscepit me.
Non timebo milia populi circumdantis me.
Exsurge, Domine, salvum me fac, Deus meus;
quoniam tu percussisti omnes adversantes mihi sine causa,
dentes peccatorum contrivisti.
Domini est salus, et super populum tuum benedictio tua.

   Liber Psalmorum iii

Past Time; Volition; Pronouns

FAMILIAR ABBREVIATIONS

fl. or **flor., floruit,** he (she) flourished. Used with the date at which artists produced their work.

I.H.S., In hoc signo, In this sign. Or, **Iesus Hominum Salvator,** Jesus Savior of Men.

I.N.R.I., Iesus Nazarenus, Rex Iudaeorum, Jesus of Nazareth, King of the Jews.

pinx., pinxit, he (she) painted it.

sculp., sculpsit, he (she) carved it.

op. cit., opere citato, in the work cited. Used in footnotes instead of repeating the title of a book already referred to.

ibid. or **ib., ibidem,** in the same place. Used in footnotes, if the reference is the same as one made just previously.

Reading Vocabulary

Nouns

ignis, ignis, m., fire (**ignium**) (ignite)

audacia, audaciae, f., boldness, bravery, daring (audacity)

pretium, pretii or **preti, n.,** price (precious)

Tarquinius, Tarquini, m., Tarquinius

liber, liberi, m., book (library)

Adjectives

Sibyllinus, Sibyllina, Sibyllinum, Sibylline

superbus, superba, superbum, proud (superb)

novem, nine (November)

sex, six (sextet)

Verbs

rogo, rogare, rogavi, rogatus, ask, ask for (interrogate)

Conjunctions

postquam, after, when

Reading Grammar

Introduction to the Perfect Tense

A. The third principal part of the verb is used to form the active voice **perfect, pluperfect,** and **future perfect tenses.** The third principal part is the first person singular of the perfect active indicative tense.

B. In Latin, as in English, the **perfect** tenses differ from the **imperfect** tense, because the action of the perfect tenses happens once, at a definite point in time, and is finished, while the action of the imperfect tense takes place over a longer period of time, and is often repeated. Thus, the first person singular of **pugno** in the perfect, **pugnavi,** means *I have fought*. The fighting took place at one time in the past and was finished. However, the first person imperfect, **pugnabam,** means *I used to fight/did fight/was fighting*. The fighting still took place in the past, but it happened repeatedly. It is not made clear when the fighting stopped.

C. The basic endings for the three perfect active tenses are as follows:

		PERFECT	PLUPERFECT	FUTURE PERFECT
Singular:	1st person	-i	-eram	-ero
	2nd person	-isti	-eras	-eris
	3rd person	-it	-erat	-erit
Plural:	1st person	-imus	-eramus	-erimus
	2nd person	-istis	-eratis	-eritis
	3rd person	-erunt	-erant	-erint

These endings are added on to the perfect stem, which is derived by omitting the -**i** of the third principal part. Thus, the perfect stem of **amo** is **amav-.**

D. The perfect tense shows action completed in the past — *I have loved* — and the third principal part is the first person singular of this tense.

A-CONJUGATION		E-CONJUGATION	
amavi	I have loved; I loved	habui	I have had; I had
amavisti	you have loved	habuisti	you have had
amavit	he, she, it has loved	habuit	he, she, it has had
amavimus	we have loved	habuimus	we have had
amavistis	you have loved	habuistis	you have had
amaverunt	they have loved	habuerunt	they have had

E. The pluperfect tense is formed by adding the imperfect forms of **sum** to the perfect stem. It shows action completed at a definite point of time in the past — *I had loved*. The word *pluperfect* means *more perfect*. Thus, since the perfect tense describes action taking place in the past, the pluperfect describes action taking place even more in the past, or before the action of the perfect tense. Thus, the pluperfect is occasionally called the *past perfect*.

A-CONJUGATION		E-CONJUGATION	
amaveram	I had loved	habueram	I had had
amaveras	you had loved	habueras	you had had
amaverat	he, she, it had loved	habuerat	he, she, it had had
amaveramus	we had loved	habueramus	we had had
amaveratis	you had loved	habueratis	you had had
amaverant	they had loved	habuerant	they had had

F. The **future perfect** tense is formed by adding the future forms of **sum** to the perfect stem. The one exception is the third person plural of the future perfect active tense. This is formed by adding **-erint** to the perfect stem, to avoid confusion with the third person plural of the perfect active tense, which is formed by adding **-erunt** to the perfect stem.

The **future perfect** tense shows action to be completed before a definite point of time in the future — *I shall have loved*. Thus, it differs from the **future tense** in the same way that the **perfect** and **pluperfect** tenses differ from the **imperfect** tense.

A-CONJUGATION		E-CONJUGATION	
amavero	I shall have loved	habuero	I shall have had
amaveris	you will have loved	habueris	you will have had
amaverit	he/she/it will have loved	habuerit	he/she/it will have had
amaverimus	we shall have loved	habuerimus	we shall have had
amaveritis	you will have loved	habueritis	you will have had
amaverint	they will have loved	habuerint	they will have had

G. The verbs **sum**, **possum**, and **eo** are regular in the perfect tenses.

1. The forms of **sum** are as follows:

PERFECT TENSE		PLUPERFECT TENSE	
fui	I have been	fueram	I had been
fuisti	you have been	fueras	you had been
fuit	he/she/it has been	fuerat	he/she/it had been
fuimus	we have been	fueramus	we had been
fuistis	you have been	fueratis	you had been
fuerunt	they have been	fuerant	they had been

FUTURE PERFECT TENSE	
fuero	I shall have been
fueris	you will have been
fuerit	he/she/it will have been
fuerimus	we shall have been
fueritis	you will have been
fuerint	they will have been

2. The third principal part of **possum** is **potui**, and the perfect stem is **potu-**. Thus:

PERFECT TENSE		PLUPERFECT TENSE	
potui	I have been able	potueram	I had been able
potuisti	you have been able	potueras	you had been able
potuit	he/she/it has been able	potuerat	he/she/it had been able
etc.		etc.	

FUTURE PERFECT TENSE	
potuero	I shall have been able
potueris	you will have been able
potuerit	he/she/it will have been able
etc.	

3. The third principal part of **eo** is **ii** or **ivi**. The perfect stem is **i-**. Thus:

PERFECT TENSE

ii, ivi	I have gone
iistis, istis	you have gone
iit, it	he/she/it has gone
iimus	we have gone
iistis, istis	you have gone
ierunt	they have gone

PLUPERFECT TENSE

ieram	I had gone
ieras	you had gone
ierat	he/she/it had gone
ieramus	we had gone
ieratis	you had gone
ierant	they had gone

FUTURE PERFECT TENSE

iero	I shall have gone
ieris	you will have gone
ierit	he/she/it will have gone
ierimus	we shall have gone
ieritis	you will have gone
ierint	they will have gone

As you can see, some forms of the perfect active have alternatives. The **ii-** stem may be changed to **i-** if there is no other form of **eo** with which it can be confused. Thus, the first person plural, **iimus** would not be written as **imus;** it might be confused with the first person plural of the present active.

Reading

Libri Sibyllini

1. Inter antiquos erat fabula de libris Sibyllinis.

2. Tarquinius Superbus urbem Romam regnabat.

3. Femina ad Tarquinium libros novem portavit et pro libris pecuniam rogavit.

4. Tarquinius feminae pecuniam non dedit.

5. Femina in igni libros tres tum locavit.

6. Pro sex libris pretium librorem novem rogavit.

7. Tarquinius feminae pecuniam non dedit.

8. Postquam femina in igni libros sex locaverit Tarquinius feminae pro libris pecuniam dedit quod audacia feminae movebatur.

9. Libri erant libri Sibyllini.

10. Cum populus Romanus periculo incitabatur aut cum Roma oppugnabatur ad libros properabant.

The Sibylline Books

1. Among the ancients, there was a story about the Sibylline books.

2. Tarquinius the Proud was ruling the city of Rome.

3. A woman brought nine books to Tarquinius and asked for money for the books.

4. Tarquinius did not give the money to the woman.

5. The woman then put three books in the fire.

6. For the six books, she asked the price of the nine books.

7. Tarquinius did not give the money to the woman.

8. After the woman had placed six books in the fire, Tarquinius gave the money to the woman for the books because he was moved by the woman's boldness.

9. The books were the Sibylline books.

10. When the Roman people were aroused by danger, or when Rome was being attacked, they hurried to the books.

11. Libri Romanis auxilium multum semper dabant.
12. Erantne libri deorum?

11. The books always gave much help to the Romans.
12. Were they the books of the gods?

Practice Exercises

No. 84. Complete these principal parts:
1. ambulo, ambulare, _____, ambulatus
2. laudo, laudare, _____, laudatus
3. moneo, monere, _____, monitus
4. debeo, debere, _____, debitus
5. porto, portare, _____, portatus
6. servo, servare, _____, servatus
7. voco, vocare, _____, vocatus
8. moveo, movere, _____, motus
9. do, dare, _____, datus
10. rogo, rogare, _____, rogatus

No. 85. Translate these perfect tenses:
1. rogavit
2. spectaverunt
3. monuimus
4. iuvi
5. fuisti
6. necavisti
7. narravistis
8. habitavi
9. vidi
10. timuerunt
11. doluisti
12. habuistis
13. debuimus
14. laboraverunt
15. superavisti
16. monstravit
17. narraverunt
18. occupavistis
19. paravimus
20. volavit

No. 86. Translate these pluperfect tenses:
1. ambulaveram
2. adoraverant
3. araverat
4. moverant
5. manseramus
6. videratis
7. paraveras
8. dederas
9. tenueratis
10. steteram
11. paraverat
12. locaverant
13. incitaveras
14. curaveratis
15. nataveram
16. dolueramus
17. rogaverat
18. spectaverant
19. viderat
20. vocaveratis

No. 87. Translate these future perfect tenses:
1. amaveris
2. curaverit
3. laudavero
4. locaverimus
5. habuerint
6. terruerit
7. moverit
8. dederint
9. steteris
10. tenuerit
11. vocaverimus
12. servavero
13. portaverit
14. paraverint
15. nuntiaveris
16. narraverimus
17. habueritis
18. debuerit
19. adoraverint
20. ambulaveris

Perfect Passive Tenses

Reading Vocabulary

Nouns

rex, regis, m., king (regal)
nomen, nomenis, n., name (nomenclature)
mulier, mulieris, f., woman
mons, montis, m., mountain, mount (**montium**)
finis, finis, m., end, border (**finium**). In the plural, boundaries (finish)

lex, legis, f., law (legal)
pugna, pugnae, f., fight
murus, muri, m., wall (mural)
flumen, flumenis, n., river, stream (flume)
collis, collis, m., hill (collium)

Adjectives

proximus, proxima, proximum, next, nearest (approximate)
ultimus, ultima, ultimum, last, farthest (ultimate)   **septem,** seven (September)

Verbs

augeo, augere, auxi, auctus, increase, enlarge (augment)

Adverbs

postea, afterwards

Reading Grammar

A. The fourth principal part of the verb is the perfect passive participle. It is a verbal adjective. Since it is an adjective, it must agree with the word it modifies in case, number, and gender. Thus, **amatus,** *loved,* is really the adjective **amatus, amata, amatum,** and it is declined like any other first and second declension adjective. However, since it is a verbal adjective, it also has some of the qualities of a verb, such as tense and person, as usually occurs when it is used with the verb **sum.** When it is used with **sum** to form the perfect passive tenses, it is always in the nominative case, but it must agree with the subject in gender and number.

> **mulier amata est,** the woman has been loved
> **mulieres amatae sunt,** the women have been loved
> **vir amatus est,** the man has been loved
> **viri amati sunt,** the men have been loved
> **nomen vocatum est,** the name has been called
> **nomina vocata sunt,** the names have been called

FAMILIAR PHRASES

carpe diem, seize the day. Often used to mean "seize the opportunity" or "seize the chance."
cave canem, beware of the dog. Literally, beware the dog.
ex libris, from the library of. Used often on bookplates.
ex officio, because of an office (held previously).
in toto, in the whole; completely.
per capita, by heads; per person or individual.
post mortem, after death
exeunt omnes, all go out. Used as a stage direction in plays.
ultimatum, the last thing; the farthest thing. Used for the final terms offered by one party to another.

B. The perfect passive tense is formed by using the fourth principal part with the present tense of **sum.**

A-CONJUGATION		E-CONJUGATION	
amatus sum,	*I* (masc.) *have been loved*	**habita sum,**	*I* (fem.) *have been told*
amatus, -a, -um sum	I have been loved	**habitus, -a, -um sum**	I have been held
amatus, -a, -um es	you have been loved	**habitus, -a, -um es**	you have been held
amatus, -a, -um est	he/she/it has been loved	**habitus, -a, -um est**	he/she/it has been held
amati, -ae, -a sumus	we have been loved	**habiti, -ae, -a sumus**	we have been held
amati, -ae, -a estis	you have been loved	**habiti, -ae, -a estis**	you have been held
amati, -ae, -a sunt	they have been loved	**habiti, -ae, -a sunt**	they have been held

C. The pluperfect passive tense is formed by using the fourth principal part with **eram,** the imperfect tense of **sum.**

A-CONJUGATION		E-CONJUGATION	
amatus eram,	*I* (masc.) *had been loved*	**habita eram,**	*I* (fem.) *had been held*
amatus, -a, -um eram	I had been loved	**habitus, -a, -um eram**	I had been held
amatus, -a, -um eras	you had been loved	**habitus, -a, -um eras**	you had been held
amatus, -a, -um erat	he/she/it had been loved	**habitus, -a, -um erat**	he/she/it had been held
amati, -ae, -a eramus	we had been loved	**habiti, -ae, -a eramus**	we had been held
amati, -ae, -a eratis	you had been loved	**habiti, -ae, -a eratis**	you had been held
amati, -ae, -a erant	they had been loved	**habiti, -ae, -a erant**	they had been held

D. The future perfect passive tense is formed by using the fourth principal part with **ero,** the future tense of **sum.**

A-CONJUGATION		E-CONJUGATION	
amatus ero,	*I* (masc.) *shall have been loved*	**habita ero,**	*I* (fem.) *shall have been held*
amatus, -a, -um ero	I shall have been loved	**habitus, -a, -um ero**	I shall have been held
amatus, -a, -um eris	you will have been loved	**habitus, -a, -um eris**	you will have been held
amatus, -a, -um erit	he/she/it will have been loved	**habitus, -a, -um erit**	he/she/it will have been held
amati, -ae, -a erimus	we shall have been loved	**habiti, -ae, -a erimus**	we shall have been held
amati, -ae, -a eritis	you will have been loved	**habiti, -ae, -a eritis**	you will have been held
amati, -ae, -a erunt	they will have been loved	**habiti, -ae, -a erunt**	they will have been held

E. The verbs **sum** and **possum** do not have perfect passive tenses. **possum** only has three principal parts, while in **sum,** the fourth principal part, **futurus,** is the future active participle.

F. The fourth principal part of **eo** is **itus. eo** does have perfect passive forms, but these are rarely used.

Reading

Reges Romae	The Kings of Rome
1. Urbs Roma septem reges habuit. Romulas urbem parvam in monte Palatino aedificavit.	1. The city of Rome had seven kings. Romulus built a small city on the Palatine mount.
2. Urbi nomen Romam dedit. Romulus ob sapientam suam urbem bene regnabat.	2. To the city he gave the name Rome. Romulus ruled the city well because of his wisdom.
3. Populo consilium bonum dedit.	3. He gave good advice to the people.

4. Quod in urbe non erant mulieres Romani finitimos suos ad ludos vocaverunt.

4. Because there were not women in the city, the Romans called their neighbors to games.

5. Tum feminas puellasque pugna obtinuerunt.

5. Then they got women and girls by a fight.

6. Et Sabini et socii sui contra Romanos bella multa pugnaverunt, sed copiae Romanae hostes superaverunt.

6. Both the Sabines and their allies fought many wars against the Romans, but the Roman forces conquered the enemy.

7. Postea Numa Pompilius erat rex Romanorum.

7. Afterward, Numa Pompilius was king of the Romans.

8. Pacem amavit et populo erat gratus quod Romanis leges multas bonasque dedit.

8. He liked peace and he was pleasing to the people because he gave many and good laws to the Romans.

9. Aedificia templaque etiam aedificavit.

9. He also built buildings and temples.

10. Tum Romani ad Anco Marcio regnabantur.

10. Then the Romans were ruled by Ancus Marcius.

11. Multos bello superavit et murum circum montem Caelium aedificavit.

11. He defeated many people in war and he built a wall around the Caelian mount.

12. Postea Roma a Prisco Tarquinio regnabatur.

12. Afterwards, Rome was ruled by Tarquinius Priscus.

13. Circum Maximum, ubi Romani ludos habebant, aedificavit.

13. He built the Circus Maximus, where the Romans held their games.

14. Contra Sabinos bellum pugnavit et agris finitimis et monte Capitolio fines urbis auxit.

14. He fought a war against the Sabines and increased the territory of the city by neighboring fields and the Capitoline mount.

15. Proximus rex, Servius Tullius, Sabinos superavit.

15. The next king, Servius Tullius, overcame the Sabines.

16. Colles Romae ad septem auxit. Circum colles murum et circum murum fossas aedificavit.

16. He increased the hills of Rome to seven. Around the hills, he built a wall, and around the wall, ditches.

17. Multi in urbe habitaverunt et multi erant agricolae in agris et post colles et post flumen.

17. Many people lived in the city and many were farmers in the fields both in back of the hills and in back of the river.

18. Tarquinius Superbus erat ultimus rex Romae, sed bene diuque regnavit.

18. Tarquinius the Proud was the last king of Rome, but he ruled well and for a long time.

19. Copiae Tarquini Superbi bella multa pugnaverunt et nationes proximas Romae superaverunt.

19. The troops of Tarquinius the Proud fought many wars and defeated the nations next to Rome.

Practice Exercises

No. 88. Give the English for these perfect tenses:

1. fuerunt	6. laudatae sunt	11. vocati sumus	16. timuisti
2. ambulavit	7. monitus sum	12. natavi	17. paratus est
3. portatus est	8. debuimus	13. servatae estis	18. locata sunt
4. amati sunt	9. stetistis	14. nuntiatum est	19. laudaverunt
5. curata es	10. narratum est	15. moti sunt	20. movistis

No. 89. Give the English for these pluperfect tenses:

1. dederant
2. moverat
3. territus erat
4. manseratis
5. tenueras
6. pugnaverat
7. laudata eram
8. curati erant
9. amata eras
10. incitati eratis
11. parati erant
12. occupaveras
13. liberati eratis
14. necatus erat
15. servati eramus
16. monuerat
17. habueratis
18. tenueras
19. iuti eramus
20. adoraverant

No. 90. Give the English for these future perfect tenses:

1. monuero
2. fuerit
3. portatum erit
4. moniti erunt
5. habuerint
6. terrueris
7. moverimus
8. visi eritis
9. timuerit
10. mota erit
11. dederimus
12. steterint
13. fuerimus
14. necati eritis
15. laudatae erimus
16. armatus eris
17. curati erunt
18. locatum erit
19. fuerint
20. servata erit

No. 91. Translate these verb forms:

1. habitum erat
2. videro
3. oppugnata erunt
4. laudata eris
5. portata eras
6. debitum erit
7. debuerant
8. exspectavisti
9. vidistis
10. monstratum est
11. moniti sunt
12. rogatae sumus
13. spectaverunt
14. moti sumus
15. paraveramus
16. monitus est
17. steterat
18. dati erant
19. narraverunt
20. tenuero

Volo, Nolo, Malo

Reading Vocabulary

Nouns

Hesperides, Hesperidum, f., the Hesperides
Hercules, Herculis, m., Hercules
hortus, horti, m., garden (horticulture)
serpens, serpentis, f., snake, serpent (serpentium) (serpentine)
mille passus, a mile. Literally, a thousand paces. Pl.: **milia passuum**, miles
locus, loci, m., place, position. Sometimes neuter in the plural. (location, local)

Atlas, Atlantis, m., Atlas
Pythia, Pythiae, f., Pythia
corpus, corporis, n., body (corporeal)
hora, horae, f. hour (horology)
amor, amoris, m., love (amorous)
Apollo, Apollinis, m., Apollo
Eurystheus, Eurysthei, m., Eurystheus
Iuno, Iunonis, f., Juno

Adjectives

aureus, aurea, aureum, golden, of gold (aureate)

duodecim, twelve (duodecimal)

Verbs

volo, velle, volui, wish, want, be willing (volition)
nolo, nelle, nolui, not to wish, be unwilling
malo, malle, malui, prefer
doceo, docere, docui, doctus, teach, show (docile)
iubeo, iubere, iussi, iussus, order, command (jussive)
demonstro, demonstrare, demonstravi, demonstratus,
        point out, show (demonstrate)

Adverbs

domi, at home (domicile)   **quam diu,** how long
ruri, in the country (rural)

Prepositions

in, into, onto (inhale). With the accusative case.

Reading Grammar

A. Both the accusative and ablative cases are used to show time.
 1. The accusative case is used to show *how long* something goes on.
multos annos	for many years	**duodecim horas**	for twelve hours
 2. The ablative case is used to show **when** something happens.
anno	in (during) a year	**sex annis**	in (during) six years
hora	in (during) an hour		

B. Both the accusative and ablative cases are used to show place.
 1. The accusative case shows *to* or *into* what place motion is directed, or *how far*.
ad urbem	to the city	**in oppidum**	into the town
multa milia passuum	many miles, for many miles		
 2. The ablative case shows *where* the place is, or *from where* the motion is directed.
in oppido	in the town	**in mare**	on the sea
ab oppido	away from the town	**ex urbe**	out of the city
de muro	down from the wall		

C. With the names of cities, towns, and small islands, and with the words **ruri** (in the country) and **domi** (at home), no preposition is used.
Romam	to Rome	**Roma**	from Rome

D. Numbers are adjectives. There are two kinds of numbers. One, two, five, ten, etc. are called **cardinal** numbers. First, second, fifth, tenth, etc. are called **ordinal numbers.** You will learn more about numbers in a later chapter. For now, all you need to remember is that most **cardinal** numbers are not declined.
duodecim puellae	twelve girls	**duodecim puellarum**	of twelve girls
duodecim horti	twelve gardens	**duodecim hortorum**	of twelve gardens
duodecim corpora	twelve bodies	**duodecim corporum**	of twelve bodies

E. The Irregular Verbs **volo, nolo,** and **malo.**
  1. These three verbs are conjugated similarly, and are closely related in meaning.
    a. **Volo** means to wish for something, to want something, or to be willing to do something.
    b. **Nolo** means to wish not to have or to do something, or to be unwilling to do something.
    c. **Malo** means to prefer something.
  2. These verbs are almost always used with the infinitive of another verb:

volo ire   I want to go   **nolo pugnare**   I do not want to fight   **malo manere**   I prefer to stay

  3. These verbs only have the first three principal parts:

volo, velle, volui   **nolo, nelle, nolui**   **malo, malle, malui**

  4. None of these verbs have passive forms.
  5. Present tense:

volo	I want/am willing	**nolo**	I do not want/am not willing
vis	you want	**non vis**	you do not want
vult	he, she, it wants	**non vult**	he, she, it does not want
volumus	we want	**nolumus**	we do not want
vultis	you want	**non vultis**	you do not want
volunt	they want	**nolunt**	they do not want

malo	I prefer
mavis	you prefer
mavult	he, she, it prefers
malumus	we prefer
mavultis	you prefer
malunt	they prefer

Present active infinitives:

velle   to want, to be willing   **malle**   to prefer   **nelle**   not to want, to be unwilling

    a. Only **nolo** has imperative forms.
    Singular: **noli**   do not want! be unwilling!   Plural: **nolite**   do not want! be unwilling!
These forms are generally used to command someone *not* to do something.

      noli ire   do not go! (literally, do not want to go!)
      nolite pugnare   do not fight! (literally, do not want to fight!)

    b. As you may have suspected from the present forms, **nolo** was originally **non volo.** The two words contracted, or became one word, **nolo.** However, some forms of the present tense remain uncontracted.
    c. Similarly, **malo** was originally **mavolo.** This form does appear occasionally, but usually, the contracted form **malo** is used. The other forms of the present tense are not contracted.
  6. **volo** uses the stem **vol-** for the imperfect and future tenses; **nolo** uses **nol-** and **malo** uses **mal-.**
    a. Imperfect:

volebam	I used to want/was wanting	**nolebam**	I did not want/was unwilling
volebas	you used to want	**nolebas**	you did not want
volebat	he, she, it used to want	**nolebat**	he, she, it did not want
etc.		etc.	

malebam	I used to prefer/was preferring
malebam	you used to prefer
malebat	he, she it used to prefer
etc.	

b. Future:

volam	I shall want/be willing	nolam	I shall not want/be unwilling
voles	you will want	noles	you will not want
volet	he, she, it will want	nolet	he, she, it will not want
volemus	we shall want	nolemus	we shall not want
voletis	you will want	noletis	you will not want
volent	they will want	nolent	they will not want

malam	I shall prefer
males	you will prefer
malet	he, she, it will prefer
malemus	we shall prefer
maletis	you will prefer
malent	they will prefer

You will notice that the future endings for these verbs are different from those you have previously encountered. These are the normal future endings for third and fourth conjugation verbs. These conjugations will be introduced later in this chapter.

6. In the perfect tenses, **volo, nolo,** and **malo** are conjugated normally. The perfect stems are **volu-, nolu-,** and **malu-.**

Reading

Labores Herculis	The Labors of Hercules
1. Pythia ab Apolline docebatur et populo consilium dei dedit.	1. Pythia was taught by Apollo and gave the advice of the god to the people.
2. Hercules a femina amorem suum Apollinis demonstrare iussus est.	2. Hercules was ordered by the woman to show his love for Apollo.
3. Hercules ad urbem regis, Eurysthei, properavit. Ibi Eurystheus Herculi labores duodecim dedit.	3. Hercules hurried to the city of the king, Eurystheus. There, Eurystheus gave Hercules twelve labors.
4. Sunt multae fabulae de laboribus Herculis.	4. There are many stories about the labors of Hercules.
5. Duodecim annos laborabat quod erat servus regis, sed Hercules de laboribus suis minime dolebat.	5. He labored for twelve years because he was the servant of the king, but Hercules grieved very little about his labors.
6. Corpus robustum habebat et regem laboremque non timebat.	6. He had a strong body and did not fear the king and the work.
7. A rege diu tenebatur, sed post duodecim annos liberatus est quod regem bene iuverat.	7. He was held for a long time by the king, but after twelve years, he was freed because he had helped the king well.
8. Deo Apollini amorem suum demonstraverat.	8. He had shown the god, Apollo, his love.

Poma Aurea Hesperidum	The Golden Apples of the Hesperides
1. Hercules pro rege, Eurystheus, bene laboravit, sed etiam tum non erat liber et domi non mansit.	1. Hercules worked well for the king, Eurytheus, but even then he was not free and did not stay at home.
2. Rex Herculem poma aurea ex horto Hesperidum obtinere iussit.	2. The king ordered Hercules to get the apples from the garden of the Hesperides.
3. Hesperides erant filiae pulchrae Atlantis et in loco ultimo in fini terrae ruri habitabant.	3. The Hesperides were the beautiful daughters of Atlas and lived in the country in the farthest place on the end of the earth.
4. Pro Iunone pome aurea ibi curabant.	4. They took care of the golden apples there for Juno.
5. Multi praemio pomorum moti erant, sed Hesperides poma semper bene servabant.	5. Many people had been moved by the reward of the apples, but the Hesperides always preserved the apples well.
6. Erat murus magnus altusque circum hortum ubi erant poma, atque ante horum erat serpens.	6. There was a large and high wall around the garden where the apples were, and in front of the garden was a serpent.
7. Serpens capita multa habuit.	7. The serpent had many heads.
8. Hercules multa milia passuum ambulavit. Post annum ad hortum venit.	8. Hercules walked many miles. After a year, he came to the garden.
9. Erat in fini ultimo terrae et proximus Oceano.	9. It was on the farthest end of the earth and next to the Ocean.
10. Hercules Atlantem, virum robustum et amicum, ibi vidit.	10. Hercules saw Atlas there, a strong and friendly man.
11. Auxilium rogavit.	11. He asked for help.

ACADEMIC DEGREES AND TERMS

We use many Latin words and phrases in academic degrees and terms, as shown below.

cum laude, with praise. Given with a diploma that has been earned with a grade of work higher than ordinary.

magna cum laude, with great praise.

summa cum laude, with highest praise.

Alumnus, pl. **Alumni,** male graduate or graduates.

Alumna, pl. **Alumnae,** female graduate or graduates.

Alma Mater, Foster Mother. Refers to one's school or college.

M.A. or, A.M. Artium Magister, Master of Arts.

B.A. or A.B., Baccalaureus Artium, Bachelor of Arts.

B.S., Baccalaureus Scientiae, Bachelor of Science.

D.D., Divinitatis Doctor, Doctor of Divinity.

D.Litt. or Litt.D., Doctor Litterarum, Doctor of Literature or Letters.

M.D., Medicinae Doctor, Doctor of Medicine.

Ph.D., Philosophiae Doctor, Doctor of Philosophy.

LL.D., Legum Doctor, Doctor of Laws.

D.M.D., Dentariae Medicinae Doctor, Doctor of Dental Medicine.

ASSIMILATION

Some prefixes take on the first letter of the word to which they are attached. This process is called assimilation and often smooths out pronunciation. Assimilation occurs with these prefixes:

ad   **ad** and **pono** (put, place) become **appono,** put to, put near
con   **con** and **mitto** (send) become **committo,** send together
in   **in** and **mortalis** become **immortalis,** immortal

Sometimes there is a change to a different letter:

in and **porto** become **importo,** carry in, bring in
con and **pono** become **compono,** put together

Practice Exercises

No. 92. Give the English for these expressions of time:

1. multos annos
2. proximo anno
3. multas horas
4. proxima hora
5. septem horas
6. medio anno
7. sex horis
8. annos longos
9. hora
10. duodecim horas

No. 93. Give the English for these expressions of place:

1. ad urbes
2. ex oppidis
3. Roma
4. Romam
5. in castra
6. ante forum
7. post hortum
8. in agro
9. in agros
10. de collibus
11. ex casa
12. ruri
13. domi
14. ab flumine
15. sub maribus
16. sub muris
17. in fossam
18. ab templo
19. e viis
20. de sole

No. 94. Translate these verbs:

1. videbo
2. pugnaverat
3. stabatis
4. laborabimus
5. fuerat
6. obtinebunt
7. natabamus
8. erit
9. videmus
10. spectatum est
11. movebitur
12. aedificata erant
13. fuisti
14. oppugnabamur
15. manserunt
16. vult
17. non vis
18. malo habere
19. malebam
20. noles

No. 95. Translate these sentences:

1. Proximo anno Romam movebimus.
2. Sex horas in urbe manserunt.
3. Medio in colle oppugnati erant.
4. Multas horas in Italia manebam.
5. Ibi erit horam.
6. Nonne multos annos laborabunt?
7. Ad oppidum multas horas longas ambulabat.
8. Ab rege non liberatus est.
9. Suntne in horto cum pueris?
10. Septem milia passuum ab urbe movi.
11. Nolite ad urbem ire.
12. Malo in oppidum manere.

Pronouns; Third Conjugation Verbs

Reading Vocabulary

Nouns

causa, causae, f., cause, reason (causeless)
signum, signi, n., signal, standard (signify)
Hippomenes, Hippomenis, m., Hippomenes
iter, itineris, n., journey, march, way, route
       (itinerary)

mora, morae, f., delay (moratorium)
umerus, umeri, m., shoulder (humerus)
pes, pedis, m., foot (pedal)
nox, noctis, f., night (**noctium**) (nocturnal)
Atalanta, Atalantae, f., Atalanta

Pronoun and Adjective

is, ea, id, he, she, it; this, that. Can be used either as a pronoun or as an adjective.

Verbs

duco, ducere, duxi, ductum, lead (conduct, aqueduct)
mitto, mittere, misi, missus, send (mission, manumit)
peto, petere, petivi, petitus, seek, ask (petition)

curro, currere, cucurri, cursus, run (current)
dico, dicere, dixi, dictus, say, speak (diction)

Adverbs

paene, almost, nearly (peninsula)

Reading Grammar

    A. **e/i-conjugation** or third conjugation verbs follow the same rules as the regular verbs you have met so far, except in the future tense. The predominant vowels are **e** and **i**.
    Consider the verb **duco.**
       1. Principal parts: **duco, ducere, duxi, ductus,** lead
    The first two principal parts show that **duco** is a third conjugation verb. The infinitive ends in **-ere,** like a second conjugation verb; however, there is no **-e-** in the first person singular of the present active tense. The stem for the present, imperfect, and future forms is **duc-.** The stem for the perfect active forms is **dux-,** while the perfect passive forms are derived from **ductus.**
       2. Present Tense:

ACTIVE (I lead, am leading, do lead)		PASSIVE (I am being led, am led)	
Singular	Plural	Singular	Plural
duco	ducimus	ducor	ducimur
ducis	ducitis	duceris	ducimini
ducit	ducunt	ducitur	ducuntur

As you can see, the vowel connecting the stem to the ending varies, depending on the form. You will have to memorize which forms use which vowels.

Imperatives: Singular: **duc**   Plural: **ducite**

For the imperative singular, the **-ere** is dropped. In the plural, the basic ending -te is added on to the present stem plus the vowel -i-.

3. Imperfect Tense:

ACTIVE (I led, was leading)

Singular	Plural
ducebam	ducebamus
ducebas	ducebatis
ducebat	ducebant

PASSIVE (I was being led, was led)

Singular	Plural
ducebar	ducebamur
ducebaris	ducebamini
ducebatur	ducebantur

The vowel used between the stem and the imperfect endings is -e-.

4. Future Tenses:

The active future tense endings of third conjugation verbs are:

SINGULAR	PLURAL
-am	-emus
-es	-etis
-et	-ent

These are the same as the basic endings of the present tense added to the vowel -e-, with the exception of the first person singular. The basic ending for this form is -m, and it is added to the vowel -a-. The future passive endings are the basic passive endings added to the vowel used for the active future tense:

SINGULAR:	PLURAL:
-ar	-emur
-eris	-emini
-etur	-entur

Thus, the future tense of **duco** is:

ACTIVE (I shall lead)

Singular	Plural
ducam	ducemus
duces	ducetis
ducet	ducent

PASSIVE (I shall be led)

Singular	Plural
ducar	ducemur
duceris	ducemini
ducetur	ducentur

5. Perfect Tense:

ACTIVE (I led, have led)

Singular	Plural
duxi	duximus
duxisti	duxistis
duxit	duxerunt

PASSIVE (I have been led)

Singular	Plural
ductus, -a, -um sum	ducti, -ae, -a sumus
ductus, -a, -um es	ducti, -ae, a estis
ductus, -a, -um est	ducti, -ae, -a sunt

6. Pluperfect Tense:

ACTIVE (I had led)		PASSIVE (I had been led)	
Singular	Plural	Singular	Plural
duxeram	**duxeramus**	**ductus, -a, -um eram**	**ducti, -ae, -a eramus**
duxeras	**duxeratis**	**ductus, -a, -um eras**	**ducti, -ae, -a eratis**
duxerat	**duxerant**	**ductus, -a, -um erat**	**ducti, -ae, -a erant**

7. Future Perfect Tense:

ACTIVE (I shall have led)		PASSIVE (I shall have been led)	
Singular	Plural	Singular	Plural
duxero	**duxerimus**	**ductus, -a, -um ero**	**ducti, -ae, -a erimus**
duxeris	**duxeritis**	**ductus, -a, -um eris**	**ducti, -ae, -a eritis**
duxerit	**duxerint**	**ductus, -a, -um erit**	**ducti, -ae, -a erunt**

B. **is, ea, id** can be used as either a pronoun (*he, she, it;* plural: *they*) or an adjective (*this, that;* plural: *these, those*). The declension is given below.

1. As a **pronoun,** it has the same gender and number as the noun it replaces, but its case is determined by its use in the sentence, and may not always agree with the case of the noun it replaces.

Puerum video, I see the boy. **Eum video,** I see him. Same case (accusative), number (singular), and gender (masculine) as **puerum. Is in casa est,** He is in the house. Same number and gender as **puerum.** However, the case is different. It is nominative, not accusative, because **is** is the subject of the verb **est,** and the subject is put in the nominative case.

SINGULAR

CASE	MASCULINE		FEMININE		NEUTER	
Nom.	**is**	he	**ea**	her	**id**	it
Gen.	**eius**	his	**eius**	hers	**eius**	its
Dat.	**ei**	to, for him	**ei**	to, for her	**ei**	to, for it
Acc.	**eum**	him	**eam**	her	**eum**	it
Abl.	**eo**	from/with/by/in him	**ea**	from/with/by/in her	**eo**	from/with/by/in it

PLURAL

CASE	MASCULINE	FEMININE	NEUTER	
Nom.	**ei or ii**	**eae**	**ea**	they
Gen.	**eorum**	**earum**	**eorum**	their
Dat.	**eis or iis**	**eis or iis**	**eis or iis**	to, for them
Acc.	**eos**	**eas**	**eos**	them
Abl.	**eis or iis**	**eis or iis**	**eis or iis**	from/with/by/in them

Note that most pronouns are not used in the vocative case.

2. As an **adjective, is, ea, id** must have the same gender, number, and case as the noun it modifies. It is declined in the same way as the pronoun.

is puer, this boy, that boy   **ea puella,** this girl, that girl   **id bellum,** this war, that war

As an **adjective,** the singular means *this* or *that,* and the plural means *these* or *those.*

CASE	SINGULAR	PLURAL
Nom.	this, that	these, those
Gen.	of this, of that	of these, of those
Dat.	to, for this; to, for that	to, for these; to, for those
Acc.	this, that	these, those
Abl.	from/with/by/in this; from/with/by/in that	from/with/by/in these; from/with/by/in those

C. The use of **eius**.

    1. The possessive form of the pronoun **is, ea, id** is **eius**; plural, **eorum**. It does not refer to the subject.

      Pomum eius videmus.   We see his (her) apple.

      Pomum eius videt.   He (she) sees someone else's apple.

Note that **eius** might still be translated as *his* or *her,* but the person it refers to is somone other than the subject of **videt**.

    2. When the possessor is the same as the subject, the adjective **suus** is used.

      Pomum suum habet.   He has his (own) apple.

Reading

Poma Aurea Hesperidum (concl'd)

1. Postquam Hercules auxilium petiverat, causam itineris sui ad finem terrae Atlantem docuit.

2. Atlas erat pater Hesperidum et Herculi de loco ubi erant poma aurea narravit, sed Atlas caelum in umeris suis tenebat.

3. Atlas Herculi caelum dedit et Herculum in umeris caelum tenere iussit.

4. Atlas ad hortum Hesperidum properavit.

5. Diu Hercules in umeris suis caelum tenebat. Diu Atlantem non viderat.

6. Hercules famam de Atlante non habuerat. Et timebat et dolebat.

7. Pretium pomorum erat certe magnum.

8. Post multas noctes Atlantem vidit et laetus erat.

9. Mox poma aurea habuit. Tum Atlas caelum in umeris suis locavit et Hercules erat liber.

10. Ad Graecam cum pomis properavit.

Atalanta

1. Atalanta erat puella Graeciae et vero pulchra.

2. Multi viri contra eam cucurrerant, sed magnam celeritatem habebat et non superata erat.

3. Venus consilium habebat. Puella erat praemium victoriae et pedibus eos currere iussit.

4. Hippomenes contra eam currere paratus est.

5. Multi spectabant et eum incitabant.

6. Signum datum est.

7. Atalanta celeritatem suam demonstrabat. Paene volabat.

8. Quam longe ante eum currit!

9. Sed Venus Hippomeni viam ad victoriam docuerat. Ei poma aurea dederat.

10. Hippomenes pomum ad terram misit.

The Golden Apples of the Hesperides (concl'd)

1. After Hercules had sought help, he showed Atlas the cause of his journey to the end of the earth.

2. Atlas was the father of the Hesperides and he told Hercules about the place where the golden apples were, but Atlas was holding the sky on his shoulders.

3. Atlas gave the sky to Hercules and he ordered Hercules to hold the sky on his shoulders.

4. Atlas hurried to the garden of the Hesperides.

5. For a long time Hercules held the sky on his shoulders. He had not seen Atlas for a long time.

6. Hercules had not had a report about Atlas. He was both afraid and grieving.

7. The price of the apples was certainly great.

8. After many nights, he saw Atlas and he was happy.

9. Soon he had the golden apples. Then Atlas placed the sky on his own shoulders and Hercules was free.

10. He hurried to Greece with the apples.

Atalanta

1. Atalanta was a girl of Greece and truly beautiful.

2. Many men had raced against her, but she had great speed and had not been surpassed.

3. Venus had a plan. The girl was the reward of victory and she ordered them to run on foot.

4. Hippomenes was prepared to run against her.

5. Many were watching and urging him on.

6. The signal is given.

7. Atalanta was showing her speed. She was almost flying.

8. How far in front of him she runs!

9. But Venus had shown Hippomenes the way to victory. She had given him golden apples.

10. Hippomenes threw an apple to the ground.

11. Atalanta ad moram movebatur.
12. Hippomenes celeritatem suam auxit.
13. Finis erat propinquus.
14. Venus, dea amoris, eum bene iuverat.
15. Hippomenes consilio donoque deae puellam superaverat.

11. Atalanta was moved toward delay.
12. Hippomenes increased his speed.
13. The end was near.
14. Venus, goddess of love, had helped him well.
15. Hippomenes had overtaken the girl by the plan and gift of the goddess.

Practice Exercises

No. 96. Translate these verb forms:

1. mittunt	6. parati erunt	11. iubebit	16. mittet
2. doctus sunt	7. duxit	12. spectabamur	17. servavi
3. petimur	8. liberavisti	13. demonstratis	18. timueras
4. debet	9. adorabam	14. rogabunt	19. petiveratis
5. moniti eratis	10. miserit	15. ducebas	20. mansuerunt

No. 97. Translate these phrases:

1. ob iniuriam	6. ad Galliam
2. ex proeliis	7. ab colle
3. sex horas	8. in litteris
4. in itinere	9. ab hominibus
5. e finibus	10. in ripam

No. 98. Translate the following:

1. Eas peto.	6. Eum vidistis.	11. ea hora	16. eorum poma
2. eorum librorum	7. in eis locis	12. sua signa	17. suos reges
3. hortus eius	8. patri eius	13. ex eis urbibus	18. cum eis
4. Ea eis dedi.	9. Ab eo mittuntur.	14. eam mulierem	19. id iter
5. Is pugnabat.	10. Eos misisti.	15. Ab eis ducimur.	20. eam causam

No. 99. Change these verb forms to the active (if they are passive) or to the passive (if they are active):

1. ducit	6. misisti	11. petiverunt	16. current
2. duxi	7. mittebantur	12. petiti erimus	17. cucurrit
3. ducebar	8. mittemini	13. petet	18. curritur
4. ducti sunt	9. missus es	14. petitur	19. currebant
5. ducam	10. miserat	15. petebaris	20. cursum erat

Chapter Five Review

Vocabulary Review

Nouns

1. amor	11. fines	21. lex	31. nox
2. Apollo	12. flumen	22. liber	32. pes
3. Atalanta	13. Hercules	23. locus	33. pomum
4. Atlas	14. Hesperides	24. mille passus	34. pretium
5. audacia	15. Hippomenes	25. milia passuum	35. pugna
6. causa	16. hora	26. mons	36. Pythia
7. collis	17. hortus	27. mora	37. rex
8. corpus	18. ignis	28. mulier	38. serpens
9. Eurystheus	19. iter	29. murus	39. signum
10. finis	20. Iuno	30. nomen	40. Tarquinius

Pronouns

1. is	2. ea	3. id

Adjectives

1. aureus	6. sex
2. duodecim	7. Sibyllinus
3. novem	8. superbus
4. proximus	9. ultimus
5. septem	10. is, ea, id

Verbs

1. augeo	4. dico	7. iubeo	10. nolo
2. curro	5. doceo	8. malo	11. peto
3. demonstro	6. duco	9. mitto	12. rogo

Adverbs

1. domi	2. paene	3. postea	4. quam diu	5. ruri

Prepositions

1. in

Conjunctions

1. postquam

Practice Exercises

No. 100. Give the English for these phrases:

1. in pedibus	4. ex agris	7. de corpore	10. Romam
2. ab colli	5. in ignem	8. ruri	11. domi
3. ad flumina	6. in muris	9. Roma	12. ex nocte

No. 101. Translate these perfect tenses:

1. fuerat	7. data sunt	13. incitati erant	19. laudati erimus
2. regnavimus	8. misistis	14. properaveratis	20. habuerat
3. rogatus est	9. petitum erit	15. fuerint	21. maluit
4. portaveris	10. auctum erat	16. rogatus sum	22. voluerunt
5. dederunt	11. movimus	17. stetit	23. malueram
6. locaverunt	12. fuimus	18. vocavisti	24. nolueritis

No. 102. Give the English for these phrases:

1. proximo anno	6. eo nocte
2. horas septem	7. eas noctes
3. proximis horis	8. eos annos
4. multo anno	9. eo anno
5. sex annos	10. ea hora

No. 103. Give the English for these pronouns:

1. eius	4. ei	7. ea	10. eum
2. eos	5. id	8. eorum	11. ii
3. eae	6. eas	9. eis	12. eo

No. 104. Translate these adjective phrases:

1. eum amorem	4. eas causas	7. ea poma	10. eius loci
2. eius audaciae	5. eis finibus	8. ei mulieri	11. ei regi
3. ea nomina	6. eorum itinerum	9. id corpus	12. eam noctem

Reading

Marcus Valerius Martialis

Martial was born in Spain about A.D. 40 and went to Rome as a young man. He was a master of the epigram, and his poems, depicting scenes of everyday life, are full of wit, freshness, and satire. Martial died about A.D. 103, after returning to Spain.

Non amo te, Sabidi, nec possum dicere quare;
      hoc tantum possum dicere: non amo te.
          Epigrammaton Liber I, xxxii

Cras te victurum, cras dicis, Postume, semper.
    Dic mihi, cras istud, Postume, quando venit?
Quam longe cras istud, ubi est? aut unde petendum?
    Numquid apud Parthos Armeniosque latet?
Iam cras istud habet Priami vel Nestoris annos.
    Cras istud quanti, dic mihi, posset emi?
Cras vives? Hodie iam vivere, Postume, serum est;
    ille sapit, quisquis, Postume, vixit heri.
        Epigrammaton Liber V, lviii

The Bible

    Omnia tempus habent,
et suis spatiis transeunt universa sub caelo.
Tempus nascendi et tempus moriendi,
tempus plantandi et tempus evellendi quod plantatum est,
tempus occidenti et tempus sanandi,
tempus destruendi et tempus aedificandi,
tempus flendi et tempus ridendi,
tempus plangendi et tempus saltandi,
tempus spargendi lapides et tempus colligendi,
tempus amplexandi et tempus longe fieri ab amplexibus,
tempus adquirendi et tempus perdendi,
tempus custodiendi et tempus abiciendi,
tempus scindendi et tempus consuendi,
tempus tacendi et tempus loquendi,
tempus dilectonis et tempus odii,
tempus belli et tempus pacis.
Quid habet amplius homo de labore suo?
        Liber Ecclesiastes III, i-ix

Irregular Verbs; Pronouns; Infinitives

LATIN IN THE CONSTITUTION OF THE UNITED STATES

The following Latin phrases are used in the Constitution:

In Section 3, dealing with Officers of the Senate:

"The Senate shall choose their officers, and also a president **pro tempore**, in the absence of the Vice-President, or when he shall exercise the office of President of the United States." **pro tempore** means *for the time.*

In Section 9, dealing with Powers Forbidden to the United States:

"The privilege of the writ of **habeas corpus** shall not be suspended, unless when in cases of rebellion or invasion the public safety may require it." **habeas corpus** means *thou shalt have the body.* A writ of habeas corpus is a legal document making it mandatory that an accused person be brought to court to be told the reason for his or her detention.

"No bill of attainder or **ex-post-facto** law shall be passed." **ex post facto** means *from what is done afterwards.* An ex post facto law is passed after a crime has been committed. Thus, a person who has committed a crime must be tried under the laws as they existed at the time of the commission of the crime.

Reading Vocabulary

Nouns

timor, timoris, m., fear, dread (timorous)
poena, poenae, f., punishment, fine (penal)
Bacchus, Bacchi, m., Bacchus (bacchanalian)
mors, mortis, f., death (**mortium**) (mortality)
diligentia, diligentiae, f., diligence, care (diligent)
studium, studii or studi, n., zeal, eagerness (studio)
tempus, temporis, n., time (temporary, ex tempore)

aurum, auri, n., gold (auriferous)
arena, arenae, f., sand (arena)
Silenus, Sileni, m., Silenus
Midas, Midae, m., Midas
cibus, cibi, m., food
arbor, arboris, f., tree (arboretum)

Verbs

capio, capere, cepi, captus, take, seize, capture (caption)
pono, ponere, posui, positus, put, place (position, postpone)

fero, ferre, tuli, latum, carry, bear
facio, facere, feci, factus, make, do (factory)
verto, vertere, verti, versus, turn (vertical)

Prepositions

propter, because of, on account of

Reading Grammar

A. Some **e/i-conjugation** verbs have **-io** in the first principal part. These also have an **-i-** in most forms of the present, imperfect, and future tenses. Compare **capio** with **ducio**.

1. Present Tense:

ACTIVE		PASSIVE	
duco, *I lead*	capio, *I seize*	ducor, *I am led*	capior, *I am seized*
ducis	capis	duceris	caperis
ducit	capit	ducitur	capitur
ducimus	capimus	ducimur	capimur
ducitis	capitis	ducimini	capimini
ducunt	capiunt	ducuntur	capiuntur

capio has an **-i-** in all forms of the present tense, except for the second person singular in the passive voice.
Imperatives:

	lead!	seize!
Singular:	duc	cape
Plural:	ducite	capite

You will notice that although the imperative plurals are formed the same way, the imperative singular of **capio** ends in **-e**. This is true of all **-io** verbs.

2. Imperfect Tense:

ACTIVE		PASSIVE	
ducebam, *I was leading*	capiebam, *I was seizing*	ducebar, *I was led*	capiebar, *I was seized*
ducebas	capiebas	ducebaris	capiebaris
ducebat	capiebat	ducebatur	capiebatur
ducebamus	capiebamus	ducebamur	capiebamur
ducebatis	capiebatis	ducebamini	capiebamini
ducebant	capiebant	ducebanutur	capiebantur

Where the forms of **duco** have **-e-**, the forms of **capio** have **-ie-**.

3. Future Tense:

ACTIVE		PASSIVE	
ducam, *I shall lead*	capiam, *I shall seize*	ducar, *I shall be led*	capiar, *I shall be seized*
duces	capies	duceris	capieris
ducet	capiet	ducetur	capietur
ducemus	capiemus	ducemur	capiemur
ducestis	capietis	ducemini	capiemini
ducent	capient	ducentur	capientur

The future forms of **capio** have **-ie-** and **-ia-** instead of **-e-** and **-a-**.

4. The perfect tenses are all regular. The active endings are added on to the perfect stem, just as with all other verbs. The perfect stem of **capio** is **cep-**, derived from the third principal part, **cepi**. The passive endings are formed with the fourth principal part, **captus**, and the verb **sum**.

B. The irregular verb **fero**.
1. The principal parts of this verb are **fero, ferre, tuli, latus**.
2. Most of the irregularities are found in the present forms:

ACTIVE	PASSIVE
fero, *I carry, am carrying, do carry*	**feror,** *I am being carried, am carried*
fers	**ferris**
fert	**fertur**
ferimus	**ferimur**
fertis	**ferimini**
ferunt	**feruntur**

Some of these forms are quite strange, so you will have to memorize them.

Present Infinitive: **ferre**
Imperative: Singular: **fer**
                 Plural: **ferte**

2. The imperfect and future forms of **fero** add the basic endings for third conjugation verbs to the present stem, **fer-.**

IMPERFECT TENSE:

ACTIVE	PASSIVE
ferebam, *I was carrying, carried*	**ferebar,** *I was being carried, was carried*
ferebas	**ferebaris**
ferebat	**ferebatur**
etc.	etc.

FUTURE TENSE:

ACTIVE	PASSIVE
feram, *I shall carry*	**ferar,** *I shall be carried*
feres	**fereris**
etc.	etc.

3. The perfect tenses are regular. However, you must remember the principal parts of the verb! The third principal part is **tuli** and the perfect stem is **tul-.** The fourth principal part is **latus.** Thus:

PERFECT TENSE:

ACTIVE	PASSIVE
tuli, *I have carried, carried*	**latus, -a, -um sum,** *I have been carried*
tulisti	**latus, -a, -um es**
etc.	etc.

PLUPERFECT TENSE:

ACTIVE	PASSIVE
tuleram, *I had carried*	**latus, -a, -um eram,** *I had been carried*
tuleras	**latus, -a, -um eras**
etc.	etc.

FUTURE PERFECT TENSE:

ACTIVE	PASSIVE
tulero, *I shall have carried*	**latus, -a, -um ero,** *I shall have been carried*
tuleris	**latus, -a, -um eris**
etc.	etc.

C. When **cum** is used to show how something was done, it often follows the adjective.

Cum diligentia laborat.   He works with diligence.
Laborat magna cum diligentia.   He works with great diligence.

D. The cause of an action may be shown by either the ablative case alone, or by **ob** or **propter** followed by the accusative case.

timore,   because of (on account of) fear
ob timorem,   because of (on account of) fear
propter timorem,   because of (on account of) fear

Reading

Midas et Aurum
1. Temporibus antiquis erat rex, Midas.
2. Nomen eius regis erat clarum quod amicus Bacchi erat.
3. Silenus Bacchum docebat, sed ab hostibus captus erat.
4. A Mida liberatus erat. Bacchus vero fuit laetus.
5. Bacchus ei nuntiavit: "Donum dabo."
6. Midas bonam fortunam, sed non multam sapientam habebat.
7. Rex id donum accepit: Postea ea proxima ei in aurum vertebantur.
8. Rex donum dei bene amabat.
9. Midas aurum facere properavit.
10. In aurum arbores altas atque terram aquamque in eis locis ubi stabat aut ambulabat vertit.
11. Ob donum suum deum laudavit.
12. Rex superbus auro suo factus erat.
13. Nunc Midas domi est. Magno cum studio multa in aurum vertit.
14. Tum cibus aquaque ante eum a servo suo ponebantur.
15. Ea petivit, sed sine mora in aurum versa sunt.
16. Tum Midas timore magno capiebatur. Suam mortem vero timebat.
17. In locis ultimis proximisque aurum videbat.
18. Ad Bacchus vocavit: "Id donum rogavi, sed non est donum bonum. Est poena magna malaque. Nunc auxilium peto."

Midas and the Gold
1. In ancient times, there was a king, Midas.
2. The name of this king was famous because he was a friend of Bacchus.
3. Silenus taught Bacchus, but he had been captured by the enemy.
4. He had been freed by Midas. Bacchus was indeed happy.
5. Bacchus told him: "I shall give a gift."
6. Midas had good fortune, but not much wisdom.
7. The king received this gift: Afterwards, those things nearest to him were turned into gold.
8. The king liked the gift of the god very much.
9. Midas hurried to make gold.
10. He turns into gold the high trees and also the land and water in those places where he was standing or walking.
11. He praised the god because of his gift.
12. The king had been made proud by his gold.
13. Now Midas is at home. With great eagerness, he turns many things into gold.
14. Then food and water were placed in front of him by his servants.
15. He sought these things, but without delay, they were turned into gold.
16. Then Midas was seized with great fear. He indeed feared his death.
17. He saw gold in the farthest and nearest places.
18. He called on Bacchus: "I asked for this gift, but it is not a good gift. It is a great and evil punishment. Now I seek help."

19. Deus ei auxilium mox dedit.
20. Corpus caputque in flumine ponere eum iussit.
21. Midas magna cum diligentia id fecit. Mox liberatus est, sed flumini suum donum dederat.
22. Post id tempus arenae fluminis erant aureae.
23. Bacchus laetus erat quod nunc liber erat et arena ab eo tempore erat pulchra.

19. The god soon gave him help.
20. He ordered him to place his body and head in a river.
21. Midas did this with great care. Soon he was free, but he had given his own gift to the river.
22. After that time, the sands of the river were golden.
23. Bacchus was happy because now he was free and the sand was beautiful from that time on.

Practice Exercises

No. 105. Translate these phrases, showing cause or reason:
1. ob moram
2. cura mea
3. propter pericula
4. propter timorem
5. ob mortem
6. diligentia
7. celeritate
8. ob audaciam
9. propter moras
10. tempore

No. 106. Translate these phrases, showing manner:
1. cum studio
2. magna cura
3. magna cum diligentia
4. magno cum timore
5. cum celeritate
6. studio multo
7. magno cum studio
8. cum mora
9. magna celeritate
10. magna cum mora

No. 107. Complete these principal parts:
1. pono, ponere, _____, positus
2. supero, _____, superavi, superatus
3. do, dare, _____, datus
4. capio, _____, cepi, captus
5. servo, servare, servavi, _____
6. _____, facere, feci, factus
7. verto, vertere, _____, versus
8. terreo, terrere, _____, territus
9. _____, ducere, duxi, ductus
10. fero, ferre, _____, latus

No. 108. Translate these verb forms:
1. iussit
2. duxisti
3. demonstraverunt
4. rogabam
5. fecimus
6. docetur
7. mitteris
8. capimini
9. spectabit
10. augebimus
11. petent
12. ferebant
13. obtinebas
14. vertebatur
15. terruerat
16. petiveratis
17. ceperant
18. moti erunt
19. ducti eramus
20. capiebat

No. 109. Translate these prepositional phrases:
1. ob horam
2. propter telum
3. ante castra
4. a timore
5. de arbore
6. ab rege
7. ex arboribus
8. in eum locum
9. cum patre
10. cum cura
11. in aqua
12. sub oceano
13. circum muros
14. contra eum
15. inter oppida
16. per agrum
17. post castra
18. sine eis
19. trans mare
20. de viris

THE PRONUNCIATION OF CHURCH LATIN

The pronunciation of Church Latin may follow classical Latin pronunciation, or the general patterns of Italian pronunciation. The rules are by no means fixed and standardized, but, with widened oral communication, the Italian pronunciation of liturgical Latin increased in the Roman Catholic Church and also in the singing of all Church Latin.

1. Vowels

The vowels have the same pronunciation, except that **u** is voiced as **ou**.

meus, me**ous**

2. Consonants

The most noticeable difference is that **c** before **e** or **i** is not **k**, but **ch**.

cibus, **ch**ibous

If **c** before **e** or **i** is preceded by an **s**, the **s** is dropped.

scio, **chio**

ti between two vowels is **tsi**.

nationem, na**tsi**onem

ti after a consonant (except **s, t,** or **x**) is **ci**.

amanti, aman**ci**

g before **e** or **i** is soft, like **j**.

gens, **j**ens

All double consonants are pronounced definitely, with equal stress on each.

anno, an-no

Pronouns and Adjectives

Reading Vocabulary

Nouns

classis, classis, f., a fleet (classium) (class)
animus, animi, m., mind, spirit (animosity)
iniuria, iniuriae, f., injury, harm (injurious)
Minotaurus, Minotauri, m., the Minotaur
eques, equitis, m., horseman, knight (equestrian)
labyrinthus, labyrinthi, m., labyrinth
    (labyrinthine)
impedimentum, impedimenti, n., hindrance.
    In the plural, baggage. (impediment)

Hannibal, Hannibalis, m., Hannibal
navis, navis, f., ship (navium) (navy)
pedes, peditis, m. foot soldier
Minos, Minois, m., Minos
Africa, Africae, f., Africa
adulescens, adulescentis, m., youth
    (adulescentium) (adolescent)
imperator, imperatoris, m., general,
    commander, emperor (imperative)

Adjectives

hic, haec, hoc, this
idem, eadem, idem, the same

ille, illa, illud, that
ipse, ipsa, ipsum, himself, herself, itself; very
(This last use is somewhat archaic.)

Pronouns

idem, eadem, idem, he, she, it
ipse, ipsa, ipsum, he (himself), she (herself), it (itself)

ille, illa, illud, he, she, it
hic, haec, hoc, he, she, it

Verbs

interficio, interficere, interfeci, interfectus, kill
fio, fieri, factus sum, be made, become, be done
contendo, contendere, contendi, contentus, hasten,
     arrive, contend (contender)

gero, gerere, gessi, gestus, carry on, wage
vinco, vincere, vici, victus, conquer

Conjunctions

itaque, and so, therefore

Reading Grammar

A. These words are used as both pronouns and adjectives, in the same way as **is, ea, id.**

	PRONOUN	ADJECTIVE		
hic, haec, hoc	he, she, it (here)	this	**hic vir,** this man	**hic,** he
ille, illa, illud	he, she, it (there)	that	**ille homo,** that man	**ille,** he
idem, eadem, idem	he, she, it (the same)	same	**idem homo,** the same man	**idem,** he
ipse, ipsa, ipsum	he, she, it (-self)		**vir ipse,** the man himself	**ipse,** he

The declension of these words is very much the same as the declension of **is, ea, id.**

  1. hic, haec, hoc:

SINGULAR:

CASE	MASCULINE		FEMININE		NEUTER	
Nom.	**hic**	he	**haec**	she	**hoc**	it; this
Gen.	**huius**	his	**huius**	her	**huius**	its; of this
Dat.	**huic**	to/for him	**huic**	to/for, her	**huic**	to/for it; to, for this
Acc.	**hunc**	him	**hanc**	her	**hoc**	it; this
Abl.	**hoc**	from/with/by/in him	**hac**	from/with/by/in her	**hoc**	from/with/by/in it, from/with/by/in this

PLURAL:

CASE	MASCULINE	FEMININE	NEUTER	
Nom.	hi	hae	haec	they; these
Gen.	horum	harum	horum	their; of these
Dat.	his	his	his	to/for them; to/for these
Acc.	hos	has	haec	them; these
Abl.	his	his	his	from/with/by/in them; from/with/by/in these

As a pronoun, **hic, haec, hoc** means *he, she, it*. As an adjective, it means *this*.

2. **ille, illa, illud:**

	SINGULAR			PLURAL		
CASE	MASC.	FEM.	NEUT.	MASC.	FEM.	NEUT.
Nom.	ille	illa	illud	illi	illae	illa
Gen.	illius	illius	illius	illorum	illarum	illorum
Dat.	illi	illi	illi	illis	illis	illis
Acc.	illum	illam	illud	illos	illas	illa
Abl.	illo	illa	illo	illis	illis	illis

Ille, illa, illud has the same meanings (he, she, it) as **is, ea, id** or **hic, haec, hoc** when used as a pronoun. When used as an adjective, **ille, illa, illud** means *that*.

3. **ipse, ipsa, ipsum** is declined just like **is, ea, id** or **ille, illa, illud** after the first few forms:

	SINGULAR			PLURAL		
CASE	MASC.	FEM.	NEUT.	MASC.	FEM.	NEUT.
Nom.	ipse	ipsa	ipsum	ipsi	ipsae	ipsa
Gen.	ipsius	ipsius	ipsius	ipsorum	ipsarum	ipsorum
Dat.	ipsi	ipsi	ipsi	ipsis	ipsis	ipsis
Acc.	ipsum	ipsam	ipsum	ipsos	ipsas	ipsa
Abl.	ipso	ipsa	ipso	ipsis	ipsis	ipsis

As a pronoun, **ipse, ipsa, ipsum** means *he* (himself), *she* (herself), *it* (itself). As an adjective, it means *himself, herself, itself, very*.

4. **idem, eadem, idem** is based on **is, ea, id** and declined in much the same way:

	SINGULAR			PLURAL		
CASE	MASC.	FEM.	NEUT.	MASC.	FEM.	NEUT.
Nom.	idem	eadem	idem	eidem, iidem	eaedem	eadem
Gen.	eiusdem	eiusdem	eiusdem	eorumdem	earumdem	eorumdem
Dat.	eidem	eidem	eidem	eisdem, iisdem [in all genders]——————→		
Acc.	eundem	eandem	idem	eosdem	easdem	eadem
Abl.	eodem	eadem	eodem	eisdem, iisdem [in all genders]——————→		

As you can see, **isdem, eadem, idem** are made up of **is, ea, id** and the suffix **-dem**. Only the first part of the word is declined; **-dem** remains unchanged throughout. Any changes in the first part from the normal declension of **is, ea, id** are made for ease of pronunciation.

As a pronoun, **idem, eadem, idem** means (the same) *he,* (the same) *she,* (the same) *it*. As an adjective, it means *same*.

5. Remember that when **hic, ille, idem,** and **ipse** are used as pronouns, they must agree with the nouns they replace in number and gender, but not necessarily in case. When they are used as adjectives, they must agree with the nouns they modify in case, number, and gender.

B. The verb **possum, posse, potui** must always have a completing infinitive.

> **ducere potest,** he is able to lead, he can lead
> **vincere posse debet,** he ought to be able to conquer

C. The verb **facio, facere, feci, factus** does not have a real passive voice, even though it has all four principal parts. Instead, the verb **fio, fieri, factus sum** is used to express the passive voice of **facio.**

Fio conjugates in the active voice, but its meanings are all passive. It only needs three principal parts, because the active meanings of the perfect tense of **fio** are expressed by the verb **facio.**

1. Present Tense:

Singular:		Plural:	
fio	I am made; I become	——	
fis	you are made; you become	——	
fit	he, she, it is made; he, she, it becomes, it is done	**fiunt**	they are made; they become

You will note that **fio** does not have the first or second person plural in the present tense. It is said to be *defective* in those forms.

Present Passive Infinitive: **fieri,** to be done, to become, to be made

Since **fio** exists only in the passive, there is no present active infinitive, only a present passive infinitive.

Imperative:

Singular:	**fi**	be made! become! be done!
Plural:	**fite**	be made! become! be done!

2. The imperfect and future tenses are conjugated the same way as those of a regular **e/i-conjugation** verb. The stem used is **fi-.**

IMPERFECT		FUTURE	
SINGULAR	PLURAL	SINGULAR	PLURAL
fiebam, *I was made; I was becoming*	**fiebamus**	**fiam,** *I shall be made; I shall become*	**fiemus**
fiebas	**fiebatis**	**fies**	**fietis**
fiebat	**fiebant**	**fiet**	**fient**

3. Since **fio** has only a passive voice, the third principal part is the first person singular of the perfect passive, **factus sum.** It is made by using the fourth principal part of **facio** and the verb **sum.**

PERFECT TENSE:	PLUPERFECT TENSE:	FUTURE PERFECT TENSE
I have been made/become	I had been made/become	I shall have been made/become
factus, -a, -um sum	**factus, -a, -um eram**	**factus, -a, -um ero**
factus, -a, -um es	**factus, -a, -um eras**	**factus, -a, -um eris**
etc.	etc.	etc.

Reading

Hannibal

1. Adulescens, Hannibal, erat inimicus Romanis quod a patre suo ductus est.
2. In Africa habitaverunt, sed mox Hannibal cum suis trans aquam in navibus multis ad Hispaniam navigavit.
3. Ipse multas copias et classem bonam habuit.
4. In Hispania multa oppida oppugnavit et praedam captivosque cepit.
5. Tum ad Italiam viros suos duxit, sed inter Hispaniam Italiamque erant montes.
6. Eidem montes pedites equitusque eius minime iuverunt.
7. Multa impedimenta portabantur. Ad imperatorem Romanorum is nuntius portatus est.
8. Romani ad hostes iter facere properaverunt.
9. Romani proelio hostes non vicerunt, sed bellum ad Africam mox portatum est et Romani ad victoriam ab imperatore suo ibi ducti sunt.

Hannibal

1. The youth, Hannibal, was unfriendly to the Romans because he had been led by his father.
2. They lived in Africa, but soon Hannibal, with his men, sailed across the water in many ships to Spain.
3. He himself had many troops and a good fleet.
4. In Spain, he attacked many towns and took booty and captives.
5. Then he led his men to Italy, but between Spain and Italy, there were mountains.
6. These same mountains did not help his foot soldiers and horsemen at all.
7. They were carrying much baggage. This message was carried to the general of the Romans.
8. The Romans hurried to travel toward the enemy.
9. The Romans did not conquer the enemy in battle, but soon the war was carried to Africa and the Romans were led to victory there by their general.

Theseus et Minotaurus

1. Populus Graeciae contra populum insulae Cretae multos annos bellum gesserat.
2. Graeci magno cum animo diu contendebant, sed ab copiis Minois, regis Cretae, victi erant.
3. Haec fuerat causa belli: Filius Minois a Graecis interfectus erat. Itaque rex ob iniuriam illam ab his poenam petebat.
4. Septem puellas et septem pueros rogavit.
5. Graeci erant miseri, sed illos miserunt.
6. Minos, rex, labyrinthum habebat. In labyrintho animal barbarum, Minotaurum, tenebat.
7. In labyrinthum puellas puerosque duxit.
8. In illo loco terrbantur quod contra eum sine armis pugnare non poterant et mortem acceperunt.

Theseus and the Minotaur

1. The people of Greece had waged war against the people of the island of Crete for many years.
2. The Greeks fought for a long time with great spirit, but they had been conquered by the forces of Minos, the king of Crete.
3. This was the cause of the war: the son of Minos had been killed by the Greeks. And so, the king sought punishment from them because of that injury.
4. He asked for seven boys and seven girls.
5. The Greeks were unhappy, but they sent them.
6. Minos, the king, had a labyrinth. In the labyrinth, he kept a savage animal, the Minotaur.
7. He led the girls and boys into the labyrinth.
8. In that place, they were terrified because they were not able to fight against him without weapons, and they received death.

Practice Exercises

No. 110. Translate these phrases which use **hic** and **ille**:

1. hic murus	8. illa consilia	15. ex illa arbore	22. harum partium
2. illam urbem	9. illius oceani	16. hunc impedimentum	23. de illa pace
3. in illo loco	10. horum hominum	17. his patribus	24. illarum arenarum
4. hi duces	11. in illo horto	18. has naves	25. his annis
5. illis militibus	12. illa dea	19. ille liber	26. illam horam
6. illi legato	13. illius peditis	20. illi puellae	27. illud signum
7. hos imperatores	14. de hoc domino	21. haec arma	28. huius equi

No. 111. Translate these pronouns:

1. huius	4. hos	7. hoc	10. hi	13. has
2. ille	5. illis	8. huic	11. haec	14. illum
3. illi	6. harum	9. illa	12. hanc	15. illos

No. 112. Translate these phrases which use **idem** and **ipse**:

1. dea ipsa	8. nocte ipsa	15. eadem hora	22. pax ipsa
2. ex templis ipsis	9. eadem itinera	16. lex ipsa	23. eadem oppida
3. urbem eandem	10. iisdem viris	17. mons ipse	24. in urbibus ipsis
4. homines ipsos	11. ex agro ipso	18. puellae ipsae	25. eiusdem populi
5. ab eodem adulescenti	12. annis ipsis	19. idem iter	26. iidem homines
6. idem nomen	13. pueri ipsi	20. ab mulieribus ipsis	27. ex iisdem locis
7. eiusdem nationis	14. legati ipsius	21. eodem tempore	28. iisdem annis

No. 113. Translate these pronouns:

1. ipsi	6. eadem
2. eiusdem	7. eundem
3. idem	8. eorundem
4. ipsa	9. ex iisdem
5. ipsos	10. ipsius

No. 114. Give the English for these verb forms:

1. ducere poterant	7. iubere potueram	13. vocare non potuerunt	19. factae erant
2. manere potes	8. docere potes	14. laborare non possum	20. fiebam
3. adorare non potuit	9. rogare poteramus	15. manere potuistis	21. facimus
4. liberare poterit	10. augere non potui	16. fiunt	22. facietis
5. curare possunt	11. iuvare poterimus	17. factus est	23. faciunt
6. necare non potuimus	12. pugnare poteris	18. fies	24. faciebant

---

SUFFIXES

Some of the more common suffixes used to form adjectives are:
-eus, denoting the material. English, *of.* **aureus,** of gold
-osus, denoting fullness. English, *full of.* **periculosus,** full of danger
-bilis, denoting possibility. English, *able.* **amabilis,** able to be loved, lovable
-anus, -icus, -alis, -inus, denoting connection.

    -anus becomes *-ane* or *an* in English. **Romanus,** Roman.
    -icus becomes *-ic* in English. **publicus,** public
    -alis becomes *-al* in English. **mortalis,** mortal
    -inus becomes *-in* or *-ine* in English. **Latinus,** Latin

---

Third Declension Adjectives

Reading Vocabulary

Nouns

civis, civis, m. or f., citizen (**civium**) (civic)
Polyphemus, Polyphemi, m., Polyphemus
Ariadne, Ariadnes, f. Ariadne (a Greek noun)
Cyclops, Cyclopis, m., Cyclops
tempestas, tempestatis, f., storm, bad weather (tempest)

Theseus, Thesei, m. Theseus
poeta, poetae, m. poet (poetical)
opus, operis, n., work (opera)
Homerus, Homeri, m., Homer
Ulixes, Ulixis, m., Ulysses

Adjectives

celer, celeris, celere, quick, swift (celerity)
acer, acris, acre, sharp, active, keen (acid)
brevis, breve, short, brief (brevity)
alter, altera, alterum, the one, the other (alternate)
solus, sola, solum, alone, only (solitude)
alius, alia, aliud, other, another (alien)
audax, audacis, gen. **audacis,** bold (audacious)

ullus, ulla, ullum, any
neuter, neutra, neutrum, neither
unus, una, unum, one (unite)
omnis, omne, all, every
uter, utra, utrum, which (of two)
totus, tota, totum, all, whole (total)
nullus, nulla, nullum, no, none (null)

Verbs

fugio, fugere, fugi, fugitus, flee, run away, escape
scribo, scribere, scripsi, scriptus, write (scribe)

Adverbs

interea, meanwhile

Prepositions

apud, in the presence of. With the accusative case.
pro, in front of; for; instead. With the ablative case.

Reading Grammar

A. Some adjectives that belong to the **a-** and **o-declension** have the genitive singular ending in **-ius** and the dative singular ending in **-i** for all genders. Otherwise, they are regular. For example, consider the declension of **unus, una, unum:**

CASE	MASCULINE	FEMININE	NEUTER
Nom.	unus	una	unum
Gen.	unius	unius	unius
Dat.	uni	uni	uni
Acc.	unum	unam	unum
etc.			

All forms other than the genitive and dative singular are regular.

These adjectives are declined like **unus:**

alius, alia, aliud, other, another
alter, altera, alterum, the one, the other
neuter, neutra, neutrum, neither
nullus, nulla, nullum, no, none

solus, sola, solum, alone, only
totus, tota, totum, whole, all
ullus, ulla, ullum, any
uter, utra, utrum, which (of two)

B. Sometimes **alius** or **alter** may be used in pairs. When this happens, their meaning is slightly different:

alius . . . alius, one . . . another
alter . . . alter, the one . . . the other (of two)
Alterum iter longum est, alterum non est.
Alii sunt boni, alii sunt mali.

alii . . . alii, some . . . others

One road is long, the other is not.
Some are good, some are bad.

C. Those adjectives that do not belong to the **a-** and **o-declension** belong to the **i-** or third declension. These adjectives are of three kinds, according to the number of spellings in the nominative singular, but all have the **i-declension** endings. The masculine and feminine genders are declined like **urbs;** the neuter like **mare.** See pages 72–73 if you need to review these endings.

The three kinds of adjectives are:

1. Those that have one spelling for the nominative singular for all genders:

SINGULAR:

CASE	MASCULINE	FEMININE	NEUTER
Nom.	audax	audax	audax
Gen.	audacis	audacis	audacis
Dat.	audaci	audaci	audaci
Acc.	audacem	audacem	audacem
Abl.	audaci	audaci	audaci
Voc.	audax	audax	audax

PLURAL:

CASE	MASCULINE	FEMININE	NEUTER
Nom.	audaces	audaces	audacia
Gen.	audacium	audacium	audacium
Dat.	audacibus	audacibus	audacibus
Acc.	audaces (-is)	audaces (-is)	audacia
Abl.	audacibus	audacibus	audacibus
Voc.	audaces	audaces	audacia

Note the alternatives, -es and -is,. for the masculine and feminine accusative plural.

2. Two spellings for the nominative singular, one for the masculine and feminine, and one for the neuter:

CASE	MASCULINE	FEMININE	NEUTER
Nom.	omnis	omnis	omne
Gen.	omnis	omnis	omnis
Dat.	omni	omni	omni
etc.			

3. Three spellings for the nominative singular, one for each gender:

CASE	MASCULINE	FEMININE	NEUTER
Nom.	celer	celeris	celere
Gen.	celeris	celeris	celeris
Dat.	celeri	celeri	celeri
etc.			

Remember that an adjective, regardless of its declension, must agree with the word it modifies in case, number, and gender.

The vocabulary in this book gives an adjective's nominative singular case. If the adjective has more than one spelling for this case, all spellings will be given, as is usual in most Latin dictionaries.

Reading

Theseus et Minotaurus (concl'd)

1. Interea in Graecia Theseus fortuna misera puerorum puellarumque Graecorum incitatus est.
2. Rogavit: "Estne nullum auxilium pro his filiis civium nostrorum?"
3. Itaque ad Cretam cum sociis suis navi contendit.
4. Ariadne, filia regis, eum vidit et ob virtutem eius illum amavit.
5. Sine mora ille de labyrintho eum docuit.
6. Tum Theseus solus ad labyrinthum properavit. Arma portabat et bonum consilium Ariadnes memoria tenebat.
7. Mox Minotaurum spectabat. Cum illo animali diu contendebat, sed id interficere potuit.

Theseus and the Minotaur (concl'd)

1. Meanwhile, in Greece, Theseus was aroused by the unhappy fortune of the Greek boys and girls.
2. He asked: "Is there no help for these children of our citizens?"
3. And so he hurried to Crete by ship with his comrades.
4. Ariadne, the daughter of the king, saw him and loved him because of his courage.
5. Without delay, she showed him about the labyrinth.
6. Then Theseus alone hurried to the labyrinth. He carried weapons and he remembered the good advice of Ariadne.
7. Soon he saw the Minotaur. He struggled with that animal for a long time, but was able to kill it.

8. Minotaurus necatus erat. Pueri puellaeque liberati erant.

8. The Minotaur had been killed. The boys and girls had been freed.

9. Totos annos postea populus Graeciae laetus erat quod regi malo Cretae nullas poenas dabat.

9. For all the years afterwards, the people of Greece were happy because they paid no penalties to the evil king of Crete.

Ulixes et Cyclops

Ulysses and the Cyclops

1. Homerus, poeta antiquus, de bello inter viros Graeciae Troiaeque in suo magno opere scripsit.

1. Homer, an ancient poet, wrote in his great work about the war between the men of Greece and Troy.

2. Post multos annos longos Troia ab Graecis capta erat.

2. After many long years, Troy had been captured by the Greeks.

3. Graeci ab illo loco navigabant. Apud eos erat Ulixes, homo audax, sed brevi tempore navis eius tempestate ad aliam partem maris portata est.

3. The Greeks were sailing away from that place. Among them was Ulysses, a bold man, but in a short time, his ship was carried by a storm to another part of the sea.

4. Ex navi ad terram cum sociis suis Ulixes contendit.

4. Ulysses hurried from his ship to the land with his comrades.

5. Non longe ab illo loco ubi stabant corpus magnum Polyphemi, Cyclopis, mox viderunt. Ille in colli habitabat.

5. Not far from that place where they were standing, they soon saw the large body of Polyphemus, the Cyclops. He lived on a hill.

6. Graeci iniuriam timebant.

6. The Greeks feared injury.

7. Polyphemus eos a mari celeribus pedibus duxit.

7. Polyphemus led them away from the sea at a swift pace.

8. Viri cibum exspectabant, sed Cyclops pro cibo suo unum hominem, tum alterum, et alium cepit.

8. The men waited for food, but the Cyclops, for his own food, took one man, then another, and another.

9. Alii pro sociis suis dolebant.

9. The others grieved for their comrades.

10. Illine ab Polyphemo fugere poterunt?

10. Will they be able to flee from Polyphemus?

Practice Exercises

No. 115. Give the English for these phrases:

1. uno anno
2. nullam curam
3. utrius doni
4. ulli navi
5. totos annos
6. cum patre solo
7. nullarum mortium
8. neutri nationi
9. in altera via
10. alio nomine
11. ad utrum flumen
12. ullius collis
13. uni libro
14. ob nullas causas
15. ab neutro homine

No. 116. Translate these verb forms:

1. timuerant
2. fuistis
3. mittent
4. cepit
5. timebit
6. spectabant
7. tenebuntur
8. mittar
9. laudati sunt
10. factum erat
11. navigabas
12. dabantur
13. gerit
14. fuerant
15. habuerunt

No. 117. Give the English for the following:
1. alter puer est, alter non est.
2. nullo tempore
3. ullius belli
4. ad utra castra
5. mulieres ipsae solae
6. neutrius adulescentis
7. alias urbes
8. unam partem
9. de neutra puella
10. aliud inter

No. 118. Give the English for these phrases:
1. hora breve
2. servi audacis
3. eques celer
4. in flumine celeri
5. ab viris audacibus
6. tempora omnia
7. a legato acri
8. vita brevis
9. omnibus horis
10. in navi celeri
11. opus audax
12. brevi tempore
13. copiae acres
14. equi celeris
15. acres feminae
16. mortem celerem
17. itinera brevia
18. audaci homini
19. brevem annum
20. omni in loco

Present Passive Infinitive; Interrogatives

Reading Vocabulary

Nouns

oculus, oculi, m., eye (oculist)
saxum, saxi, n., stone, rock (saxatile)
porta, portae, f., gate, door, entrance (portal)

telum, teli, n., weapon
fuga, fugae, f., flight, escape

Pronouns

quis, quid, who?, what?

Adjectives

fortis, forte, brave, strong (fort)
uterque, utraque, utrumque, each, every
gravis, grave, heavy, severe, serious (grave, gravity)

facilis, facile, easy (facility)
novus, nova, novum, new (novel)

Verbs

clamo, clamare, clamavi, clamatus, shout (clamor)
cognosco, cognoscere, cognovi, cognitus, learn, recognize, know (cognizance)

iacio, iacere, ieci, iactus, throw (project)
simulo, simulare, simulavi, simulatus, pretend (simulate)

Adverbs

noctu, at night (noctambular)

FAMILIAR QUOTATIONS

Nil homini certum est, Nothing is certain to man. Ovid.
Virtus praemium est optimum, Virtue is the best reward. Plautus.
Omnia praeclara rara, All the best things are rare. Cicero.
Possunt quia posse videntur, They can because they think they can. Virgil.
Alea iacta est, The die is cast. Caesar.
Mens sana in copore sano, A sound mind in a sound body. Juvenal.
Carmina morte carent, Songs do not die. Ovid.

Reading Grammar

A. **uterque, utraque, utrumque,** is declined by adding -que to the forms of **uter, utra, utrum.**
    uterque vir, each man   **utriusque viri,** of each man
    utrique viro, to, for each man   **utrumque virum,** each man   etc.

B. The declension of the interrogative pronoun, **quis, quid,** *who?, what?,* is similar to that of **is, ea, id.**

SINGULAR

CASE	MASC.	FEM.	NEUT.	
Nom.	quis	quis	quid	who?, what?
Gen.	cuius	cuius	cuius	of whom?, whose?, of what?
Dat.	cui	cui	cui	to, for whom?, to, for what?
Acc.	quem	quem	quid	whom?, what?
Abl.	quo	quo	quo	from, with, by, in whom?, from, with, by, in what?

PLURAL

CASE	MASC.	FEM.	NEUT.	
Nom.	qui	quae	quae	who?, what?
Gen.	quorum	quarum	quorum	of whom?, whose?, of what?
Dat.	quibus	quibus	quibus	to, for whom?, to, for what?
Acc.	quos	quas	quae	whom?, what?
Abl.	quibus	quibus	quibus	from, with, by, in whom?, from, with, by, in what?

Quis, quid is called an interrogative pronoun because it is used in questions.
    Quis est? Who is it?   **Qui sunt?** Who are they?
    Cuius est? Whose is it?   **Quorum est?** Whose is it?
    Quem vides? Whom do you see?   **Quid vides?** What do you see?

C. When **cum** is used with the ablative case, it is generally added to the end of the word.
    quocum, with whom   **quibuscum,** with whom

D. The verb **fio** has a present passive infinitive, **fieri,** to be made, but not a present active infinitive. With rare exceptions, verbs have both active and passive infinitives.

1. The present passive infinitive of the **a-** and **e-conjugation** verbs is the same as the present active infinitive, except that it ends in -**i**:

      amare, to love   **amari,** to be loved

      habere, to have   **haberi,** to be had

2. In the **e/i-conjugation,** the -**i** of the present passive infinitive is added directly on to the stem.

      ducere, to lead   **duci,** to be led

      capere, to take   **capi,** to be taken

3. The verbs **sum, possum, eo, volo, nolo,** and **malo** have no present passive infinitives. The present passive infinitive of **fero** is **ferri,** to be carried.

Reading

Ulixes et Cyclops (concl'd)

1. **Postquam Cyclops haec fecerat, Graeci fortes mortem exspectabant, sed Ulixes Polyphemum interficere in animo habebat.**

2. **Ob magnitudinem viri non erat ullum iter facile ex periculo eorum, sed consilium parabant et suos animos bonos tenebant.**

3. **Ante hoc tempus alia pericula gravia superaverant et hoc periculum novum superare in animo habuerunt.**

4. **Uterque Cyclopem timebat, sed Polyphemus inimicus omnibus erat.**

5. **Eum incitare non debebant. Itaque Ulixes suum consilium eis demonstravit.**

6. **Partem arboris in igni posuerunt. Post breve tempus finis arboris erat acer.**

7. **Hoc erat telum eorum contra Cyclopem. Id magna cum diligentia paraverant.**

8. **Hoc telo Cyclops poenas dabit.**

9. **Polyphemus unum oculum solum habuit. Magna cum audacia Ulixis et socii sui in oculo eius finem arboris posuerunt.**

10. **Iniuria erat gravis et Cyclops postea videre non poterat.**

11. **Polyphemus etiam multa animalia habebat.**

12. **Ante portam ille saxum grave et magnam posuerat.**

13. **Id a Graecis moveri non potuit, sed Cyclops ab porta saxum movebat, cum animalia cibus petebant.**

14. **Hoc erat consilium: Ulixes et sui amici fugam suam noctu paraverunt.**

15. **Cyclops eos videre non potuit.**

16. **Saxum ab porta movit.**

Ulysses and the Cyclops (concl'd)

1. After the Cyclops had done these things, the brave Greeks waited for death, but Ulysses had in mind to kill Polyphemus.

2. Because of the great size of the man, there was not any easy way out of their danger, but they prepared a plan and kept their good spirits.

3. Before this time, they had overcome other serious dangers and they had in mind to overcome this new danger.

4. Each feared the Cyclops, but Polyphemus was unfriendly to all.

5. They ought not to arouse him. And so, Ulysses showed them his plan.

6. They placed part of a tree in the fire. After a short time, the end of the tree was sharp.

7. This was their weapon against the Cyclops. They had prepared it with great care.

8. With this weapon, the Cyclops will pay the penalty.

9. Polyphemus had only one eye. With great boldness, Ulysses and his companions put the end of the tree in his eye.

10. The injury was serious, and the Cyclops was not able to see after that.

11. Polyphemus also had many animals.

12. He put a heavy and large stone in front of the door.

13. This could not be moved by the Greeks, but the Cyclops moved the stone away from the door when the animals sought food.

14. This was the plan: Ulysses and his friends prepared their flight at night.

15. The Cyclops was not able to see them.

16. He moved the stone away from the door.

17. Animalia per portam cucurrerunt. Sub animalibus erant Graeci.

17. The animals ran through the door. Under the animals were the Greeks.

18. Graeci simulabant et Polyphemus eos non cognovit.

18. The Greeks pretended and Polyphemus did not recognize them.

19. Tum Ulixes clamavit. Itaque Cyclops fugam eorum cognovit.

19. Then Ulysses shouted. And so, the Cyclops learned of their flight.

20. Cyclops ad mare properavit. Saxum magnum ad Graecos iecit.

20. The Cyclops hurried to the sea. He threw a large stone toward the Greeks.

21. Polyphemus dixit: "Quis es?"

21. Polyphemus said: "Who are you?"

22. Ulixes clamavit: "Nullus homo sum," sed Graeci in navi erant et laeti erant quod a Polyphemo fugerant et ad Graeciam navigabant.

22. Ulysses shouted: "I am no man," but the Greeks were on the ship and were happy because they had escaped from Polyphemus and were sailing to Greece.

23. Postea de oculo suo Polyphemus dicebat: "Nullus id fecit."

23. Afterwards, Polyphemus said about his eye: "No one did it."

Practice Exercises

No. 119. Translate these adjectival phrases:
1. solis aurei
2. ex neutro loco
3. summo in monte
4. itineris facilis
5. ullae horae
6. poenas graves
7. nationum proximarum
8. civem audacem
9. corpus robustem
10. fluminum celerium
11. libros latinos
12. homines alii
13. navis vestra
14. patrum multorum
15. utriusque regis

No. 120. Give the English for these interrogative phrases and clauses:
1. Qui estis?
2. Cui ea dedit?
3. Quos videbo?
4. Cuius oculi?
5. Quae cognoscit?
6. Quocum ambulabat?
7. A quo captus est?
8. Quis clamat?
9. Quis pugnat?
10. Quorum tela?
11. Quid habes?
12. Quem necavit?
13. Quibus id dabo?
14. Quid rogatum est?
15. Cui donum misisti?
16. Quem amas?
17. Quis fugit?
18. Quid facile est?
19. Cuius est?
20. Quibuscum?
21. Quos mittet?
22. Quid facit?
23. Qui contendunt?
24. A quo gestum est?

No. 121. Give the active form of these present passive infinitives:
1. pugnari
2. mitti
3. regi
4. dari
5. laudari
6. rogari
7. scribi
8. videri
9. cognosci
10. necari
11. capi
12. timeri
13. haberi
14. moveri
15. parari
16. duci
17. augeri
18. servari
19. vinci
20. terreri

No. 122. Give the passive forms of these present active infinitives:
1. demonstrare
2. ducere
3. movere
4. iubere
5. vertere
6. armare
7. amare
8. ferre
9. docere
10. occupare
11. mittere
12. gerere
13. accipere
14. timere
15. vocare
16. interficere
17. iuvare
18. tenere
19. cognoscere
20. simulare

Chapter Six Review

Vocabulary Review

Nouns

1. adulescens
2. Africa
3. animus
4. arbor
5. arena
6. Ariadne
7. aurum
8. Bacchus
9. cibus
10. civis
11. classis
12. Cyclops
13. diligentia
14. eques
15. fuga
16. Hannibal
17. Homerus
18. impedimentum
19. imperator
20. iniuria
21. labyrinthus
22. Midas
23. Minos
24. Minotaurus
25. mors
26. navis
27. oculus
28. opus
29. pedes
30. poena
31. poeta
32. Polyphemus
33. porta
34. saxum
35. Silenus
36. studium
37. telum
38. tempestas
39. tempus
40. Theseus

Pronouns

1. hic, haec, hoc
2. idem, eadem, idem
3. ille, illa, illud
4. ipse, ipsa, ipsum

Adjectives

1. acer
2. alius
3. alter
4. audax
5. brevis
6. celer
7. facilis
8. fortis
9. gravis
10. hic
11. idem
12. ille
13. ipse
14. neuter
15. novus
16. nullus
17. omnis
18. solus
19. totus
20. ullus

Verbs

1. capio
2. clamo
3. cognosco
4. contendo
5. facio
6. fero
7. fio
8. fugio
9. gero
10. iacio
11. interficio
12. pono
13. scribo
14. simulo
15. verto

Adverbs

1. interea
2. noctu

Prepositions

1. apud
2. pro
3. propter

Conjunctions

1. itaque

Practice Exercises

No. 123. Translate these verbs:

1. capiunt
2. cognitum erat
3. victi sunt
4. vertent
5. interficiebamus
6. fecerunt
7. ceperas
8. fugiebat
9. ponetur
10. gesserint
11. scribit
12. iacis
13. contendent
14. positi sunt
15. gestum est
16. fis

No. 124. Translate these phrases:

1. propter mortem
2. ob iniuriam
3. diligentia magna
4. ob imperatorem
5. propter cibum
6. ob classes
7. parva cum poena
8. magno cum studio
9. ob impedimentum
10. propter arenam

No. 125. Translate these pronouns:

1. hunc
2. huius
3. illos
4. illud
5. ipse
6. illorum
7. eadem
8. eiusdem
9. hic
10. ipsorum
11. quem
12. quid
13. cuius
14. cui
15. quocum

No. 126. Translate these verb forms:

1. clamare potuit
2. capere poterant
3. facere potes
4. ponere possumus
5. vincere potuistis
6. contendere poterit
7. scribere potuerunt
8. cognoscere poteramus
9. vertere potes
10. gerere possunt

No. 127. Translate these adjective phrases:

1. unius operis
2. omnium civium
3. aliud impedimentum
4. nova tela
5. brevi tempore
6. toti saxo
7. nullius timoris
8. ullam iniuriam
9. audaces equites
10. celeris poena

Reading

Marcus Tullius Cicero

Cicero was born into an upper middle class family living near Arpinum, in Latium, the province in which Rome was located, in 106 B.C. He studied law, philosophy, and rhetoric in Rome, Athens, and Rhodes, and became consul in 63 B.C. It was in this office that he disclosed Catiline's conspiracy to overthrow the government and, in four orations delivered in the Senate, persuaded the Senators to decree the death penalty for the conspirators. After Caesar's assassination in 44 B.C. and the formation of the Second Triumvirate, Cicero was murdered in 43 B.C., while trying to escape from his political enemies.

O tempora! O mores! Senatus haec intellegit, consul vidit; hic tamen vivit. Vivit? Immo vero etiam in senatum venit, fit publici consili particeps, notat et designat oculis ad caedam unum quemque nostrum. Nos autem, fortes viri, satis facere rei publicae videmur, si istius furorem ac tela vitamus. Ad mortem te, Catilina, duci iussu consilis iam pridem oportebat; in te conferri pestem, quam tu in nos machinaris.

In Catilinam Oratio Prima, ii

Odo de Cerinton

The following two stories were written by Odo de Cerinton, who lived in the twelfth century and composed a work called **Narrationes,** which drew stories from various fables and other sources, giving a mystical interpretation to tales about animals.

De Hydro

Quoddam animal dicitur hydrus, cuius natura est se invovere luto, ut melius posset labi. Tandem in os crocodili, quando dormit, intrat et sic, ventrem eius ingrediens, cor eius mordet et sic crocodilum intermit.

Mistice: Hydrus significat filium Dei, qui assumpsit lutum nostrae carnis ut facilius laberetur in os diaboli, et sic, ventrem eius ingrediens et cor eius mordens, ipsum interficit.

De Antilope

Quoddam animal est quod vocatur antilops; quod cum virgultis ludit cum cornibus, tandem cornua eius implicantur cum virgultis quod non potest ea extrahere et tunc incipit clamare; quo audito veniunt venatores et interficiunt eum.

Mistice: Sic contigit quod plerique delectati sunt et ludunt cum negotiis huius mundi et sic in eisdem implicantur quod evelli non possunt et sic a venatoribus, id est a daemonibus, capiuntur et interficiuntur.

More Verbs, Nouns, and Pronouns

FAMILIAR PHRASES

status quo or **status in quo,** the state in which. That is, the existing condition.
mirabile dictu, wonderful to tell, wonderful to relate.
per se, by itself, of itself; by its own force.
cum grano salis, with a grain of salt.
modus vivendi, manner of living (often temporary).
post scriptum, written after. Abbreviated, **P.S.** or **p.s.**
inter nos, among us, among ourselves.
sine qua non, something indispensible or necessary. Literally, without which not.

Reading Vocabulary

Nouns

Orpheus, Orphei, m., Orpheus (a Greek name)
nihil or **nil, n.,** nothing **nihil** (or **nil**), has the same spelling in all cases (nihilist)

natura, naturae, f., nature (natural)
regnum, regni, n., kingdom (interregnum)
Eurydice, Eurydices, f., Eurydice (a Greek name)

Adjectives

primus, prima, primum, first (prime, primary)

difficilis, difficile, difficult, hard (difficulty)

Verbs

audio, audire, audivi, auditus, hear (audio)
relinquo, relinquere, reliqui, relictus, leave, leave behind (relinquish)
discedo, discedere, discessi, discessus, withdraw, go away, leave
trado, tradere, tradidi, traditus, give up, surrender (tradition)

rego, regere, rexi, rectus, rule (regent)
educo, educere, eduxi, eductus, lead out (educate)
reduco, reducere, reduxi, reductus, lead back (reduce)

Adverbs

parum, too little, not enough

magnopere, greatly

Reading Grammar

A. In Latin, adverbs are generally formed from adjectives.

1. Adverbs formed from **a-** and **o-declension** adjectives end in **-e.**

ADJECTIVE	ADVERB
altus, high	**alte,** high, on high
latus, wide	**late,** widely
longus, long	**longe,** far, distant
miser, wretched	**misere,** wretchedly
pulcher, beautiful	**pulchre,** beautifully

Note that when an adjective ending in **-er** in the masculine nominative singular keeps the **-e-** in all other forms, the adverb also keeps the **-e-,** as in the case of **misere.** When an adjective ending in -er in the masculine nominative singular drops the -e- in all other forms, the adverb also drops it, as in the case of **pulchre.**

2. Adverbs formed from **i-declension** adjectives end in **-ter,** or **-iter.** You will notice that the adverbial ending is added to the stem of the adjective, which is derived from the genitive singular.

ADJECTIVE		ADVERB
Nom. Sing.	Gen. Sing.	
acer, keen	**acris,** of a keen man/woman/object	**acriter,** keenly
audax, bold	**audacis,** of a bold man/woman/object	**audacter,** boldly
celer, swift	**celeris,** of a swift man/woman/object	**celeriter,** swiftly
fortis, brave	**fortis,** of a brave man/woman/object	**fortiter,** bravely

3. Some adverbs are irregular.

ADJECTIVE	ADVERB
bonus, good	**bene,** well
difficilis, difficult	**difficile,** with difficulty
facilis, easy	**facile,** easily
magnus, great	**magnopere,** greatly
malus, bad	**male,** badly
parvus, little	**parvum,** too little, not enough
primus, first	**primum,** at first, or **primo,** at first
solus, alone	**solum,** alone, only

4. Other adverbs are not based on any adjective; e.g.,

nunc, now   **semper,** always   **non,** not

B. **i-conjugation** verbs, also known as fourth conjugation verbs, have **-i** as the predominant vowel between the stem and the endings. Consider the verb **audio,** *hear.*

1. Principal parts: **audio, audire, audivi, auditus.**

2. Present tense:

ACTIVE	PASSIVE
audio, *I hear, do hear, am hearing*	**audior,** *I am being heard, I am heard*
audis	**audiris**
audit	**auditur**
audimus	**audimur**
auditis	**audimini**
audiunt	**audiuntur**

3. Imperfect Tense:

ACTIVE	PASSIVE
audiebam, *I was hearing, heard*	audiebar, *I was being heard, was heard*
audiebas	audiebaris
audiebat	audiebatur
audiebamus	audiebamur
audiebatis	audiebamini
audiebant	audiebantur

4. Future Tense:

ACTIVE	PASSIVE
audiam, *I shall hear*	audiar, *I shall be heard*
audies	audieris
audiet	audietur
audiemus	audiemur
audietis	audiemini
audient	audientur

You will note that fourth conjugation verbs are conjugated like **capio** in the future tense.

5. Perfect Tense:

ACTIVE	PASSIVE
audivi, *I have heard, heard*	auditus, -a, -um sum, *I have been heard*
audivisti	auditus, -a, -um es
etc.	etc.

6. Pluperfect Tense:

ACTIVE	PASSIVE
audiveram, *I had heard*	auditus, -a, -um eram, *I had been heard*
audiveras	auditus, -a, -um eras
etc.	etc.

7. Future Perfect Tense

ACTIVE	PASSIVE
audivero, *I shall have heard*	auditus, -a, -um ero, *I shall have been heard*
audiveris	auditus, -a, -um eris
etc.	etc.

Reading

Orpheus et Eurydice

1. Orpheus erat vir fortis, sed dolebat quod Eurydice morte capta erat et eum solum et miserum reliquerat.

Orpheus and Eurydice

1. Orpheus was a brave man, but he grieved because Eurydice had been taken by death and had left him alone and wretched.

2. Orpheus animalia omnia et naturam bene amabat et laetus esse simulabat, sed Eurydicen semper petebat.

2. Orpheus loved all animals and nature very much and he pretended to be happy, but he always looked for Eurydice.

3. Orpheus ipse sine ea esse non poterat. Itaque auxilium ab deis petivit.

3. Orpheus himself could not be without her. And so, he sought help from the gods.

4. Nihil ab Iove facti poterat. Eurydice ab terra discesserat et apud Inferos nunc habitabat.

4. Nothing could be done by Jupiter. Eurydice had departed from the earth and was now living among Those Below.

5. Iter ad regnum Plutonis erat difficile.

5. The journey to the kingdom of Pluto was difficult.

6. Pluto suos non saepe tradit, sed Orpheus erat audax et paene nullum timorem habebat.

6. Pluto does not often give up his own, but Orpheus was bold and had almost no fear.

7. Sub terram magna cum celeritate contendit. Ante regem, Plutonem, mox stat.

7. He hurries below the earth with great speed. He soon stands before the king, Pluto.

8. Orpheus ab Plutone petivit: "Cur Eurydicen hic tenes? Non solum ei amorem summum semper docebam sed etiam mors et non est idonea. Eurydice ipsa nihil fecerat."

8. Orpheus asked Pluto: "Why do you keep Eurydice here? Not only did I always show the greatest love for her, but also death is not suitable for her. Eurydice herself had done nothing."

9. Tum Pluto ipse pro illo acriter dolebat, sed Orpheum iussit: "Eam tradam, sed iter ex regno Inferorum difficile est. Ille ad terram tuam reduci poterit, sed eam spectare non debes. Cum primus eam ad terram educes, tum eam spectare poteris."

9. Then Pluto himself felt keenly sorry for him, but he instructed Orpheus: "I shall give her up, but the way out of the kingdom of Those Below is difficult. She can be led back to your land, but you ought not to look at her. When you, going first, lead her back to earth, then you can look at her."

10. Ab Plutone grate discesserunt et iter ab illo loco malo celeriter faciebant.

10. They departed from Pluto gratefully and quickly made the journey away from that evil place.

11. Primo ille fortiter ambulabat, sed Orpheus amore regebatur. Non diu postea ad eam oculos suos vertit.

11. At first he walked bravely, but Orpheus was ruled by love. Not long afterwards, he turns his eyes toward her.

12. Ob eam causam Pluto magna cum celeritate illam cepit et eam ad Inferos reduxit.

12. For this reason, Pluto seized her with great speed and led her back to Those Below.

13. Ab illo tempore in terra non visa est.

13. From that time, she was not seen on earth.

Practice Exercises

No. 128. Form the adverbs and give the English meanings:

1. pulcher	6. gravis	11. miser
2. longus	7. brevis	12. proximus
3. magnus	8. altus	13. fortis
4. novus	9. gratus	14. celer
5. acer	10. audax	15. liber

No. 129. Translate these verb forms:

1. portas	7. visi erant	13. audiet	19. capientur
2. habeo	8. auditi sunt	14. petiverunt	20. audieris
3. ducunt	9. acceptus es	15. audiunt	21. audiris
4. iacit	10. auditis eram	16. iuvabamini	22. fecit
5. audivistis	11. audiebant	17. audiebamur	23. rogabunt
6. liberatus est	12. paratus erit	18. vertebamus	24. audivimus

No. 130. Give the English for these phrases and clauses:

1. fortiter pugnant
2. proxime vidimus
3. difficile gessit
4. late accipientur
5. longe ambulat
6. bene stant
7. facile cognovit
8. magnopere amabat

No. 131. Translate these sentences:

1. Locus facile defendetur.
2. Primo nihil parari poterat.
3. Ob timorem non fortiter contendistis.
4. Utramque portam amas?
5. Terra natura difficile defensa est.
6. Non solum rex sed etiam regina id audivit.

Relative and Interrogative Pronouns; Deponent Verbs

Reading Vocabulary

Nouns

turris, turris, f., tower (**turrium**) (turret)
regio, regionis, f., region, boundary (regional)
Hellespontus, Hellesponti, m., Hellespont

Leander, Leandri, m., Leander
Hero, Herus, f., Hero (a Greek name)
inopia, inopiae, f., want, scarcity

Pronoun and Adjective

qui, quae, quod, who, which, that; which, what

Verbs

venio, venire, veni, ventus, come (venture)
pervenio, pervenire, perveni, perventus, arrive
accido, accidere, accidi, happen (accident)
reperio, reperire, repperi, repertus, find, discover (repertory)
conspicio, conspicere, conspexi, conspectus, observe (conspectus)
prohibeo, prohibere, prohibui, prohibitus, keep off, hinder, prohibit, prevent, forbid (prohibition)
cupio, cupere, cupivi, cupitus, desire, wish, want (cupidity)

vereor, vereri, veritus sum, fear
sequor, sequi, secutus sum, follow
morior, mori, mortuus sum, die (mortal)
impedio, impedire, impedivi, impeditus, hinder (impede)
hortor, hortari, hortatus sum, urge, encourage (exhort)
experior, experiri, expertus sum, try, test (experience)

Adverbs

tamen, however, nevertheless

iam, already, now

Conjunctions

ut, as

PREFIXES

prae, before. **praepono,** put before.
re, again, back. **remitto, send back.**
con, together, with; very thoroughly. **convoco,** call together (convene). **conficio,** finish (thoroughly do).
pro, out, forth. **provoco,** call forth.

Reading Grammar

A. Antecedents.

An antecedent is a word or a group of words to which a pronoun refers. The word *antecedent* comes from the Latin word **antecedo,** which means *stand before* or *precede,* and an antecedent usually does precede the pronoun which refers to it. Consider the following sentence:

I saw the girl who was swimming.

The relative pronoun *who* refers to *the girl.* Thus, *the girl* is the antecedent of *who.* You will notice that the case of the pronoun is not necessarily the same as the case of its antecedent. In Latin, *the girl* will be in the accusative case, because it is the direct object of the verb *saw.* However, the pronoun *who* will be in the nominative case because it is the subject of the verb *was swimming.*

B. A relative clause is used to tell something about its antecedent. It is, therefore, introduced by a relative pronoun which has the same number and gender (but not necessarily the same case) as its antecedent.

vir qui, the man who	Antecedent: **vir**	Relative pronoun: **qui**
puella quae, the girl who	Antecedent: **puella**	Relative pronoun: **quae**
bellum quod, the war that	Antecedent: **bellum**	Relative pronoun: **quod**

The case of a relative pronoun is determined by its use in its own clause.

vir quem video, the man whom I see

Antecedent: **vir.** Relative clause: **quem video.** Relative pronoun: **quem.**
quem is accusative because it is used as the direct object of **video.** It is masculine and singular to agree with **vir.**

puella quam video, the girl whom I see

Antecedent: **puella.** Relative clause: **quam video.** Relative pronoun: **quam.**

quam is accusative because it is used as the direct object of **video.** It is feminine and singular to agree with **puella.**
The relative pronoun is declined as follows:

SINGULAR

CASE	MASC.	FEM.	NEUT.	
Nom.	**qui**	**quae**	**quod**	who, which, that
Gen.	**cuius**	**cuius**	**cuius**	whose, of which
Dat.	**cui**	**cui**	**cui**	to, for whom, which
Acc.	**quem**	**quam**	**quod**	whom, which, that
Abl.	**quo**	**qua**	**quo**	from, with, by, in which, whom

PLURAL

CASE	MASC.	FEM.	NEUT.	
Nom.	**qui**	**quae**	**quae**	who, which, that
Gen.	**quorum**	**quarum**	**quorum**	whose, of which
Dat.	**quibus**	**quibus**	**quibus**	to, for whom, which
Acc.	**quos**	**quas**	**quae**	whom, which, that
Abl.	**quibus**	**quibus**	**quibus**	from, with, by, in which, whom

To express *with,* **cum** is added to the end of the ablative case: **quocum, quacum, quibuscum.**

C. An interrogative adjective modifies a noun and asks a question. It is, therefore, in the same case, number, and gender as the noun it modifies.

qui vir? which man?   **quae puella?** which girl?   **quod bellum?** which war?

Do not confuse the interrogative adjective **qui, quae, quod,** *who?* with the relative pronoun, **qui, quae, quod,** *who, which.* The interrogative adjective has the same spellings in some cases when *who?* not *which?* is meant. When *which?* is meant, the **quis, quis, quid** spelling provides a clue.

D. Deponent Verbs.
1. Several verbs in Latin use passive forms to express the active voice; they have no active voice forms. These verbs are called deponent verbs. They can easily be recognized from their prinicipal parts, which are passive in form, but active in meaning:

a-conjugation: **hortor, hortari, hortatus sum,** urge, encourage (exhort)
e-conjugation: **vereor, vereri, veritus sum,** fear
e/i-conjugation: **sequor, sequi, secutus sum,** follow (sequential)
e/i-conjugation -io verbs: **morior, mori, mortuus sum,** die (mortal)
i-conjugation: **experior, experiri, expertus sum,** try, test (experience)

You will notice that deponent verbs only have three principal parts. This is because the third principal part (first person singular of the perfect active) is identical with the fourth principal part.
2. Since the forms of deponent verbs are the same as the passive forms of regular verbs, the only form you need to learn is the imperative.
a. The imperative singular is formed in the same way the present active infinitive is formed for a regular verb:

hortare, urge!   **verere,** fear!   **sequere,** follow!
morere, die!   **experire,** try!

b. The imperative plural is formed in the same was as the second person plural of the present tense. Remember that though the form is passive, the meaning is active.

hortamini, urge!   **veremini,** fear!   **sequimini,** follow!
morimini, die!   **experimini,** try!

Reading

Hero et Leander

1. Sunt multae fabulae de amore Leandri Herusque.

2. Haec fuit puella pulchra, quae in Graecia habitat et quae omnia in templo, quod erat in oppido suo, curabat.

3. Ille in altera regione, quae erat trans Hellespontum, pontem Graeciae, habitabat, sed, cum eam videre cupiebat, trans mare quod non erat latum natabat.

4. Ob leges templi cum ea videri non poterat, sed illa lex eum non impedivit. Itaque ad eam semper noctu veniebat.

5. Etiam longum et difficile iter trans aquam ab puella eum non prohibuit.

6. Hero ad mare de alto turri omnibus noctibus spectabat.

7. Leander sine periculo ullo saepe veniebat et tum Hero ipsa vero laeta erat, quod eum bene amabat.

8. Diu Leander bonam fortunam habebat et omnibus noctibus ad Graeciam facile natabat atque ad illam terram sine ullo periculo perveniebat.

9. Nullam inopiam celeritatis aut studi habebat. Ut accidit tamen uno tempore, cum natabat, tempestate magna victus est.

10. Primo trans aquam turris Herus ab illo videri poterat, sed iam iter erat difficile et mox tempestate sub mare mittebatur.

11. Hero totam noctem eum misere exspectabat.

12. Tum ad mare contendit et corpus illius petebat. Id primo non conspexit.

13. Tum in loco non longe ab mari corpus Leandri repperit.

14. Misera Hero in mare cucurrit et illa eum morte sua repperit.

Hero and Leander

1. There are many stories about the love of Hero and Leander.

2. She was a beautiful girl, who used to live in Greece and who took care of everything in the temple that was in her town.

3. He lived in another region, which was across the Hellespont, the sea of Greece, but, when he wished to see her, he used to swim across the sea, which was not wide.

4. Because of the laws of the temple, he could not be seen with her, but that law did not hinder him. And so, he used to come to her always at night.

5. Even the long and difficult journey across the water did not keep him from the girl.

6. Hero used to watch every night from a high tower toward the sea.

7. Leander often came without any danger and then Hero herself was truly happy, because she loved him well.

8. For a long time, Leander had good fortune and swam easily to Greece every night and came to that land without any danger.

9. He had no lack of speed or eagerness. As it happened, however, one time, when he was swimming, he was overcome by a great storm.

10. At first, Hero's tower could be seen by him across the water, but already the way was difficult and soon he was sent under the sea by the storm.

11. Hero waited for him unhappily all night.

12. Then she hurried to the sea and sought his body. She did not see it at first.

13. Then in a place not far from the sea, she found the body of Leander.

14. The unhappy Hero ran into the sea and she found him by her own death.

Practice Exercises

No. 132. In the following sentences, translate (a) the relative clause, and (b) the whole sentence:
1. Homines qui cum copiis suis iter faciunt sunt fortes.
2. Turris quam aedificavit ex oppido barbaros prohibebat.
3. Femina quacum ambulabam mater mea est.
4. Navis cuius nomen conspicere non possumus ad Italiam navigat.
5. Puer cui litteras dedi celeriter veniet.
6. Timor quem habebitis mox non memoria tenebitur.
7. Flumen ad quod fugiebant erat altum latumque.
8. Locus de quo scripsit longe est ab urbe.
9. Omnia quae habuit nunc mea sunt.
10. Viri quorum pueros vides sunt amici.

No. 133. Translate these phrases containing interrogative adjectives:
1. in quibus locis?
2. qui homo?
3. quod oppidum?
4. quae praeda?
5. quos viros?
6. qua celeritate?
7. quo anno?
8. cuius nominis?
9. qua hora?
10. quo tempore?
11. cum quibus militibus?
12. quorum civium?
13. quae impedimenta?
14. cuius magnitudinis?
15. quo consilio?

No. 134. Give the English for these verb forms:
1. faciunt
2. iubebit
3. repperisti
4. perveniet
5. haberi
6. currebat
7. fuerat
8. cepit
9. conspexerunt
10. accidebat
11. auditis
12. pervenisti
13. contendebat
14. dederant
15. videri
16. prohibuerunt
17. erunt
18. videbor
19. rogari
20. habebo

No. 135. a. Translate these phrases and clauses:
1. non potuit
2. illius loci
3. filios tuos
4. alii veniunt
5. venire cupit
6. fortis populus
7. ob tempestatem
8. magno studio
9. domi mansit
10. eius nationis
11. proximo anno
12. mi amice
13. omnes homines
14. nihil timet
15. non solum mater tua

No. 135. b. Translate these verb forms:
1. verebamini
2. sequeris
3. experti erunt
4. verita ero
5. sequuntur
6. hortor
7. veretur
8. morti eritis
9. hortata erat
10. moriebantur
11. hortabuntur
12. experiris
13. verebuntur
14. expertus erat
15. hortabaris
16. sequebamur
17. mortuus est
18. moriemur
19. secutus eram
20. experta est

FAMILIAR ABBREVIATIONS

A.D., Anno Domini, in the year of (our) Lord.
a.m., ante meridiem, before noon.
p.m., post meridiem, after noon.
cf., confer, compare.
et al., et alii, or **et alia,** and other people or other things; **et alibi,** and elsewhere
vs, v., versus, against.
c., circ., circa, circum, about. Used with dates.

Fourth and Fifth Declension Nouns

Reading Vocabulary

Nouns

exercitus, exercitus, m. army (exercise)
impetus, impetus, m., attack (impetuous)
manus, manus, f., hand, group (manual)
res, rei, f., thing, matter, affair (re)
Persae, Persarum, m., the Persians
cornu, cornus, n., horn, wing (of an army) (cornucopia)
Athenae, Athenarum, f., Athens
     (declined in plural; meaning is singular)

domus, domus, f., house (domicile)
spes, spei, f., hope
acies, aciei, f., line of battle
passus, passus, m., pace (passage)
Sparta Spartae, f., Sparta
dies, diei, m. or **f.,** day (diet)
adventus, adventus, m., arrival, approach
     (adventure)

Adjectives

Marathonius, Marathonia, Marathonium, of Marathon

Verbs

instruo, instruere, instruxi, instructus, draw up, form, train (instruct)

Conjunctions

neque, and . . . not

neque . . . neque, neither . . . nor

Reading Grammar

A. Nouns that end in **-us** in the genitive singular are of the **u-declension,** or fourth declension. With a few exceptions, fourth declension nouns ending in **-us** in the nominative singular are masculine; those ending in **-u** in the nominative singular are neuter.

The endings are:

SINGULAR:

CASE	MASC. & FEM.	NEUT.
Nom.	-us	-u
Gen.	-us	-us
Dat.	-ui	-u
Acc.	-um	-u
Abl.	-u	-u
Voc.	-us	-u

PLURAL:

CASE	MASC. & FEM.	NEUT.
Nom.	-us	-ua
Gen.	-uum	-uum
Dat.	-ibus	-ibus
Acc.	-us	-ua
Abl.	-ibus	-ibus
Voc.	-us	-ua

Thus, the declensions of **exercitus** and **cornu** are as follows:

SINGULAR:

Nom.	exercitus	the army	cornu	the horn, wing
Gen.	exercitus	of the army	cornus	of the horn, wing
Dat.	exercitui	to, for the army	cornui	to, for the horn, wing
Acc.	exercitum	the army	cornu	the horn, wing
Abl.	exercitu	from/with/by/in the army	cornu	from/with/by/in the horn, wing
Voc.	exercitus	O army	cornu	O horn, wing

PLURAL:

Nom.	exercitus	the armies	cornua	the horns, wings
Gen.	exercituum	of the armies	cornuum	of the horns, wings
Dat.	exercitibus	to, for the armies	cornibus	to, for the horns, wings
Acc.	exercitus	the armies	cornua	the horns, wings
Abl.	exercitibus	from/with/by/in the armies	cornibus	from/with/by/in the horns, wings
Voc.	exercitus	O armies	cornua	O horns, wings

B. **Domus,** *house, home,* has endings in both the **o-declension** and the **u-declension.**

CASE	SINGULAR		PLURAL	
Nom.	domus	house	domus	houses
Gen.	domus, domi	of the house	domuum, domorum	of the houses
Dat.	domui, domo	to, for the house	domibus	to, for the houses
Acc.	domum	house	domus, domos	houses
Abl.	domu, domo	from/with/by/in the house	domibus	from/with/by/in the houses
Voc.	domus	O house	domus	O houses

Note that the nominative, dative, ablative and vocative plurals use only the **u-declension** ending.

C. Nouns that end in **-ei** in the genitive singular are of the **e-declension,** or fifth declension. These nouns are all feminine, except for **dies** (day), which is generally masculine.

The basic endings for this declension are:

CASE	SINGULAR	PLURAL
Nom.	-es	-es
Gen.	-ei	-erum
Dat.	-ei	-ebus
Acc.	-em	-es
Abl.	-e	-ebus
Voc.	-es	-es

Consider the declension of **spes, f.,** *hope:*

CASE	SINGULAR		PLURAL	
Nom.	spes	the hope	spes	the hopes
Gen.	spei	of the hope	sperum	of the hopes
Dat.	spei	to, for the hope	spebus	to, for the hopes
Acc.	spem	the hope	spes	the hopes
Abl.	spe	from, with, by, in the hope	spebus	from, with, by, in the hopes
Voc.	spes	O hope	spes	O hopes

Reading

Equus Troiae

1. Graeci novem annos Troiam oppugnaverunt et iam domi esse cupiebant.

2. Bellum diu et fortiter gesserant, sed neque urbem ceperant neque illum locum relinquere potuerant.

3. Itaque consilium ceperunt. Magno studio laboreque equum magnum fecerunt. Multi milites Graeci, qui bene pugnare poterant, a sociis suis in equo ipso noctu locati sunt.

4. Exercitus urbis Troiae, qui post muros urbis erat, equum illa nocte non vidit.

5. Cives Troiae tamen, adventu solis in caelo, equum viderunt et eum in urbem duxerunt, sed mox Graeci, qui in equo positi erant, clamabant et in cives exercitumque Troiae impetum faciabant.

6. Populus terrebatur.

7. Graeci telis suis et igni urbem ceperunt. Tum Graeci ad mare, ubi alii Graeci naves suas instruxerant, cucurrerunt.

The Trojan Horse

1. The Greeks had attacked Troy for nine years and now they wanted to be at home.

2. They had carried on war for a long time and bravely, but they had neither captured the city nor had they been able to leave that place.

3. And so, they decided on a plan. With great zeal and work, they made a large horse. Many Greek soldiers, who were able to fight well, were placed in the horse itself by their comrades at night.

4. The army of the city of Troy, which was behind the walls of the city, did not see the horse that night.

5. The citizens of Troy, however, at the arrival of the sun in the sky, saw the horse and led it into the city, but soon the Greeks, who had been placed in the horse, shouted and made an attack on the citizens and army of Troy.

6. The people were terrified.

7. With their weapons and fire, the Greeks took the city. Then the Greeks ran to the sea, where the other Greeks had drawn up their ships.

8. Post breve tempus, manus Graecorum cum captivis multis a Troia navigavit.

8. After a short time, the band of Greeks sailed from Troy with many captives.

Proelium Marathonium

1. Anno XD Ante Christum, Graecis ab exercitu Persarum graviter oppugnabatur.
2. Persae trans mare ad Graeciam navigaverant et multa oppida occupaverant.
3. Hostes ad locum, qui non multa milia passuum Athenis erat, iam iter fecerant, et ob hanc rem cives Athenarum et in aliis urbibus propinquis illi loco adventum hostium timebant.
4. Populus Athenarum ad Spartam virum misit.
5. Ille totum iter cucurrit et ab populo Spartae auxilium petivit, sed Sparta legem habebat. Hac lege, illi sine luna in caelo bellum gerere non poterant, et illo tempore luna non erat.
6. Itaque milites soli Athenarum aciem suam instruxerunt et sagittis ac telis gravibus hostes vicerunt. Illo die populus Athenarum spem victoriae magnae videbat.
7. Postea ob virtutem viri, qui Athenis Spartam cucurrerat, ludos habebant. His ludis nomen proeli, quod in agro Marathonio fuerat, dederunt.
8. Etiam hodie ludo pedibus id nomen damus.

The Battle of Marathon

1. In the year 490 B.C., Greece was heavily attacked by the army of the Persians.
2. The Persians had sailed across the sea to Greece and had seized many towns.
3. The enemy had made the journey to a place which was not many miles from Athens, and for this reason, the citizens of Athens and in other cities near to that place feared the arrival of the enemy.
4. The people of Athens sent a man to Sparta.
5. He ran the whole way and sought help from the people of Sparta, but Sparta had a law. By this law, they were not able to carry on war without a moon in the sky, and at that time, there was no moon.
6. And so the soldiers of Athens drew up their battle line alone and conquered the enemy with arrows and heavy weapons. On that day, the people of Athens saw the hope of a great victory.
7. Afterwards, because of the courage of the man who had run from Athens to Sparta, they held games. To these games they gave the name of the battle that had been on the field of Marathon.
8. Even today, we give this name to a contest on foot.

Practice Exercises

No. 136. Give the English for these phrases:
1. multos passus
2. vestra manus
3. longum impetum
4. ob adventum eius
5. utrumque cornu
6. exercituum nostrorum
7. in cornu tuo
8. ex exercitu
9. in domum
10. sex milia passuum
11. contra exercitus
12. ob adventum tuum
13. impetus hostium
14. manus militum
15. ab exercitu

No. 137. Give the English for these phrases:
1. acies suas
2. multo die
3. proximo die
4. ob has res
5. ullius spei
6. totam rem
7. unam diem
8. quarum rerum?
9. nostrae acies
10. quas res?
11. in qua acie?
12. utriusque diei
13. ob eam rem
14. in his aciebus
15. multam spem

No. 138. Translate these verb forms:
1. ambulavit
2. videmur
3. erant
4. fecerat
5. fugiebat
6. reperit
7. datum erat
8. potest
9. instructum est
10. videri
11. relicti sunt
12. pugnabunt
13. instruxit
14. iter facit
15. audientur

No. 139. Translate these sentences:
1. Omnes res faciles esse videntur.
2. Post sex dies neuter miles ullam spem habebat.
3. Captivi quos reduxisti ex eorum exercitu venerunt.
4. Quis fortem impetum magnopere impedivit?
5. Una hora homines domum venient.
6. Quam ob rem aciem suam in colli instruebat?
7. Inter has res quas habemus est parva copia aquae.
8. Milites in illo cornu equos suos ad agrum vertunt.
9. Neque cornu neque acies spem videbat.
10. Qui inter hos populos regnum tenebat?

Personal and Reflexive Pronouns

Reading Vocabulary

Nouns

Thermopylae, Thermopylarum, f. pl., Thermopylae
praesidium, praesidii or praesidi, n., guard, garrison
    (presidial, preside)

civitas, civitatis, f., state

Pronouns

ego, mei, I (egotist)
nos, nostrum, we (nostrum)

tu, tui, you (sing.)
vos, vestrum, you (pl.)

Adjectives

decem, ten (decimal)

Verbs

scio, scire, scivi, scitus, know (sciolist)
appello, appellare, appellavi, appellatus, address, call, name (appellation)
conloco, conlocare, conlocavi, conlocatus, place, station (collocate, collate)

Conjunctions

enim, for. Never the first word in a Latin sentence.

LEGAL TERMS

a vinculo matrimonii, from the bond of marriage. Used in a decree of absolute divorce.

caveat emptor, let the buyer beware. The buyer buys at his or her own risk.

inter vivos, between the living. Used to indicate a gift from a living person to another living person.

compos mentis, sound or sane of mind. **non compos mentis** or **non compos,** not sound or sane of mind.

nolo contendere, I do not wish to contend. A plea by which a defendant is subject to conviction, but does not admit guilt.

nolle prosequi, to be unwilling to prosecute. Abbr. **nol pros.** A court record stating that the prosecutor will not carry the suit further.

non prosequitur, he or she does not prosecute. Abbr. **non pros.** Used to indicate a decision against a plaintiff who does not appear in court to prosecute.

obiter dictum, something said along the way. Used of remarks made by a judge that are not part of the legal decision, but are personal comments and observations on matters relating to the case and decision.

nisi, if not, unless. Used to indicate that an order or decree will go into effect at a specified time unless modified by further evidence or cause presented before that time.

sui iuris or **suo iure,** of one's own right or in one's own right. Used of a person who has full capacity and ability to act for him- or herself in legal proceedings.

Reading Grammar

A. Personal pronouns are used to show emphasis or to make a clear distinction.

      Emphasis: **ego scio,** I (myself) know

      Clarity: **ego et tu scimus,** I and you know

    1. Personal Pronouns of the First Person.

CASE	SINGULAR		PLURAL	
Nom.	**ego**	I	**nos**	we
Gen.	**mei**	of me	**nostrum** or **nostri**	of us
Dat.	**mihi**	to, for me	**nobis**	to, for us
Acc.	**me**	me	**nos**	us
Abl.	**me**	from, with, by, in me	**nobis**	from, with, by. in us

    2. Personal Pronouns of the Second Person.

CASE	SINGULAR		PLURAL	
Nom.	**tu**	you	**vos**	you
Gen.	**tui**	of you	**vestrum** or **vestri**	of you
Dat.	**tibi**	to, for you	**vobis**	to, for you
Acc.	**te**	you	**vos**	you
Abl.	**te**	from, with, by, in you	**vobis**	from, with, by, in you
Voc.	**tu**	O you	**vos**	O you

3. You have already learned the Personal Pronouns of the Third Person.

SINGULAR		PLURAL	
is, ea, id	he, she, it	**ei, eae, ea,**	they
ille, illa, illud	he, she, it	**illi, illae, illa**	they
hic, haec, hoc	he, she, it	**hi, hae, haec**	they

B. Adjectives are more commonly used to show possession than is the genitive case of the personal pronoun, except in the third person. In other words, *my horse* would be more likely to be expressed as **meus equus** than as **mei equus.**

1st person	**meus, mea, meum**	my, mine
	noster, nostra, nostrum	our, ours
2nd person	**tuus, tua, tuum**	your, yours
	vester, vestra, vestrum	your, yours

These adjectives must agree with the nouns they modify in case, number and gender.
But there are exceptions to the rule when we use:

3rd person	**eius, eius, eius**	his, her, its
	eorum, earum, eorum	their; *or*
	illius, illius, illius	his, her, its
	illorum, illarum, illorum	their; *or*
	huius, huius, huius	his, her, its
	horum, harum, horum	their

With these pronouns, the genitive of the third person is used, regardless of the case of the noun it modifies, e.g., **eius filiam,** *his (her) daughter.* However, this only applies when the third person possessor is not the same as the subject of the sentence, e.g., *The man loves his daughter,* where *his* does not refer to *The man.* If the third person possessor is the subject, then the adjective is used:

suus, sua, suum   his, her, its (own)

The adjective must agree with the noun it modifies in case, number, and gender, e.g., **suam filiam,** *his (her) own daughter.*

When **cum** is used, it is added to the end of the personal pronouns.

mecum, with me	**nobiscum,** with us
tecum, with you	**vobiscum,** with you

C. Reflexive pronouns reflect back to the subject and, therefore, have no nominative case.

Me video, I see myself   **Te vides,** you see yourself

1. Reflexive Pronouns of the First Person.

CASE	SINGULAR		PLURAL	
Gen.	**mei**	of myself	**nostri**	of ourselves
Dat.	**mihi**	to/for myself	**nobis**	to/for ourselves
Acc.	**me**	myself	**nos**	ourselves
Abl.	**me**	from/with/by/in myself	**nobis**	from/with/by/in ourselves

2. Reflexive Pronouns of the Second Person.

CASE	SINGULAR		PLURAL	
Gen.	**tui**	of yourself	**vestri**	of yourselves
Dat.	**tibi**	to/for yourself	**vobis**	to/for yourselves
Acc.	**te**	yourself	**vos**	yourselves
Abl.	**te**	from/with/by/in yourself	**vobis**	from/with/by/in yourselves

3. The reflexive pronoun for the third person is the same in Latin for the singular and plural. Only the meaning changes.

CASE	SINGULAR AND PLURAL	
Gen.	**sui**	of himself/herself/itself/themselves
Dat.	**sibi**	to/for himself/herself/itself/themselves
Acc.	**se**	himself, herself, itself, themselves
Abl.	**se**	from/with/by/in himself/herself/itself/themselves

Reading

Proelium Thermopylarum	The Battle of Thermopylae
1. Post decem annos Persae ad Graeciam navibus suos reduxerunt.	1. After ten years, the Persians led their men back to Greece by ship.
2. Proelium Marathonium anno XD Ante Christum fuerat.	2. The Battle of Marathon had been in the year 490 B.C.
3. Hic annus erat XXD Ante Christum et hoc proelium appellatur Proelium Thermopylarum.	3. This year was 480 B.C. and this battle is called the Battle of Thermopylae.
4. Persae magnum copiam et cibi et frumenti, quam trans mare portare in animo habebant, decem annos paraverant atque exercitum fortem acremque habuerunt.	4. The Persians for ten years had prepared a great supply both of food and grain, which they intended to carry across the sea, and they also had a brave and keen army.
5. Illi in impetu hoc omnem spem suam posuerant, sed illo tempore erat apud Graecos nulla pax. Alia civitas contra aliam contendebat.	5. They had placed all their hope in this attack, but at that time there was no peace among the Greeks. One state was fighting against another.
6. Itaque Athenae Spartaque Graeciam totam aegre defendere poterant.	6. And so, Athens and Sparta were able to defend all Greece with difficulty.
7. Exercitus hostium ad partem montium quae Thermopylae appellata est pervenit.	7. The army of the enemy came to the part of the mountains which is called Thermopylae.
8. Hic locus natura fortis est quod iter parvum inter montes ab non multis militibus teneri poterat.	8. This place is stong by nature because the small road between the mountains was able to be held by a few soldiers.
9. In eo loco manus parva Graecorum conlocata erat et adventum hostium exspectabat.	9. In this place, a small group of Greeks had been stationed and was waiting for the arrival of the enemy.
10. Graeci in montibus facile pugnare poterant. Ei enim patriam suam bene sciebant.	10. The Greeks were able to fight easily in the mountains. For they knew their native country well.
11. Iter per montes erat difficile et angustum. Itaque Graeci praesidium ibi conlocaverant.	11. The way through the mountains was both difficult and narrow. And so the Greeks had stationed a garrison there.

12. Hi contra milites fortes hostium, qui spem iam relinquebant, diu et fortiter contenderunt, sed erat unus homo, qui Persis auxilium dedit.

12. They fought for a long time against the brave soldiers of the enemy, who were already giving up hope, but there was one man, who gave help to the Persians.

13. Hic vir hostibus iter, quod erat post locum ubi praesidium Graecum instructum erat, trans montes demonstravit.

13. This man pointed out to the enemy a way across the mountains, which was in back of the place where the Greek guard had been drawn up.

14. Exercitus hostium ad locum post aciem Graecam noctu iter fecit.

14. The army of the enemy made its way at night to a place in back of the Greek battle line.

15. Alii Graeci fugere potuerunt, sed alii milites Spartae et sociorum eius nullum timorem demonstraverunt.

15. Some Greeks were able to escape, but other soldiers of Sparta and her allies showed no fear.

16. Hi gladiis et aliis telis pugnabant, sed post breve tempus Graeci omnes ab hostibus interfecti erant et Persae trans corpora eorum Athenas iter fecerunt.

16. These men fought for a time with swords and other weapons, but after a short time, all the Greeks had been killed by the enemy and the Persians made their way to Athens over their bodies.

Practice Exercises

No. 140. Give the English for these personal pronouns:

1. vos	7. te	13. vobis	19. illorum	25. illis
2. nos	8. ego	14. eos	20. ad vos	26. de his
3. a te	9. eum	15. illud	21. tibi	27. illa
4. eorum	10. mihi	16. huic	22. vestrum	28. cum ea
5. ea	11. nobiscum	17. eius	23. nostri	29. horum
6. ei	12. tu	18. tecum	24. de me	30. illos

No. 141. Give the English for these reflexive pronouns:

1. sibi	6. vobis
2. te	7. mihi
3. a me	8. nobis
4. vos	9. me
5. se	10. nos

No. 142. Translate these sentences:

1. Homo ipse non scit.
2. Ego tibi auxilium misi.
3. Nos in hoc loco te repperimus.
4. Venietisne vos mecum?
5. Tu nobis libros das.
6. Vos eum non auditis.
7. Illi ad nos fugiebant.
8. Is mihi haec misit.
9. Tecum domum ambulare non poterit.
10. Haec est patria nostra.
11. Tu id illis narrabis
12. Nos hanc domum reducemus.
13. Illi ab his pacem petebant.
14. Ego a te et tuo gladio terrebar.
15. Nos illo tempore nos servaveramus.
16. Nonne tu nos iuvare potes?
17. Ille urbem eorum vidit.
18. Nos ipsi eos venire iubebimus.
19. Vos nobis ea demonstrabitis.
20. Animus eius me non diu terrebat.

Chapter Seven Review

Vocabulary Review

Nouns

1. acies
2. adventus
3. Athenae
4. civitas
5. cornu
6. dies
7. domus
8. Eurydice
9. exercitus
10. Hellespontus
11. Hero
12. impetus
13. inopia
14. Leander
15. manus
16. natura
17. nihil, nil
18. Orpheus
19. passus
20. Persae
21. praesidium
22. regio
23. regnum
24. res
25. Sparta
26. spes
27. Thermopylae
28. turris

Pronouns

1. ego
2. nos
3. qui
4. tu
5. vos

Adjectives

1. decem
2. difficilis
3. Marathonius
4. primus

Verbs

1. accido
2. appello
3. conloco
4. conspicio
5. cupio
6. discedo
7. educo
8. impedio
9. instruo
10. pervenio
11. prohibeo
12. reduco
13. rego
14. relinquo
15. reperio
16. scio

Adverbs

1. iam
2. magnopere
3. parum
4. primum, primo
5. solum

Conjunctions

1. enim
2. neque
3. neque . . . neque
4. ut

Practice Exercises

No. 143. Give the adverbs of these adjectives, with their meanings:

1. latus
2. acer
3. difficilis
4. miser
5. longus
6. magnus
7. laetus
8. liber
9. parvus
10. angustus

No. 144. Translate these verbs:

1. veniam
2. sciebat
3. auditus est
4. perveniebamus
5. impedientur
6. reperiunt
7. audiebaris
8. scitum erat
9. cupiverunt
10. audieris

No. 145. Translate these pronouns:

1. cuius
2. quem
3. quae
4. qui
5. quibuscum
6. nos
7. mihi
8. me
9. vestrum
10. tibi
11. tecum
12. eius
13. eorum
14. illum
15. hanc

No. 146. Translate these nouns:

1. exercitui
2. res
3. cornus
4. aciem
5. spem
6. manuum
7. die
8. impetibus
9. adventum
10. domum
11. rebus
12. cornua
13. exercituum
14. manui
15. spei

Reading

Publius Vergilius Maro

Virgil was born in 70 B.C. near Mantua, in the north of Italy, and was educated in Milan, Rome, and Naples, where he studied philosophy and rhetoric. During the latter part of his life, he lived near Naples, where he composed his epic poem *The Aeneid*. Virgil died in 19 B.C. at Brundisium, while returning from Greece.

Ibant obscuri, sola sub nocte, per umbram
perque domos Ditis vacuas, et inania regna;
quale per incertam lunam sub luce maligna
est iter in silvis, ubi caelum condidit umbra
Iuppiter, et rebus nox abstulit atra colorem.
Vestibulum ante ipsum primisque in faucibus
Orci
Luctus et ultrices posuere cubilia Curae,
pallentesque habitant Morbi, tristisque
Senectus,
et Metus, et malesuada Fames, ac turpis Egestas,
terribiles visu formae, Letumque Labosque,
tum consanguineus Leti Sopor, et mala mentis
Gaudia, mortiferumque adverso in limine
Bellum,
ferreique Eumenidum thalami, et Discordia
demens,
vipereum crinem vittis innexa cruentis.

Aeneidos VI, 268–281

Jacques de Vitry

These two stories are found in the sermons of Jacques de Vitry, who was the Cardinal Bishop of Tusculum and died in A.D. 1240. The stories were used to illustrate a point as well as to entertain the listeners.

De Arbore In Qua Se Suspendebant Mulieres
De quodam alio audivi, qui habebat arborem in horto suo, in qua duae eius uxores suspenderant semetipsas. Cui quidam eius vicinus ait: "Valde fortunata est arbor illa et bonum omen habet. Habeo autem uxorem pessimam; rogo te, da mihi surculum ex ea, ut plantem in horto meo."

De Bachone Qui Pendebat In Quadam Villa
Aliquando transivi per quandam villam in Francia, ubi suspenderant pernam seu bachonem in platea hac condicione ut, qui vellet iuramento firmare quod uno integro anno post contractum matrimonium permansisset cum uxore ita quod de matrimonio non paenituisset, bachonem haberet. Et cum per decem annos ibi pependisset non est unus solus inventus qui bachonem lucraretur, omnibus infra annum de matrimonio contracto paenitentibus.

Numbers and Comparisons

MORE STATE MOTTOES

E Pluribus Unum, One From Many. United States of America.

Nil Sine Numine, Nothing Without Divine Power. Colorado.

Qui Transtulit Sustinet, He Who Has Transplanted Sustains. Connecticut.

Scuto Bonae Voluntatis Tuae Coronasti Nos, You Have Crowned Us With The Shield Of Thy Will. Maryland.

Si Quaeris Paeninsulam Amoenam, Circumspice, If You Seek A Pleasant Peninsula, Look Around. Michigan.

Crescit Eundo, It Increases As It Goes. New Mexico.

Esse Quam Videri, To Be Rather Than To Seem. North Carolina.

Labor Omnia Vincit, Labor Conquers All. Oklahoma.

Alis Volat Propriis, It Flies On Its Own Wings. Oregon.

Animis Opibusque Parati, Prepared In Mind And Resources. South Carolina.

Sic Semper Tyrannis, Thus Always To Tyrants. Virginia.

Reading Vocabulary

Nouns

onus, oneris, n., burden, weight (onerous)
hiems, hiemis, f., winter
portus, portus, m., harbor (port)
multitudo, multitudinis, f., great number, multitude (multitudinous)

Creusa, Creusae, f., Creusa
ventus, venti, m., wind
aestas, aestatis, f., summer

Verbs

opprimo, opprimere, oppressi, oppressus, overcome, crush (oppressive)
convenio, convenire, conveni, conventus, come together, assemble (convene, convention)
incendo, incendere, incendi, incensus, set fire to, burn (incendiary)

cogo, cogere, coegi, coactus, collect, drive, compel (cogent)
recipio, recipere, recepi, receptus, take back, receive (reception)
dedo, dedere, dedidi, deditus, give up, surrender
suscipio, suscipere, suscepi, susceptus, take up, undertake (susceptible)

Adverbs

bis, twice (bicycle)

Conjunctions

nam, for

Reading Grammar

A. Cardinal numbers are one, two, three, four, and so on; they answer the question *how many?* Ordinal numbers are first, second, third, fourth, and so on; they answer the question *which one?*

B. The cardinal numbers one to twenty, one hundred, and one thousand are as follows:

1—**unus, una, unum**	6—**sex**	11—**undecim**	16—**sedecim**
2—**duo, duae, duo**	7—**septem**	12—**duodecim**	17—**septendecim**
3—**tres, tria**	8—**octo**	13—**tredecim**	18—**duodeviginti**
4—**quattuor**	9—**novem**	14—**quattuordecim**	19—**undeviginti**
5—**quinque**	10—**decem**	15—**quindecim**	20—**viginti**

100—**centum**   1000—**mille**

The following cardinal numbers are declined:

1—

CASE	MASC.	FEM.	NEUT.
Nom.	unus	una	unum
Gen.	unius	unius	unius
Dat.	uni	uni	uni
Acc.	unum	unam	unum
Abl.	uno	una	uno

2—

CASE	MASC.	FEM.	NEUT.
Nom.	duo	duae	duo
Gen.	duorum	duarum	duorum
Dat.	duobus	duabas	duobus
Acc.	duos, duo	duas	duo
Abl.	duobus	duabus	duobus

3—

CASE	MASC./FEM.	NEUT.
Nom.	tres	tria
Gen.	trium	trium
Dat.	tribus	tribus
Acc.	tres, tris	tria
Abl.	tribus	tribus

1000—

CASE	SINGULAR	PLURAL
Nom.	mille	milia
Gen.	mille	milium
Dat.	mille	milibus
Acc.	mille	milia
Abl.	mille	milibus

1. **Unus** is only declined in the singular. **Duo** and **tres** are only declined in the plural. **Mille** is declined in both the singular and the plural. The other cardinal numbers are not declined.

2. **Mille** is an adjective in the singular and a noun in the plural.

mille homines, a thousand men   **milia hominum,** thousands of men

3. The other cardinal numbers may be used as either adjectives or nouns.

tres homines, three men   **tres hominum,** three of the men

tres de hominibus, three (from the) men   **tres ex hominibus,** three (from the) men

C. The ordinal numbers first to tenth are as follows:

first	**primus, prima, primum**	sixth	**sextus, sexta, sextum**
second	**secundus, secunda, secundum**	seventh	**septimus, septima, septimum**
third	**tertius, tertia, tertium**	eighth	**octavus, octava, octavum**
fourth	**quartus, quarta, quartum**	ninth	**nonus, nona, nonum**
fifth	**quintus, quinta, quintum**	tenth	**decimus, decima, decimum**

All ordinal numbers are **a-** and **o-declension** adjectives.
sexto die, on the sixth day

quartum annum, for the fourth year

Reading

Aeneas in Igni Troiae

1. Aeneas in vias Troiae una nocte cucurrit et multitudinem militum Graecorum, qui vero laeti erant, quod urbem vicerant, ibi videbat.

2. Aeneas cum parva manu sociorum suorum contra hostes primo contendit, sed nihil faci poterat.

3. Tum patrem suum, qui domi erat, memoria tenuit et domum properavit.

4. Troia eo tempore acriter incendebatur. Populus Troiae dediderat. Bellum contra Graecos pugnatum erat.

5. Aeneas patrem suum secum venire coegit et in umeris suis totum onus corporis eius portabat. Hi tres, Aeneas atque pater suus atque suus filius parvus, ex igni contendebant.

6. Ob victoriam hostium magnopere opprimebantur.

7. Post breve tempus, Aeneas matrem fili sui, Creusam, memoria tenuit. Illa enim erat in urbe. Itaque in urbem celeriter cucurrit.

8. Bis centum tempora eam appellabat, sed illa ibi non erat. A Morte educta erat.

Iter Ulixis

1. Decem annos Ulixes ab portu Troiae ad patriam suam navigabat. Ipse et socii sui ad multa loca illo tempore pervenerunt.

2. Primus locus erat eis acriter gratus idoneusque.

3. Secundus locus erat terra in qua Polyphemus habitabat.

Aeneas in the Fire of Troy

1. Aeneas ran into the streets of Troy one night and he saw there a great number of Greek soldiers, who were truly happy, because they had conquered the city.

2. Aeneas, with a small band of his comrades, at first struggled against the enemy, but nothing could be done.

3. Then he remembered his father, who was at home, and he hurried home.

4. Troy, at that time, was being fiercely burned. The people of Troy had surrendered. The war against the Greeks had been finished.

5. Aeneas had forced his father to come with him and he carried the whole burden of his body on his shoulders. These three, Aeneas and his father and his small son, hurried from the fire.

6. Because of the victory of the enemy, they were greatly oppressed.

7. After a short time, Aeneas remembered the mother of his son, Creusa. For she was in the city. And so, he ran quickly into the city.

8. He called her twice a hundred times, but she was not there. She had been carried off by Death.

The Journey of Ulysses

1. Ulysses sailed for ten years from the harbor of Troy to his native country. He and his comrades arrived at many places during that time.

2. The first place was keenly pleasing and suitable to them.

3. The second place was the land in which Polyphemus lived.

4. Tertio in loco, venti eis ab rege ventorum dati sunt.

4. In the third place, winds were given to them by the king of the winds.

5. Quarto in loco, multi viri ab illo, quem ibi reppererunt, necati sunt.

5. In the fourth place, many of the men were killed by him, whom they found there.

6. Ob feminam pulchram ab quinto loco difficile se recipere potuerunt.

6. They were able to depart from the fifth place with difficulty because of a beautiful woman.

7. Sexto in loco, omnes qui apud Inferos convenerant viderunt.

7. In the sixth place, they say all those who had come together among Those Below.

8. Septimo in loco, multas res pulchras audiverunt et ibi manere cupiverunt.

8. In the seventh place, they heard many beautiful things and wished to stay there.

9. Ab octavo loco celeriter fugerunt. Nam duo animalia ibi habitabant. Unum ex his erat serpens et alterum erat magnum saxum.

9. They fled from the eighth place quickly. For two animals lived there. One of these was a serpent and the other was a large rock.

10. Nono in loco animalia dei solis tenebantur.

10. In the ninth place, the animals of the god of the sun were held.

11. Tum omnes socii eius in mari necati sunt. Itaque ille solus ad decimum locum pervenit.

11. Then all his comrades were killed on the sea. And so, he arrived alone at the tenth place.

12. Iter difficile susceperat, sed post decem aestates atque decem hiemes servatus erat et domum venit.

12. He had undertaken a difficult journey, but after ten summers and ten winters, he had been saved and he came home.

Practice Exercises

No. 147. Give the English forms for these cardinal numbers:

1. quindecim	6. decem	11. centum	16. tredecim
2. novem	7. tres	12. quattuordecim	17. septem
3. viginti	8. septendecim	13. octo	18. unus
4. quinque	9. quattuor	14. undeviginti	19. duodeviginti
5. sedecim	10. undecim	15. duo	20. mille

No. 148. Give the English forms for these ordinal numbers:

1. quartus	6. secundus
2. octavus	7. quintus
3. decimus	8. nonus
4. tertius	9. primus
5. septimus	10. sextus

No. 149. Translate these phrases which contain cardinal numbers:

1. mille naves	6. viginti milia passuum	11. centum annis	16. duae de provinciis
2. tres homines	7. centum pueros	12. octo ex pueris	17. duodecim diebus
3. milium militum	8. quinque annos	13. duos dies	18. sex animalium
4. quattuordecim dies	9. sex de militibus	14. decem legum	19. duodeviginti ex regibus
5. unius viri	10. septem horis	15. tria loca	20. tribus annis

No. 150. Translate these phrases which contain ordinal numbers:

1. decimae puellae
2. octavo die
3. sexta hora
4. septima navis
5. quinta aestate

6. tertium diem
7. decima hieme
8. septimus impetus
9. nonae horae
10. primo anno

Comparison of Adjectives

Reading Vocabulary

Nouns

fons, fontis, m., spring, fountain (fontium) (font)
Psyche, Psyches, f., Psyche (a Greek name) (psychic)
oraculum, oraculi, n., oracle (oracular)
matrimonium, matrimonii or matrimoni, n.,
    marriage (matrimony)

Cupido, Cupidinis, m., Cupid
difficultas, difficultatis, f., difficulty
soror, sororis, f., sister (sorority)
in matrimonium ducere, marry
    (literally, to lead into marriage)

Adjectives

aequus, aequa, aequum, equal, level, fair (equality)
immortalis, immortale, immortal (immortality)

dulcis, dulce, sweet (dulcet)
similis, simile, like, similar (similarity)

Verbs

deligo, deligere, delegi, delectus, choose, select
dormio, dormire, dormivi, dormitus, sleep
    (dormant, dormitory)

tango, tangere, tetigi, tactus, touch (tangent)
constituo, constituere, constitui, constitutus,
    decide, establish (constitution)

Adverbs

olim, formerly, once upon a time

quoque, also

Conjunctions

quamquam, although

FAMILIAR QUOTATIONS

Laudator temporis acti. A praiser of past times. Horace.
Abeunt studia in mores. Pursuits pass over into habits. Ovid.
Factum fieri infectum non potest. What is done cannot be undone. Terence.
O tempora! O mores! Oh the times! Oh the customs! Cicero.
Tu ne cede malis. Do not yield to misfortunes. Virgil.
Docendo discitur. We learn by teaching. Seneca.
In hoc signo vinces. By this sign shalt thou conquer. Constantine.
Non datur ad Musas currere lata via. It is not granted to run to the Muses on a wide road. Propertius.
Est modus in rebus. There is a middle course in things. Horace.
Forsan et haec olim meminisse iuvabit. Perhaps some time it will be pleasant to remember even these things. Virgil.

Reading Grammar

A. Adjectives have three degrees of comparison—positive, comparative, and superlative.

	POSITIVE	COMPARATIVE	SUPERLATIVE
good:	*good* food	*better* food	the *best* food
pretty:	a *pretty* girl	a *prettier* girl	the *prettiest* girl
fast:	a *fast* train	a *faster* train	the *fastest* train
slow:	a *slow* boat	a *slower* boat	the *slowest* boat

Many adjectives end in *-er* in the comparative degree and in *-est* in the superlative degree. However, some adjectives modify their spelling in these two degrees. The comparative of *pretty* is *prettier,* and the superlative is *prettiest.* The *-y* becomes an *-i-.*

Some adjectives have irregular comparative and superlative degrees, for example, *good, better, best,* and *bad, worse, worst.*

B. In Latin, as in English, most adjectives have regular endings in the comparative and superlative degrees. However, some adjectives will have modified spellings, while others will be irregular in these degrees.

1. The positive degree is alway the simple form of the adjective.

longus, longa, longum, long
miser, misera, miserum, wretched
acer, acris, acre, keen

fortis, forte, brave
pulcher, pulchra, pulchrum, pretty
facilis, facile, easy

The positive degree of an adjective is declined regularly in the **a-** and **o-declension** or in the **i-declension.** There are no **u-declension** or **e-declension** adjectives.

2. The comparative degree of most adjectives ends in **-ior** or **-ius**. The ending is added to the stem of the positive degree.

> **longior, longius,** longer, rather long, too long, quite long
> **fortior, fortius,** braver, rather brave, too brave, quite brave
> **miserior, miserius,** more wretched, rather wretched, quite wretched
> **pulchrior, pulchrius,** prettier, more pretty, rather pretty, quite pretty
> **acrior, acrius,** keener, more keen, rather keen, quite keen
> **facilior, facilius,** easier, more easy, rather easy, quite easy

The comparative degree is declined as follows:

CASE	SINGULAR		PLURAL	
	MASC./FEM.	NEUT.	MASC./FEM.	NEUT.
Nom.	longior	longius	longiores	longiora
Gen.	longioris	longioris	longiorum	longiorum
Dat.	longiori	longiori	longioribus	longioribus
Acc.	longiorem	longius	longiores	longiora
Abl.	longiore	longiore	longioribus	longioribus
Voc.	longior	longius	longiores	longiora

As you can see, the comparative degree belongs to the **i-declension**. Since it is an adjective, it **must agree** in case, number, and gender with the word it modifies.

3. The superlative degree endings are as follows:

> a. **-rimus, -rima, -rimum** for those adjectives that end in **-er,**
>> **miserrimus, -a, -um,** very wretched, most wretched
>> **pulcherrimus, -a, -um,** very pretty, most pretty, prettiest
>> **acerrimus, -a, -um,** very keen, most keen, keenest
> b. for **facilis, difficilis,** and **similis,**
>> **facillimus, -a, -um,** very easy, most easy, easiest
>> **difficillimus, -a, -um,** very difficult, most difficult
>> **simillimus, -a, -um,** very similar, most similar
> c. for most other adjectives, the ending is **-issimus, -a, -um.**
>> **longissimus, -a, -um,** very long, most long, longest
>> **fortissimus, -a, -um,** very brave, bravest, most brave

The superlative endings are added on to the stem of the positive degree. The superlative degree is declined regularly in the **a-** and **o-declension** and must agree with the word it modifies in case, number, and **gender**.

Reading

Cupido et Psyche	Cupid and Psyche

1. **Erant olim tres sorores pulchrae, quae erant filiae regis reginaque. Harum Psyche erat clarissima. Itaque fama eius in regionibus, quae finitimae erant domui suae, erat aequa illi Veneris.**

1. There were once three beautiful sisters, who were daughters of the king and queen. Of these, Psyche was the most famous. And so, her reputation in the regions that were neighboring to her home was equal to that of Venus.

2. Venus non solum immortalis sed etiam superbissima erat. Itaque contra puellam, quae neque dea neque immortalis erat, poenam reperire constituit.

3. Dea pulchra nullam inopiam consili habebat. Postquam ipsa iter ex hac difficultate delegerat, filium suum, Cupidem, deum amoris, ad se vocavit.

4. Ei difficultatem suam demonstrat et dicit: "Omnes Psychen petunt et illi nunc me adorare non etiam simulant. Ob iniurias, quas matri tuae fecit, poenas dare debet. Hoc opus tibi idoneum est."

5. Cupido matrem suam iuvare celeriter parabat.

6. Ad hortum Veneris, in quo erant duo fontes, quorum alter dulcis erat alterque non dulcis, properavit.

7. Postquam ex utroque fonte aquam obtinuerat, Psychen, quae domi dormiebat, petivit.

8. Ipse, ubi illam vidit, paene motus est quod pulcherrima erat, sed deus matrem memoria tenebat et puellam aqua, quae non dulcis erat, et sagitta sua tetigit.

9. Psyche incitata est, sed Cupidinem videre non poterat. Ipse territus est et in illa aquam dulcem posuit.

10. Postea Psyche, quamquam pulchra erat, miserrima quoque erat. Quod illa a Venere non amabatur nullus eam in matrimonium ducere cupiebat.

11. Itaque Psyche domi manebat et pater materque puellae simillimam inopiam spei demonstrabant.

12. Hoc ab oraculo dictum erat: "Non a viro, sed ab uno contra quem nullus stare potest tu in matrimonium duceris."

2. Venus was not only immortal, but also very proud. And so, she decided to find a punishment against the girl, who was neither a goddess nor immortal.

3. The beautiful goddess had no lack of plan. After she had chosen a way out of this difficulty, she called her son, Cupid, the god of love, to her.

4. To him, she pointed out her difficulty and said: "All seek Psyche and they do not even pretend to worship me now. Because of the injuries which she has done to your mother, she ought to pay penalties. This work is suitable to you."

5. Cupid quickly prepared to help his mother.

6. He hurried to the garden of Venus, in which there were two fountains, one of which was sweet and the other not sweet.

7. After he had obtained water from each fountain, he sought Psyche, who was asleep at home.

8. He himself, when he saw her, was almost moved, because she was very pretty, but the god remembered his mother and touched the girl with the water that was not sweet and with his arrow.

9. Psyche was aroused, but she was not able to see Cupid. He was frightened and placed the sweet water on her.

10. Afterwards, Psyche, although she was pretty, was also very unhappy. Because she was not loved by Venus, no one wanted to marry her.

11. And so, Psyche remained at home and the father and mother of the girl showed a similar lack of hope.

12. This had been said by the oracle: "You will be married not by a man, but by one against whom no one can stand."

Practice Exercises

No. 151. Translate these phrases with positive degree adjectives:

1. iter difficile
2. domum miseram
3. virorum liberorum
4. timores acres
5. exercitus similes
6. diem longum
7. in monte alto
8. flumina celeria
9. vias latas
10. puellarum puchrarum

No. 152. Translate these phrases with comparative degree adjectives:

1. viae angustiores
2. puer altior
3. puellarum laetiorum
4. populus amicior
5. iter longius
6. in locis gratioribus
7. sororum clariorum
8. hiemem longiorem
9. flumina latiora
10. virum audaciorem

No. 153. Translate these phrases with superlative degree adjectives:

1. fontis dulcissimi
2. ex hortis pulcherrimis
3. templum angustissimum
4. ob memoria miserrimas
5. oracula clarissima
6. civis laetissimus
7. ex agro latissimo
8. cum matribus pulcherrimis
9. in navi novissima
10. nomina brevissima

No. 154. Translate these sentences:

1. Is est locus miserrimus.
2. Fortissimi homines ad insulam pervenerunt.
3. Acerrimi equi erant inter primos.
4. Quid ad Graeciam est iter facilius?
5. Populus Italiae est liberrimus.
6. Haec est angustior pars aquae.
7. Hae res sunt quoque simillimae.
8. Flumen altissimum et latius vidimus.
9. Nostri ad urbem viam breviorem delegerunt.
10. Aedificium altum ab hoc loco videre potestis.

Comparison of Irregular Adjectives

Reading Vocabulary

Nouns

maritus, mariti, m., husband (marital)
Zephyrus, Zephyri, m., Zephyr, west wind

vox, vocis, f., voice

Adjectives

posterus, postera, posterum, next, following (posterior)

Adverbs

quam, than
multo, much
maxime, most, especially (maximum)

antea, before
magis, more

Conjunctions

aut . . . aut, either . . . or

MATHEMATICAL TERMS DERIVED FROM LATIN

plus, more, increased by.
minus, less, diminished by.
multiplication, from **multiplicare,** to make manifold or many fold.
division, from **dividere,** divide.
subtraction, from **subtrahere,** withdraw, draw from beneath.
addition, from **addere,** add to, or **additio,** adding.
ratio, from **ratio,** reason.
quotient, from **quotiens,** how often, how many times.
sum, from **summa,** sum or total, or **summus,** highest.
number and numeral, from **numerus,** number.
integer, from **integer,** whole, untouched.
fraction, from **frangere,** break.
percent and per centum, from **per centum,** by the hundred, in the hundred.

Reading Grammar

A. Latin has two ways to show comparison between two things.

1. Use **quam,** with the same case for the two things being compared.

Ego altior sum quam tu, I am taller than you.

Ego and **tu** are both in the nominative case.

amicior illi quam huic, more friendly to that one than to this one.

illi and **huic** are both in the dative case.

2. Use the ablative case after the comparative degree, without **quam.**

Ego altior sum te, I am taller than you.

Ego is in the nominative case; **te** is in the ablative case.

amicior illi hoc, more friendly to that one than to this one.

illi is in the dative case; **hoc** is in the ablative case.

B. Some adjectives have irregular comparative and superlative degrees; this is known as irregular **comparison.**

POSITIVE	COMPARATIVE	SUPERLATIVE
bonus, -a, -um, good	melior, melius, better	optimus, -a, -um, best
magnus, -a, -um, large	maior, maius, larger	maximus, -a, -um, largest
malus, -a, -um, bad	peior, peius, worse	pessimus, -a, -um, worst
parvus, -a, -um, small	minor, minus, smaller	minimus, -a, -um, smallest
multus, -a, -um, much	——-, plus, more	plurimus, -a, -um, most
multi, -ae, -a, many	plures, plura, more	plurimi, -ae, -a, most

The superlative degree of **posterus** is **postremus, -a, -um** or **postumus, -a, -um.**

Although the comparison of the above adjectives is irregular, the declension of the comparative and superlative degrees is regular, with the exception of **plus.**

C. **Plus** is a neuter noun in the singular and an adjective in the plural.

CASE	SINGULAR		PLURAL
	Neut.	Masc./Fem.	Neut.
Nom.	plus	plures	plura
Gen.	pluris	plurium	plurium
Dat.	——	pluribus	pluribus
Acc.	plus	plures	plura
Abl.	plure	pluribus	pluribus
Voc.	plus	plures	plura

D. Most adjectives ending in a vowel and -us are compared this way:

POSITIVE	COMPARATIVE	SUPERLATIVE
idoneus, -a, -um	magis idoneus, -a, -um	maxime idoneus, -a, -um
suitable	more suitable	most suitable

idoneus, -a, -um is declined regularly in all three degrees. **Magis** and **maxime** are adverbs; therefore, they are not declined.

Reading

Cupido et Psyche (cont'd)

1. Locus, quem oraculum demonstraverat et in quo maritus illam exspectabat, summo in monte erat.

2. Illa ipsa etiam miserior aut patre aut matre erat. Itaque ad suam fortunam malam se dedere constituit.

3. Mox postea puella, cum matre patreque atque multis ex amicis suis, ad montem a populo oppidi, in quo habitabat, ducta est.

4. Hi eam solam ibi relinquerunt, quamquam pro ea magnopere dolebant, et se receperunt.

5. Psyche, quae summo in monte diu steterat et omnia in eo loco timebat, ab uno ex ventis, Zephyro, a monte ad terram pulcherrimam celeriter portata est.

6. Postquam breve tempus dormiverat, circum se spectabat et in silvam, quae propinqua erat agro, in quo a Zephyro relicta erat, audacter ambulavit.

7. In silva domum, quae pulchrior erat ulla quam antea viderat, repperit. Ad domum cucurrit.

8. Omnia in domo ei erant gratissima et ipsa tum vero laetissima erat.

Cupid and Psyche (cont'd)

1. The place which the oracle had pointed out and in which her husband was waiting for her, was on the top of a mountain.

2. She herself was more unhappy than either her father or mother. And so, she decided to surrender herself to her bad fortune.

3. Soon afterwards, the girl, with her mother and father and many of her friends, was led to the mountain by the people of the town in which she lived.

4. They left her there alone, although they felt very sorry for her, and departed.

5. Psyche, who had stayed on top of the mountain for a long time and was afraid of everything in that place, was carried quickly from the mountain to a very beautiful land by one of the winds, Zephyr.

6. After she had slept for a short time, she looked around her and boldly walked into the forest, which was near the field in which she had been left by Zephyr.

7. In the forest, she found a house, which was prettier than any that she had seen before.

8. All the things in the house pleased her very much and she herself was then truly very happy.

9. Mox vocam audivit, sed neque virum neque mulierem vidit. Vox dixit: "Haec domus tua est et nos servi tui erimus. Omnia quae rogabis faciemus."

10. Postea in domo habitabat et laetior erat quam ulla puella in terra illa. Nil cupiebat.

11. Domum, servos, omnia bona, et maritum habebat, sed hunc non videbat. Noctu veniebat et ab ea ante diem properabat.

12. Quam ob rem maxime dolebat, sed maritum suum bene amabat. Ipse dixit: "Me nunc amas quod aequi sumus. Hoc iter optimum est."

13. Diu tamen laetissima erat, sed posteriore tempore matrem patremque sororesque quoque memoria tenebat et oppressa est quod ibi non erant.

14. Una nocte, ubi maritus eius venit, ab eo viam e difficultate sua petivit.

9. Soon she heard a voice, but she saw neither man nor woman. The voice said: "This house is yours and we shall be your servants. We shall do everything that you ask."

10. Afterwards, she lived in the house and she was happier than any girl in that land. She wished for nothing.

11. She had a house, servants, all good things, and a husband, but she did not see him. He came at night and hurried away from her before day.

12. For this reason, she grieved greatly, but she loved her husband well. He said: "You love me now because we are equal. This way is best."

13. For a long time, however, she was very happy, but at a later time, she remembered her father and mother and also her sisters and was oppressed because they were not there.

14. One night, when her husband came, she sought from him a way out of her difficulty.

Practice Exercises

No. 155. Translate these sentences:
1. Hae turres altiores sunt quam illae.
2. Es altior patre tuo.
3. Illa itinera aliis faciliora non sunt.
4. Patri tuo quam matri similior es.
5. Homines multo fortiores mulieribus sunt.
6. Domus eius ruri novior est illa in urbe.
7. Puer laetior est quam soror.
8. Barbari multo audaciores sunt finitimis suis.
9. Ille vobis amicior quam mihi erit.
10. Estne manus celerior quam oculus?

No. 156. Give the English for these verb forms:
1. erunt
2. demonstratum est
3. constituit
4. parabitur
5. ducebant
6. relictus est
7. mittetur
8. portaris
9. videbamus
10. ambulavit

No. 157. Give the English for these adjectives:
1. plura
2. melior
3. pessimorum
4. maioris
5. minorum
6. plurimorum
7. pluribus
8. posteros
9. magis idonei
10. maxime idoneum

No. 158. Translate these adjective phrases:
1. in pluribus urbibus
2. ex fontibus minoribus
3. virtutem maximam
4. vox optima
5. de muris altioribus
6. plus aquae
7. tempus magis idoneum
8. rei pessimae
9. ad partem meliorem
10. cum maiore exercitu
11. die longiore
12. plurimas civitates
13. finem peiorem
14. annos optimos
15. soror minima

GEOMETRICAL TERMS DERIVED FROM LATIN

perpendicular, from **per**, through, and **pendere**, hang.
circumference, from **circum**, around, and **ferre**, carry
radius, from **radius**, staff, rod, ray.
arc, from **arcus**, bow, arc.
tangent, from **tangere**, touch.
angle, from **angulus**, angle, corner.
obtuse, from **obtundere**, strike.
acute, from **acuere**, sharpen.
triangle, from **tri**, three, and **angulus**, angle.
rectangle, from **rectus**, right, and **angulus**, angle.
Q. E. D., abbreviation of **quod erat demonstrandum**, which was to be demonstrated.

Comparison of Adverbs

Reading Vocabulary

Nouns

imperium, imperii or imperi, n., command (imperial)
verbum, verbi, n., word (verb)

uxor, uxoris, f., wife (uxorial)
lux, lucis, f., light (lucent)

Adjectives

mortalis, mortale, mortal (mortality)

Verbs

conficio, conficere, confeci, confectus, finish,
      complete, carry out (confection)
plurimum posse, be most powerful
cado, cadere, cecidi, casurus, fall (cadence)

excito, excitare, excitavi, excitatus,
      arouse, stir up (excitement)
plus posse, be more powerful

Adverbs

quam, as possible. With the superlative degree.
umquam, ever
supra, over, above. Also a preposition with the accusative case.

numquam, never
postridie, on the next day

Conjunctions

dum, while. With the present tense.

Reading Grammar

A. Adverbs are compared in much the same way as adjectives, but have only one form for each degree. In other words, adverbs are not declined.

1. Regular adverbs are compared as follows:

POSITIVE		COMPARATIVE		SUPERLATIVE	
longe	far	longius	farther	longissime	farthest
misere	unhappily	miserius	more unhappily	miserrime	most unhappily
pulchre	beautifully	pulchrius	more beautifully	pulcherrime	most beautifully
acriter	keenly	acrius	more keenly	acerrime	most keenly
fortiter	bravely	fortus	more bravely	fortissime	most bravely
facile	easily	facilius	more easily	facillime	most easily

As you can see, in the positive degree, most adverbs end in -e, -ter, or -iter. In the comparative degree, most adverbs end in -ius and in the superlative degree, most adverbs end in -e.

2. These adverbs are irregular:

POSITIVE		COMPARATIVE		SUPERLATIVE	
bene	well	melius	better	optime	best
magnopere	greatly	magis	more	maxime	most
male	badly	peius	worse	pessime	worst
multum	much	plus	more	plurimum	most
parum	little	minus	less	minime	least
diu	long	diutius	longer	diutissime	longest
saepe	often	saepius	more often	saepissime	most often

B. When **quam** is used with the superlative degree of an adjective or adverb, it means *as . . . as possible*.

quam pulcherrimus, as pretty (beautiful) as possible
quam pulcherrime, as prettily (beautifully) as possible

Reading

Cupido et Psyche (cont'd)

1. Postridie ad Zephyrum quam celerrime contendit et illi id quod maritus suus dixerat narrabat.

2. Imperia Cupidinis facillime confecit et brevi tempore duae sorores eius ad domum eius a Zephyro celeriter portatae sunt.

3. Psyche adventu earum laetissima erat et illis omnia sua demonstravit. Ipsae tamen postquam domum atque servos illius viderant inopiam eius bonae fortunae acerrime cognoverunt.

4. Multa rogabant: "Esne uxor laeta?" "Quis es maritus tuus?"

5. Magno cum studio verba eius audiebant. Vita eius melior quam vita earum esse videbatur.

Cupid and Psyche (cont'd)

1. On the next day, she hurried as quickly as possible to Zephyr and told him what her husband had said.

2. He very easily carried out the commands of Cupid and in a short time, her two sisters were carried quickly to her house by Zephyr.

3. Psyche was very happy at their arrival and showed them all her possessions. They, however, after they had seen her house and servants, clearly recognized her lack of good fortune.

4. They asked many things: "Are you a happy wife?" "Who is your husband?"

5. They listened to her words with great eagerness. Her life seemed to be better than their life.

6. Eam misserime conspiciebant. Eodem tempore spem maiorem videbant: "Num tu maritum tuum umquam vidisti? Maritus quem uxor numquam vidit optimus maritus esse non potest. Nonne verba oraculi memoria tenes? Ille aut serpens aut animal est."

7. Psyche consilio sororum suarum coacta est quod ab eis semper facillime ducebatur. Itaque lucem ac gladium cepit et haec in loco idoneo conlocavit.

8. Psyche consilium sororum suarum minime amabat, sed verba earum quam verba sua plus poterant. Illae plus facile quam ipsa dicere poterant.

9. Itaque ipsa lucem gladiumque paravit et maritus eius ad eam noctu venit. Ipsa maxime timebat, sed ei timorem suum non demonstrabat.

10. Dum ille dormit, lucem cepit et supra eum id tenebat. Quid vidit? Neque serpentem neque animal ante se conspexit. Erat unus ex deorum pulcherrimus atque gratissimus.

11. A timore liberata erat. Eum non diutius timebat, sed magis amabat.

12. Ut accidit tamen umerum eius luce tetegit et ille excitatus est. Ipse nullum verbum dixit, sed oculis suis eam monuit et alis celeribus eam reliquit.

13. Psyche ad terram cecidit. Cupido supra eam breve tempus volebat et dixit: "Contra imperia matris meae te amavi. Immortales mortales non saepe amant, sed te in matrimonium duxi et me interficere nunc cupis. Amor tuus minus fortis meo est."

14. His verbis puellam miserrimam reliquit et ad caelum volavit.

6. They looked at her most unhappily. At the same time, they saw a greater hope: "You haven't ever seen your husband, have you? A husband whom his wife has never seen can not be the best husband. You remember the words of the oracle, don't you? He is either a serpent or an animal."

7. Psyche was convinced by the plan of her sisters because she was always very easily influenced by them. And so, she took a light and a sword, and placed these things in a suitable place.

8. Psyche did not like her sisters' plan at all, but their words were more powerful than her own words. They were able to talk more easily than she.

9. And so she got the light and the sword ready, and her husband came to her at night. She was very much afraid, but she did not show her fear to him.

10. While he slept, she took the light and held it above him. What did she see? She saw in front of her neither a serpent nor an animal. He was one of the most handsome and pleasing of the gods.

11. She had been freed from fear. She no longer feared him, but loved him more.

12. As it happened, however, she touched his shoulder with the light and he was aroused. He said no word, but warned her with his eyes and left her on swift wings.

13. Psyche fell to the ground. Cupid flew above her for a short time and said: "I have loved you against the commands of my mother. Immortals do not often love mortals, but I married you and now, you want to kill me. Your love is less strong than mine."

14. With these words, he left the very unhappy girl and flew to the sky.

Practice Exercises

No. 159. Give the English for these adjectives and adverbs:

1. latus	8. libere	15. pulcherrimus	22. celerius
2. late	9. liberior	16. pulchre	23. celerrimus
3. latior	10. liberrimus	17. pulchrius	24. celerrime
4. latius	11. liberius	18. pulcherrime	25. acer
5. latissimus	12. liberrime	19. celer	26. acriter
6. latissime	13. pulcher	20. celeriter	27. acrior
7. liber	14. pulchrior	21. celerior	28. acrius

No. 160. Translate these sentences containing adverbs:

1. Gravissime oppugnabantur.
2. Fortius pugnat.
3. Celeriter incensi sunt.
4. Multo brevius dicent.
5. Audacissime monebitur.
6. Difficile aciem instruxerunt.
7. Acrius bellum gessit.
8. Superbe ambulant.
9. Gratius dabat.
10. Altissime laudatur.
11. Latius missis sunt.
12. Liberrime dedit.
13. Longissime navigat.
14. Miserius movet.
15. Nove videbantur.
16. Pulchrius movent.
17. Acerrime timebit.
18. Audacter capti sunt.
19. Brevissime dicebat.
20. Fortiter pugnant.

No. 161. Give the English for these adverbs:

1. bene
2. magnopere
3. male
4. multum
5. parum
6. diu
7. saepe
8. diutius
9. plus
10. magis
11. melius
12. peius
13. minus
14. saepius
15. maxime
16. plurimum
17. diutissime
18. saepissime
19. optime
20. pessime

No. 162. Translate these sentences containing adverbs:

1. Saepius perveniunt.
2. Quam diutissime pugnavit.
3. Magis excitatus est.
4. Plus impediebatur.
5. Optime amatus es.
6. Id saepissime auditum est.
7. Minus difficile ambulat.
8. Apud nos plurimum possunt.
9. Plus celeriter volat.
10. Multum diutius manebit.

Chapter Eight Review

Vocabulary Review

Nouns

1. aestas
2. Creusa
3. Cupido
4. difficultas
5. fons
6. hiems
7. imperium
8. lux
9. maritus
10. matrimonium
11. multitudo
12. onus
13. oraculum
14. plus
15. portus
16. Psyche
17. soror
18. uxor
19. ventus
20. verbum

Adjectives

1. aequus
2. dulcis
3. immortalis
4. maior
5. maximus
6. melior
7. minimus
8. minor
9. mortalis
10. optimus
11. peior
12. pessimus
13. plurimus
14. posterus
15. postumus

Verbs

1. cado	6. dedo	11. opprimo
2. cogo	7. deligo	12. plurimum posse
3. conficio	8. dormio	13. plus posse
4. constituo	9. excito	14. recipio
5. convenio	10. incendo	15. suscipio

Adverbs

1. antea	6. numquam
2. bis	7. olim
3. magis	8. postridie
4. maxime	9. quam
5. multo	10. supra

Conjunctions

1. aut . . . aut   2. dum   3. nam   4. quamquam   5. quoque

Practice Exercises

No. 163. Translate these phrases:

1. una ex sororum	6. centum verba	11. secundo anno
2. tria flumina	7. unius vocis	12. septimum verbum
3. duos annos	8. viginti fontes	13. primum oraculum
4. mille anni	9. quarta hora	14. in quarto portu
5. duas uxores	10. quinto die	15. ex sexta porta

No. 164. Translate these adjective phrases:

1. longiorem hiemem
2. pulcherrima aestas
3. longissimorum annorum
4. dulcis verbum
5. onus simillimum

6. vocis immortalis
7. iter facilius
8. luces clariores
9. difficultatis acerrimae
10. maritorum fortiorum

No. 165. Give the English for these adjectives:

1. dulcis, dulcior, dulcissimus
2. acer, acrior, acerrimus
3. longus, longior, longissimus
4. similis, similior, simillimus
5. altus, altior, altissimus

6. liber, liberior, liberrimus
7. celer, celerior, celerrimus
8. latus, latior, latissimus
9. clarus, clarior, clarissimus
10. audax, audacior, audacissimus

No. 166. Give the English for these adjectives:

1. magnus, maior, maximus
2. parvus, minor, minimus
3. bonus, melior, optimus

4. malus, peior, pessimus
5. multus, plus, plurimus
6. multi, plures, plurimi

No. 167. Translate into English:

1. longius ambulabat
2. misere oppressus est
3. parum dormit
4. diutissime incendet
5. acrius excitati sunt
6. magis tangebant
7. facilius dediderunt
8. plurimum possunt
9. plus poterit
10. minus facile cogentur

Reading

Phaedrus

Phaedrus, a freedman of Augustus, lived in the first half of the first century A.D. Five books of his **Fables** are extant. These are based on early folk tales and on the Greek fables of Aesop. Phaedrus' work, in turn, furnished the material for the French fabulist, La Fontaine.

Qui se laudari gaudet verbis subdolis,
sera dat poenas turpes paenitentia.
Cum de fenestra corvus raptum caesum
comesse vellet, celsa residens arbore,
vulpes hunc vidit; deinde sic coepit loqui:
"O qui tuarum, corve, pinnarum est nitor.
Quantum decoris corpore et vultu geris.

Si vocem haberes, nulla prior ales foret."
At ille stultus, dum vult vocem ostendere,
emisit ore caesum, quem celeriter
dolosa vulpes avidis rapuit dentibus.
Tum demum ingemuit corvi deceptus stupor.
Phaedrus I, xiii

Stabat Mater

The thirteenth-century scholar and mystic St. Bonaventura is sometimes credited with writing the **Stabat Mater,** which has been set to music by many composers during the last three centuries.

Stabat mater dolorosa
iuxta crucem lacrimosa,
dum pendebat filius,
cuius animam gementem,
contristantem et dolentem
pertransivit gladius.
O quam tristis et afflicta
fuit illa benedicta
mater unigenti,
quae maerebat et dolebat
et tremebat, dum videbat
nati poenas incliti!
Quis est homo qui non fleret,
matrem Christi si videret
in tanto supplicio?
Quis non posset contristari
piam matrem contemplari
dolentem cum filio?
Pro peccatis suae gentis
vidit Iesum in tormentis

et flagellis subditum;
vidit suum dulcem natum
morientem, desolatum,
dum emisit spiritum
Eia mater, fons amoris!
Me sentire vim doloris
fac, ut tecum lugeam.
Fac ut ardeat cor meum
in amando Christum Deum,
ut sibi complaceam.
Sancta mater, istud agas,
crucifixi fige plagas
cordi meo valide;
tui nati vulnerati,
tam dignati pro me pati,
poenas mecum divide.
Fac me vere tecum flere,
crucifixo condolere,
donec ego vixero;
iuxta crucem tecum stare,

meque tibi sociare
in planctu desidero.
Virgo virginium praeclara,
mihi iam non sis amara,
fac me tecum plangere;
fac ut portem Christi mortem,
passionis fac consortem
et plagas recolere.
Fac me plagis vulnerari,
cruce had inebriari,
et cruore filii;
per te, Virgo, sim defensus
inflammatus et accensum
in die iudicii.
Fac me cruce custodiri
morte Christi praemuniri,
confoveri gratia.
Quando corpus morietur,
fac ut animae donetur
paradisi gloria.

Infinitives and Participles

MEDICAL ABBREVIATIONS DERIVED FROM LATIN

R, **recipe**, take

d., da, give

gtt., guttae, drops

Lb., libra, pound

ol., oleum, oil

pulv., pulvis, powder

c̄, cum, with

os., os, ora, mouth

t.i.d., ter in die, three times a day

quotid., quotidie, every day

omn. hor., omni hora, every hour

noct., nocte, at night

t.i.n., ter in nocte, three times a night.

h.s., hora somni, at the hour of sleep, at bedtime

non rep., non repetatur, do not repeat (literally, let it not be repeated)

Sig., S., signetur, let it be marked (direction to patient)

Q.v., quantum vis, as much as you wish

a.c., ante cibum, before food, before meals

Q.s., quantum sufficiat, a sufficient quantity

bib., bibe, drink

cap., capsula, capsule

gr., granum, grain

mist., mistura, mixture

ung., unguentum, ointment

aq., aqua, water

no., numero, number

p.o., per os, by mouth

q.i.d., quater in die, four times a day

stat., statim, immediately

H., hora, hour

omn. noct., omni nocte, every night

q.i.n., quater in nocte, four times a night

Q.h., quaque hora, every hour. **Q.2h.**, every two hours

p.r.n., pro re nata, as the occasion arises, as needed

alt. dieb., alternis diebus, every other day, on alternate days

rep., repetatur, let it be repeated

p.c., post cibum, after food, after meals

Reading Vocabulary

Nouns

numerus, numeri, m., number (numeral)

satis, n., enough. Same spelling in all cases. (satisfy)

modus, modi, m., manner, way (mode)

ordo, ordinis, m., rank, order (order, ordinal)

vulnus, vulneris, n., wound (vulnerable)

formica, formicae, f., ant

genus, generis, n., kind, class (genus)

dux, ducis, m., leader (duke)

Verbs

invenio, invenire, inveni, inventus, find, come upon (invent)

Adverbs

tam, so
satis, enough (satisfaction)

tandem, finally

Reading Grammar

A. Regular Latin verbs have six different infinitives, three in the active voice, three in the passive. All infinitives are formed on the same pattern. For example, the infinitives for **amo** are:

Active: **amare**, to love
              amavisse, to have loved
              amaturus esse, to be about to love
Passive: **amari**, to be loved
              amatus esse, to have been loved
              amatum iri, to be about to be loved

1. The present active infinitive is the second principal part:

amare, to love	**habere**, to have	**ducere**, to lead
capere, to seize	**audire**, to hear	**esse**, to be
posse, to be able	**ire**, to go	**velle**, to wish
ferre, to carry		

The verb **fio** does not have a present active infinitive.

2. The present passive infinitive ends in -i-. Note that the **e/i-conjugation** drops the -er-.

amari, to be loved	**haberi**, to he had	**duci**, to be led
capi, to be seized	**audiri**, to be heard	**ferri**, to be carried
fieri, to be made		

The verbs **sum, possum, volo, nolo,** and **malo** do not have present passive infinitives. **eo** does have a present passive infinitive, **iri,** but this is only used with the future passive infinitive.

3. The perfect active infinitive is formed from the third principal part and the ending **-isse.**

amavisse, to have loved	**habuisse**, to have had	**duxisse**, to have led
cepisse, to have seized	**audivisse**, to have heard	**fuisse**, to have been
isse, to have gone	**voluisse**, to have wanted	**tulisse**, to have carried
potuisse, to have been able		

4. The perfect passive infinitive is formed with the fourth principal part and **esse,** the present active infinitive of the verb **sum.**

amatus, -a, -um esse, to have been loved	**habitus, -a, -um esse**, to have been had
ductus, -a, -um esse, to have been led	**capitus, -a, -um esse**, to have been seized
auditus, -a, -um esse, to have been heard	**latus, -a, -um esse**, to have been carried
factus, -a, -um esse, to have been made	

The verbs **sum, possum, eo, volo, nolo,** and **malo** do not have a perfect passive infinitive.

5. The future active infinitive is formed by adding **-ur-** to the fourth principal part before the **regular** ending, and by **esse**. This modification of the fourth principal part creates the future active participle, **which** will be considered in the next chapter.

amaturus, -a, -um esse, to be about to love
habiturus, -a, -um esse, to be about to have
docturus, -a, -um esse, to be about to lead
capturus, -a, -um esse, to be about to seize

futurus, -a, -um esse, to be about to be
iturus, -a, -um esse, to be about to go
laturus, -a, -um esse, to be about to carry

The verbs **possum, volo, nolo,** and **malo** do not have a future active infinitive.

6. There is a future passive infinitive in Latin, but this is rarely used. It is formed from the **neuter** nominative singular of the fourth principal part and **iri,** the present passive infinitive of **eo.** The future **passive** infinitive is also called the supine. It is not declined.

amatum iri, to be about to be loved
ductum iri, to be about to be led
auditum iri, to be about to be heard
factum iri, to be about to be made

habitum iri, to be about to be had
captum iri, to be about to be seized
latum iri, to be about to be carried

B. You have already met the completing infinitive.

Id capere cupit.	He wants *to take* it.
Amari cupit.	He wants *to be loved.*

The infinitive is also used to express:
1. A subject.

Id invenire difficile est.	It is difficult *to find* it. *To find* it is difficult.

In this sentence, the infinitive, **invenire,** can be considered the subject of the verb, **est.**

2. A direct object.

Natare amat.	He likes *to swim.*

In this sentence, the infinitive, **natare,** is the direct object of the verb, **amat.**

3. An indirect statement after a verb showing mental processes such as saying, thinking, knowing, or hearing. In English, an indirect statement is generally introduced by the word *that.*

Virum laborare dico.	I say *that* the man *is working.*

virum laborare, *that the man is working,* is an indirect statement. A direct statement would be **vir laborat,** *The man is working.* Since the main verb is not **laborat,** but **dico,** the infinitive, **laborare** is used.

The tense of the infinitive is detemined by when the action of the indirect statement takes place.

a. If the action of the indirect statement takes place at the same time as the action of the main **verb,** the present infinitve is used, regardless of the tense of the main verb.

Virum laborare dico.	I say that the man is working.
Virum laborare dixi.	I said that the man was working.
Virum laborare dicam.	I shall say that that the man is working.
Virum amari dico.	I say that the man is loved.
Virum amari dixi.	I said that the man was loved.
Virum amari dicam.	I shall say that the man is loved.

b. If the action of the indirect statement takes place earlier than the action of the main verb, the perfect infinitive is used, regardless of the tense of the main verb.

Virum laborisse dico.	I say that the man worked.
Virum laborisse dixi.	I said that the man had worked.
Virum laborisse dicam.	I shall say that the man worked.
Virum amatum esse dico.	I say that the man was loved.
Virum amatum esse dixi.	I said that the man had been loved.
Virum amatum esse dicam.	I shall say that the man was loved.

c. If the action of the indirect statement takes place later than the action of the main verb, the future infinitive is used, regardless of the tense of the main verb. Note, however, that the future passive infinitive is rarely used.

Virum laboraturum esse dico.	I say that the man will work.
Virum laboraturum esse dixi.	I said that the man would work.
Virum laboraturum esse dicam.	I shall say that the man will work.

C. Subjects of infinitives are in the accusative case.

virum laborare	viros laborare	agrum arari	agros arari

D. The perfect passive and future active infinitives must be in the accusative to agree with their accusative subjects. They must also agree in number and gender with their subjects.

Agrum aratum esse dicit.	He says that the field has been plowed.
Agros aratos esse dicit.	He says that the fields have been plowed.
Virum laboraturum esse dicit.	He says that the man is going to work.
Viros laboraturos esse dicit.	He says that the men are going to work.

Reading

Cupido et Psyche (cont'd)

1. Postquam Cupido uxorem suam tam celeriter reliquerat, illa circum se spectavit. Omnis spes ab ea interea cecidit atque sua vita laeta discessit, nam horti pulchri ac domus magna nunc ibi non erant.

2. Non longe ab urbe, ubi antea habitaverat, erat sola. Maxime dolebat.

Cupid and Psyche (cont'd)

1. After Cupid had left his wife so quickly, she looked around her. All hope fell from her meanwhile and her happy life departed, for the beautiful gardens and large house were not there now.

2. She was alone, not far from the city where she had lived before. She grieved very much.

3. Sorores fabulam eius magno cum studio audiverunt. Sibi dixerunt: "Cupido unam ex nobis nunc certe deliget."

4. Prima luce postridie illae duae ad montem properaverunt et Zephyrum audacissime appellabant. Utraque tamen ad terram sub monte cecidit et interfecta est, quod deus venti eam non iuvit.

5. Psyche interea maritum suum noctu dieque petebat. Montem altissimum, in quo templum magnum erat, conspexit. Eratne templum Cupidinis?

6. In templo aliud genus rei invenit. Omnibus in partibus aedifici frumentum videbat.

7. Quo modo multa genera frumenti in ordine ponere poterit?

8. Nunc etiam magis dolebat, sed erat puella fortissima.

9. Dum illa laborat, Ceres, dea frumenti, in templum venit, nam id erat templum Cereris. Ceres puellam miserrimam iuvare cupiebat quod Psyche bene laboraverat et frumentum in templo in ordine bene posuerat.

10. Dea ei auxilium dare cupiebat quod illa pro ea satis iam fecerat. Dixit: "Venus tibi auxilium non dat. Dea bona est, sed filium suum, maritum tuum, maxime amat et eum dedere non cupit."

11. Psyche nullam spem habebat, sed tamed ad domum deae pulcherrimae properavit.

12. Ibi Venerem superbam invenit, quae dixit: "Nonne tu me tandem memoria tenes? Maritus tuus vulnus quod tu luce ei dedisti nunc curat. Postquam hunc laborem confecisti tibi eum dare cupio."

13. Hoc opus erat: Magnum numerum et multa genera frumenti sine ordine ante se videbat.

14. Mors melior quam hoc opus esse videbatur. Ipsa nil fecit. Labor maximus erat, sed Cupido uxorem suam mox vidit et ei auxilium misit.

15. Parva formica, quae erat dux sociorum amicorumque suorum, ad eam venit.

16. Omnes hae formicae brevissimo tempore frumentum in ordine conlocaverunt. Fugerunt postquam hoc fecerant.

3. Her sisters heard her story with great eagerness. They said to themselves: "Cupid will now certainly choose one of us."

4. At dawn the next day, those two hurried to the mountain and very boldly called Zephyr by name. Each, however, fell to the ground at the foot of the mountain and was killed, because the god of the wind did not help her.

5. Psyche, meanwhile, sought her husband night and day. She saw a very high mountain, on which there was a large temple. Was it the temple of Cupid?

6. In the temple, she found another kind of thing. In all parts of the building, she saw grain.

7. How will she be able to put many kinds of grain in order?

8. Now she grieved even more, but she was a very brave girl.

9. While she was working, Ceres, the goddess of grain, came into the temple, for this was the temple of Ceres. Ceres wished to help the very unhappy girl, because Psyche had worked well and had put the grain in the temple in order well.

10. The goddess wished to give help to her because she had already done enough for her. She said: "Venus does not give help to you. The goddess is good, but she loves her son, your husband, very much and does not want to give him up."

11. Psyche had no hope, but nevertheless, she hurried to the house of the very beautiful goddess.

12. There she found the proud Venus, who said: "You finally remember me, don't you? Your husband is now caring for the wound that you gave him with the light. After you have finished this work, I want to give him to you."

13. This was the task: She saw in front of her a great amount and many kinds of grain without order.

14. Death seemed to be better than this task. She did nothing. The work was very great, but Cupid soon saw his wife and sent help to her.

15. A small ant, that was the leader of his comrades and friends, came to her.

16. All these ants placed the grain in order in a very short time. They fled after they had done this.

Practice Exercises

No. 168. Give the English for these infinitives:

1. monere	9. manisse	17. tangi
2. auxisse	10. auditurum esse	18. oppugnatum esse
3. iaci	11. scripsisse	19. sciri
4. positurum esse	12. pugnaturum esse	20. gesturum esse
5. fugisse	13. laudaturum esse	21. accipi
6. impedire	14. excitari	22. victum esse
7. natavisse	15. petitum esse	23. dici
8. territurum esse	16. mittere	24. ambulaturum esse

No. 169. Change these infinitives to the active and give the English meanings:

1. peti	6. vocatum esse
2. captum esse	7. ferri
3. haberi	8. datum esse
4. rectum esse	9. instrui
5. portari	10. verti

No. 170. Change these infinitives to the passive and give the English meanings:

1. narrare	6. movisse
2. defendisse	7. vocare
3. videre	8. invenire
4. iuvare	9. necavisse
5. pugnavisse	10. relinquere

No. 171. Give the future active infinitive of these verbs and the English meanings:

1. esse	6. properare
2. iubere	7. capere
3. facere	8. invenire
4. defendere	9. dare
5. oppugnare	10. ponere

No. 172. Translate these sentences:
1. Illi milites viros auxilium portaturos esse dixerunt.
2. Putatisne opus vestrum factum esse?
3. Nos hostes quam celerrime venturos esse sperabamus.
4. Puellae latae esse videntur.
5. Hic rex bene regere cupiebat.
6. Ille appellari non cupiet.
7. Oppidum nostrum defendere optimum est.
8. Spem habuisse melius erat quam se recepisse.
9. Celeritatem augeri posse nuntiavit.
10. Nos locum meliorem invenire iussit.

FAMILIAR ABBREVIATIONS

i.e., id est, that is.
pro and **con, pro et contra,** for and against
etc., et cetera, and the rest; and so forth.
e.g., exempli gratia, for (the sake of) example.
no., numero, by number.
viz., videlicet, namely, that is to say; introduces further explanation.
d.v. or **D.V., Deo volente,** God willing; if God is willing.
vox pop., vox populi, the voice of the people.

Forming and Using Participles

Reading Vocabulary

Nouns

lana, lanae, f., wool
ovis, ovis, f., sheep
pulchritudo, pulchritudinis, f., beauty (pulchritude)

Adjectives

utilis, utile, useful (utility)

Verbs

spero, sperare, speravi, speratus, hope (aspire)
puto, putare, putavi, putatus, think, believe (putative)
reporto, reportare, reportavi, reportatus, carry back, bring back (reporter)

Reading Grammar

A. Regular Latin verbs have four participles or verbal adjectives. They have some of the qualities of verbs and some of the qualities of adjectives. They are not used as the main verb of a sentence, but in addition to the main verb. In English, participles generally end in *-ing*: singing, dancing, having, going, doing. The participles of **amo** are:

Active: **amens**   loving   **amaturus**   about to love
Passive: **amatus**   having been loved   **amandus**   deserving to be loved, being loved

1. The present active participle is formed from the present stem and **-ns**.

amens	loving	**habens**	having
ducens	leading	**capiens**	seizing
audiens	hearing	**potens**	having
iens	going	**volens**	wishing
nolens	not wishing	**ferens**	carrying

Sum, malo, and **fio** do not have present active participles.
The action of the present active participle occurs at the same time as the action of the main verb, as in the sentence *I am carrying the book.*

2. The perfect passive participle is the fourth principal part.

amatus, -a, -um	having been loved	**habitus, -a, -um**	having been had
ductus, -a, -um	having been led	**captus, -a, -um**	having been seized
auditus, -a, -um	having been heard	**factus, -a, -um**	having been made
latus, -a, -um	having been carried		

Sum, possum, volo, nolo, and **malo** do not have perfect passive participles. The perfect passive participle of eo is **itus, -a, -um.**
The action of the perfect passive participle occurs before the action of the main verb, as in *The woman, having been loved, was happy.*

3. The future active participle is the fourth principal part ending in **-urus, -a, -um.**

amaturus, -a, -um	about to love	**habiturus, -a, -um**	about to have
ducturus, -a, -um	about to lead	**capturus, -a, -um**	about to seize
auditurus, -a, -um	about to hear	**futurus, -a, -um**	about to be
iturus, -a, -um	about to go	**laturus, -a, -um**	about to carry

Futurus is used as the fourth principal part of **sum.** The verbs **possum, volo, nolo, malo,** and **fio** do not have future active participles.
The action of the future active participle occurs after the action of the main verb, as in *The army was about to seize the town.*

4. The future passive participle is formed from the present stem and **-ndus.**

amandus, -a, -um	deserving to be loved, being loved
habendus, -a, -um	deserving to be had, being had
ducendus, -a, -um	deserving to be led, being led
capiendus, -a, -um	deserving to be taken, being taken
audiendus, -a, -um	deserving to be heard, being heard
eundus, -a, -um	deserving to be gone, being gone
faciendus, -a, -um	deserving to be made, being made
ferendus, -a, -um	deserving to be carried, being carried

Sum, possum, volo, molo, and **malo** do not have future passive participles.

The action of the future passive participle occurs after the action of the main verb, as in *The song is deserving to be heard/being heard/worthy to be heard.*

The future passive participle is also known as the gerundive. You will learn more about this participle later in this chapter.

B. The participles are verbal adjectives. Thus, they have voice and tense, like verbs, and they must agree with their nouns in case, number, and gender, like adjectives.

1. The present participle is of the **i-declension.**

CASE	SINGULAR		PLURAL		
	MASC./FEM.	NEUT.	MASC./FEM.	NEUT.	
Nom.	amans	amans	amantes	amantia	the loving
Gen.	amantis	amantis	amantium	amantium	of the loving
Dat.	amanti	amanti	amantibus	amantibus	to, for the loving
Acc.	amantem	amans	amantes	amantia	the loving
Abl.	amanti	amanti	amantibus	amantibus	from/with/by/in the loving

Note with **eo** that the genitive of **iens** is **euntis.**

2. The perfect passive and future active and passive participles are of the **a-** and **o-** declension.

C. Participles are best translated by a clause in English, beginning with *when, who, because, if,* or *although.*

Miles captus non timebat.	The soldier, although he was captured, was not afraid.
Miles captus timebat.	The soldier, because he was captured, was afraid.
Miles pugnans necatus est.	The soldier, when he was fighting, was killed, *or*
	The soldier, who was fighting, was killed.

Reading

Cupido et Psyche (cont'd)	Cupid and Psyche (cont'd)
1. **Venus ad templum suum multo die venit et ad illam partem templi ubi puellam reliquerat sine mora properavit. Ipsa puellam miseram ante se etiam tum laborem difficile habere sperabat.**	1. Venus came to her temple late in the day and hurried without delay to that part of the temple where she had left the girl. She hoped that the unhappy girl had difficult work ahead of her even then.
2. **Ubi laborem confectum esse vidit, filium suum id fecisse putabat et puellae cibum minimum dedit.**	2. When she saw that the work had been finished, she thought that her son had done it and she gave the girl very little food.
3. **Postridie puellam ad se venire iussit. Dea ad silvam in qua erant multae oves, quarum lana erat aurea, currere et lanam reportare illam iussit.**	3. On the next day, she ordered the girl to come to her. The goddess ordered her to run to the forest in which there were many sheep, whose wool was golden, and to bring back the wool.
4. **Cum illa ad flumen pervenit non solum oves sed etiam deum fluminis invenit.**	4. When she came to the river, she found not only the sheep, but also the god of the river.

5. Ille dixit flumen celerrimum esse atque oves die maxime inimicas esse, sed demonstravit oves noctu futuras esse dulciores. Quam ob rem illa ad noctem exspectavit et oves dormire invenit.

6. Labor eius facillimus erat quod lana ovium in arboribus erat. Oves non etiam tetigerat, sed auxilio dei multam lanam auream ab arboribus obtinuit et eodem die ad Venerem, dominam suam, properavit, quod pro illa omnia bene facere cupiebat.

7. Postquam ad Venerem venerat et sub pedibus illius lanam posuerat, Psyche deam eam liberaturam esse atque se maritum suum recepturam esse sperabat.

8. Qua de causa spes eius celeriter fugit nam domina eius illam sine auxilio alterius lanam non obtinuisse dixit.

9. Puellam esse utilem cupiebat. Itaque eam apud Inferos iter facere iussit. Ei arcam parvam dedit.

10. Psyche miser templum Veneris reliquit et se mortem certe inventuram esse putabat quod dea partem pulchritudinis Proserpinae ex terra mortis ad se reportari cupiebat.

11. Psyche tamen fortissima erat et ad turrem altissimam venit. Celerrimum iter ad Inferos petebat, sed vox ex turre eam appellavit et ipsam illo modo se necare non debere dixit.

12. Vox quoque id ei futurum esse postremum laborem nuntiavit. Puellae iter facile celereque ad regnum Plutonis demonstravit et illa ex timore ab eodem amico qui eam antea servaverat nunc liberata est.

5. He said that the river was very swift and the sheep were especially unfriendly in the daytime, but he pointed out that the sheep would be more gentle at night. For this reason, she waited until night and found that the sheep were sleeping.

6. Her work was very easy because the wool of the sheep was on the trees. She had not even touched the sheep, but with the help of the god, she obtained much golden wool from the trees and the same day she hurried to Venus, her mistress, because she wished to do everything well for her.

7. After she came to Venus and placed the wool at her feet, Psyche hoped that the goddess would free her and that she would get back her husband.

8. For this reason, her hope quickly fled, for her mistress said that she had not obtained the wool without the help of another.

9. She wanted the girl to be useful. And so, she ordered her to make a journey among Those Below. She gave her a small box.

10. The unhappy Psyche left the temple of Venus and thought that she would certainly find death, because the goddess wished a part of Proserpina's beauty to be brought back to her from the land of death.

11. Psyche, however, was very brave and came to a very high tower. She was seeking the fastest way to Those Below, but a voice out of the tower called to her and said that she ought not to kill herself in that manner.

12. The voice also announced that this would be the last task for her. It pointed out to the girl an easy and quick way to the kingdom of Pluto and she was now freed from fear by the same friend who had saved her before.

FAMILIAR QUOTATIONS

Veni, vidi, vici, I came, I saw, I conquered. Caesar.
Vae victis, Woe to the vanquished. Livy.
In medias res, Into the middle of things. Horace.
Finis coronat opus, The end crowns the work. Ovid.
Non omnia possumus omnes, We can't all do everything. Virgil.
Diem perdidi, I have lost a day. Titus.
Pares cum paribus facillime congregantur, Equals very easily congregate with equals. Cicero.

Practice Exercises

No. 173. Translate these participles:
1. vocans
2. motus
3. missurus
4. accipiens
5. venturus
6. spectatus
7. perveniens
8. capturus
9. ponens
10. nuntiatus

No. 174. Translate these participial phrases:
1. naves navigantes
2. ducem iussurum
3. illi oppugnati
4. viros perventuros
5. petentes pacem
6. canem currentem
7. urbes captae
8. templa aedificata
9. portus inventos
10. flumina currentia

No. 175. Translate these sentences:
1. Populus urbium captarum quam fortissimus erat.
2. Viri perventuri iter quam celerrime faciebant.
3. Rex patriam vestram nunc regens timidus esse videtur.
4. Mulier difficultatem tuam videns auxilium dabit.
5. Tempestas non auctura non acerrima erit.
6. Pater filios suos visurus magnum gaudium habebat.
7. Ei nostros timentes quam celerrime currebant.
8. Homines victi maxime territi sunt.
9. In oppido perveniens illa fabulam suam narravit.
10. Illi portam defendentes amici non erant.

No. 176. Translate these adverbs:
1. fortiter
2. quam celerrime
3. minime
4. diutissime
5. acrius
6. difficile
7. facillime
8. melius
9. male
10. magnopere

Participial Clauses

Reading Vocabulary

Nouns

carcer, carceris, n., prison (incarcerate)
gaudium, gaudii or gaudi, n., joy (gaudy)
Cerberus, Cerberi, m., Cerberus

somnus, somni, m., sleep (insomnia)
canis, canis, m. and f., dog (canine)
Charon, Charontis, m., Charon

Adjectives

timidus, timida, timidum, timid (timidity)
reliquus, reliqua, reliquum, remaining, rest of

apertus, aperta, apertum, open (aperture)

Reading Grammar

A. Clauses.

A clause is a group of words that contains a subject and a verb. If the clause can stand alone, as a complete sentence, it is called a primary clause, or an independent clause:

> I went to the city.

If the clause cannot stand alone, it is called a subordinate clause, or a dependent clause:

> While I was going to the city,

This clause has a subject, *I*, and a verb, *was going*. However, it is not a complete sentence. It needs a main clause, for example, *I lost my watch*. Therefore, the first clause is a subordinate clause.

In the sentence *I saw the woman who was speaking*, the main clause is *I saw the woman*, because this clause can stand alone as a complete sentence. The clause *who was speaking* is a subordinate clause because it cannot do this.

B. A participle with a noun or a pronoun, both in the ablative case, may be used as a clause. The participle may be replaced by a noun or an adjective. This use of the participle in the ablative is known as the ablative absolute.

1. The clause must have a noun or pronoun subject that is different from the subject of the main part of the sentence.

2. The clause may be translated with *because, when, although,* or *if.*

3. The verb *to be* must sometimes be supplied in English.

Oppidis captis, pacem petebant.	When the towns had been captured, they sought peace.
Hoc viro duce, vincemur.	If this man is leader, we shall be conquered.
Navibus gravibus, celerius navigabant.	Although the ships were heavy, they were sailing quite quickly.

C. The Gerundive and the Gerund.

1. You have already learned about the gerundive, or the future passive participle, earlier in this chapter. It is a verbal adjective, used to express an action that ought to be done, or that will be done.

   a. When used to express an action that should or must be taken, the gerundive is usually in the nominative case, although it may occasionally be in the accusative case instead.

Puella tibi amanda est.	The girl must be loved by you, *or* You must love the girl.
Puellam tibi amandam est.	I say that the girl must be loved by you, *or* I say that you must love the girl.

You will notice that the person or object who must perform the action is put in the dative case.

   b. The gerundive is also used in certain constructions where the gerund would normally be used.

2. The gerund is a verbal noun. It is formed in the same way as the gerundive. However, since it is a verbal noun, it has gender, just like a noun does. The gerund is neuter. It is conjugated only in the singular, and it does not have a nominative or a vocative form. It is declined as follows:

CASE	ENDING
Gen.	**-ndi**
Dat.	**-ndo**
Acc.	**-ndum**
Abl.	**-ndo**

Thus, the gerund of **amo** is:

Gen.	**amandi**	of loving
Dat.	**amando**	to, for loving
Acc.	**amandum**	loving
Abl.	**amando**	from, with, by, in loving

As you can see, the gerund is essentially a participle used as a noun.

    a. When the gerund is used in the accusative, it always comes after a preposition:

    Aures ad audiendum facti sunt.   Ears were made for hearing.

    b. The gerund can take a direct object, because it is a verbal noun. However, in practice, when a gerund would take a direct object, Latin uses the gerundive instead:

    Spes est casam inveniendi.   There is hope of finding the house.

    Spes est casae inveniendae.   There is hope of finding the house.

The first sentence uses the gerund; the second uses the gerundive. Both mean the same thing, although the second sentence would be found most often. Note that when the gerund takes a direct object, the **object** is put into the accusative case, as **casam** is. However, when the gerundive is used, the noun is put into the case that the gerund would have taken (the genitive in this example). Remember that because it is a verbal adjective, the gerundive must agree with the noun.

Reading

Cupido et Psyche (concl'd)

1. Psyche, timida videri non cupiens, verba vocis magno cum gaudio audivit et hunc laborem difficillimum futurum esse sperabat.

2. Itaque haec omnia, quae demonstraverant, facere contendit. Sine plurimo periculo enim ad regnum Inferorum iter facere magnopere cupiebat.

3. Cerberus, ante portam quae ad terram mortis ducit positus, canis erat audacissimus qui tria capita habebat, sed Psyche voce monita eum non timebat.

4. Charon tum nave minima trans flumen illam, in regnum Plutonis venturam, duxit.

5. Ante Proserpinam, reginam pulcherrimam Inferorum, stans illa Venerem donum cupire nuntiavit.

6. Regina arcam a puella cepit et in eandem arcam partem parvam suae pulchritudinis posuit. Dea, puella arcam dans, illam monuit.

Cupid and Psyche (concl'd)

1. Psyche, who did not wish to seem timid, heard the words of the voice with great joy and hoped that this task would be very difficult.

2. And so, she hurried to do all these things that they had pointed out to her. For she greatly wished to make the journey to the kingdom of Those Below without very great danger.

3. Cerberus, who was placed in front of the door that leads to the land of death, was a very bold dog who had three heads, but Psyche, because she had been warned by the voice, was not afraid of him.

4. Charon then led her, as she was about to come into the kingdom of Pluto, across the river in a very small boat.

5. Standing in front of Proserpina, the very beautiful queen of Those Below, she reported that Venus wanted a gift.

6. The queen took the box from the girl and put a small part of her own beauty into the same box. The goddess, as she gave the box to the girl, warned her.

7. Illam in arcam spectantem, in periculum magnum casuram esse dixit, sed Psyche, ex terra Inferorum iter facere cupiens, verbis reginae ad timorem non excitata est.

8. Ad terram mortalium eadem viam cepit, sed postquam ad lucem pervenerat in arcam spectare et pulchritudinem videre atque habere cupiebat, sed nil pulchritudinis ib invenit, arca aperta.

9. Psyche dolens pulchritudinem ibi non invenit quod id quod Proserpina in arca posuerat somnus altus Inferorum erat.

10. Somno ex carcere suo liberato, puella somno celeriter capta est et ipsa sine ulla mora, modo simili corpori quod a Morte delectum, erat, media in via cecedit. Nil sciebat atque nil faciebat. Solum dormiebat.

11. Cupido tamen, vulnere eius curato, magno cum gaudio uxorem suam vidit. Ad locum ubi illa dormiebat quam celerrime volavit.

12. Ipse, supra illam stans, somnum qui illam opprimebat cepit et, hoc in arca posito, una ex sagittis suis uxorem tetegit.

13. Ipse dixit: "Tu, multis temporibus e morte servata, omnes labores tuos conficere debes. His factis, omnia reliqua faciam."

14. Illa satis poena habuerat. Hic ad Iovem properavit et ab eo auxilium petivit. Iuppiter ad Venerem eodem die iter fecit et illa tandem puellam dedidit.

15. Psyche, ad regnum deorum a Mercurio ducta, immortalis facta est.

16. Matrimonium ab illo tempore ad finem temporis omnis, illa immortali facta, laetissimum erat.

17. Mortales hac fabula animum esse immortalem atque se gaudium per omnes difficultates semper inventuros esse docentur.

7. She said that she would fall into great danger, if she looked into the box, but Psyche, who wished to make the journey out of the land of Those Below, was not aroused to fear by the words of the queen.

8. She took the same road to the land of mortals, but after she had arrived at the light, she wished to look into the box and to see and have the beauty, but she found no beauty there, when the box was opened.

9. The grieving Psyche did not find beauty there, because what Proserpina had placed in the box was the deep sleep of Those Below.

10. When sleep had been freed from its prison, the girl was quickly overcome by sleep and without any delay, in a manner similar to a body that had been chosen by Death, she fell in the middle of the road. She knew nothing and she did nothing. She only slept.

11. Cupid, however, when his wound had been healed, saw his wife with great joy. He flew as quickly as possible to the place where she was sleeping.

12. He, standing above her, took the sleep that was oppressing her and, when this had been placed in the box, he touched his wife with one of his arrows.

13. He said: "You, because you have been saved from death many times, ought to finish all your tasks. When these have been done, I shall do all the other things."

14. She had had enough punishments. He hurried to Jupiter and begged aid from him. Jupiter made the journey to Venus the same day and, at last, she surrendered the girl.

15. Psyche, after she had been led to the kingdom of the gods by Mercury, was made immortal.

16. The marriage from that time to the end of all time was very happy, because she had been made immortal.

17. Mortals are taught by this story that the spirit is immortal and that they will always find joy through all difficulties.

Practice Exercises

No. 177. Translate these sentences:
1. Multi, oraculo audito, ad terram nostram venire constituerunt.
2. Signo dato, in agrum impetum fecerunt.
3. Homines, armis non multis, tamen fortiter pugnaverunt.
4. Militibus multis interfectis, duces pacem petiverunt.
5. Viri, praeda magna, magno cum gaudio domi accipientur.
6. Hac re gesta, pueri domum venient.

7. Illo duce, id sine difficultate faciemus.
8. His mihi nuntiatis, ex urbe iter facere cupiebam.
9. His necatis, populus melius regetur.
10. Die dicto, omnia quam celerrime paraverunt.
11. Porta aperta, in casam venire potuit.
12. Nullam spem habebat, oppido capto.
13. His rebus factis, rex plus poterat.
14. Reliquis visis, ad silvam curremus.
15. Patre eius duce, omnia audacter faciunt.
16. Pace facta, ab insula navigabit.
17. Multis timidis, flumina invenire non poterunt.
18. Tempore nunc brevi, nullum auxilium perveniet.
19. Loco idoneo, hic diutius manere cupitis.
20. Auxilio dato, gaudium magnum erat.
21. Arma utila est pugnando.
22. Habes spem natandi.
23. Ierant causa urbis oppugnandae.
24. Veni ad audiendum.

Chapter Nine Review

Vocabulary Review

Nouns

1. canis	6. formica	11. numerus
2. carcer	7. gaudium	12. ordo
3. Cerberus	8. genus	13. ovis
4. Charon	9. lana	14. pulchritudo
5. dux	10. modus	15. satis

Adjectives

1. apertus	2. reliquus	3. timidus	4. utilis

Verbs

1. invenio	2. puto	3. reporto	4. spero

Adverbs

1. satis	2. tam	3. tandem

Practice Exercises

No. 178. Translate these infinitives:

1. esse	6. putavisse	11. duci	16. cupi
2. fuisse	7. reportare	12. duxisse	17. potuisse
3. inventurum esse	8. reportaturum esse	13. habitum esse	18. posse
4. inveniri	9. speravisse	14. habere	19. pugnavisse
5. putatum esse	10. speraturum esse	15. cupere	20. pugnatum esse

No. 179. Translate these participles:

1. ducens	8. inventa	15. venientium	22. missus
2. ducturus	9. reportantium	16. ventura	23. visuris
3. habentes	10. reportaturus	17. timenti	24. videntium
4. habitos	11. sperantia	18. territus	25. dicturos
5. putata	12. speratam	19. posituros	26. dicens
6. putaturis	13. moturos	20. ponentibus	27. monentes
7. invenientem	14. moventes	21. mittens	28. moniti

No. 180. Translate these ablative clauses:

1. eis visis	6. puella ambulanti	11. urbe capta
2. illo capto	7. ducibus timidis	12. reliquis dicentibus
3. his dictis	8. numero parvo	13. verbo audito
4. bello facto	9. somno venienti	14. spe inventa
5. viris timentibus	10. carcere magno	15. generibus multis

Reading

Quintus Horatius Flaccus

Horace, the son of a freedman, was born in 65 B.C. at Venusia, in southern Italy, and studied in Rome and Athens. He was a friend of Virgil and of Augustus, through his literary patron, Maecenas. Before his death in 8 B.C., he had gained enduring popularity from the quality and universality of his poetry and philosophy.

> Integer vitae scelerisque purus
> non eget Mauris iaculis neque arcu
> nec venenatis gravida sagittis, Fuscae, pharetra,
> sive per Syrtis iter aestuosas
> sive facturus per inhospitalem
> Caucasum vel quae loca fabulosus lambit Hydaspes.
> Carminum Liber Primus, xxii

Carmina Burana

In the early nineteenth century, a thirteenth-century manuscript was found in the monastery of Benedictburen in Bavaria. These **carmina,** or songs, called **Carmina Burana** after the monastery (Buren), were mostly poems, chiefly in Latin or German, or a combination of both, composed by the goliards, or wandering students and monks, on a wide variety of topics. By the Middle Ages, the classical pronunciation and meter had changed and the use of rhyme had been introduced in poetry. These poems provided both inspiration and text for the German composer Carl Orff's famous "Carmina Burana."

Omnia sol temperat
purus et subtilis,
nova mundo reserat
facies Aprilis,
ad amorem properat
animus erilis,
et iucundis imperat
deus puerilis.
Rerum tanta novitas
in sollemni vere
et veris auctoritas
iubet nos gaudere,
vias praebet solitas,
et in tuo vere
fides est et probitas
tuum retinere.
Ama me fideliter,
fidem meam nota,

de corde totaliter
et ex mente tota,
sum praesentialiter
absens in remota;
quisquis amat taliter,
volvitur in rota.
Ecce gratum
et optatum
ver reducit gaudia,
purpuratum
floret pratum,
sol serenat omnia,
iam iam cedunt tristia.
aestas redit,
nunc recedit
hiemis saevitia.
Iam liquescit
et decrescit

grando, nix, et cetera,
bruma fugit,
et iam sugit
ver aestatis ubera;
illi mens est misera,
qui nec vivit,
nec lascivit
sub aestatis dextera.
Gloriantur
et laetantur
in melle dulcedinis
qui conantur
ut utantur
praemio Cupidinis;
simus iussu Cypridis
gloriantes
et laetantes
pares esse Paridis.

The Subjunctive Mood

IMPORTANT DATES IN ROMAN HISTORY

753 B.C. Legend says in this year Romulus and Remus founded Rome. The Romans figured dates from this year, which they called **anno urbis conditae,** *from the year of the founding of the city,* abbreviated to A.U.C. Thus, the year 20 A.U.C. is the same as the year 733 B.C., and the year 763 A.U.C. is the same as the year A.D. 10.

509 B.C. (244 A.U.C.) The Romans set up a republic and drive out Tarquinius the Proud, the last king of the Etruscans.

264–241 B.C. (489–512 A.U.C.) The First Carthaginian War ends in victory for the Romans.

218–201 B.C. (535–552 A.U.C.) The Second Carthaginian War ends in victory for the Romans.

44 B.C. (709 A.U.C.) The assassination of Julius Caesar.

27 B.C. (726 A.U.C.) Augustus Caesar becomes the first emperor of Rome and its provinces.

14 A.D. (767 A.U.C.) Augustus Caesar dies. Tiberius becomes the second emperor.

64 A.D. (817 A.U.C.) The Great Fire of Rome.

79 A.D. (832 A.U.C.) Pompeii is destroyed by the eruption of Mount Vesuvius.

313 A.D. (1066 A.U.C.) Emperor Constantine grants religious toleration to the Christians.

395 A.D. (1148 A.U.C.) The Roman Empire splits into the Eastern and Western Empires. Rome is part of the Western Empire.

410 A.D. (1163 A.U.C.) Rome is sacked by the Visigoths.

455 A.D. (1208 A.U.C.) Rome is sacked again, this time by the Vandals.

476 A.D. (1229 A.U.C.) The last emperor of the Western Empire is deposed.

Reading Grammar

A. So far, the tenses you have learned have been in the indicative mood of verbs, for the active and passive voices. However, Latin has another mood, the subjunctive. The subjunctive has four tenses: present, perfect, imperfect, and pluperfect in both the active and the passive voice. In general, the subjunctive (depending on the tense and voice) is used to express doubt, hope, probability, improbability, and unreal situations or events. First we will learn the forms of the subjunctive and the sequences of tenses, and then we will consider specific uses of this mood.

B. Present Subjunctive.

1. Active Voice.

amo	habeo	duco	capio	audio
amem	habeam	ducam	capiam	audiam
ames	habeas	ducas	capias	audias
amet	habeat	ducat	capiat	audiat
amemus	habeamus	ducamus	capiamus	audiamus
ametis	habetis	ducatis	capiatis	audiatis
ament	habeant	ducant	capiant	audiant

2. Passive Voice.

amer	habear	ducar	capiar	audiar
ameris	habearis	ducaris	capiaris	audiaris
ametur	habeatur	ducatur	capiatur	audiatur
amemur	habeamur	ducamur	capiamur	audiamur
amemini	habeamini	ducamini	capiamini	audiamini
amentur	habeantur	ducantur	capiantur	audiantur

As you can see, for **a-conjugation** verbs the basic endings are added to the present stem plus the vowel **-e-**. For the other conjugations, the basic endings are added to the present stem plus the vowel **-a-**.

3. Present Subjunctive of **sum**.

The verb **sum** has no passive voice. The active voice of the present subjunctive is as follows:

Singular:	sim	Plural:	simus
	sis		sitis
	sit		sint

C. Perfect Subjunctive.

1. Active Voice.

amaverim	habuerim	duxerim	ceperim	audiverim
amaveris	habueris	duxeris	ceperis	audiveris
amaverit	habuerit	duxerit	ceperit	audiverit
amaverimus	habuerimus	duxerimus	ceperimus	audiverimus
amaveritis	habueritis	duxeritis	ceperitis	audiveritis
amaverint	habuerint	duxerint	ceperint	audiverint

You will notice that the perfect active subjunctive is formed in the same way as the future active indicative, with the exception of the first person singular. However, there is no danger of confusing the two tenses. The context will always provide you with enough information to figure out which tense is being used.

2. Passive Voice.

The perfect passive subjunctive is formed by using the fourth principal part and the present subjunctive of **sum.**

amatus, -a, -um sim	habitus, -a, -um sim	ductus, -a, -um sim
amatus, -a, -um sis	habitus, -a, -um sis	ductus, -a, -um sis
amatus, -a, -um sit	habitus, -a, -um sit	ductus, -a, -um sit
amati, -ae, -a simus	habiti, -ae, -a simus	ducti, -ae, -a simus
amati, -ae, -a sitis	habiti, -ae, -a sitis	ducti, -ae, -a sitis
amati, -ae, -a sint	habiti, -ae, -a sint	ducti, -ae, -a sint

captus, -a, -um sim	auditus, -a, -um sim
captus, -a, -um sis	auditus, -a, -um sis
captus, -a, -um sit	auditus, -a, -um sit
capti, -ae, -a simus	auditi, -ae, -a simus
capti, -ae, -a sitis	auditi, -ae, -a sitis
capti, -ae, -a sint	auditi, -ae, -a sint

3. The perfect subjunctive of **sum** is formed regularly.

Singular: **fuerim**   Plural: **fuerimus**
fueris   **fueritis**
fuerit   **fuerint**

D. Imperfect Subjunctive.

1. Active Voice.

The imperfect active subjunctive is formed by adding the basic endings onto the second principal part, the present active infinitive.

amarem	haberem	ducerem	caperem	audirem
amares	haberes	duceres	caperes	audires
amaret	haberet	duceret	caperet	audiret
amaremus	haberemus	duceremus	caperemus	audiremus
amaretis	haberetis	duceretis	caperetis	audiretis
amarent	haberent	ducerent	caperent	audirent

2. Passive Voice.

The imperfect passive subjunctive is formed by adding the passive endings onto the second principal part, the present active infinitive.

amarer	haberer	ducerer	caperer	audirer
amareris	habereris	ducereris	capereris	audireris
amaretur	haberetur	duceretur	caperetur	audiretur
amaremur	haberemur	duceremur	caperemur	audiremur
amaremini	haberemini	duceremini	caperemini	audiremini
amarentur	haberentur	ducerentur	caperentur	audirentur

3. The imperfect subjunctive of **sum** is formed regularly.

Singular: **essem**   Plural: **essemus**
esses   **essetis**
esset   **essent**

E. Pluperfect Subjunctive.

1. Active Voice.

The pluperfect active subjunctive is formed by using the perfect active infinitive (the third principal part plus **-isse-**) and the basic endings.

amavissem	habuissem	duxissem	cepissem	audivissem
amavisses	habuisses	duxisses	cepisses	audivisses
amavisset	habuisset	duxisset	cepisset	audivisset
amavissemus	habuissemus	duxissemus	cepissemus	audivissemus
amavissetis	habuissetis	duxissetis	cepissetis	audivissetis
amavissent	habuissent	duxissent	cepissent	audivissent

2. Passive Voice.

The pluperfect passive subjunctive is formed by using the fourth principal part and the imperfect subjunctive of **sum.**

amatus, -a, -um essem	habitus, -a, -um essem	ductus, -a, -um essem
amatus, -a, -um esses	habitus, -a, -um esses	ductus, -a, -um esses
amatus, -a, -um esset	habitus, -a, -um esset	ductus, -a, -um esset
amati, -ae, -a essemus	habiti, -ae, -a essemus	ducti, -ae, -a essemus
amati, -ae, -a essetis	habiti, -ae, -a essetis	ducti, -ae, -a essetis
amati, -ae, -a essent	habiti, -ae, -a essent	ducti, -ae, -a essent

captus, -a, -um essem	auditus, -a, -um essem
captus, -a, -um esses	auditus, -a, -um esses
captus, -a, -um esset	auditus, -a, -um esset
capti, -ae, -a essemus	auditi, -ae, -a essemus
capti, -ae, -a essetis	auditi, -ae, -a essetis
capti, -ae, -a essent	auditi, -ae, -a essent

3. The pluperfect subjunctive of **sum** is formed normally.

Singular:		Plural:	
	fuissem		fuissemus
	fuisses		fuissetis
	fuisset		fuissent

F. Sequences of Tenses.

When a Latin sentence has a verb in the indicative and one in the subjunctive, the verb in the indicative will be the main verb and its tense limits the choice of tenses that can be used for the subjunctive.

Latin has two sequences of verbs. The primary sequence consists of verbs whose action takes place either in the **present** or in the **future.** The secondary sequence consists of verbs whose action takes place in the **past.** When the subjunctive is used in the same sentence as the indicative, the subjunctive must be of the same sequence as the indicative. Examples of this will follow.

In the indicative, the primary tenses are the present, perfect, and future perfect. In the subjunctive, the primary tenses are the present and the perfect. When indicative and subjunctive verbs are used in the same sentence, the **present subjunctive** is used if the action of the subjunctive verb takes place at the same time as the action of the indicative verb. If the action of the subjunctive verb takes place before the action of the indicative verb, the **perfect subjunctive** is used.

In the indicative, the secondary tenses are the imperfect, perfect, and pluperfect. In the subjunctive, the secondary tenses are the imperfect and the pluperfect. The **imperfect** is used when the action of the subjunctive verb takes place at the same time as the action of the indicative verb. The **pluperfect** is used when the action of the subjunctive verb takes place before the action of the indicative verb.

The above information can be summarized as follows:

PRIMARY SEQUENCE

INDICATIVE	SUBJUNCTIVE
Present	Present — if action takes place at the same time
Future	Perfect — if action takes place earlier

Thus, if the action of the subjunctive verb takes place at the same time as the action of the indicative verb, you will see a sentence like this:

> **Rogo/Rogabo/Rogavero quid mulier audiat.**
> *I ask/will ask/shall have asked what the woman hears.*

However, if the action of the subjunctive verb takes place earlier than the action of the indicative verb, you will see a sentence like this:

> **Rogo/Rogabo/Rogavero quid mulier audiverit.**
> *I ask/will ask/shall have asked what the woman heard.*

SECONDARY SEQUENCE

INDICATIVE	SUBJUNCTIVE
Imperfect	Imperfect — if action takes place at the same time
Perfect	Pluperfect — if action takes place earlier

Thus, if the action of the subjunctive verb takes place at the same time as the action of the indicative verb, you will see a sentence like this:

> **Rogabam/Rogavi/Rogaveram quid mulier audiret.**
> *I was asking/have asked/had asked what the woman heard.*

However, if the action of the subjunctive verb takes place earlier than the action of the indicative verb, you will see a sentence like this:

> **Rogabam/Rogavi/Rogaveram quid mulier audivissit.**
> *I was asking/have asked/had asked what the woman had heard.*

Note that the tense of the subjunctive verbs is not determined only by the tense of the indicative verb, but also by when the action of the subjunctive takes place in relation to the action of the main verb. Thus, if the main verb is from the primary sequence and the action of the subjunctive occurs at the same time, the present tense of the subjunctive is used, regardless of whether the main verb is in the present, future, or future perfect.

Practice Exercises

No. 181. Change these verbs to the subjunctive:

1. debuerunt	6. facis	11. ventae estis	16. debes
2. relinquebat	7. iacta erant	12. fuit	17. fuerat
3. oppugnatis	8. debitus sum	13. rogamini	18. oppungnabant
4. es	9. veniebat	14. conspicimur	19. relicta est
5. eram	10. relinquebamur	15. veni	20. debebatur

No. 182. Change these verbs to the indicative:

1. sint	6. debeam	11. debita esses	16. conspecti essetis
2. veniamus	7. fuerimus	12. reliquerit	17. fuissem
3. rogata sint	8. conspexissent	13. rogaverit	18. oppugnaveris
4. oppugnaret	9. veniretur	14. venisses	19. relinquas
5. conspicerem	10. debuerim	15. esses	20. deberetur

No. 183. Tell which tense of the subjunctive would be used to indicate the following:
1. Action happening at the same time as one requiring a present tense verb.
2. Action happening before one requiring a pluperfect tense verb.
3. Action happening before one requiring a future tense verb.
4. Action happening at the same time as one requiring a perfect tense verb.

No. 184.
1. Give the present subjunctive, active and passive, of **laudo**.
2. Give the perfect subjunctive, active and passive, of **video**.
3. Give the imperfect subjunctive, active and passive, of **peto**.
4. Give the pluperfect subjunctive, active and passive, of **dormio**.

The Jussive Subjunctive

Reading Vocabulary

Nouns

severitas, severitatis, f., severity, strictness (severe)
coniuratio, coniurationis, f., conspiracy, plot
res publica, rei publicae, f., republic, common good
desiderium, desiderii, or desideri, n., longing, loss, need (desire)

vespera, vesperae, f., evening
senatus, senatus, m., senate (senator)
lenitas, lenitatis, f., mercy, mildness, gentleness gentleness (lenient)

Adjectives

Aurelius, Aurelia, Aurelium, Aurelian
tantus, tanta, tantum, so great
pristinus, pristina, pristinum, former, earlier
    (pristine)
superior, superius, higher, past, preceding (superior).
    Comparative of **superus**, high, upper

hesternus, hesterna, hesternum, yesterday
tot, so many (indeclinable)
perpetuus, perpetua, perpetuum, continuous,
    perpetual, uninterrupted (perpetuity)

Verbs

accelero, accelerare, acceleravi, acceleratus, hurry
    (accelerate)
concedo, concedere, concessi, concessum, grant,
    allow, withdraw (concede)
erro, errare, erravi, erratus, be mistaken, lose
    one's way (error)
patefacio, patefacere, patefeci, patefactus, throw
    open, bring to light. Conjugated like **facio**;
    the passive verb is **patefio, patefieri,
    patefactus sum**, which is conjugated like **fio**.
patior, pati, passus sum, allow, grant, suffer
    (patience)
proficiscor, proficisci, profectus sum, go forth,
    depart
tabesco, tabescere, tabescui, decay, melt away

adsequor, adsequi, adsecutus sum, gain,
    obtain, reach
consequor, consequi, consecutus sum, follow,
    catch up with (consequence)
exeo, exire, exii, exitus, avoid, go away,
    depart (exit). Conjugated like **eo**.
profugio, profugere, profugi, run away, flee,
    escape
perfero, perferre, pertuli, perlatus, report.
    Conjugated like **ferro**.
pertimesco, pertimescere, pertimui, fear,
    be alarmed at
sentio, sentire, sensi, sensum, feel, perceive,
    realize (sense)
flagito, flagitare, flagitavi, flagitatus, demand

Adverbs

ita, so
vehementer, violently, eagerly (vehemently)

sic, so, thus

Adverb and Conjunction

ut, or uti, as; that, so that

Conjunctions

ne, that not, lest

Reading Grammar

A. Clauses may be defined by and named for what they express. For example, consider this sentence:

I ran so fast that I arrived early.

There are two clauses in this sentence, *I ran so fast* and *I arrived early.* The word *that* serves to link the two clauses and show how they are related. Arriving early is a result of running fast. Thus, *that* becomes part of the second clause. *that I arrived early* is a result clause because it shows the result of the action the took place in the earlier clause.

B. Uses of the Subjunctive Mood.

You have learned the indicative mood, used to state a fact, or to ask a direct question, and the imperative mood, used to give commands. The subjunctive mood has many different uses. This is why only the briefest explanation about the uses of the subjunctive was given ealier in this chapter. When you meet or use the subjunctive in Latin, you must determine how it is being used before you can decide how to translate it. The first three uses of the subjunctive are called the jussive subjunctive (or hortatory subjunctive), the purpose clause, and the result clause.

1. The **jussive subjunctive.** *Jussive* is derived from the Latin verb **iubeo,** meaning *command.* However, in Latin, as you have already learned, you use the imperative mood to issue commands. In fact, the jussive subjunctive is used to recommend an action strongly; not quite a command, but stronger than a suggestion. For this reason, the jussive subjunctive is often called the *hortatory* subjunctive. The word comes from the verb **hortor,** meaning *urge.* When the subjunctive is translated into English, the word *let* is supplied. This construction uses only the present subjunctive, usually in the first person plural or in the third person.

Vocemus eum.	Let us call him.
Dicat.	Let him (her) speak.
Mulieres id audiant.	Let the women hear it.

The hortatory subjunctive can also be used to strongly recommend that an action not be taken. In this case, the word **ne** is used.

Ne vocemus virum.	Let us not call the man.
Ne dicat.	Let him (her) not speak.
Mulieres id ne videant.	Let the women not see it.

2. The **Subjunctive of Purpose** (Purpose Clause). In English, the infinitive is used to express purpose:

I am going to the store to buy food.

The infinitive, *to buy,* expresses the purpose of going to the store. You could also say, *I am going to the store for the purpose of buying food,* or, *I am going to the store so that I can buy food.*

In Latin, the infinitive is not used to express purpose. Instead, you use the present and the imperfect tenses of the subjunctive. As the previous chapter stated, the **present tense** is used if the main verb is from the primary sequence, and the **imperfect tense** is used if the main verb is from the secondary sequence. The word **ut** is usually used to introduce purpose clauses.

Urbam eunt ut matrem suam videant.	They go to the city to see (in order to see, for the purpose of seeing, so that they might see) their mother.
Urbam ibis ut patrem tuum videas.	You will go to the city to see your father.
Urbam iero ut sorores meas videam.	I shall have gone to the city to see my sisters.
Urbam ductus est ut a sorore sua videretur.	He was led to the city to be seen by his sister.
Urbam ibam ut viros audirem.	I was going to the city to hear the men.
Currerant ut ludos viderent.	They were running to see the games.

If the purpose clause is negative, the word **ne** is used instead of **ut**.

Pugnant ne necentur.	They fight so that they will not be killed (in order not to be killed, for the purpose of not being killed).
Domi manebam ne viros audirem.	I remained at home so that I would not hear the men.

3. The **Subjunctive of Result** (Result Clauses). Result clauses show the result of an action.

I ran so fast that I caught the train.

The result clause is *that I caught the train*. You could also say: *I ran so fast with the result that I caught the train,* or *I ran so fast that the result was that I caught the train.*

Result clauses are formed in the same way as purpose clauses. Often, you will have to decide from the context whether a clause expresses result or purpose. However, there are two instances when this will be easier.

The first instance is if the clause is negative. A negative purpose clause uses the word **ne**. A negative result clause uses the words **ut** and **non** in the same sentence.

Purpose Clause:	**Pugnant ne necentur.** They fight so that they will not be killed.
Result Clause:	**Pugnant ut non necentur.** They fight with the result that they are not killed.

The other instance is when certain words appear in the main clause that precedes the result clause. These words are **ita,** *so;* **tam,** *so;* **tantus,** *so great;* **tot,** *so many;* **talis,** *such;* and **sic,** *so.*

Purpose Clause:	**Pugnabant bene ne necarentur.** They fought well so that they would not be killed.
Result Clause:	**Pugnabant tam bene ut non necarentur.** They fought so well that they were not killed.
Purpose Clause:	**Cucurreram celeriter ut eam viderem.** I had run swiftly so that I might see her.
Result Clause:	**Cucurreram ita celeriter ut eam viderem.** I had run so swiftly that I saw her.

C. Subjunctive of Irregular Verbs.

1. You have already learned the subjunctive of **sum**. Like **sum**, the verbs **possum, eo, volo, nolo,** and **malo** only have the active voice.

a. Present Subjunctive.

possum	eo	volo	nolo	malo
possim	eam	velim	nolim	malim
possis	eas	velis	nolis	malis
possit	eat	velit	nolit	malit
possimus	eamus	velimus	nolimus	malimus
possitis	eatis	velitis	nolitis	malitis
possint	eant	velint	nolint	malint

The present tense is the most irregular; the other three subjunctive tenses are more straightforward.

b. Perfect Subjunctive.

potuerim	ierim	voluerim	noluerim	maluerim
potueris	ieris	volueris	nolueris	malueris
potuerit	ierit	voluerit	noluerit	maluerit
etc.	etc.	etc.	etc.	etc.

c. Imperfect Subjunctive.

possem	irem	vellem	nollem	mallem
posses	ires	velles	nolles	malles
posset	iret	vellet	nollet	mallet
etc.	etc.	etc.	etc.	etc.

d. Pluperfect Subjunctive.

potuissem	issem	voluissem	noluissem	maluissem
potuisses	isses	voluisses	noluisses	maluisses
potuisset	isset	voluisset	noluisset	maluisset
etc.	etc.	etc.	etc.	etc.

2. The verb **fio** only has the passive voice in the subjunctive.

PRESENT	PERFECT	IMPERFECT	PLUPERFECT
fiam	factus, -a, -um sim	fierem	factus, -a, -um essem
fias	factus, -a, -um sis	fieres	factus, -a, -um esses
fiat	factus, -a, -um sit	fieret	factus, -a, -um esset
etc.	etc.	etc.	etc.

Note that, although the imperfect of **fio** is translated as passive, it is formed by adding the active endings to **fier-.** Only the stem of the second principal part is used, not the whole infinitive.

3. The verb **fero** has both the active and the passive voice in the subjunctive.

PRESENT		PERFECT	
ACTIVE	PASSIVE	ACTIVE	PASSIVE
feram	ferar	tulerim	latus, -a, -um sim
feras	feraris	tuleris	latus, -a, -um sis
ferat	feratur	tulerit	latus, -a, -um sit
etc.	etc.	etc.	etc.

IMPERFECT		PLUPERFECT	
ACTIVE	PASSIVE	ACTIVE	PASSIVE
ferrem	ferrer	tulissem	latus, -a, -um essem
ferres	ferreris	tulisses	latus, -a, -um esses
ferret	ferretur	tulisset	latus, -a, -um esset
etc.	etc.	etc.	etc.

D. Regular deponent verbs form the subjunctive with the usual passive endings. They are, of course, translated in the active voice.

Reading

From this point on, the readings will all be drawn directly from actual writings in Classical Latin. Some of the more complicated constructions will occasionally be simplified, but for the most part, you will be reading the same words that literate citizens of the Roman Empire read centuries ago.

Often, words that would be used in English are left out in Latin. Such words are supplied in the translation where necessary. If they are not obvious, they are placed in square brackets [].

In the Sixth Review Section, you read an excerpt from Cicero's First Oration Against Cataline, who had formed a conspiracy to overthrow the government. This excerpt is taken from Cicero's second oration against Cataline, which was delivered before the people of Rome. In this section, Cicero is trying to convince Cataline's fellow conspirators to leave Rome. Refer to the Sixth Review Section to refresh your memory on Cicero and Cataline.

In Catilinam II, 6–7.

Against Cataline 2, 6–7,
adapted from the Second Oration Against Cataline, delivered before the people.

Omnia superioris noctis consilia ad me perlata esse sentiunt, patefeci in senatu hesterno die, Catalina ipse pertimuit, profugit: hi quid exspectant? Ne illi vehementer errant, si illam meam pristinam lenitatem perpetuam sperant futuram.

They realize that all their plans of the past night have been reported to me; I brought them to light yesterday in the senate; Cataline himself was alarmed; he fled: for what do these men wait? Indeed, they are violently mistaken if they hope that that earlier mildness of mine will exist forever.

Quod exspectavi iam sum adsecutus, ut vos omnes factam esse aperte coniurationem contra rem publicam videretis. Non est iam lenitati locus; severitatem res ipsa flagitat.

What I have waited for I have now obtained: that you all may see that a conspiracy has been made openly against the republic. There is not now a place for mildness; the matter itself demands severity.

Unum etiam nunc concedam: exeant, proficiscantur, ne patiantur desidero sui Catalinam miserum tabescere. Demonstrabo iter: Aurelia via profectus est; si accelerare volent, ad vesperam consequentur.

I will grant one thing even now: let them go away; let them depart; let them not allow wretched Cataline to waste away from their lack. I will point out the road: He has set out by the Aurelian Road; if they wish to hurry, they will catch up at evening.

CHURCH HOURS

When monasteries were established during the Middle Ages, the religious rules required the monks to say prayers at specific times of the day. The names of the prayers, derived from Latin, reflected the names of the times at which they were recited. These times were the seven canonical hours. Time keeping was not fixed and standard in the Middle Ages, and often depended on the time of year and on the location of the monastery. However, the following is an approximate guide to the canonical hours.

Matins, from the adjective **matutinus,** *of the morning.* Despite the meaning, Matins is supposed to be recited at midnight, although it is often recited at dawn instead. As a canonical hour, Matins falls between midnight and 3 a.m.

Lauds, from **laus,** *praise.* This refers to the prayers said at dawn, and to an hour within the 3 a.m. to 6 a.m. period.

Prime, from **primus,** *first.* This refers to the first daylight hour, falling between 6 a.m. and 9 a.m. It begins at sunrise.

Terce, from **tertius,** *third.* This refers to the third hour after sunrise, and to the prayers recited then. This hour falls between 9 a.m. and noon.

Sext, from **sextus,** *sixth.* This refers to the sixth hour after sunrise, or noon, and to the prayers recited then. It falls between noon and 3 p.m.

Nones, from **nonus,** *ninth.* This refers to the ninth hour of daylight and to the prayers recited then. It falls between 3 p.m. and 6 p.m.

Vespers, from **vesper,** *the evening.* This refers to the evening hour, which falls between 6 p.m. and 9 p.m., and to the prayers recited then. It starts at sunset.

Compline, from **completus,** the fourth principal part of the verb **compleo,** *complete.* This refers to the final canonical hour and to the prayers recited then. It falls between 9 p.m. and midnight.

The canonical hours do not last for sixty minutes. Their duration, as well as their starting and finishing times, is determined by the times of sunrise, midday, sunset, and midnight.

Practice Exercises

No. 185. Change these indicative tenses to the subjunctive:

1. possum	6. non vult	11. factus est	16. volebat
2. eunt	7. isti	12. ferebantur	17. maluit
3. tulit	8. malebant	13. malo	18. fio
4. fiebatis	9. potuit	14. ierant	19. fertis
5. volueramus	10. noluistis	15. potueras	20. nolueritis

No. 186. Translate these jussive clauses:

1. concedamus	6. ne scribat
2. ne veniat	7. ne arment
3. pugnebant	8. ne flagitemus
4. profugiant	9. conficiat
5. maneamus	10. dormiamus

No. 187. Translate these sentences containing purpose clauses:
1. **Pugnant ut urbem capiant.**
2. **Accelerabam ut consequerer.**
3. **Daedalus alas paraverat ut ipse et filius suus volarent.**
4. **Urbem existi ne pugnares.**
5. **Haec patefacit ut sciamus.**
6. **Instruimus ut cognoscatis.**
7. **Audiunt ut cognoscant.**
8. **Mulier profugerat ne necerat.**

No. 188. Translate theses sentences containing result clauses:
1. **Cicero tam bene narravit ut Catilina Roma profisceretur.**
2. **Catalina pertimescebam ut non urbem oppugnaret.**
3. **Psyche Cupidinem tam magnopere amavit ut ad Inferos iret.**
4. **Cupid Psychem tam magnopere amavit ut non verba matris suae audiret.**
5. **Vidistis tam longe ut coniurationem inveniretis.**
6. **Viri tam celere cucurrerant ut consequerent.**
7. **Severitas rei tanta eras ut non lenitas daretur.**
8. **Soror tua ita bene instruit ut multo cognoscamus.**

Subjunctive in Noun Clauses

Reading Vocabulary

Nouns

Allobroges, Allobrogum, m. pl., Allobroges
fames, famis, f., famine, hunger
Helvetii, Helvetiorum, m. pl., Helvetii
Latobrigi, Latobrigorum, m. pl., Latobrigi
bonitas, bonitatis, f., goodness, kindness, benevolence

deditio, deditionis, f., surrender
fructus, fructus, m., produce, fruit
vicus, vici, m., village, street
obses, obsidis, m., or f., hostage
Tulingi, Tulingorum, m. pl., Tulingi
Rhenus, Rheni, m., the Rhine

Adjectives

quantus, quanta, quantum, how much

Verbs

accipio, accipere, accepi, acceptus, take, receive (accept)
amitto, amittere, amisi, amissum, lose
dubito, dubitare, dubitavi, dubitatus doubt, hesitate, be uncertain (dubious)
permitto, permittere, permisi, permissus, allow, permit (permission)
purgo, purgare, purgavi, purgatus, clean, remove, excuse (purge)

conquiro, conquirere, conquisivi, conquisitus, look for, collect
incolo, incolere, incolui, live in, reside
impero, imperare, imperavi, imperatus, command, order (imperial)
persuadeo, persuadere, persuasi, persuasus, persuade (persuasion)
restituo, restituere, restitui, restitutus, restore, rebuild (restitution)

rescisco, rescīscere, rescii, rescitus, learn, find out
revertor, reverti, reversus sum, turn back, return (revert)
vaco, vacare, vacavi, vacatus, be empty (vacant)
transeo, transire, transivi, transitus, pass over, cross, desert. Conjugated like **eo.**

oro, orare, oravi, oratus, beg, pray
tolero, tolerare, toleravi, toleratus, bear, endure (tolerate)
veto, vetare, vetavi, vetatus, forbid (veto)

Adverbs

unde, from where, whence

Conjunctions

an, or   **si,** if   **num,** whether

Reading Grammar

A. Noun Clauses.

1. Noun clauses are sometimes called indirect commands. The main verb usually expresses an action of commanding or asking. The main verb is in the indicative, and the subordinate verb is in the subjunctive. If the noun clause is positive, **ut** is used; if negative, **ne** is used.

Imperaverunt nobis ut hoc faceremus.	They commanded us to do this.
Eam rogis ut Romam eat.	You ask her to go to Rome.
Ab eis petivi ne pugnarent.	I begged of them not to fight.
Monet ne illud facias.	He (she) warns you not to do that.

As you see, noun clauses are formed the same way as purpose clauses. However, you will not confuse the two because the indicative verb will show what kind of clause you are dealing with.

The following are some of the verbs that can be used with noun clauses:

constituo	decide	**impero**	command
moneo	warn	**oro**	beg
permitto	allow	**persuadeo**	persuade
peto	ask, seek	**rogo**	ask

The following verbs are *not* used in noun clauses:

volo	wish	**nolo**	wish not
malo	prefer	**cupio**	desire
iubeo	command	**patior**	allow
veto	forbid		

Instead, these verbs are used with the accusative and the completing infinitive:

Vos manere iubeo.	I order you to remain.
Te amari volo.	I want you to be loved.

2. Verbs which express actions of preventing, forbidding, and hindering also use the subjunctive in noun clauses. These clauses are introduced by **ne, quin,** or **quominus.** They are otherwise identical with noun clauses.

Pueros prohibui ne domi irent.	I have forbidden the boys to go home.
Mulierem non impediam quin dicat.	I will not prevent the woman from speaking.

3. Verbs which express fear form noun clauses with the subjunctive and the word **ne** if the clause is positive. If the clause is negative, the word **ut** is used. Note that this is the opposite of the way most noun clauses are formed.

Timent ne milites veniant.	They fear that the soldiers will come, *or* They fear lest the soldiers come.
Timent ut milites veniant.	They fear that the soldiers will not come.

4. Verbs expressing doubt form noun clauses with the subjunctive and **quin** if the clause is negative. If the clause is positive, **an,** *or, whether;* **num,** *whether;* or **si,** *if* is used.

Non dubitat quin puella pulchra sit.	He (she) does not doubt that the girl is pretty.
Dubito si veniam.	I doubt if I shall come.

B. Indirect Questions.

Where are you going? is a direct question.
I ask where you are going is an indirect question.

You already know that a direct question is formed by using the indicative mood and adding **-ne** to the end of the first word, as in **Amatne vir mulierem?** *Does the man love the woman?*

An indirect question is formed by using the indicative for the main verb, which expresses the action of asking, knowing, showing, or perceiving. The subjunctive is used for the other verb. This is different from an indirect statement, where the infinitive is used instead of the subjunctive.

Remember to use the proper sequence of tenses in indirect questions.

Scio quid velis.	I know what you want, *or* I know what you will want.
Scio quid volueris.	I know what you wanted.
Rogavi ubi irent.	I have asked where they were, *or* I have asked where they would be.
Rogavi ubi issent.	I have asked where they had been.
Rogabunt quid faciamus.	They will ask what we are doing, *or* They will ask what we will do.
Rogabunt quid fecerimus.	They will ask what we did.
Cognoscabatis cur oppugnarentur.	You learned why they attacked, *or* You learned why they were attacked.
Cognoscabatis cur oppugnati essent.	You learned why they had been attacked.

It is easy to recognize an indirect question. One of the following words will generally be present in the sentence:

quis, who (relative pronoun)	**quid,** what (relative pronoun)
ubi, where, when (adverb)	**unde,** whence, from where (adverb)
cur, why (adverb)	**quantus, -a, -um,** how much (adjective)

qui, quae, quod, which (interrogative adjective)
quo modo, how, in what way (interrogative adjective plus noun)

Reading

In the third review section, you read an excerpt from Book I of Caesar's *Commentaries on the Gallic War.* Gaul was the name of what is now France. The Helvetii had surrendered to Caesar. However, one group attempted to sneak away and escape across the upper Rhine.

Comentarii de Bello Gallico I

Commentaries on the Gallic War 1, adapted from chapter 28.

Quod ubi Caesar resciit, quorum per fines ierant, his uti conquirerent et reducerent, si sibi purgati esse vellent, imperavit. Reductos in hostium numero habuit; reliquos omnes obsidibus, armis, perfugis traditis in deditionem accepti.

When Caesar learned this, he ordered those [tribes] through whose borders they [the Helvetii] had gone to look for them and lead them back, if they wanted to be excused. He held the men led back into the number of the enemy; he received all those remaining in surrender, when the hostages, weapons, and deserters were handed over.

Helvetios, Tulingos, Latobrigos in fines suos, unde erant profecti, reverti iussit, et quod omnibus fructibus amissis domique nihil erat, quo famem tolerarent, Allobrogius imperavit ut his frumenti copiam facerent.

He ordered the Helvetii, the Tulingi, and the Latobrigi to return to their own borders from where they had set forth, and, because they had lost all their produce and nothing was at home by which they might endure famine, he ordered the Allobroges to make an abundance of grain for them.

Ipsos oppida vicosque, quos incenderant, restituere iussit quod noluit eum locum, unde Helvetii discesserant vacare, ne propter bonitatem agrorum Germani, qui trans Rhenum incolunt, e suis finibus in Helvetiorum fines transirent et finitimi Galliae provinciae Allobrogibusque essent.

He ordered them [the tribes] to rebuild themselves the towns and villages which they had burned, because he did not wish that place from where the Helvetii had departed to be empty, lest, on account of the goodness of the fields, the Germans, who live across the Rhine, cross over from their own borders into the borders of the Helvetii and be neighbors to the province of Gaul and to the Allobroges.

Practice Exercises

No. 189. Translate these sentences:
1. Monuerat ne Romam veniretis.
2. Tulingos persuadetis ut arma sua tradant.
3. Oro ne patrem meum necatur.
4. Mater tua imperavit ne equos amitteres.
5. Caesar milites suos reverti vetat.
6. Caesar Allobroges prohibuit ne urbem captam rescicerent.
7. Timemus ne vicos vacent.
8. Cicero pertimescet ut Catilina Roma proficiscatur.
9. Helvetii dubitant si Caesar deditiones suas accipiat.
10. Non dubitant quin Germani fines suos transeant.

No. 190. Translate the following sentences which contain indirect questions:
1. Non scio quis sis.
2. Cicero vos narrabit cur Catilina Roma discesseris.
3. Mulier rogavit quo modo hoc rescisses.

4. Rescierant quid cuperemus.
5. Sciamus unde milites oppugnent.
6. Cognosco cur mulierem ames.
7. Me dixisti quo modo vici restituissentur.
8. Rogabas quem amavero.
9. Vir scit quid soror tua viderit.
10. Helvetii casa incenderant in quos incoluerint.

No. 191.
1. Give the present subjunctive, active and passive, of **accipio.**
2. Give the perfect subjunctive of **revertor.**
3. Give the imperfect subjunctive of **eo.**
4. Give the pluperfect subjunctive, active and passive, of **veto.**

THE MONTHS OF THE YEAR

The names of all of our months come from Latin.
January, from **Januarius.** Named after Janus, the two-headed god of beginnings.
February, from **Februarius.**
March, from **Martius.** Named after Mars, the god of war, it was originally the first month of the Roman year.
April, from **Aprilis.**
May, from **Maius.** Named after Maia, the mother of Mercury, the messenger of the gods.
June, from **Junius.** Named after Juno, the queen of the gods.
July, from **Julius.** Named after Julius Caesar, the month was originally called **Quintilis,** a word related to the adjective **quintus,** meaning *fifth.* **Quintilis** was the fifth month of the year when the calender started with **Martius.**
August, from **Augustus.** Named after Augustus Caesar, this month was originally called **Sextilis,** related to **sextus,** *sixth,* because it was origininally the sixth month of the year.
September, October, November, and **December** are taken directly from Latin. The words for these months are related to **septimus, octavus, nonus,** and **decimus,** because they were originally the seventh, eighth, ninth, and tenth months of the year.

Optative Subjunctive

Reading Vocabulary

Nouns

ius, iuris, n., right, authority
Nicaea, Nicaeae, f., Nicaea
annua, annuorum, n. pl., pension, yearly pay
(annuity)
magnitudo, magnitudinis, f., greatness, vastness
(magnitude)

nemo, neminis, m. or f., no one, nobody
Nicomedia, Nicomediae, f., Nicomedia
officium, officii or offici, n., official job,
official position
ministerium, ministerii or ministeri, n., service,
work, employment (ministry)

Pronouns

quidam, quaedam, quiddam, a certain one; pl., some.
Declined like the relative pronoun plus **dam,**
except that the neuter nominative, accusative,
and vocative singular are **quid.**

aliquis, aliquid, someone, something; anyone,
anything. Declined like the interrogative
pronoun **quis, quid.**

Adjectives

publicus, publica, publicum, public, common
salvus, salva, salvum, safe, well (salvation)
otiosus, otiosa, otiosum, free, at leisure, not
working
plerusque, plerasque, plerumque, most.
Declined like **plerus** plus **que.**

inutilis, inutile, useless, harmful
senex, senix, old, aged (senile)
periculosus, periculosa, periculosum, dangerous,
perilous
honestus, honesta, honestum, honored,
respected (honest)

Verbs

adfirmo, adfirmare, adfirmavi, adfirmatus, strengthen, affirm, assert
arbitror, arbitrari, arbitratus sum, think, judge (arbitrate)
comperio, comperire, comperi, compertus, learn, ascertain (compare)
credo, credere, credidi, creditus, believe, trust (credit, credence)
damno, damnare, damnavi, damnatus, condemn, find guilty (damnation)
desceno, descendere, descendi, descensus, descend, come down (descent)
evenio, evenire, eveni, evenitus, happen, come out
existimo, existimare, existimavi, existimatus, think, judge
exsolvo, exsolvere, exsolvi, exsolutus, release, free
fungor, fungi, functus sum, perform, do
haesito, haesitare, haesitavi, haesitatus, hesitate, be at a loss (hesitant)
lego, legere, legi, lectus, read (legible)
nescio, nescire, nescivi, nescitus, not know, be ignorant of
pascor, pasci, pastus sum, feed on, eat

quaero, quaerere, quaesivi, quaesitus, ask, look for (quest, question)
reddeo, reddere, reddidi, reditus, return, restore
refero, referre, retuli, relataus, report, bring back (refer). Conjugated like **fero.**
retineo, retinere, retinui, retentus, keep back, retain
vivo, vivere, vixi, victus, live (vivacious)
oportet, oportere, oportuit, it is right, it is proper. This is an impersonal verb.
    The subject is always *it;* thus, it is used only in the third person.

Adverbs

fortasse, perhaps
modeste, moderately, modestly
quantum, as much as

frugaliter, temperately, frugally (frugal)
nimis, very much, too much
rursus, backward, on the other hand

Conjunctions

utinam, if only, would that

vel, or **vel . . . vel,** either . . . or

Reading Grammar

A. Relative Characteristic Clauses.

In a sentence containing a relative characteristic clause, the clause tells you something about its antecedent. It is like an adjective in this way. In such sentences, the antecedent is usually indefinite, negative, general, or interrogative, and the verb of the clause is put into the subjunctive.

> **Nemo est qui te credat.**
> There is no one who believes you.

In this sentence, the relative characteristic clause is: *who believes you.* It describes a characteristic of *no one,* the antecedent. Thus, the sentence might be translated as follows: There is no one with the characteristic of believing you. Other examples follow:

> **Aliquis est qui puerum nesciat?**
> Is there anyone who does not know the boy?
>
> **Multi sunt qui illa credant.**
> There are many who believe those things.
>
> **Sunt qui libros legant.**
> There are those who have read the books.
>
> **Hic est vir quem omnes ament.**
> He is the kind of man whom all like.

Note that, in the last example, **omnes,** *all,* is the subject of the relative clause, and of the verb **ament; quem,** referring to the antecedent **vir,** is in the accusative because it is the direct object of the verb **ament.**

B. Optative Subjunctive.

The optative subjunctive expresses a wish. The word **ne** is used when the wish is negative. The adverb **utinam** may be used whether the optative is positive or negative.

    1. If it is possible for the wish to come true, the present subjunctive is used. **Utinam** may or may not be used. It is easy to recognize the optative, whether or not **utinam** is used.

> **Utinam veniant!**
> If only they would come!
>
> **Ne miles necetur!**
> May the soldier not die!

2. If the wish refers to the present time, and it cannot come true, the imperfect subjunctive is used. Note that this is different from the usual sequence of tenses.

Utinam regina diceret!	If only the queen were speaking!
Utinam ne ibi essem!	If only I were not here!

3. If the wish refers to the past, and if it did not come true, the pluperfect subjunctive is used.

Utinam casam vidissetis!	If only you had seen the house!
Utinam ne Romam venissent!	If only they had not come to Rome!

C. **Cum** and the Subjunctive.

a. You have already learned that, when it is a conjunction, **cum** can be used with the indicative. In this case, **cum** means *when* or **while,** and the verb is in the present or future tense.

Cum Romam eo, patrem meum video.   When I go to Rome, I see my father.

If the verb is in the past, the indicative is used if the clause with **cum** refers to the point in time at which something occurred.

Cum Romam veni, patrem meum vidi.   When I went to Rome, I saw my father, *or*
At the time when I went to Rome, I saw my father.

b. The subjunctive is used in a **cum** clause if the action took place in the past and the clause refers to the situation or the circumstances under which the main action took place. The verb describing the main action stays in the indicative. In this context, the word **cum** can be translated as *when, since,* or *although.* The subjunctive **cum** clause is used in almost the same way as the ablative absolute, and can often be replaced by it.

As always, the proper sequence of tenses must be followed. Since the main verb will be in one of the past tenses (otherwise, there would be no need for the subjunctive), the imperfect is used if the action of **cum** clause occurs at the same time as the main action. The pluperfect is used if the action of the clause occurs before the action of the main verb.

Cum pugnarent, timebamus.	When they were fighting, we were afraid.
Cum bene pugnarent, timebamus.	Although they were fighting well, we were afraid.
Cum bene pugnarent, non timebamus.	Since they fought well, we were not afraid.
Cum dixissem, mansisti.	When I had spoken, you remained.
Cum bene pugnavissent, urbs capta est.	Since they had fought well, the city was captured, *or*
	Although they had fought well, the city was captured.

You will notice that it is not always immediately obvious how **cum** is to be translated. You will have to rely on the context of the sentence for help.

Reading

Gaius Plinius Caecilius Secundus, known as Pliny the Younger, was born in North Italy in A.D. 61 or 62. In A.D. 109, he was appointed by the Emperor Trajan to represent him in the province of Bithynia, in northern Turkey. Pliny wrote several letters to Trajan, discussing the various problems of Bithynia.

Gaius Plinius Traiano Imperatori

Gaius Pliny to Emperor Trajan,
adapted from Pliny's Letters, 10, 31.

Salva magnitudine tua, domine, descendas oportet ad meas curas, cum ius mihi dederis referendi ad te, de quibus dubito. In plerisque civitatibus, maxime Nicomediae et Nicaeae, quidam vel in opus damnati vel in ludum similiaque his genera poenarum publicorum servorum officio ministerioque funguntur, atque etiam ut publici servi annua accipiunt.

Saving your greatness, lord, it is right that you should descend to my cares, since you have given to me the right of reporting to you about what I am in doubt. In most cities, especially those of Nicomedia and Nicaea, some of those condemned either to work or to the [gladiatorial] games and similar types of punishments to these, perform the job and ministry of public servants, and even receive a pension as public servants.

Quod ego cum audissem, diu multumque haesitavi, quid facere deberem. Nam et reddere poenae post longum tempus plerosque iam senes et, quantum adfirmatur, frugaliter modesteque viventes nimis severum arbitrabar, et in publicis officiis retinere damnatos non satis honestum putabam; eosdem rursus a re publica pasci otiosos inutile, non pasci etiam periculosum existimabam.

When I had heard this, I was for long at a great loss as to what I ought to do. Now, I thought that to return them to punishment after a long time, most of them already old and, as far as can be affirmed, living frugally and moderately, [would be] too severe, and I thought that to retain the condemned men in public jobs was not sufficiently honest; on the other hand, I thought for these same men to eat at [the expense of] the republic wasteful; [for them] not to eat, [I thought] even perilous.

Quares fortasse quem ad modum evenerit, ut poenis in quas damnati erant exsoluerentur: et ego quaesivi, sed nihil comperi quod adfirmare tibi possim.

You will ask, perhaps, in what way it happened that those condemned to these penalties were freed, and I have asked, but I learned nothing which I am able to affirm to you.

Note: Trajan's response to Pliny was that the elderly men, and those who had been sentenced more than ten years ago, could be employed in jobs traditionally reserved for criminals, but that the rest of those sentenced must return until they had completed the term of their sentences.

Practice Exercises

No. 192. Translate these sentences:
1. Nemo erat qui haec existimaret.
2. Illa est quam omnes credunt.
3. Aliquis est qui non exsolutus sit?
4. Sunt quo illud adfirment.
5. Utinam pater meus viveret!

6. Utinam reddeant!
7. Utinam libros meos legisses!
8. Ne haec quaerant!
9. Ne in ludum damnatus esset!
10. Ne pugnandi nescirem!

No. 193. Translate the following sentences which contain **cum** clauses:
 1. **Cum armes obsidesque tradidissent, Caesar vicos restituit.**
 2. **Cum damnatus esset, miserus erat.**
 3. **Cum exsolutae essent, non laetae erant.**
 4. **Cum mulierem amarem, urbem exii.**
 5. **Cum periculosum essent, non pertimescimus.**
 6. **Cum acceleravissent, non consecuti sunt.**
 7. **Cum acceleravisset, consecutus est.**
 8. **Cum Cicero erraret, bene dixit.**
 9. **Cum agri incensi essent, Helvetii non ibi incolebant.**
10. **Cum id concessum esset, Catilina Roma discessit.**

No. 194.
 1. Give the present indicative of **consequor.**
 2. Give the imperfect perfect subjunctive, active and passive, of **erro.**
 3. Give the perfect subjunctive, active and passive, of **perfero.**
 4. Give the pluperfect indicative, active and passive, of **flagito.**

SPECIAL DAYS IN THE ROMAN MONTHS

Each month in the Roman calendar had three special days which were used to keep track of when an event had happened or was to happen.

Kalendae, the *Kalends,* fell on the first day of every month. It is abbreviated **Kal.**

Idus, the *Ides,* fell on the fifteenth in March, May, July, and October, and on the thirteenth in all other months. It is abbreviated to **Id.** One of the most famous dates in Roman history is the Ides of March, the date of the assassination of Julius Caesar.

Nonae, the *Nones,* comes from the adjective **nonus,** *ninth.* It fell on the ninth day before the Ides. However, when the Romans counted days, they added in the day they started with and the day they ended with. Thus, the Nones fell on the seventh in March, May, July, and October, and on the fifth of all other months.

The names of these days are given in the plural. **Kalendae** and **Nonae** are first declension nouns. **Idus** is a fourth declension noun.

Days were counted backwards from whichever of these three days was closest. The starting and ending days were counted as well. Thus, **ante diem septimum Kalendas Augustas,** *the seventh day before the Kalends of August,* would be July 26. The Latin would be abbreviated to A.D. VII. Kal. Aug. You will notice that the date is put into the accusative.

The day immediately before one of the three special days is indicated by using the word **pridie,** followed by the accusative. Thus, **pridie Idus Martias** is March 14.

Conditional Sentences

Reading Vocabulary

Nouns

aspectus, aspectus, m., look, sight (aspect)
misericordia, misericordiae, f., sympathy, pity
odium, odii, or **odi, n.,** hatred (odius)
praesentia, praesentiae, f., presence, effect
sensus, sensus, m., sense, sensation, feeling
iudicium, iudicii, or **iudici, n.,** judgment, sentence
contumelia, contumeliae, f., mistreatment,
    outrage, injury
necessarius, necessarii, or **necessari, m.,** or
    necessaria, necessariae, f., relative, friend

frequentia, frequentiae, f., crowd
mens, mentis, f., mind (mental)
pactum, pacti, n., way, manner
parens, parentis, m. or **f.,** parent
ratio, rationis, f., manner, fashion, reason
taciturnitas, taciturnitatis, f., silence (taciturn)
parricidium, parricidii or **parricidi, n.,** parricide,
    murder, treason

Pronoun and Adjective

iste, ista, istud, that, that one of yours.
    Conjugated like **ille, illa, illud,** this generally
    has negative or derogatory connotations.

Adjectives

infestus, infesta, infestum, threatening, dangerous,
    hostile (infested)

communis, commune, common, public

Verbs

absum, abesse, abfui, be absent, be away from
careo, carere, carui, be without, be absent from
loquor, loqui, locutus sum, say, speak (loquacious)
opinor, opinari, opinatus sum, think, suppose
    (opinion)
placo, placare, placavi, placatus, calm, reconcile
    (placate)
saluto, salutare, salutavi, salutatus, greet, welcome
    (salute, salutations)
suspicio, suspicere, suspexi, suspectus, mistrust,
    suspect (suspicion)

metuo, metuere, metui, fear, be afraid
permoveo, permovere, permovi, stir, move
vito, vitare, vitavi, vitatus, avoid
adsum, adesse, adfui, be present, be here.
    Conjugated like **sum.**
cogito, cogitare, cogitavi, cogitatus, consider,
    think (cogitate)
iudico, iudicare, iudicavi, iudicatus, judge,
    sentence, examine
vulnero, vulnerare, vulneravi, vulneratus, wound,
    hurt (vulnerable)

Adverbs

paulo, a little

Conjunctions

etiamsi, even if
quamvis, although

etsi, even if, although
tametsi, even if

nisi, if not, unless

Interjections

mehercule, by Hercules!

Reading Grammar

A. Conditional Sentences.
In a English, a sentence is conditional if it speaks of an action that will occur if another action occurs.

If he eats, he will not be hungry.

If he eats is the conditional clause of the sentence. *he will not be hungry* is the conclusion.

1. Conditional clauses are introduced by the following words:

si, if   nisi, if not, unless   etsi, even if   tametsi, even if   etiamsi, even if

2. The indicative is used if the conditional sentence refers to a definite fact. The same tense is used in both halves of the sentence.

Si audit, multa cognoscit.	If he is listening, he is learning many things.
Etsi audivit, nulla congnovit.	Even if he has listened, he has learned nothing.
Si audiet, multa cognoscet.	If he will listen, he will learn many things.

3. If a conditional sentence deals with a future event that probably will not happen, the present subjunctive is used. This kind of conditional sentence is called the future less vivid. (If there is a high probability of the condition being fulfilled, the future indicative (the future more vivid) is used instead.)

Si audiat, cognoscat.	If he were to listen (he will not), he would learn.
Si ad urbem eas, laetus sim.	If you were to come to the city, I would be happy.
Tametsi non ad urbem eas, laetus sim.	Even if you were not coming to the city, I would be happy.

4. The third kind of conditional sentence deals with conditions contrary to fact. The condition expressed in the sentence has not been met.

a. If the action takes place in the present, the imperfect subjunctive is used in both parts of the sentence. Note that this does not break the rules for sequences of tenses since the indicative is not used in the sentence.

Si veniret, adesset.	If he were coming, he would be here.
Nisi oppugnarent, non timeremus.	If they were not attacking, we should not be afraid.

b. If the action takes place in the past, the pluperfect subjunctive is used.

Si adfuisset, eam vidisses.	If she had been here, you would have seen her.
Nisi hoc dixisset, non oppugnavissent.	If he had not said this, they would not have attacked.

B. Concessive Clauses.

Concessive clauses are introduced by words such as *although, nevertheless, even though, despite the fact that,* and so forth. You have already learned how **cum** is used in a concessive clause in the subjunctive, and how the ablative absolute is used in a concessive clause with a participle. The words **quamquam, etsi, tametsi, etiamsi,** or **quamvis** may also be used. The word **tamen,** *nevertheless,* is often used in the second half of the sentence.

1. If **quamquam** is used, or if **etsi,** meaning *although,* is used, then the sentence deals with a definite fact and the indicative is used.

Quamquam diu acriterque vidimus, mulierem non invenimus.
Although we have looked for a long time and keenly, we have not found the woman.

Etsi bene pugnabunt, tamen urbs capietur.
Although they will fight well, nevertheless, the city will be captured.

2. If **quamvis** is used, then the sentence deals with a possibility instead of with a fact. The subjunctive is used in the concessive clause and the indicative is used for the main verb.

Quamvis mulierem non veniamus, diu acriterque videbimus.
Although we may not find the woman, we shall look long and keenly.

3. If **etiamsi, tametsi,** or **etsi** meaning *even if* are used, then the sentence is a conditional sentence, and follows the rules for conditionals given above.

Reading

The following section is taken from Cicero's First Oration Against Cataline. In this passage, he attempts to convince Cataline, as he will later attempt to convince Cataline's cohorts, to leave Rome.

In Catalinam II	Against Cataline 2, 16–18, adapted from the Second Oration Against Cataline, delivered in the senate.

Nunc vero quae tua est ista vita? Sic enim iam tecum loquar, non ut odio permotus esse videar, quo debeo, sed ut misericordia quae tibi nulla debetur.	Now, truly, what is this life of yours? For I shall speak with you thus, not as if I seemed to be moved by hatred, which I ought, but as if by pity, of which none is owed to you.

Venisti paulo ante in senatum. Quis te ex hac tanta frequentia, tot ex tuis amicis ac necessariis salutavit? Vocis exspectas contumeliam, cum sis gravissimo iudicio taciturnitatis oppressus?

You came, a little before, into the Senate. Who welcomed you out of such a crowd as this, out of so many of your friends and relatives? Do you wait for an insult of the voice when you have been crushed by the most grave judgment of silence?

Servi mehercule mei si me isto pacto metuerent ut te metuunt omnes cives tui, domum meam relinquerem: tu tibi urbem non arbitraris? Et si me meis civibus suspectum tam graviter viderem, carere civium quam infestis omnium oculis conspici mallem: dubitas quorum mentus sensusque vulneras, eorum aspectum praesentiamque vitare?

By Hercules, if my slaves feared me in that manner as all your fellow citizens fear you, I should leave my house: Do you not think that [you should leave] the city? And if I saw that I was suspected so gravely by my fellow citizens, I should prefer to avoid my fellow citizens than to see the unfriendly eyes of all: Do you hesitate to avoid the looks and the presence of those whose minds and senses you are wounding?

Si te parentes timerent tui neque eos ratione ulla placere posses, ut opinor, ab eorum oculis concederes. Nunc te patria quae communis est parens omnium nostrum metuit et iam diu nihil te iudicat nisi de parricidio suo cogitare.

If your parents feared you, nor were you able to calm them by any manner, you would withdraw from their eyes, as I think. Now your native land, which is the common parent of all of us, fears you and judges that for a long time now, you consider nothing except her murder.

Practice Exercises

No. 195. Translate these conditional sentences:
1. Si me vulneraveris, te vitavero.
2. Tametsi non salutatus esset, venisset.
3. Nisi metuerim, pugnaverim.
4. Tametsi milites Caesaris metuissent, urbes vicosque Helvetiorum oppugnavissent.
5. Tametsi Catilina non Roma discedat, Cicero populum de coniuratio eius moneat.
6. Si te amavissem, te narravissem.
7. Si illa adfuerit, nos crediderit.
8. Tametsi ibi adfuisses, nihil fecisses.
9. Tametsi litteras scribamus, non eas legant.
10. Nisi Allobroges arma tradidissent, Caesar casas suas incendisset.

No. 196. Translate the following sentences, which contain concessive clauses:
1. Quamquam me suspicis, tamen te credo.
2. Etsi mulieram nescivisti, eam audivisti.
3. Quamvis non audiant, Cicero loquetur.
4. Quamvis Catilina non salutetur, tamen in senatum veniet.
5. Etsi miles vitatus est, vivit.
6. Quamvis urbs capiatur, tamen non metuemus.
7. Quamquam corpus tuum abest, mens tua adest.

No. 197.
1. Give the present subjunctive of adsum.
2. Give the future perfect indicative, active and passive, of exsolvo.
3. Give the pluperfect subjunctive, active and passive, of suscipio.
4. Give the imperfect subjunctive, active and passive, of vulnero.
5. Give the perfect indicative, active and passive, of vivo.

AN OVERVIEW OF LATIN LITERATURE

Latin literature is usually divided into six periods. The first of these is the *Early Period,* and it covers Latin literature before 80 B.C. The second period, the *Golden Age,* lasted from 80 B.C. until A.D. 14. During this period, Classical Latin reached its height as a written language. The Golden Age is further subdivided into the *Ciceronian* period and the *Augustan* period. The Ciceronian period, named after the orator Cicero, whose command of Latin few could equal, ran from 80 B.C. through 43 B.C. The Augustan period, named after Augustus Caesar, lasted from 43 B.C. until A.D. 14.

The *Silver Age* of Latin literature ran from A.D. 14 through A.D. 138. It shows a decline in standards. The fourth period, called the *Patristic Period,* ran from the late second century through the fifth century. The major writers included the Church Fathers (**patres**). During this period the Romance languages were developing from local dialects of Latin. The fifth period ran from the sixth through the fourteenth centuries. It is called the *Medieval Period,* and the literature of this period was written in looser, more flexible Medieval Latin rather than in Classical Latin. However, your knowledge of Classical Latin will enable you to read the literature of this period with little difficulty.

The sixth and final period runs from the fifteenth century until the present day. It is called the *Modern Period.* Much of the literature from this period is written in Classical Latin, as people rediscovered the literature of the earlier periods.

Indirect Speech

Reading Vocabulary

Nouns

Carnutes, Carnutum, m. pl., Carnutes
initium, initii or initi, n., beginning, start (initiation)
maiores, maiorum, m. pl., ancestors, forefathers
salus, salutis, f., health, safety (salutary)

casus, casus, m., downfall, overthrow, fate
Acco, Acconis, m., Acco
pollicitatio, pollicitationis, f., promise
legio, legionis, f., legion

Noun and Adjective

princeps, principis, m. (as noun,) chief; first, foremost (principal)

Adjectives

postremus, postrema, postremum, last, finally
clandestinus, clandestina, clandestinum, secret,
    hidden (clandestine)

vetus, veteris, old, aged (veteran)

Verbs

recido, recidere, recepi, receptus, recoil, fall

sancio, sancire, sanxi, sanctus, consecrate

absum, abesse, abfui, be absent, be away from

recupero, recuperare, recuperavi, recuperatus, recover, get back (recuperate)

vindico, vindicare, vindicavi, vindicatus, defend, protect; in libertatem vindicare, set free

deleo, delere, delevi, deletus, destroy, obliterate (delete)

effero, efferre, extuli, elatus, carry forth, bring out. Conjugated like fero.

intercludo, intercludere, interclusi, interclusus, shut off, stop

misereor, misereri, miseritus sum, pity, feel sorry for

profiteor, profiteri, professus sum, declare, acknowledge, say

recuso, recusare, recusavi, recusatus, refuse, reject (recusant)

posco, poscere, poposci, ask, beg, demand

audeo, audere, ausus sum, dare (audacity)

polliceor, polliceri, pollicatus sum, promise

agito, agitare, agitavi, agitatus, consider, discuss

caveo, cavere, cavi, cautus, beware of, guard against (caution)

desero, deserere, deserui, deseritus, desert, abandon

egredior, egredi, egressus sum, quit, surpass, go beyond (egress)

iureiuro, iureiurare, iureiuravi, iureiuratus, swear by an oath

praesto, praestare, praestavi, praestatus, be better than, be superior to

queror, queri, questus sum, complain about (querulous)

Conjunctions

priusquam, before

quoniam, because, now that

Reading Grammar

The subjunctive is used in subordinate clauses in indirect speech.

A direct statement uses the indicative:

Urbs deleta est.   The city was destroyed.

An indirect statement uses the indicative and the infinitive. The subject of the infinitive is put into the accusative:

Putavi urbem deli.   I thought that the city was destroyed.

However, if the indirect statement has a subordinate clause, the subjunctive is used in that clause, even if the indicative would be used in direct speech.

Putavi urbem qui capta esset deli.   I thought that the city which had been captured was destroyed.

The subordinate clause is **qui capta esset,** *which had been captured.* **qui** is in the nominative because it is the subject of this clause. The verb, **capta esset,** is in the pluperfect subjunctive because the action in the subordinate clause takes place before the action of the main verb, which is from the secondary sequence.

More examples follow:

1. Direct speech:

Scribit libros.	He writes the books.
Scripsit libros.	He wrote the books.

2. Direct speech with a subordinate clause:

Scribit libros quos legis.	He writes the books *which you read.*
Scribit libros quos legisti.	He writes the books *which you have read.*
Scipsit libros quos legis.	He wrote the books *which you read.*
Scripsit libros quos legisti.	He wrote the books *which you have read.*

You will note that the subordinate clauses in the sentences above are in the indicative, because this is direct speech.

3. Indirect speech:

Dico eum libros scribere.	I say that he writes the books.
Dico eum libros scripsisse.	I say that he wrote the books.
Dixi eum libros scribere.	I said that he wrote the books.
Dixi eum libros scripsisse.	I said that he had written the books.

Both **eum** and **libros** are in the accusative. **libros** is accusative because it is the direct object of the infinitve, and **eum** is accusative because it is the subject of the infinitive. The present infinitive is used when the action takes place at the same time as that of the main verb, **dico.** The perfect infinitive is used when the action takes place before that of the main verb.

4. Indirect speech with a subordinate clause:

Dico eum libros quos legas scribere.	I say that he writes the books which you read.
Dixi eum libros quos lectus sis scribere.	I said that he wrote the books which you read.
Dixi eum libros quos lectus esses scripsisse.	I said that he had written the books which you had read.

Reading

The following is another excerpt from Caesar's *Commentaries on the Gallic War.* This reading is drawn from the seventh book, where the leaders of the Gauls are attempting to conspire against Caesar.

Commentarii de Bello Gallico

Commentaries on the Gallic War,
adapted from 7, 1–2.

Inter se principes Galliae de Acconis morte queruntur; posse hunc casum ad ipsos recidere demonstrant, miserantur communem Galliae fortunam, omnibus pollicitationibus ac praemiis deposcunt qui belli initium faciant et sui capitis periculo Galliam in libertatem vindicent.

The chiefs complained among themselves about the death of Acco; they pointed out that this fate could fall on themselves; they pitied the common fortune of Gaul; they asked with all [kinds of] promises and rewards for those who would make a beginning of the war and free Gaul at the risk of their own heads.

In primis rationem esse habendam dicunt, priusquam eorum clandestina consilia efferantur, ut Caesar ab exercitu intercludatur. Id esse facile quod neque legiones audeant absente imperatore egredi, neque imperator sine praesidio ad legiones pervenire possit. Postremo in acie praestare interfici quam non veterem belli gloriam libertatemque quam a maioribus acceperint recuperare.

His rebus agitatis profitentur Carnutes se nullum periculum communis salutis causa recusare principesque ex omnibus bellum facturos pollicentur et, quoniam in praesentia obsidibus cavere inter se non possint ne res efferatur, ut iureiurando sanciatur, petunt, ne facto initio belli ab reliquis deserantur.

First, they said that there would have to be a way, before their secret plans were carried abroad, for Caesar to be shut off from the army. [They said that] this would be easy because neither would the legions dare to go out when the general was absent nor could the general arrive at the legions without a guard. At last, [they said that] to die in battle is better than not to recover the old glory of war and freedom which they had received from their ancestors.

When these matters had been considered, the Carnutes said that they themselves refused no danger for the cause of the common safety and they promised that they, first of all, would make war, and, because in the present situation, they could not guard against [betrayal] among themselves with hostages, lest the matter be carried abroad, they sought that it be consecrated by swearing an oath, lest, when a beginning of war had been made, they be deserted by those remaining.

Practice Exercises

No. 198. Translate these sentences:
1. Dixit Helvetios qui in agris incolerent urbem delevisse.
2. Dicunt mulierem quam sciam adesse.
3. Professus est milites quos Caesar imperavisset arma obsidesque tradidisse.
4. Dico puellas quae haec pollicatae sint in libertatem vindicatas esse.
5. Dices sagittam quae puerum necaverit in silva amissam esse.
6. Putaverunt legionem quae Caesarem deservisset redituram esse.
7. Putamus coniurationem quam Cicero patefecerit Romam volneraturam esse.
8. Sentio verbi qui ab te narreris ab omnibus credi.
9. Putavisti pollicitationes quae ab frequentia Carnutum factae essent parricidium cauturas esse.
10. Imperavit virum qui filios filiasque eius pastus sit laudari.

No. 199.
1. Give all six infinitives of recido.
2. Give the four participles of recuso.
3. Give the imperfect active indicative of queror.
4. Give the perfect subjunctive, active and passive, of praesto.

Chapter Ten Review

Vocabulary Review

Nouns

1. Acco
2. Allobroges
3. annua
4. aspectus
5. bonitas
6. Carnutes
7. casus
8. coniuratio
9. contumelia
10. deditio
11. desiderium
12. fames
13. frequentia
14. fructus
15. Helvetii
16. initium
17. iudicium
18. ius
19. Latobrigi
20. legio
21. lenitas
22. magnitudo
23. maiores
24. mens
25. ministerium
26. misercordia
27. necessarius
28. nemo
29. Nicaea
30. Nicomedia
31. officium
32. obses
33. odium
34. pactum
35. parens
36. parricidium
37. pollicitatio
38. princeps
39. praesentia
40. ratio

41. res publica
42. Rhenus
43. salus
44. senatus
45. sensus
46. severitas
47. taciturnitas
48. Tulingi
49. vespera
50. vicus

Pronouns

1. aliquis, aliquid
2. iste, ista, istud
3. quidam, quaedam, quiddam

Adjectives

1. Aurelius
2. clandestinus
3. communis
4. hesternus
5. honestus
6. infestus
7. inutilis
8. iste
9. otiosus
10. periculosus
11. perpetuus
12. plerusque
13. postremus
14. princeps
15. pristinus
16. publicus
17. quantus
18. salvus
19. senex
20. superior

Verbs

1. absum
2. accipio
3. accelero
4. adfirmo
5. adsequor
6. adsum
7. agito
8. amitto
9. arbitror
10. audeo
11. careo
12. caveo
13. cogito
14. comperio
15. concedo
16. conquiro
17. consequor
18. credo
19. damno
20. deleo
21. desceno
22. deseo
23. vulnero
24. dubito
25. effero
26. egredior
27. erro
28. evenio
29. exeo
30. existimo
31. exsolvo
32. flagito
33. fungor
34. haesito
35. impero
36. incolo
37. intercludo
38. iudico
39. iureiuro
40. lego

41. loquor
42. metuo
43. misereor
44. nescio
45. opinor
46. oportet
47. oro
48. pascor
49. patefacio
50. patior
51. perfero
52. permitto
53. permoveo
54. persuadeo
55. pertimesco
56. placo
57. polliceor
58. posco
59. praesto
60. proficiscor
61. profiteor
62. profugio
63. purgo
64. quaero
65. queror
66. recido
67. recupero
68. recuso
69. reddeo
70. refero
71. rescisco
72. restituo
73. retineo
74. revertor
75. saluto
76. sentio
77. suspicio
78. tabesco
79. tolero
80. transeo

Adverbs

1. fortasse
2. frugaliter
3. ita
4. modeste
5. nimis
6. paulo
7. quantum
8. rursus
9. sic
10. unde
11. ut, uti
12. vehementer

Conjunctions

1. an
2. etiamsi
3. etsi
4. ne
5. nisi
6. num
7. priusquam
8. quamvis
9. quoniam
10. si
11. tametsi,
12. ut, uti
13. utinam
14. vel . . . vel

Interjections

1. mehercule

Practice Exercises

No. 200.
1. Give all the subjunctive forms of **loquor.**
2. Give all the infinitives of **oro.**
3. Give all the participles of **concedo.**
4. Give all the subjunctive forms of **possum.**
5. Give all the indicative forms of **sentio.**

Reading

Publius Vergilius Maro

You have already read one passage from *The Aeneid* in the Seventh Review Section. In the following passage, Jupiter prophesies the founding of Rome to Venus, the mother of Aeneas.

Parce metu, Cytherea, manent immota tuorum
fata tibi; cernes urbem et promissa Lavini
moenia sublimemque feres ad sidera caeli
magnanimum Aenean; neque me sententia vertit.
Hic tibi (fabor enim, quando haec te cura remordet,
longius et volvens fatorum arcana movebo)
bellum ingens geret Italia populosque ferocis
contundet moresque viris et moenia ponet,
tertia dum Latio regnantem viderit aestas,
ternaque transierint Rutulis hiberna subactis.
At puer Ascanius, cui nunc cognomen Iulo
additur (Ilus erat, dum res stetit Ilia regno),
triginta magnos volvendis mensibus orbis
imperio explebit, regnumque ab sede Lavini
transferet, et Longam multa vi muniet Albam.
Hic iam ter centum totos regnabitur annos
gente sub Hectorea, donec regina sacerdos
Marte gravis geminam partu dabit Ilia prolem.
Inde lupae fulvo nutricis tegmine laetus
Romulus excipiet gentem et Mavortia condet
moenia Romanosque suo de nomine dicet.

His ego nec metas rerum nec tempora pono;
imperium sine fine dedi. Quin aspera Juno,
quae mare nunc terrasque metu caelumque fatigat,
consilia in melius referet, mecumque fovebit
Romanos, rerum dominos gentemque togatam.
Sic placitum. Veniet lustris labentibus aetas
cum domus Assaraci Phthiam clarasque Mycenas
servitio premet ac victis dominabitur Argis.
Nascetur pulchra Troianus origine Caesar,
imperium Oceano, famam qui terminet astris,
Iulius, a magno demissum nomen Iulo.
Hunc tu olim caelo spoliis Orientis onustum
accipies secura; vocabitur hic quoque votis.
Aspera tum positis mitescent saecula bellis;
cana Fides et Vesta, Remo cum fratre Quirinus
iura dabunt; dirae ferro et compagibus artis
claudentur Belli portae; Furor impius intus
saeva sedens super arma et centum vinctus aenis
post tergum nodis fremet horridus ore cruento.

Aeneidos, I, 257–296

ANSWERS

Chapter One

Grammar Practice No. 1

puella	the girl	casa	the cottage
puellae	of the girl	casae	of the cottage
puellae	to, for the girl	casae	to, for the cottage
puellam	the girl	casam	the cottage
puella	from, with, by, in the girl	casa	from, with, by, in the cottage
puella	O girl	casa	O cottage
puellae	the girls	casae	the cottages
puellarum	of the girls	casarum	of the cottages
puellis	to, for the girls	casis	to, for the cottages
puellas	the girls	casas	the cottages
puellis	from, with, by in the girls	casis	from, with, by, in the cottages
puellae	O girls	casae	O cottages
terra	the land	femina	the woman
terrae	of the land	feminae	of the woman
terrae	to, for the land	feminae	to, for the woman
terram	the land	feminam	the woman
terra	from, with, by, in the land	femina	from, with, by, in the woman
terra	O land	femina	O woman
terrae	the lands	feminae	the women
terrarum	of the lands	feminarum	of the women
terris	to, for the lands	feminis	to, for the women
terras	the lands	feminas	the women
terris	from, with, by, in the lands	feminis	from, with, by, in the women
terrae	O lands	feminae	O women
aqua	the water	agricola	the farmer
aquae	of the water	agricolae	of the farmer
aquae	to, for the water	agricolae	to, for the farmer
aquam	the water	agricolam	the farmer
aqua	from, with, by, in the water	agricola	from, with, by, in the farmer
aqua	O water	agricola	O farmer
aquae	the waters	agricolae	the farmers
aquarum	of the waters	agricolarum	of the farmers
aquis	to, for the waters	agricolis	to, for the farmers
aquas	the waters	agricolas	the farmers
aquis	from, with, by, in the waters	agricolis	from, with, by, in the farmers
aquae	O waters	agricolae	O farmers

Grammar Practice No. 2

porto	I carry, do carry, am carrying	laudo	I praise, do praise, am praising
portas	you carry	laudas	you praise
portat	he, she, it carries	laudat	he, she, it praises
portamus	we carry	laudamus	we praise
portatis	you carry	laudatis	you praise
portant	they carry	laudant	they praise
laboro	I work, do work, am working	voco	I call, do call, am calling
laboras	you work	vocas	you call
laborat	he, she, it works	vocat	he, she, it calls
laboramus	we work	vocamus	we call
laboratis	you work	vocatis	you call
laborant	they work	vocant	they call

Practice Exercise No. 1

1. aquas, the waters	3. terrae, the lands	5. stellis, by the stars	7. laboratis, you work
2. puellarum, of the girls	4. agricolis, for the farmers	6. vocant, they call	8. portamus, we carry

Practice Exercise No. 2

1. of the farmers	4. for the woman	7. you call
2. the, a girl	5. by the lands	8. they are working
3. the cottages	6. he, she, it is praising	9. we like

Practice Exercise No. 3

1. we	2. he, she, it	3. I	4. you	5. they

Practice Exercise No. 4
1. direct object, acc.
2. prepositional phrase, abl.
3. subject, nom.
4. indirect object, dat.
5. possession, gen.

Practice Exercise No. 5
1. portamus
2. amat
3. porto
4. laudamus
5. vocant
6. laboratis
7. portat
8. vocas
9. amamus
10. laudatis

Practice Exercise No. 6
1. casam parvam
2. mearum filiarum
3. pulchras stellas
4. tua terra
5. filiae malae
6. casis Romanis
7. puellas parvas
8. aquam bonam
9. feminae parvae
10. casarum pulchrarum

Practice Exercise No. 7
1. you are
2. he, she, it is; there is
3. they are; there are
4. I am
5. you are
6. we are

Practice Exercise No. 8
1. natantne? Do they swim?
2. portasne? Are you carrying?
3. amamusne? Do we like?
4. laboratne? Does he (she, it) work?
5. vocatisne? Are you calling?
6. suntne? Are they? Are there?
7. natamusne? Do we swim?
8. portatne? Is he (she, it) carrying?
9. estisne? Are you?
10. laudasne? Do you praise?
11. laudatne? Does he (she, it) praise?
12. vocantne? Are they calling?
13. estne? Is he (she, it) there? Is there?
14. natasne? Do you swim?
15. amantne? Do they love?

Practice Exercise No. 9
1. you love/are loving/do love
2. we praise
3. you call
4. I work
5. they love
6. you call
7. he (she, it) swims
8. we carry
9. you work
10. he (she, it) praises

Check on Roman Numeral Practice No. 1

13	1100	43	502	120
300	25	610	420	10300
9	900	36	95	74

Check on Roman Numeral Practice No. 2

LIX	XLII	LXV	MMCCXXII	DCCCXVIII or CCMXVIII
CCCIV	VXL	MLXVI	XXVI	CCLXXI
LXXXV, XXCV	MCDXCII	DCCLIII	CMLX	CI

Practice Exercise No. 10
1. the girl's cottage
2. a supply of water
3. the farmers' land
4. the women's cottages
5. the sailor's native country
6. the sailor's island
7. the farmer's daughter
8. the sailors' cottages
9. an abundance of stars

Practice Exercise No. 11
1. Feminae, the women
2. Puella, the girl
3. Agricolae, the farmers
4. Nauta, the sailor
5. Agricola, the farmer
6. Filiae, the daughters
7. Patria, the native country
8. Insulae, the islands
9. Filia, the daughter

Practice Exercise No. 12
1. magna, big
2. pulchrae, pretty
3. bonae, good
4. Romanae, Roman
5. mala, bad
6. tua, yours
7. parvae, small
8. pulchra, beautiful
9. bona, good

Practice Exercise No. 13
1. agricola, a farmer
2. nautae, sailors
3. patria, native country
4. casae, cottages
5. nauta, a sailor
6. feminae, women
7. puella, a girl
8. agricolae, farmers
9. silva, a forest

Practice Exercise No. 14
1. toward the road
2. in the cottage
3. with the woman
4. into the wood
5. out of the cottages
6. away from the land
7. away from the cottages
8. out of the forests
9. into the islands
10. toward the streets
11. into the forests
12. with the girl
13. in or on the water
14. toward the water
15. away from the girls
16. toward the island
17. out of the land
18. with the farmer
19. in the native country
20. with the girls

Practice Exercise No. 15

1. aquam, water
2. fabulam, a story
3. aquam, water
4. Nautam, the sailor
5. Agricolas, the farmers
6. fabulam, a story
7. viam, the road
8. Terram, the land
9. terram, the land

Practice Exercise No. 16

1. Feminae, to the women
2. Nautae, to the sailor
3. Nautis, to the sailors
4. Puellae, to the girl
5. Puellis, to the girls
6. Feminis, to the women
7. Agricolis, to the farmers
8. Feminae, to the woman
9. Puellis, to the girls

Practice Exercies No. 17

1. you walk; you are walking, you do walk
2. he, she, it tells / is telling / does tell.
3. they walk; they do walk; they are walking
4. I dwell; I am dwelling; I do dwell
5. we sail; we are sailing; we do sail
6. you give; you are giving; you do give
7. he, she, it gives / is giving / does give
8. they call; they are calling; they do call
9. you work; you are working; you do work
10. we carry; we are carrying; we do carry
11. you praise; you are praising; you do praise
12. they love; they are loving; they do love
13. you are
14. we are
15. they swim; they are swimming; they do swim
16. you swim; you are swimming; you do swim
17. he, she, it fights / is fighting / does fight.
18. we fight; we are fighting; we do fight
19. I attack; I am attacking; I do attack
20. they attack; they are attacking; they do attack

Chapter One Review

Vocabulary Review

Nouns

1. farmer
2. water
3. Britain
4. cottage
5. supply, abundance
6. troops
7. Europe
8. story
9. rumor, renown, report
10. woman
11. daughter
12. Germany
13. inhabitant
14. island
15. Italy
16. Julia
17. sailor
18. peninsula
19. native country
20. girl
21. forest, woods
22. star
23. land, earth
24. road, way, street

Adjectives

1. ancient, old
2. good
3. clear, bright, famous
4. wide
5. long
6. large, great
7. bad, evil
8. my, mine
9. much
10. many
11. small
12. pretty, beautiful
13. Roman
14. your, yours

Verbs

1. walk
2. love, like
3. give
4. dwell, live
5. help, aid
6. work
7. praise
8. point out, show
9. tell, relate
10. swim
11. sail, cruise
12. attack
13. carry
14. fight
15. be
16. call

Adverbs

1. well
2. why
3. badly
4. not

Prepositions

1. from, away from
2. to, toward
3. with
4. from, out from
5. in, on; into

Conjunctions

1. and
2. because

Practice Exercise No. 18

1. Europam antiquam
2. aquae pulchrae
3. silvis parvis
4. stellas claras
5. insularum multarum
6. terra Romana
7. filias bonas
8. famam malam
9. puellarum pulchrarum
10. incolis multis

Practice Exercise No. 19

1. casae, f.
2. feminae, f.
3. stellae, f.
4. aquae, f.
5. fabulae, f.
6. insulae, f.
7. puellae, f.
8. copiae, f.
9. filiae, f.
10. nautae, m.
11. terrae, f.
12. Britanniae, f.
13. famae, f.
14. Italiae, f.
15. silvae, f.
16. patriae, f.
17. incolae, m. or f.
18. Europae, f.
19. agricolae, m.
20. viae, f.

Practice Exercise No. 20

1. amare	5. vocare	9. habitare	13. natare
2. laudare	6. oppugnare	10. portare	14. pugnare
3. navigare	7. monstrare	11. narrare	15. ambulare
4. esse	8. dare	12. laborare	

Practice Exercise No. 21

1. Nominative Case, Subject; Predicate Noun or Adjective
   Genitive Case, Possession
   Dative Case, Indirect Object
   Accusative Case, Direct Object; Prepositional Phrases
   Ablative Case, Prepositional Phrases
   Vocative Case, Direct Address

2. insula lata, wide island
   insulae latae, of the wide island
   insulae latae, to, for the wide island
   insulam latam, wide island
   insula lata, from, with, by, in the wide island
   insula lata, O wide island

   insulae latae, wide islands
   insularum latarum, of the wide islands
   insulis latis, to, for the wide islands
   insulas latas, wide islands
   insulis latis, from, with, by, in the wide islands
   insulae latae, O wide islands

   via longa, long road
   viae longae, of the long road
   viae longae, to, for the long road
   viam longam, long road
   via longa, from, with, by, in the long road
   via longa, O long road

   viae longae, long roads
   viarum longarum, of the long roads
   viis longis, to, for the long roads
   vias longas, long roads
   viis longis, from, with, by, in the long roads
   viae longae, O long roads

3. laboro, I work; I am working; I do work
   laboras, you work; you are working; you do work
   laborat, he, she, it works; he, she, it is working; he, she, it does work
   laboramus, we work; we are working; we do work
   laboratis, you work; you are working; you do work
   laborant, they work; they are working; they do work.

   laudo, I praise; I am praising; I do praise
   laudas, you praise; you are praising; you do praise
   laudat, he, she, it praises; he, she, it is praising; he, she, it does praise
   laudamus, we praise; we are praising; we do praise
   laudatis, you praise; you are praising; you do praise
   laudant, they praise; they are praising; they do praise

   sum, I am
   es, you are
   est, he, she, it is; there is
   sumus, we are
   estis, you are
   sunt, they are; there are

Chapter Two

Practice Exercise No. 22

1. we are	5. you wait for	9. he, she, it overcomes	13. we build
2. they conquer	6. he, she, it builds	10. they sail	14. they walk
3. he, she, it stands	7. they are; there are	11. you give	15. you stand
4. he, she, it is; there is	8. we swim	12. you call	

Practice Exercise No. 23

1. in Italy	4. toward Italy	7. on the peninsula	10. with the girl
2. toward Britain	5. in the province	8. in front of the cottages	11. in the woods
3. with the women	6. with the troops	9. behind the cottages	12. toward the road

Practice Exercise No. 24

1. of the inhabitant; to, for the inhabitant; the inhabitants; O inhabitants
2. Why do they work?
3. You help your native country.
4. He is carrying the booty.
5. He fights well.
6. They are pretty.
7. of many victories
8. a famous native country
9. a long story
10. out of the cottage
11. away from the road
12. Where is he (she, it)?
13. Here I am.
14. in front of the island
15. after the victory
16. with the troops
17. out of the provinces
18. There are troops here.
19. toward the streets
20. There is the province.
21. There are the women.
22. There is glory.
23. There are many girls.
24. Where are they?
25. Here they are.

Practice Exercise No. 25

1. to, for, from, with, by, in the field
2. to, for, from, with, by, in the wars
3. of the battles
4. of the boy; the boys
5. the ally
6. the friends
7. the camp
8. the swords
9. the help, aid
10. to/for/from/with/by/in the message/messenger
11. the dangers
12. of the weapons, arms
13. of the town
14. the man
15. the enemies

Practice Exercise No. 26

1. **amici**, the friends
2. **puerorum**, of the boys
3. **agris**, to, for, from, with, by, in the fields
4. **bellorum**, of the wars
5. **oppida**, the towns
6. **viri**, the men
7. **pericula**, dangers
8. **gladiorum**, of the swords
9. **nuntios**, messengers
10. **auxiliis**, to, for, from, with, by, in the aids
11. **nuntiis**, to, for, from, with, by, in the messages
12. **viris**, to, for, from, with, by, in the men
13. **periculis**, to, for, from, with, by, in the danges
14. **agri**, the fields
15. **bella**, the wars

Practice Exercise No. 27

1. of the
2. the, an
3. the, a
4. about
5. through
6. of the
7. of
8. the
9. the
10. of

Practice Exercise No. 28

1. out of the field
2. Are they arming?
3. a narrow street
4. friends
5. with the boy
6. He plows there.
7. behind the camp
8. of the friends
9. with the man
10. They fight a war.
11. They point out the towns.
12. They give arms to the man.
13. We tell stories about the war.
14. He likes dangers.
15. The camp is in the field.

Practice Exercise No. 29

1. My friend is there.
2. toward your cottages
3. out of the deep ditches
4. with famous men
5. in front of the Roman camp
6. in back of my fields
7. about good water
8. through the large forest
9. of the bad friends; the bad friends

Practice Exercise No. 30

1. virorum multorum
2. filiae meae
3. frumento bono
4. meis filiis
5. pueros agros
6. puellae miserae
7. soci liberi
8. feminam miseram
9. agris pulchris

Practice Exercise No. 31

Column I
1. many **viros**
2. sick **pueri**
3. pretty **oppidum**
4. many **servorum**
5. happy **puellam**
6. good **fili**
7. bad **famam**
8. wretched **equis**
9. Roman **terrae**
10. happy **agricola**

Column II
3. multos
5. aegri
1. pulchrum
2. multorum
4. laetam
6. boni
8. malam
9. miseris
10. Romanae
7. laetus

Practice Exercise No. 32

1. curamus
2. liberas
3. laboratis
4. portat
5. aro
6. necant
7. nuntiat
8. occupamus
9. statis

Practice Exercise No. 33

1. They are free.
2. of the happy mistress
3. into deep water
4. concerning great cares
5. in wide fields
6. about good masters
7. Why are you happy?
8. There are many people.
9. We are ill.
10. with good friends
11. in free lands
12. She is pretty.
13. Are they pretty?
14. He is unhappy.
15. many things

Practice Exercise No. 34

1. nostram
2. tuas
3. sua
4. sua
5. vestrae
6. nostram
7. sui
8. suarum
9. meam

Practice Exercise No. 35

1. I fear
2. he, she, it sees
3. you fear
4. he/she/it adores
5. they rule
6. you see
7. they fear
8. we have
9. we rule
10. they have
11. he, she, it fears
12. you see
13. I have
14. you rule
15. you adore

Practice Exercise No. 36

1. ancient gods
2. of/to/for the Roman goddess; Roman goddesses
3. of my friends
4. your booty
5. our daughters
6. his, her, its, their master
7. his, her, their son
8. his/her/its/their wisdom; from/with/by/in his/her/its/their wisdom
9. our glory

Practice Exercise No. 37

1. Your glory is not great.
2. Why do you kill your enemy?
3. Is the messenger telling many things?
4. The men are walking across their own fields.
5. The women are in their cottages.
6. Your daughters are sick today.
7. Many people sail across the ocean.
8. They are our goddesses.
9. They are our gods.
10. The woman cares for her daughters.
11. I am standing in front of the cottages.
12. He does not have many things.
13. We are telling about the moon.
14. Your fortune is good.
15. The slaves fear their masters.
16. Why are you not afraid?
17. We see a beautiful temple.
18. He has a camp there.
19. We see the boys in the back of the ditch.
20. You have great wisdom.

Chapter Two Review

Vocabulary Review

Nouns

1. field
2. friend
3. arms, weapons
4. aid, help
5. war
6. sky, heaven
7. camp
8. care
9. goddess
10. god
11. mistress
12. master
13. horse
14. son
15. fortune, fate, luck
16. ditch
17. grain
18. sword
19. glory
20. Greece
21. Spain
22. (personal) enemy
23. moon
24. messenger, message
25. ocean
26. town
27. danger
28. booty, plunder
29. battle
30. province
31. boy
32. queen
33. wisdom
34. slave, servant
35. comrade, ally

Adjectives

1. sick, ill
2. high, deep
3. narrow
4. happy
5. free
6. wretched, unhappy
7. our, ours
8. his, hers, its, their
9. your, yours

Verbs

1. worship, adore
2. build
3. arm
4. plow
5. care for, cure
6. await, expect, wait for
7. have, hold
8. free, set free
9. kill
10. announce, report
11. seize, take possession of
12. rule
13. stand
14. surpass, overcome
15. fear, be afraid of

Adverbs

1. even, also
2. here, in this place
3. today
4. there, in that place
5. often
6. where, when

Prepositions

1. before, in front of
2. about, concerning, down from
3. through
4. behind, in back of
5. across

Conjunctions

1. but

Practice Exercise No. 38

1. aedificare	5. videre	9. stare	13. timere
2. nuntiare	6. liberare	10. curare	14. habere
3. exspectare	7. regnare	11. necare	15. occupare
4. superare	8. arare	12. adorare	

Practice Exercise No. 39

1. deae, f.	6. socii or soci, m.	11. pueri, m.	16. viri, m.
2. proelii or proeli, n.	7. fortunae, f.	12. agri, m.	17. gladii or gladi, m.
3. provinciae, f.	8. amici, m.	13. castrorum, n.	18. curae, f.
4. belli, n.	9. inimici, m.	14. periculi, n.	19. praedae, f.
5. oceani, m.	10. reginae, f.	15. victoriae, f.	20. equi, m.

Practice Exercise No. 40

1.   a. **Cur viris frumentum non datis?**   b. **Datne incolis insularum curam bonam?**
2.   sto   I stand; I am standing; I do stand
     stas   you stand; you are standing; you do stand
     stat   he, she, it stands; he, she, it is standing; he, she, it does stand
     stamus   we stand; we are standing; we do stand
     statis   you stand; you are standing; you do stand
     stant   they stand; they are standing; they do stand
     timeo   I fear; I am fearing; I do fear
     times   you fear; you are standing; you do stand
     timet   he, she, it fears; he, she, it is fearing; he, she, it does fear
     timemus   we fear; we are fearing; we do fear
     timetis   you fear; you are fearing; you do fear
     timent   they fear; they are fearing; they do fear

Practice Exercise No. 41

1. our farmers
2. of the happy daughters
3. high sky
4. of, to, for a free country; free countries
5. your slave
6. his, her, their sons
7. wretched people
8. narrow roads
9. your messenger; your message
10. my fortune; from, with, by, in my fortune
11. many people
12. small boy
13. of the wide fields
14. good care; from, with, by, in good care
15. of the long sword

Practice Exercise No. 42

1. O friends	5. O master	9. O messengers	13. O many friends
2. O wars	6. O mistress	10. O my slave	14. O good farmer
3. O goddesses	7. O son	11. O good man	15. O our friend
4. O god	8. O glory	12. O good girl	

Reading

Give me a thousand kisses, then a hundred,
then another thousand, then a second hundred,
then up to a thousand more, then a hundred.
At the last, when we have given many thousands,
we shall mix their count, lest we know,
or lest any wicked person might envy us,

when he learns our kisses are so many.
        Catullus 5

I hate and I love. Why I do this, perhaps you ask.
I do not know, but I feel it happen and I am tortured.
        Catullus 8

The Vulgate Bible

In the beginning was the Word, and
the Word was with God, and the Word was
God. The same was in the beginning
with God. All things were made by him;
and without him was not any thing made
that was made; in him was life,
and the life was the light of men. And the light
shineth in darkness; and the darkness
comprehended it not. There was a man sent
from God, whose name was John. The same
came for a witness, to bear witness of the Light,
that all men through him might believe. He was
not that Light, but was sent to bear witness
of that Light. That was the true Light,
which lighteth every man that cometh
into the world. He was in the world,
and the world was made by him,
and the world knew him not.

Gospel According to St. John, 1, 1–10

Chapter Three

Practice Exercise No. 43

1. You have friends, haven't you? Certainly.
2. Are they building cottages? Yes. They are building cottages.
3. You are indeed afraid, aren't you? I am indeed afraid.
4. The people are not fighting, are they? The people are not fighting.
5. The roads are not long, are they? The roads are not at all long.
6. Why are they walking toward the town?
7. Is the man staying in the building? The man is staying in the building.
8. Is the province free? The province is truly free.
9. He isn't sailing on the ocean, is he? He is not sailing on the ocean.

Practice Exercise No. 44

1. videtis
2. potest
3. habeo
4. adoras
5. video
6. eunt
7. iuvat
8. manent
9. habes
10. statis
11. parant
12. debemus
13. possunt
14. aedificas
15. oppugnant
16. ambulatis
17. timet
18. properat

Practice Exercise No. 45

1. ambulare
2. pugnare
3. necare
4. superare
5. vocare
6. natare
7. iuvare
8. laborare
9. oppugnare
10. manere
11. navigare
12. ire

Practice Exercise No. 46

1. Why is he preparing grain there?
2. You like the Latin language, don't you?
3. Where do your buildings stand?
4. You ought not to give swords to the boys.
5. The gods also have their own weapons.
6. They tell the story about the long war of Troy.
7. Aeneas is sailing with his men to Italy.
8. The god helps the people of Greece.
9. Why do the Romans fear their allies?
10. He sees the clear moon in the sky.

Practice Exercise No. 47

1. debebamus
2. parabam
3. properabant
4. manebant
5. timebat
6. videbas
7. curabam
8. adorabamus
9. locabas
10. dabatis
11. habebatis
12. stabat
13. laudabam
14. manebas
15. videbamus
16. habebas
17. portabatis
18. iuvabat
19. vocabat
20. timebamus

Practice Exercise No. 48

1. he, she, it was pointing out
2. I call
3. we prepare
4. you were ruling
5. you ought
6. you fear
7. he, she, it was; there was
8. you fight
9. I was hurrying
10. they used to see
11. you were praising
12. you carry
13. we were going
14. I was able
15. we remain
16. he, she, it was saving
17. I was placing
18. you were attacking
19. you were having
20. you were; you used to be
21. he, she, it was able
22. they were going
23. you were conquering
24. they tell

Practice Exercise No. 49

1. when he was standing
2. with the daughter
3. when we work
4. when I wait for; when I await
5. with friends
6. when he, she, it conquers
7. with a wolf
8. when you see
9. when he, she, it was; when there was
10. when you were fighting
11. with the girl
12. when they were; when there were
13. with my uncle
14. with the Romans
15. with many women

Practice Exercise No. 50

1. He does not have many men in camp, does he?
2. We were preparing today to be there.
3. Your friend has a good reputation in our town.
4. I was preparing to stay with the girls.
5. He often kills many wolves in the forests, doesn't he?
6. The Romans ought not to fear the swords of the Sabines.
7. When they build a town, they place temples and buildings there.
8. Why do they give rewards to their slaves?
9. The farmer was in the field with his friend.
10. You are without water, aren't you?

Practice Exercise No. 51

1. he, she, it attacks
2. they were setting free
3. I shall see
4. he, she, it will remain
5. they were; they used to be
6. they are; there are
7. they ought; they owe
8. to love; to like
9. you will have
10. you were fighting
11. they were giving
12. he, she, it will be; there will be
13. they will stir up
14. he, she, it will warn
15. to carry
16. he, she, it will fear
17. you will fight
18. we shall conquer
19. we were preparing
20. they will be; there will be
21. they will tell
22. he, she, it was inciting
23. you were warning
24. we are
25. we were attacking
26. he, she, it will arouse
27. they were swimming
28. you were placing
29. you will save
30. you will help
31. you will go
32. I will be able

Practice Exercise No. 52

1. down from a clear sky
2. neighboring to my country
3. near to the island
4. with our friend
5. toward the high buildings
6. in the wide ditches
7. pleasing to his comrade
8. in front of the fields
9. friendly to the slaves
10. after the war
11. unfriendly to the queen
12. concerning your victory
13. through many battles
14. suitable to the man
15. without booty

Practice Exercise No. 53

1. present
2. future
3. imperfect
4. present
5. imperfect
6. imperfect
7. future
8. present
9. future
10. future
11. future
12. imperfect
13. future
14. imperfect
15. future
16. imperfect
17. future
18. imperfect
19. imperfect
20. future

Practice Exercise No. 54

1. He (she) will walk toward the narrow streets.
2. They were standing in front of the temples.
3. You were swimming out of the ocean.
4. They will fight on the water.
5. She was pleasing to the women.
6. They ought to have a free country.
7. The girls will swim.
8. He liked his neighbors.
9. You will save your uncles.
10. They will praise the queen.
11. Where ought you to be?
12. You were calling the boy.
13. He will be unfriendly to the messenger.
14. It is not near to the province.
15. We shall not fear your swords.
16. Your slaves are helping.
17. The man will remain there.
18. We were preparing a deep ditch.
19. The master will tell a story.
20. We shall plow the field.

Practice Exercise No. 55

1. walk! sing.
2. love! pl.
3. swim! pl.
4. fight! sing.
5. praise! pl.
6. sail! pl.
7. give! pl.
8. dwell! sing.
9. fear! pl.
10. see! sing.
11. stand! pl.
12. have! pl.
13. hold! sing.
14. rule! sing.
15. hold! pl.
16. conquer! pl.
17. stand! sing.
18. help! pl.
19. warn! pl.
20. stay! sing.

Practice Exercise No. 56

1. a farmer
2. sailors
3. Britain
4. a girl
5. our allies
6. a boy
7. enemies
8. a friend
9. boys

Practice Exercise No. 57

1. The sick boy, your son, will stay in the town.
2. You ought to have allies in the battle, O friend.
3. Arouse your men, O Roman people, against war.
4. Warn the inhabitants of Gaul, O messengers.
5. I shall call the Sabines, our neighbors, to the games.
6. See the temple, O girls, beautiful buildings.
7. Rome, a town in Italy, will be famous.
8. Remember Gaul, O my son.
9. Shall we have a big forum, O friends?
10. I shall wait for my uncles, the messengers.

Chapter Three Review

Vocabulary Review

Nouns

1. building
2. chest, box
3. uncle
4. barbarian
5. neighbor
6. forum, market place
7. Gaul
8. a Gaul
9. a German
10. Latinus
11. Latium
12. lieutenant, legate
13. language
14. game
15. wolf
16. memory
17. people
18. reward
19. river bank
20. Rome
21. a Roman
22. the Sabines
23. Troy
24. life

Adjectives

1. friendly
2. savage, uncivilized, barbarian
3. neighboring
4. pleasing
5. fit, suitable
6. unfriendly
7. Latin
8. near

Verbs

1. owe, ought
2. arouse, stir up, incite
3. place, put
4. remain, stay
5. warn, advise
6. prepare, get ready
7. hurry, hasten
8. save, preserve
9. hold, keep, have
10. remember
11. go
12. be able, can

Adverbs

1. certainly, indeed, surely
2. tomorrow
3. thus, so; yes
4. not at all, by no means
5. expects the answer "yes"
6. expects the answer "no"
7. now
8. then
9. truly, in truth

Prepositions

1. against
2. on account of, because of
3. for, in behalf of
4. without

Conjunctions

1. and also, and

Practice Exercise No. 58

1. simple question
2. simple question
3. simple question
4. answer "no"
5. answer "yes"
6. answer "no"
7. simple question
8. simple question
9. simple question

Practice Exercise No. 59

1. debebam
2. locabas
3. incitabat
4. parabatis
5. tenebamus
6. servabas
7. tenebam
8. manebamus
9. monebat

Practice Exercise No. 60

1. videbo
2. stabunt
3. timebis
4. necabitis
5. habebimus
6. aedificabo
7. superabis
8. curabimus
9. nuntiabunt

Practice Exercise No. 61

1. serva, servate
2. mone, monete
3. incita, incitate
4. naviga, navigate
5. para, parate

6. tene, tenete
7. propera, properate
8. neca, necate
9. pugna, pugnate

Practice Exercise No. 62

1. popule, populi
2. memoria, memoriae
3. legate, legati
4. amice, amici
5. femina, feminae

6. bellum, bella
7. avuncule, avunculi
8. vir, viri
9. fili, filii
10. agricola, agricolae

Reading

Gaius Iulius Caesar

The entire nation of the Gauls is quite devoted to religious rites . . . They worship the god Mercury especially. There are very many statues of him; they say he is the inventor of all the arts; they believe he is the guide on roads and journeys, and that he has the greatest power over money transactions and merchants. After him come Apollo and Mars and Jupiter and Minerva. About these, they have almost the same idea as other races: Apollo dispels diseases; Minerva hands down the skills of handcrafts and arts; Jupiter holds the power over the gods, and Mars rules over wars.

Commentaries on the Gallic War, 6, 16, 17

The Bible

In the beginning, God created the heaven and the earth. And the earth was without form, and void; and darkness was upon the face of the deep. And the Spirit of God moved upon the face of the waters.

And God said: Let there be light. And there was light. And God saw the light, that it was good; and God divided the light from the darkness. And God called the light Day, and the darkeness he called Night. And the evening and the morning were the first day.

And God said: Let there be a firmament in the midst of the waters, and let it divide the waters from the waters. And God made the firmament, and divided the waters which were under the firmament from the waters which were above the firmament. And it was so. And God called the firmament Heaven. And the evening and morning were the second day.

And God said: Let the waters under the heaven be gathered together unto one place, and let the dry land appear. And it was so. And God called the dry land Earth; and the gathering together of the waters he called Seas. And God saw that it was good. And God said: Let the earth bring forth grass, the herb yielding seed, and the fruit tree yielding fruit after his kind, whose seed is in itself, upon the earth. And it was so. And the earth brought forth grass, and herb yielding seed after his kind, and the tree yielding fruit, whose seed was in itself, after his kind. And God saw that it was good. And the evening and morning were the third day.

Genesis I, 1–13

Chapter Four

Practice Exercise No. 63

1. you will be feared
2. I was praising
3. I am being cared for
4. they are praised
5. they will be related; they will be told
6. I shall stand
7. he, she, it was being armed
8. you are plowing
9. he, she, it will be seized
10. you will stand

11. he was killing
12. they will be built
13. I shall overcome; I shall conquer; I shall surpass
14. he will sail
15. I was living in
16. I was being pointed out
17. they were walking
18. he, she, it will be given
19. you are being helped; you are being aided
20. I shall be called

Practice Exercise No. 64

1. exspectabar
2. tenentur
3. monebitur
4. videbatur
5. amabitur
6. habetur
7. videbamini
8. portabitur
9. movebimini
10. parantur

11. laudabuntur
12. locamini
13. properabuntur
14. timemur
15. incitor
16. monebaris
17. servaris
18. debebatur
19. videntur
20. monebantur

Practice Exercise No. 65

1. with the lieutenant
2. with a sword
3. by the boys
4. with ditches
5. by friends
6. by a messenger
7. with uncles
8. by wars
9. by the masters
10. with a comrade
11. with horses
12. by arrows
13. by an archer
14. by a goddess
15. with a slave
16. with wisdom
17. by the people
18. with enemies
19. with water
20. by a man

Practice Exercise No. 66

1. Money will be given to the man and the girl because the boy is ill.
2. I was remembered when I was moving to the neighboring town.
3. They seem to grieve, but a gift will be brought.
4. On account of the dangers, the men were afraid of the letters.
5. Fight well for Britain, your native country.
6. Many people were walking toward the temples of the gods.
7. Where (when) will the game be given by your friend?
8. We were living in the cottage where you see the girls.
9. The man will not be attacked by a sword, will he?
10. The people were preparing to move camp, weren't they?

Practice Exercise No. 67

1. of the long peace
2. for the soldier
3. famous soldiers
4. Roman peace
5. your heads
6. to, for their dictators
7. your head
8. by happy men
9. suitable part
10. in an ancient city
11. of our sea
12. strong soldiers
13. good men
14. long peace
15. on their heads
16. against dictators
17. with the men
18. without your soldiers
19. about pleasing peace
20. friendly man

Practice Exercise No. 68

1. of the soldiers
2. of peace
3. the, a head
4. the, a part
5. in, on the cities
6. the seas
7. with the soldier
8. of the bridges
9. the enemy
10. about slaughter

Practice Exercise No. 69

1. **paces,** the peaces
2. **militibus,** from, with, by, in the soldiers
3. **capitibus,** to, for the heads
4. **partes,** parts
5. **hostibus,** to, for the enemy
6. **urbium,** of the cities
7. **caedes,** slaughters
8. **pontes,** bridges
9. **homines,** men
10. **capita,** heads
11. **militum,** of the soldiers
12. **partium,** of the parts
13. **homines,** the men
14. **pacum,** of peace
15. **dictatores,** the dictators
16. **pontibus,** to, for the bridges
17. **marium,** of the seas
18. **pontium,** of the bridges
19. **hostes,** the enemy
20. **urbibus,** from, with, by, in the cities

Practice Exercise No. 70

1. Cincinnatus was being called from his field and was giving aid.
2. Men rule on earth, but the gods rule heaven and earth.
3. Rewards will be given to a great man by the Roman people.
4. The Latin language will always be preserved.
5. He will not plow tomorrow, but he will soon save our country.
6. He was swimming toward the river bank because the bridge was not standing.
7. Fight well, O Horatius, for your country with your sword.
8. The soldiers, O my sons, will be armed with swords.
9. Because of the dangers, you ought to save your water.
10. The sailor loves the seam but the farmer loves his fields.

Practice Exercise No. 71

1. gods and goddesses
2. the god and the goddess
3. we have and we give
4. he (she, it) had and he (she, it) gave
5. a man and women
6. of the men and of the women
7. toward the sun and moon
8. toward the sun and moon
9. from the sea and land
10. from the land and sea
11. with force and weapons
12. with force and weapons

Practice Exercise No. 72

1. in the middle of the roads
2. in many towns
3. in a great war
4. on the tops of the buildings
5. in a good part
6. on (in) wide oceans
7. in many lands
8. in the middle of the sky
9. on top of the sea

Practice Exercise No. 73

1. toward the sea
2. from the cities
3. with their fathers
4. in front of the forum
5. behind the temple
6. concerning the box
7. without a plan, without advice
8. across the ocean
9. through the seas
10. because of wings
11. for your queen
12. against the people
13. among the enemy
14. by (away from) the men
15. away from the towns
16. in front of the camp
17. through the dangers
18. toward the master
19. across the field
20. concerning peace

Practice Exercise No. 74

1. he, she, it will be; there will be
2. he, she, it will be frightened
3. he, she, it was flying
4. he, she, it will swim
5. they grieve
6. we are being carried
7. he, she, it was being held
8. we shall be loved
9. I shall move
10. they were being praised
11. he, she, it was fighting
12. you will place
13. I shall be called
14. we were being warned
15. they will work
16. they are being stirred up
17. he, she, it will owe; he, she it ought
18. they are preparing
19. they were being cared for
20. you will be freed

Practice Exercise No. 75

1. The man, my uncle
2. O good friends
3. O good son
4. Of the nations, Italy and Germany
5. Because of the money, the reward
6. Of the women, of the queens
7. O famous man
8. The boy, a slave
9. To, for the girls, my daughters
10. O our father

Practice Exercise No. 76

1. vocare, to call
2. debere, to owe
3. ambulare, to walk
4. ire, to go
5. esse, to be
6. monere, to warn
7. timere, to fear
8. narrare, to tell
9. curare, to take care of
10. dolere, to grieve
11. nuntiare, to announce
12. volare, to fly
13. terrere, to frighten
14. adorare, to worship
15. movere, to move
16. parare, to prepare
17. servare, to preserve, to save
18. laudare, to praise
19. dare, to give
20. videre, to see

Practice Exercise No. 77

1. paravi, I have prepared
2. incitavi, I have aroused
3. aravi, I have plowed
4. debui, I have owed
5. liberavi, I have freed
6. ii, ivi I have gone
7. terrui, I have frightened
8. aedificavi, I have built
9. habitavi, I have lived in
10. monui, I have warned
11. properavi, I have hurried
12. habui, I have held
13. dedi, I have given
14. tenui, I have held; I have kept
15. servavi, I have preserved; I have saved
16. monstravi, I have shown; I have pointed out
17. timui, I have feared
18. natavi, I have swum
19. movi, I have moved
20. mansi, I have remained; I have stayed

Practice Exercise No. 78

1. **amatus,** having been loved
2. **habitus,** having been had
3. **liberatus,** having been freed
4. **necatus,** having been killed
5. **monitus,** having been warned
6. **exspectatus,** having been waited for
7. **narratus,** having been told
8. **territus,** having been frightened
9. **occupatus,** having been seized
10. **portatus,** having been carried
11. **datus,** having been given
12. **monitus,** having been warned
13. **servatus,** having been saved
14. **iutus,** having been helped
15. **visus,** having been seen; having seemed
16. **adoratus,** having been worshipped
17. **motus,** having been moved
18. **spectatus,** having been seen
19. **obtentus,** having been obtained
20. **locatus,** having been placed; having been put

Practice Exercise No. 79

1. Both your mother and your father were giving advice about courage.
2. In the middle of the town, there were many buildings.
3. The report about my nation will be carried by the messengers.
4. The girl and the boy are swimming under the water.
5. We ought to walk around the city and see many things.
6. You remember many bad things, don't you?
7. The sun seemed to be on the top of the water.
8. The nations of Europe will not always fight.
9. Sailors sail on seas and oceans.
10. Roman soldiers have great courage.

Chapter Four Review

Vocabulary Review

Nouns

1. wing
2. amphitheater
3. animal
4. year
5. slaughter
6. captive
7. head
8. speed, swiftness
9. wax
10. Ceres
11. Cincinnatus
12. the Colosseum
13. plan, advice
14. Crete
15. Daedalus
16. dictator
17. gift
18. gladiator
19. man
20. Horatius
21. enemy
22. Icarus
23. Those Below
24. Jupiter
25. work, toil, labor
26. letter
27. size, great size
28. sea
29. mother
30. Mercury
31. soldier
32. nation
33. part
34. father
35. peace
36. money
37. Pluto
38. bridge
39. Proserpina
40. arrow
41. archer
42. sun
43. star
44. city
45. courage, valor

Adjectives

1. middle, middle of
2. strong, robust
3. greatest, highest, top of

Verbs

1. grieve
2. move
3. secure, obtain
4. look at, watch
5. frighten, terrify, scare

Adverbs

1. long, for a long time
2. soon, presently
3. always

Prepositions

1. by; away from, from
2. around, about
3. among, between
4. under

Conjunctions

1. or
2. both . . . and
3. and

Practice Exercise No. 80

1. dolere
2. terrere
3. movere
4. vocare
5. obtinere
6. dare
7. spectare
8. volare
9. laudare
10. manere
11. debere
12. timere
13. habere
14. videre
15. necare
16. parare
17. occupare
18. stare
19. iuvare
20. monere

Practice Exercise No. 81

1. spectavi
2. curare
3. moneo
4. dedi
5. motus

6. paravi
7. servatus
8. territus
9. habito
10. laudare

Practice Exercise No. 82

1. of the animals and men
2. by the father
3. by the mothers
4. the sea and star
5. fathers and mothers

6. of speed and size
7. by Mercury
8. by the soldiers
9. by Pluto
10. war and peace

Practice Exercise No. 83

1. he, she, it was being praised
2. they will grieve
3. we were being warned
4. they are being killed
5. you are being called
6. they will be; there will be
7. we shall obtain; we shall secure
8. you are being seen; you seem
9. you were helping
10. I shall have; I shall hold
11. you will be moved
12. you can; you are able

13. they are being occupied; they are being seized
14. they were being feared
15. he, she, it will be prepared
16. you will give
17. you are being saved
18. they used to go
19. we were being prepared
20. it will be owed
21. you were being cared for
22. we were being watched; we were being looked at
23. they will frighten; they will terrify
24. I used to be; I was

Reading

Eutropius

He [Anthony] also stirred up a great Civil War, with his wife Cleopatra, queen of Egypt, urging it, since she hoped, with a womanly desire, to rule also in the City [Rome]. He ws defeated by Augustus in a famous and glorius naval battle near Actium, which is a place in Epirus, from which he escaped to Egypt and, because his future was without hope, since everyone was going over to the side of Augustus, he killed himself. Cleopatra let a snake bite her and died from its poison. Egypt was added to the Roman Empire by Octavius Augustus and Gaius Cornelius Gallus was put in command of it. Egypt had him as its first Roman judge.

Brevarium, Book 7, 7

The Bible

A Psalm of David, when he fled from Absalom his son

Lord, how are they increased that trouble me!
Many are they that rise up against me;
many there be which say of my soul:
There is no help for him in God.
But thou, O Lord, art a shield for me;
my glory, and the lifter up of mine head.
I cried unto the Lord with my voice,
and he heard me out of his holy hill.

I laid me down and slept;
I awaked; for the Lord sustained me.
I will not be afraid of ten thousands of people that have set themselves against me round about.
Arise, O Lord; save me, O my God;
for thou hast smitten all mine enemies upon the cheek bone;
thou hast broken the teeth of the ungodly.
Salvation belongeth unto the Lord; thy blessing is upon thy people.

Psalm 3

Chapter Five

Practice Exercise No. 84

1. ambulavi
2. laudavi
3. monui

4. debui
5. portavi
6. servavi

7. vocavi
8. movi
9. dedi
10. rogavi

Practice Exercise No. 85

1. he, she, it has asked
2. they have watched
3. we have warned, advised
4. I have helped, aided
5. you have been
6. you have killed
7. you have told, related
8. I have lived in, dwelt
9. I have seen
10. they have feared
11. you have grieved
12. you have had, held
13. we have owed, ought
14. they have worked
15. you have overcome, conquered
16. he, she, it has pointed out, shown
17. they have told, related
18. you have occupied, seized
19. we have prepared
20. he, she, it has flown

Practice Exercise No. 86

1. I had walked
2. they had adored
3. he, she, it had plowed
4. they had moved
5. we had remained, stayed
6. you had seen
7. you had prepared
8. you had given
9. you had held, kept
10. I had stood
11. he, she, it had prepared
12. they had placed
13. you had stirred up, aroused
14. you had cared for
15. I had swum
16. we had grieved
17. he, she, it had asked
18. they had watched, looked at
19. he, she, it had seen
20. you had called

Practice Exercise No. 87

1. you will have loved
2. he, she, it will have cared for
3. I shall have praised
4. we shall have placed
5. they will have had.
6. he, she, it will have frightened
7. he, she, it will have moved
8. they will have given
9. you will have stood
10. he, she, it will have held
11. we shall have called
12. I shall have saved
13. he, she, it will have carried
14. they will have prepared
15. you will have announced
16. we shall have told, related
17. you will have had
18. he, she, it will have owed
19. they will have worshipped
20. you will have walked

Practice Exercise No. 88

1. they have been
2. he, she has walked
3. he has been carried
4. they have been loved
5. you have been cared for
6. they have been praised
7. I have been warned
8. we have owed, ought to have
9. you have stood
10. it has been related, told
11. we have been called
12. I have swum
13. you have been saved
14. it has been announced
15. they have been moved
16. you have feared
17. he has been prepared
18. they have been placed
19. they have praised
20. you have moved

Practice Exercise No. 89

1. they had given
2. he, she, it had moved
3. he had been frightened
4. you had remained, stayed
5. you had held
6. he, she, it had fought
7. I had been praised
8. they had been cared for
9. you had been loved
10. you had been aroused, incited
11. they had been prepared
12. you had been occupied, seized
13. you had been freed
14. he had been killed
15. we had been saved
16. he had warned, advised
17. you had had
18. you had held, kept
19. we had been helped
20. they had worshipped

Practice Exercise No. 90
1. I shall have warned, advised
2. he, she, it will have been
3. it will have been carried
4. they will have been warned
5. they will have had
6. you will have frightened
7. we shall have moved
8. you will have been seen
9. he, she, it will have feared
10. she, will have been moved

11. we shall have given
12. they will have stood
13. we shall have been
14. you will have been killed
15. we shall have been praised
16. you will have been armed
17. they will have been cared for
18. it will have been placed
19. they will have been; there will have been
20. she will have been saved

Practice Exercise No. 91
1. it had been had
2. I shall have seen
3. they will have been attacked
4. you will have been praised
5. you had been carried
6. it will have been owed
7. they had owed
8. you have waited for
9. you have seen
10. it has been pointed out, shown

11. they have been warned, advised
12. we have been asked
13. they have looked at, watched
14. we have been moved
15. we had prepared
16. he has been warned, advised
17. he, she, it had stood
18. they had been given
19. they have told, related
20. I shall have held, kept

Practice Exercise No. 92
1. for many years
2. in the next year
3. for many hours
4. in the next hour
5. for seven hours

6. in the middle of the year
7. in six hours
8. for long years
9. in an hour
10. for twelve hours

Practice Exercise No. 93
1. to the cities
2. from the towns
3. from Rome
4. to Rome
5. into the camp
6. in front of the forum
7. in back of the garden
8. in the field
9. into the fields
10. down from the hills

11. out of the cottage
12. in the country
13. at home
14. away from the river
15. under the sea
16. under the walls
17. into the ditch
18. away from the temple
19. out of the roads
20. about, down from the sun

Practice Exercise No. 94
1. I shall see
2. he, she, it had fought
3. you were standing
4. we shall work
5. he, she, it had been; there had been
6. they will obtain
7. we were swimming
8. he, she, it will be; there will be
9. we see
10. it has been looked at; it has seemed

11. he, she, it will be moved
12. they had been built
13. you have been
14. we were being attacked
15. they have remained, stayed
16. he, she, it wants; he, she, it is willing
17. you do not want; you are not willing
18. I prefer to have; I prefer to hold
19. I was preferring
20. you will not want; you will be unwilling

Practice Exercise No. 95
1. Next year, we shall move to Rome.
2. For six hours, they remained in the city.
3. They had been attacked half way up the hill.
4. I stayed in Italy for many hours.
5. He (she) will be there for an hour.
6. They will work for many years, won't they?

7. He walked toward the town for many long hours.
8. He has not been freed by the king.
9. Are they in the garden with the boys?
10. I moved seven miles from the city.
11. Do not go to the city!
12. I prefer to remain in town.

Practice Exercise No. 96

1. they are sending
2. I have been shown, taught
3. we are being sought
4. he, she, it ought; owes
5. you had been warned
6. they will have been prepared
7. he, she, it has led
8. you have freed
9. I was worshipping
10. he, she, it will have sent

11. he, she, it will order
12. we were being watched, looked at
13. you are showing
14. they will ask
15. you were leading
16. he, she, it will send
17. I have been saved, preserved
18. you had feared
19. you had sought
20. they had remained, stayed

Practice Exercise No. 97

1. on account of the injury
2. from the battles
3. for six hours
4. on the road, march, journey
5. out of the territory

6. toward Gaul
7. away from the hill
8. in the letter
9. by the men; away from the men
10. into the river bank

Practice Exercise No. 98

1. I seek them.
2. of these (those) books
3. his, her garden
4. I gave these (those) things to them.
5. He was fighting.
6. You have seen him.
7. in these (those) places
8. to, for his (her) father
9. They are being sent by him.
10. You sent them.

11. this, that hour; in this, that hour
12. her, his, their own signals
13. out of these (those) cities
14. this (that) woman
15. We are being led by them.
16. their apples
17. his, her, their own kings
18. with them
19. this, that road, journey
20. this (that) cause

Practice Exercise No. 99

1. ducitur
2. ductus sum
3. ducebam
4. duxerunt
5. ducar
6. missus es
7. mittebant
8. mittetis
9. misisti
10. missus erat

11. petiti sunt
12. petiverimus
13. petetur
14. petit
15. petebas
16. currentur
17. cursus est
18. currit
19. currebantur
20. cucurrerat

Chapter Five Review

Vocabulary Review

Nouns

1. love
2. Apollo
3. Atalanta
4. Atlas
5. boldness, bravery, daring
6. cause, reason
7. hill
8. body
9. Eurystheus
10. end, border
11. territory
12. river
13. Hercules
14. the Hesperides
15. Hippomenes
16. hour
17. garden
18. fire
19. journey, march, way, route
20. Juno
21. law
22. book
23. place
24. a mile
25. miles
26. mountain, mount
27. delay
28. woman
29. wall
30. name
31. night
32. foot
33. apple
34. price
35. fight
36. Pythia
37. king
38. snake, serpent
39. signal, standard
40. Tarquinius

Pronouns

1. he
2. she
3. it

Adjectives

1. golden
2. twelve
3. nine

4. next, nearest
5. seven
6. six

7. Sibylline
8. proud, haughty
9. last, farthest

10. this, that

Verbs

1. increase, enlarge
2. run
3. point out, show

4. speak, say
5. teach, show
6. lead

7. order, command
8. prefer
9. send

10. be unwilling, wish not to
11. seek
12. ask, ask for

Adverbs

1. at home
2. almost, nearly

3. afterwards
4. how long

5. in the country

Prepositions

1. into, onto; in, on

Conjunctions

1. after, when

Practice Exercise No. 100

1. in, on the feet
2. away from the hill
3. toward the rivers
4. out of the fields
5. into the fire
6. in, on the walls

7. about the body
8. in the country
9. from Rome
10. to Rome
11. at home
12. out of the night

Practice Exercise No. 101

1. he, she, it had been; there had been
2. we have ruled
3. he has been asked
4. you will have carried
5. they have given
6. they have placed
7. they have been given
8. you have sent
9. it will have been sought
10. it had been increased
11. we have moved
12. we have been

13. they had been aroused
14. you had hurried
15. they will have been; there will have been
16. I have been asked
17. he, she, it stood
18. you have called
19. we shall have been praised
20. he had had
21. he, she, it has preferred
22. they have wanted; they have been willing
23. I had preferred
24. you will not have wanted; you will not have been willing

Practice Exercise No. 102

1. in the next year
2. for seven hours
3. in the next hours
4. late in the year
5. for six years

6. on this (that) night
7. for these (those) nights
8. for these (those) years
9. in this (that) year
10. in this (that) hour

Practice Exercise No. 103

1. his, her, its
2. them
3. they
4. to, for him, her, it; they
5. it
6. them

7. she; they; them; from, with, by, in her
8. their
9. to, for, from, with, by, in them
10. him
11. they
12. from, with, by, in him, it

Practice Exercise No. 104

1. this (that) love
2. of this (that) boldness
3. these (those) names
4. these (those) causes
5. to, for, from, with, by, in these (those) territories
6. of these (those) journeys

7. these (those) apples
8. to, for this (that) woman
9. this (that) body
10. of this (that) place
11. to, for this (that) king
12. this (that) night

Reading

Marcus Valerius Martialis

I do not love thee, Sabidius, nor can I tell you why;
    this only I can say: I do not love thee.
        Epigrams, 1, 32

Tomorrow you will live, tomorrow, you always say, Postumus.
    Tell me when, Postumus, is that tomorrow coming?
How far away is your tomorrow, where is it? or where must it be sought?
    It doesn't lie hidden among the Parthians and Armenians, does it?
Already that tomorrow of yours has the years of Priam or Nestor.

    Tell me, for how much could that tomorrow of yours be bought?
You will live tomorrow? Today it is already too late to live, Postumus;
    he is wise, whoever has lived yesterday, Postumus.
        Epigrams, 5, 58

The Bible

    To everything there is a season,
and a time to every purpose under the heaven:
A time to be born, and a time to die;
a time to plant, and a time to pluck that which is planted;
A time to kill, and a time to heal;
a time to break down, and a time to build up;
A time to weep, and a time to laugh;
a time to mourn, and a time to dance;
A time to cast away stones, and a time to gather stones together;
a time to embrace, and a time to refrain from embracing;

A time to get, and a time to lose;
a time to keep, and a time to cast away;
A time to rend, and a time to sew;
a time to keep silence, and a time to speak;
A time to love, and a time to hate;
a time of war and a time of peace.
What profit hath he that worketh in that wherein he laboureth?
    Ecclesiastes, 3, 1–9

Chapter Six

Practice Exercise No. 105

1. because of the delay
2. because of my care
3. because of the dangers
4. because of fear
5. because of death
6. because of diligence
7. because of speed
8. because of boldness
9. because of the delays
10. because of the time

Practice Exercise No. 106

1. with zeal, eagerness
2. with great care
3. with great diligence, care
4. with great fear
5. with speed
6. with much zeal, eagerness
7. with great zeal, eagerness
8. with delay
9. with great speed
10. with great delay

Practice Exercise No. 107

1. posui
2. superare
3. dedi
4. capere
5. servatus
6. facio
7. verti
8. terrui
9. duco
10. tuli

Practice Exercise No. 108

1. he, she, it has ordered
2. you have led
3. they have shown
4. I was asking
5. we have made, done
6. he, she, it is being shown
7. you are being sent; will be sent
8. you are being taken, seized
9. he, she, it will look at, watch
10. we shall increase
11. they will seek
12. they were carrying
13. you were obtaining, getting
14. he, she, it was being turned
15. he, she, it had terrified
16. you had sought
17. they had taken, seized
18. they will have been moved
19. we had been led
20. he, she, it was taking, seizing

Practice Exercise No. 109

1. because of the hour
2. because of the weapon
3. in front of the camp
4. from fear
5. down from the tree; about the tree
6. by the king; away from the king
7. out of the trees
8. into this (that) place
9. with the father
10. with care

11. in, on the water
12. under the ocean
13. around the walls
14. against him
15. between, among the towns
16. through the field
17. in back of the camp
18. without them
19. across the sea
20. about, concerning the men

Practice Exercise No. 110

1. this wall
2. that city
3. in that place
4. these leaders
5. to, for those soldiers
6. to, for that lieutenant
7. these commanders
8. those plans
9. of that ocean
10. of these men
11. in that garden
12. that goddess
13. of that foot soldier
14. about this master

15. out of that tree
16. this hindrance
17. to, for these fathers
18. these ships
19. that book
20. to that girl
21. these weapons
22. of these parts
23. about that peace
24. of those sands
25. in these years
26. for that hour
27. that sign, standard
28. of this horse

Practice Exercise No. 111

1. his, her, its
2. he
3. to, for him, her, it; they
4. them
5. to, for, from, with, by, in them
6. of them, their
7. it; from, with, by, in him, it
8. to, for him, her, it

9. she; from, with, by, in her; them; they
10. they
11. she; them; they
12. her
13. them
14. him
15. them

Practice Exercise No. 112

1. the goddess herself, the very goddess
2. out of the temples themselves, out of the very temples
3. the same city
4. the men themselves, the very men
5. by the same youth
6. the same name, the very name
.7. of the same nation
8. on the very night, in the night itself
9. the same roads, ways
10. to, for, from, with, by, in the same men
11. out of the field itself, out of the very field
12. in the years themselves, in the very years
13. the boys themselves, the very boys
14. of the lieutenant himself, of the very lieutenant

15. the same hour, in the same hour
16. the law itself, the very law
17. the mountain itself, the very mountain
18. the girls themselves, the very girls
19. the same journey, road, way
20. by the women themselves, by the very women
21. at the same time
22. peace itself, the very peace
23. the same towns
24. in the cities themselves, in the very cities
25. of the same people
26. the same men
27. out of the same place
28. in the same years

Practice Exercise No. 113

1. to, for him (himself), her (herself), it (itself); they (themselves)
2. of (the same) him, her, it
3. (the same) it
4. she (herself); they (themselves); them (themselves)
5. them (themselves)

6. (the same) she; they; them; from, with, by, in her
7. (the same) him
8. of (the same) them
9. out of (the same) them
10. of him (himself), her (herself), it (itself)

Practice Exercise No. 114

1. they were able to lead
2. you can stay
3. he, she was not able to worship
4. he, she, it will be able to free
5. they can care for
6. we were not able to kill
7. I had been able to order
8. you can show, point out
9. we were able to ask
10. I was not able to increase
11. we shall be able to help
12. you will be able to fight
13. they have not been able to call
14. I can not work
15. you have been able to stay
16. they become; they are made
17. he has been made; he has become
18. you will become; you will be made
19. they had become; they had been made
20. I was becoming; I was made
21. we make; we do
22. you will make; you will do
23. they make; they do
24. they were making; they were doing

Practice Exercise No. 115

1. in one year
2. no care
3. of which gift
4. to, for any ship
5. for all the years
6. with the father alone
7. of no deaths
8. to neither nation
9. in the other road
10. with, by another name
11. to which river
12. of any hill
13. to, for one book
14. for no reasons
15. by neither man

Practice Exercise No. 116

1. they had feared
2. you have been
3. they will send
4. he, she, it took
5. he, she, it will fear
6. they were looking at
7. they will be held
8. I shall be sent
9. they have been praised
10. it had become, been done, been made
11. you were sailing
12. they were being given
13. he, she, it carries on, bears
14. they had been; there had been
15. they have had

Practice Exercise No. 117

1. one is a boy, the other is not
2. at no time
3. of any war
4. toward which camp
5. the women themselves alone
6. of neither youth
7. other cities
8. one part
9. about neither girl
10. another road, journey, way

Practice Exercise No. 118

1. in a short hour
2. of a bold slave
3. swift horse
4. in, on a swift river
5. by bold men
6. for all times; all times
7. by a keen lieutenant
8. short life
9. at all hours
10. in a swift ship
11. bold work
12. in a short time
13. active troops
14. of a swift horse
15. active women
16. swift death, quick death
17. short journeys, roads
18. to a bold man
19. for a short year
20. in every, each place

Practice Exercise No. 119

1. of the golden sun
2. out of neither place
3. on the top of the mountain
4. of an easy journey
5. any hours
6. grave punishments
7. of the nearest nations
8. bold citizen
9. strong body
10. of swift rivers
11. Latin books
12. other men
13. your ship
14. of many fathers
15. of each king

Practice Exercise No. 120

1. Who are you?
2. To whom did he give those things?
3. Whom shall I see?
4. Whose eyes?
5. What things does he know?
6. With whom does he (she) walk?
7. By whom has he been captured?
8. Who is shouting?
9. Who is fighting?
10. Whose weapons?
11. What do you have?
12. Whom has he killed?
13. To whom shall I give it?
14. What has been asked?
15. To whom have you sent the gift?
16. Whom do you like?
17. Who is fleeing?
18. What is easy?
19. Whose is it?
20. With whom?
21. Whom will he send?
22. What is he doing?
23. Who are struggling?
24. By whom has it been carried out?

Practice Exercise No. 121

1. pugnare
2. mittere
3. regere
4. dare
5. laudare
6. rogare
7. scribere
8. videre
9. cognoscere
10. necare
11. capere
12. timere
13. habere
14. movere
15. parare
16. ducere
17. augere
18. servare
19. vincere
20. terrere

Practice Exercise No. 122

1. demonstrari
2. duci
3. moveri
4. iuberi
5. verti
6. armari
7. amari
8. ferri
9. doceri
10. occupari
11. mitti
12. geri
13. accipi
14. timeri
15. vocari
16. interfici
17. iuvari
18. teneri
19. cognosci
20. simulari

Chapter Six Review

Vocabulary Review

Nouns

1. youth
2. Africa
3. mind, spirit
4. tree
5. sand
6. Ariadne
7. gold
8. Bacchus
9. food
10. citizen
11. fleet
12. Cyclops
13. diligence, care
14. horseman, knight
15. flight, escape
16. Hannibal
17. Homer
18. hindrance
19. commander, general, emperor
20. injury, harm
21. labyrinth
22. Midas
23. Minos
24. the Minotaur
25. death
26. ship
27. eye
28. work
29. foot soldier
30. punishment, fine
31. poet
32. Polyphemus
33. gate, door, entrance
34. stone, rock
35. Silenus
36. zeal, eagerness
37. weapons
38. storm, bad weather
39. time
40. Theseus

Pronouns

1. he, she, it
2. he, she, it
3. he, she, it
4. he himself, she herself, it itself

Adjectives

1. sharp, active, keen
2. other, another
3. the one, the other
4. bold
5. short, brief
6. quick, swift
7. easy
8. brave, strong
9. heavy, severe, serious
10. this
11. the same
12. that
13. very, himself, herself, itself
14. neither
15. new
16. no, none
17. all, every
18. alone, only
19. all, whole
20. any

Verbs

1. take, seize, capture
2. shout, cry
3. learn, recognize, know
4. hasten, strive, contend
5. make, do
6. carry, bear
7. be made, be done, become
8. flee, run away, escape
9. carry on, wage
10. throw
11. kill
12. put, place
13. write
14. pretend
15. turn

Adverbs

1. meanwhile
2. at night

Prepositions

1. among, in the presence of
2. in front of; for, instead of
3. because of, on account of

Conjunctions

1. and so, therefore

Practice Exercise No. 123

1. they take, seize
2. it had been learned
3. they have been conquered
4. they will turn
5. we were killing
6. they have done, made
7. you had taken, seized
8. he, she, it was fleeing
9. he, she, it will be put
10. they will have carried on, waged
11. he, she, it writes
12. you throw
13. they will hurry
14. they have been put
15. it has been carried on, waged
16. you become, are made

Practice Exercise No. 124

1. because of death
2. because of injury
3. with great diligence
4. because of the general
5. because of food
6. because of the fleets
7. with a small punishment, fine
8. with great zeal, eagerness
9. because of the hindrance
10. because of the sand

Practice Exercise No. 125

1. him
2. his, her, its
3. them
4. that
5. he
6. their
7. the same things; she
8. his, hers, its
9. he
10. their
11. whom
12. what
13. whose
14. to, for whom
15. with whom

Practice Exercise No. 126

1. he, she was able to shout
2. they were able to take
3. you can do, make
4. we can put, place
5. you have been able to conquer
6. he, she, will be able to hurry
7. they have been able to write
8. we were able to recognize, learn
9. you are able to turn
10. they are able to carry on, wage

Practice Exercise No. 127

1. of one work
2. of all the citizens
3. another hindrance
4. new weapons
5. in a short time
6. to, for the whole stone
7. of no fear
8. any injury
9. bold horsemen, knights
10. swift punishment

Reading

Marcus Tullius Cicero

Oh what times these are! Oh what habits we have! The Senate knows these things, the consul sees them; this man, however lives. Does he live? Indeed, he even comes into the Senate, he becomes a participant in the public plans, he notes and designates with his eyes each single one of us for murder. We, however, brave men, seem to do enough for the Republic if we avoid the fury and weapons of this man. You, Catiline, should have been lead to your death by the order of the consul long ago; the destruction that you are plotting against us should have been brought against you.

First Oration Against Catiline, 2

Oro de Cerinton

About the Hydra

There is a certain animal, called the hydra, whose nature it is to bury itself in the mud so that it might be better able to glide. Finally, it enters the mouth of a crocodile, when it is sleeping, and thus, entering its stomach, it eats its heart and thus kills the crocodile.

Mystical interpretation: The hydra signifies the son of God, who has assumed the mud of our flesh so that he might slip more easily into the mouth of the devil, and thus, entering his stomach and eating his heart, he kills him.

About the Antelope

There is a certain animal that is called the antelope; when this animal plays in a thicket with its horns, finally its horns are entangled with the thicket so that it is not able to extricate them and then, it begins to cry aloud; when this is heard, hunters come and kill him.

Mystical interpretation: Thus it happens that many people are delighted and play with the occupations of this world and thus are entangled in these things so that they can not be torn away and thus by hunters, that is, by demons, they are taken and killed.

Chapter Seven

Practice Exercise No. 128
1. **pulchre**, beautifully
2. **longe**, far, distant
3. **magnopere**, greatly
4. **nove**, recently, newly
5. **acriter**, keenly
6. **graviter**, seriously
7. **breviter**, briefly
8. **alte**, on high
9. **grate**, with pleasure
10. **audacter**, boldly
11. **misere**, wretchedly
12. **proxime**, next, most recently
13. **fortiter**, bravely
14. **celeriter**, swiftly
15. **libere**, freely

Practice Exercise No. 129
1. you carry, do carry
2. I have, hold
3. they lead, are leading
4. he throws, is throwing
5. you have heard
6. he has been freed
7. they had been seen; had seemed
8. they had been heard
9. you have been received
10. I had been heard
11. they were hearing
12. he will have been prepared
13. he, she, it will hear
14. they have sought
15. they hear, do hear
16. you were being helped
17. we were being heard
18. we were turning
19. they will be taken, seized
20. you will be heard
21. you are being heard
22. he, she, it has done, made
23. they will ask
24. we have heard

Practice Exercise No. 130
1. they are fighting bravely
2. we saw very recently
3. he, she, it carried on with difficulty
4. they will be widely received
5. he, she walks far
6. they stand well
7. he easily recognized
8. he, she liked greatly

Practice Exercise No. 131
1. The place will be defended easily.
2. At first, nothing could be prepared.
3. Because of fear, you did not fight bravely.
4. Which door do you like?
5. The land by nature has been defended with difficulty.
6. Not only the king, but also the queen heard it.

Practice Exercise No. 132

1. a. who are making the journey with their forces
   b. The men, who are making the journey with their forces, are brave.
2. a. which he built
   b. The tower, which he built, was keeping the barbarians from the town.
3. a. with whom I was walking
   b. The woman, with whom I was walking, is my mother.
4. a. whose name we can not see
   b. The ship, whose name we can not see, is sailing toward Italy.
5. a. to whom I gave the letter
   b. The boy, to whom I gave the letter, will come quickly.
6. a. which you will have
   b. The fear, which you will have, will soon not be remembered.
7. a. to which they were fleeing
   b. The river, to which they were fleeing, was deep and wide.
8. a. about which he wrote
   b. The place, about which he wrote, is far from the city.
9. a. which he had
   b. Everything, which he had, now is mine.
10. a. whose boys you see
    b. The men, whose boys you see, are friends.

Practice Exercise No. 133

1. in what place?
2. which man?
3. what town?
4. what booty?
5. which men?
6. with what speed?
7. in what year?
8. of what name?
9. at what hour?
10. at what time?
11. with what soldiers?
12. of what citizens?
13. what baggage?, what hindrances?
14. of what size?
15. with what plan?

Practice Exercise No. 134

1. they make, do
2. he, she, it will order
3. you have found, learned
4. he, she, it will arrive
5. to be had
6. he, she, it was running
7. he, she, it had been
8. he, she, it took, seized
9. they have looked at
10. it was happening
11. you hear
12. you have arrived
13. he, she, it was fighting, hurrying
14. they had given
15. to be seen; to seem
16. they have prohibited
17. they will be; there will be
18. I shall be seen; I shall seem
19. to be asked
20. I shall have

Practice Exercise No. 135. a.

1. he, she, it has not been able
2. of that place
3. your sons
4. others come; some come
5. he, she wishes to come
6. brave people
7. because of the storm
8. with great zeal
9. he, she remained at home
10. of this, that nation
11. in the next year
12. my friend
13. all men
14. he, she fears nothing
15. not only your mother

Practice Exercise No. 135. b

1. you were fearing; fear!
2. you will follow
3. they will have tried
4. I shall have feared
5. they follow
6. I urge
7. he, she, it fears
8. you will have died
9. she had urged
10. they were dying
11. he, she, it will urge
12. you try
13. they will fear
14. he had tried
15. you were urging
16. we were following
17. he has died
18. we shall die
19. I had followed
20. she has tried

Practice Exercise No. 136

1. for many paces
2. your group; your hand
3. long attack
4. because of his arrival
5. each wing
6. of our armies
7. on your wing
8. out of the army
9. into the house
10. for six miles
11. against the armies
12. because of your arrival
13. the attack (attacks) of the enemy
14. group (groups) of soldiers
15. by the army

Practice Exercise No. 137

1. their battle lines
2. late in the day
3. on the next day
4. because of these things
5. of any hope
6. the whole thing
7. for one day
8. of what things?
9. our battle lines
10. what things?
11. in what battle line?
12. of each day
13. because of this (that) thing
14. in these battle lines
15. much hope

Practice Exercise No. 138

1. he, she has walked
2. we are seen; we seem
3. they were; there were
4. he, she, it had done, made
5. he, she was fleeing
6. he, she, it finds
7. it had been given
8. he, she, it can, is able
9. it has been drawn up
10. to be seen; to seem
11. they will have been left behind
12. they will fight
13. he, she, it has drawn up
14. he, she makes a journey
15. they will be heard

Practice Exercise No. 139

1. All things seem to be easy
2. After six days, neither soldier had any hope.
3. The captives whom you led back came out of their army.
4. Who greatly hindered the strong attack?
5. In one hour, the men will come home.
6. For what reason was he drawing up his battle line on the hill?
7. Among these things which we have is a small supply of water.
8. The soldiers in that wing are turning their horses toward the field.
9. Neither the wing nor the battle line saw hope.
10. Who among these peoples was holding the royal power?

Practice Exercise No. 140

1. you
2. we; us
3. by you
4. their; of them
5. she; they; them; from, with her
6. to, for her, him, it; they
7. you; from, with, by, in you
8. I
9. him
10. to, for me
11. with us
12. you
13. to, for you; from, with you
14. them
15. that; it
16. to him, her, it
17. his, hers, its
18. with you
19. their; of them
20. toward you
21. to you
22. your; of you
23. our; of us
24. about me
25. to, for them; from, with, by, in them
26. about them
27. she; from them; from, with, by, in her; they; them
28. with her
29. their; of them
30. them

Practice Exercise No. 141

1. to, for himself, herself, itself; to, for themselves
2. yourself; from, with, by, in yourself
3. by myself
4. yourselves
5. himself, herself, itself; themselves; from, with, by, in himself, herself, itself, themselves
6. to, for yourselves; from, with, by, in yourselves
7. to, for myself
8. to, for ourselves; from, with, by, in ourselves
9. myself; from, with, by, in myself
10. ourselves

Practice Exercise No. 142

1. The man himself does not know us.
2. I sent help to you.
3. We found you in this place.
4. Will you come with me?
5. You give books to us.
6. You do not hear him.
7. They were fleeing toward us.
8. He sent these things to me.
9. He (She) will not be able to walk home with you.
10. This is our native country.
11. You will tell this (that) to them.
12. We shall lead her home.
13. They were seeking peace from them.
14. I was being terrified by you and your sword.
15. We had saved ourselves at that time.
16. You can help us, can't you?
17. He saw their city.
18. We ourselves shall order them to come.
19. You will point out these things to us.
20. His spirit did not frighten me long.

Chapter Seven Review

Vocabulary Review

Nouns

1. line of battle	8. Eurydice	15. hand, group	22. region, boundary
2. arrival, approach	9. army	16. nature	23. kingdom
3. Athens	10. Hellespont	17. nothing	24. thing, matter, affair
4. state	11. Hero	18. Orpheus	25. Sparta
5. horn, wing	12. attack	19. pace	26. hope
6. day	13. want, scarcity	20. the Persians	27. Thermopylae
7. house, home	14. Leander	21. guard, garrison	28. tower

Pronouns

1. I	2. we	3. who, which, that; which, what	4. you (sing.)
			5. you (pl.)

Adjectives

1. ten	2. difficult, hard	3. of Marathon	4. first

Verbs

1. happen	5. desire, wish, want	9. draw up, form, train	12. lead back
2. address, call, name	6. withdraw, go away, leave	10. arrive	13. rule
3. place, station	7. lead out	11. keep off, hinder, prohibit, prevent, forbid	14. leave, leave behind
4. observe	8. hinder		15. find, discover
			16. know

Adverbs

1. now, already	2. greatly	3. too little, not enough	4. first, at first
			5. alone, only

Conjunctions

1. for	2. and not	3. neither . . . nor	4. as

Practice Exercise No. 143

1. **late**, widely
2. **acriter**, keenly
3. **difficile**, with difficulty
4. **misere**, wretchedly
5. **longe**, far
6. **magnopere**, greatly
7. **laete**, happily
8. **libere**, freely
9. **parum**, too little, not enough
10. **anguste**, narrowly

Practice Exercise No. 144

1. I shall come
2. he, she knew
3. he has been heard
4. we were arriving
5. they will be hindered
6. they will find, discover
7. you were being heard
8. it had been known
9. they have wished
10. you will be heard

Practice Exercise No. 145

1. whose
2. whom
3. who, which, that
4. who
5. with whom
6. we; us; ourselves
7. to, for me, myself
8. me; myself; from, with, by, in me, myself
9. of you
10. to, for you, yourself
11. with you, yourself
12. his, her, its
13. their, of them
14. him
15. her

Practice Exercise No. 146

1. to, for the army
2. the thing; things
3. of the horn, wing
4. the battle line
5. hope
6. of the hands, bands
7. on, from, with, by the day
8. to, for, from, with, by, in the attacks
9. the arrival
10. home; the house
11. to, for, from, with, by, in the things
12. horns, wings
13. of the armies
14. to, for the hand, group
15. to, for hope

Reading

Publius Vergilius Maro

They walked obscured by darkness, in the lonely night, through the shadows
and through the vacant kingdoms of Pluto, and the empty homes;
just as under the dim light of a wavering moon
is a journey in the woods, when Jupiter has hidden the sky in shadows
and black night has taken away the color from things.
Before the very entrance and in the very jaws of Orcus
Grief and avenging Cares have placed their couches,
and pale Diseases dwell, and sad Old Age,
and Fear, and Hunger persuading-evil, also base Want,
forms terrible to see, both Death and Toil,
then Sleep, the kinsman of Death, and evil Pleasures
of the mind, and death-bearing War on the threshold opposite,
and the iron chambers of the Furies, and mad Discord,
entwining her snaky hair with bloody fillets.
   Aeneid 6, 268–281

Jacques de Vitry

About a Tree on Which Women Were Hanging
I have heard about a certain other man, who had a tree in his garden, on which two of his wives had hanged themselves. A certain one of his neighbors said to him: "Certainly that tree is lucky and holds a good omen. I, however, have a very bad wife; I ask you, give me a young shoot from it, so that I may plant it in my garden."

About a Side of Bacon Which Was Hanging in a Certain Town
Once I passed through a certain town in France, where they had hung a ham or side of bacon in the street with this condition that, whoever might wish to swear on oath that he had lived one whole year with his wife after the marriage had been contracted in such a way that he had not regretted the marriage, might have the side of bacon. And although it had hung there for ten years, not one single man was found who might win the side of bacon, because all, inside of a year from the contract of marriage, regretted it.

Chapter Eight

Practice Exercise No. 147

1. fifteen
2. nine
3. twenty
4. five
5. sixteen
6. ten
7. three
8. seventeen
9. four
10. eleven
11. one hundred
12. fourteen
13. eight
14. nineteen
15. two
16. thirteen
17. seven
18. one
19. eighteen
20. one thousand

Practice Exercise No. 148

1. fourth
2. eigth
3. tenth
4. third
5. seventh
6. second
7. fifth
8. ninth
9. first
10. sixth

Practice Exercise No. 149

1. a thousand ships
2. three men
3. of thousands of soldiers
4. for fourteen days
5. of one man
6. twenty miles
7. a hundred boys
8. for five years
9. six of the soldiers
10. in seven hours
11. in a hundred years
12. eight of the boys
13. for two days
14. of ten laws; ten of the laws
15. three places
16. two of the provinces
17. in twelve days
18. of six animals
19. eighteen of the kings
20. in three years

Practice Exercise No. 150
1. to, for, of the tenth girl
2. on the eighth day
3. in the sixth hour; the sixth hour
4. the seventh ship
5. in the fifth summer
6. for the third day
7. in the tenth winter
8. the seventh attack
9. to, for, of the ninth hour; ninth hour
10. in the first year

Practice Exercise No. 151
1. a difficult way, road
2. a wretched home
3. of the free men
4. keen fears
5. similar armies
6. on a long day, for a long day
7. on a high mountain
8. swift rivers
9. wide streets
10. of pretty girls

Practice Exercise No. 152
1. narrower streets
2. a taller boy
3. of happier girls
4. a friendlier people
5. a longer road, way
6. in more pleasing places
7. of more famous sisters
8. a longer winter, for a longer winter
9. wider rivers
10. bolder man

Practice Exercise No. 153
1. of a very sweet spring
2. out of very pretty gardens
3. a very narrow temple
4. because of very wretched memories
5. very famous oracles
6. a very happy citizen
7. out of a very wide field
8. with very pretty mothers
9. on a very new ship
10. very short names

Practice Exercise No. 154
1. This is a very wretched place.
2. The bravest men arrived at the island.
3. The very keen horses were among the first.
4. What is an easier way to Greece?
5. The people of Italy are very free.
6. This is the narrower part of the water.
7. These things are also very similar.
8. We saw a very deep and rather wide river.
9. Our men chose a shorter way to the city.
10. You can see a high building from this place.

Practice Exercise No. 155
1. These towers are higher than those.
2. You are taller than your father.
3. Those roads are not easier than others.
4. You are more like your father than your mother.
5. Men are much stronger than women.
6. His house in the country is newer than that in the city.
7. The boy is happier than his sister.
8. The barbarians are much bolder than their neighbors.
9. He will be friendlier to you than to me.
10. Is the hand quicker than the eye?

Practice Exercise No. 156
1. they will be; there will be
2. it has been shown
3. he, she, it decided
4. he, she, it will be prepared
5. they were leading
6. he has been left behind
7. he, she, it will be sent
8. you are being carried
9. we were seeing
10. he, she has walked

Practice Exercise No. 157
1. more things
2. better
3. of the worst
4. of a bigger
5. of smaller
6. of very many
7. to, for, from, with, by, in more
8. the next
9. more suitable, of more suitable
10. most suitable

Practice Exercise No. 158

1. in very many cities
2. out of smaller springs
3. the greatest courage
4. best voice
5. down from higher walls
6. more water
7. more suitable time
8. of the worst thing; to, for the worst thing
9. toward a better part
10. with a bigger army
11. on a longer day
12. very many states
13. worse end
14. best years
15. smallest sister

Practice Exercise No. 159

1. wide
2. widely
3. wider
4. more widely
5. very wide
6. very widely
7. free
8. freely
9. freer
10. very free
11. more freely
12. very freely
13. pretty
14. more pretty
15. very pretty
16. prettily
17. more prettily
18. very prettily
19. swift
20. swiftly
21. swifter
22. more swiftly
23. very swift
24. very swiftly
25. keen
26. keenly
27. keener
28. more keenly

Practice Exercise No. 160

1. They were being attacked most severely.
2. He fights more bravely.
3. They have been burned quickly.
4. They will speak much more briefly.
5. He will be warned very boldly.
6. They drew up the battle line with difficulty.
7. He waged war more keenly.
8. They walk proudly.
9. He gave more pleasingly.
10. He is praised very highly.
11. They have been sent more widely.
12. He gave very freely.
13. He sails very far.
14. He moves more wretchedly.
15. They were seen recently.
16. They move more beautifully.
17. He will fear very keenly.
18. They have been taken boldy.
19. He was speaking very briefly.
20. They fight bravely.

Practice Exercise No. 161

1. well
2. greatly
3. badly
4. much
5. little
6. long
7. often
8. longer
9. more
10. more
11. better
12. worse
13. less
14. more often
15. most
16. most
17. longest
18. most often
19. best
20. worst

Practice Exercise No. 162

1. They arrive more often.
2. He fought as long as possible.
3. He has been aroused more.
4. He was being hindered more.
5. You have been loved best.
6. It has been heard most often.
7. He walks with less difficulty.
8. They are very powerful among us.
9. He flies more swiftly.
10. He will stay much longer.

Chapter Eight Review

Vocabulary Review

Nouns

1. summer
2. Creusa
3. Cupid
4. difficulty
5. spring, fountain
6. winter
7. command
8. light
9. husband
10. marriage
11. great number, multitude
12. burden, weight
13. oracle
14. more
15. harbor, port
16. Psyche
17. sister
18. wife
19. wind
20. word

Adjectives

1. equal, level, fair
2. sweet
3. immortal
4. larger
5. largest
6. better
7. smallest
8. smaller
9. mortal
10. best
11. worse
12. worst
13. most
14. next, following
15. next, following

Verbs

1. fall
2. collect, drive, compel
3. finish, complete, carry out
4. decide, establish
5. come together, assemble
6. give up, surrender
7. choose, select
8. sleep
9. arouse, stir up
10. set fire to, burn
11. overcome, crush
12. be most powerful
13. be more powerful
14. take back, receive
15. take up, undertake

Adverbs

1. before
2. twice
3. more
4. most, especially
5. much, by much
6. never
7. formerly, once upon a time
8. on the next day
9. as possible; than
10. over, above

Conjunctions

1. either . . . or
2. while
3. for
4. although
5. also

Practice Exercise No. 163
1. one of the sisters
2. three rivers
3. two years; for two years
4. a thousand years
5. two wives
6. a hundred words
7. of one voice
8. twenty springs, fountains
9. the fourth hour; in the fourth hour
10. on the fifth day
11. in the second year
12. the seventh word
13. the first oracle
14. in the fourth harbor, port
15. out of the sixth gate, door

Practice Exercise No. 164
1. the longer winter; for the longer winter
2. the very pretty summer
3. of the longest years
4. the sweeter word
5. a very similar burden
6. of an immortal voice
7. easier way, journey
8. clearer lights
9. of a very keen difficulty
10. of stronger husbands

Practice Exercise No. 165
1. sweet, sweeter, sweetest
2. keen, keener, keenest
3. long, longer, longest
4. similar, more similar, most similar
5. high, higher, highest
6. free, freer, freest
7. swift, swifter, swiftest
8. wide, wider, widest
9. clear, clearer, clearest
10. bold, bolder, boldest

Practice Exercise No. 166
1. big, bigger, biggest
2. small, smaller, smallest
3. good, better, best
4. bad, worse, worst
5. much, more, most
6. many, more, very many

Practice Exercise No. 167
1. he was walking farther
2. he has been oppressed miserably
3. he sleeps little
4. it will burn for a very long time
5. they have been more keenly aroused
6. they were touching more
7. they have surrendered more easily
8. they are very powerful
9. it, he, she will be more powerful
10. they will be forced less easily

Reading

Phaedrus

He who rejoices that he is praised by words of flattery,
to late pays his penalty with lowly repentance.
When a crow started to eat the cheese
he snatched from a window, perching in a lofty tree,
a wolf saw him; thus, with flattery, he began to speak:
"Oh what a brightness, crow, that your feathers have.
What grace of body, what charms of looks you possess.
If you should have a voice, no bird would be above you."

Then he, foolish one, while he tried to show off his voice,
dropped the cheese from his mouth. This quickly
the tricky fox snatched in his greedy teeth.
Then the crow, deceived by his stupidity, groaned, but too late.
    Phaedrus I, 13

Stabat Mater

At the Cross her station keeping,
Stood the mournful Mother weeping,
Close to Jesus at the last.
Though her soul, of joy bereaved,
Bowed with anguish, deeply grieved,
Now at length the sword hath passed.
Oh how sad and sore distressed
Was that Mother, highly blest,
Of the sole begotten One!
Oh that silent, ceaseless mourning,
Oh those dim eyes, never turning
From that wondrous, suffering Son!
Who on Christ's dear Mother gazing,
In her trouble so amazing,
Born of woman, would not weep?
Who on Christ's dear Mother thinking,
Such a cup of sorrow drinking,
Would not share her sorrow deep?
For the sins of his own nation,
Saw him hang in desolation
Till his Spirit forth he sent;
Bruised, derided, cursed, defiled,
She beheld her tender Child,
All with bloody scourges rent.
O, thou Mother, fount of love!
Touch my spirit from above,
Make my heart with thine accord.
Make me feel as thou hast felt;
Make my soul to glow and melt
With the love of Christ my Lord.

Holy Mother, pierce me through.
In my heart each wound renew
Of my Savior crucified;
Let me share with thee his pain,
Who for all my sins was slain,
Who for me in torment died.
Let me mingle tears with thee,
Mourning him who mourned for me,
All the days that I may live.
By the cross with thee to stay,
There with thee to weep and pray,
Is all I ask of thee to give.
Virgin of all virgins blest,
Listen to my fond request;
Let me share thy grief divine.
Let me to my latest breath,
In my body bear the death
Of that dying Son of thine.
Wounded with his every wound,
Steep my soul till it hath swooned
In his very blood away.
Be to me, O Virgin, nigh,
Lest in flames I burn and die
In his awful judgment day.
Christ, when thou shalt call me hence,
Be thy Mother my defense,
Be they cross my victory.
While my body here decays
May my soul thy goodness praise
Safe in Paradise with thee.

Chapter Nine

Practice Exercise No. 168

1. to warn
2. to have increased
3. to be thrown
4. to be about to place
5. to have fled
6. to hinder
7. to have swum
8. to be about to frighten
9. to have remained
10. to be about to hear
11. to have written
12. to be about to fight
13. to be about to praise
14. to be aroused
15. to have been sought
16. to send
17. to be touched
18. to have been attacked
19. to be known
20. to be about to carry on
21. to be received
22. to have been conquered
23. to be said
24. to be about to walk

Practice Exercise No. 169

1. petere, to seek
2. cepisse, to have taken
3. habere, to have
4. rexisse, to have ruled
5. portare, to carry
6. vocavisse, to have called
7. ferre, to carry
8. dedisse, to have given
9. instruere, to draw up
10. vertere, to turn

Practice Exercise No. 170

1. narrari, to be told
2. defensus, -a, -um esse, to have been defended
3. videri, to be seen; to seem
4. iuvari, to be helped
5. pugnatus, -a, -um esse, to have been fought
6. motus, -a, -um esse, to have been moved
7. vocari, to be called
8. inveniri, to be found
9. necatus, -a, -um esse, to have been killed
10. relinqui, to be left

Practice Exercise No. 171

1. futurus, -a, -umm esse, to be about to be
2. iussurus, -a, -um esse, to be about to order
3. facturus, -a, -um esse, to be about to make
4. defensurus, -a, -um esse, to be about to defend
5. oppugnaturus, -a, -um esse, to be about to attack
6. properaturus, -a, -um esse, to be about to hurry
7. capturus, -a, -um esse, to be about to take
8. inventurus, -a, -um esse, to be about to find
9. daturus, -a, -um esse, to be about to give
10. positurus, -a, -um esse, to be about to place

Practice Exercise No. 172

1. Those soldiers said that the men would carry aid.
2. Do you think that your work has been done?
3. We were hoping that the enemy would come as quickly as possible.
4. The girls seem to be happy.
5. This king wished to rule well.
6. He will not want to be called.
7. To defend our town is best.
8. To have had hope was better than to have retreated.
9. He announced that the speed could be increased.
10. He ordered us to find a better place.

Practice Exercise No. 173

1. calling
2. having been moved
3. about to send
4. receiving
5. about to come
6. having been watched
7. arriving
8. about to take
9. placing, putting
10. having been announced

Practice Exercise No. 174

1. the ships, sailing
2. the leader, about to order
3. they, having been attacked
4. the men, about to arrive
5. seeking peace
6. the dog, running
7. The temple, having been built
8. the cities, having been captured
9. the harbors, having been found
10. the rivers, running

Practice Exercise No. 175

1. The people of the cities, which had been captured, were as brave as possible.
2. The men, who were about to arrive, were making the trip as quickly as possible.
3. The king, who is now ruling your country, seems to be timid.
4. The woman will give aid, when (if) she sees your difficulty.
5. The storm will not be very fierce, if it does not increase.
6. The father had great joy, because he was about to see his sons.
7. They were running as fast as possible, because they fear our men.
8. The men, who (because they) had been defeated, were especially frightened.
9. When she arrived in the town, she told her story.
10. They, who are defending the gate, were not friends.

Practice Exercise No. 176

1. bravely
2. as quickly as possible
3. least, not at all
4. for a very long time
5. more keenly
6. with difficulty
7. very easily
8. better
9. badly
10. greatly

Practice Exercise No. 177

1. When the oracle had been heard, many people decided to come to our land.
2. When the signal had been given, they made an attack onto the field.
3. The men, although their weapons were not many, nevertheless fought bravely.
4. Because many soldiers had been killed, the leaders sought peace.
5. The men, because the booty is large, will be received at home with great joy.
6. When this thing has been done, the boys will come home.
7. If he is the leader, we shall do it without difficulty.
8. When these things had been reported to me, I wanted to make the trip from the city.
9. If these have been killed, the people will be better ruled.
10. When the day had been set, they prepared everything as quickly as possible.
11. Because the door was open, he was able to come into the cottage.
12. He had no hope, because the city had been captured.
13. When these things had been done, the king was more powerful.
14. If the rest have been seen, we shall run toward the forest.
15. When his father is the leader, they do everything boldly.
16. When peace has been made, he will sail away from the island.
17. If many are timid, they will not be able to find the rivers.
18. Because the time is now short, no help will arrive.
19. Because the place is suitable, you wish to stay here longer.
20. Because help was given, there was great joy.
21. Weapons are useful for fighting.
22. You have hope of swimming.
23. They went for the purpose of attacking the city.
24. I came to listen.

Chapter Nine Review

Vocabulary Review

Nouns

1. dog	5. leader	9. wool	13. sheep
2. prison	6. ant	10. manner, way	14. beauty
3. Cerberus	7. joy	11. number	15. enough
4. Charon	8. kind, class	12. rank, order	

Adjectives

1. open	2. remaining, rest of	3. timid	4. useful

Verbs

1. find, come upon	2. think, believe	3. carry back, bring back	4. hope

Adverbs

1. enough	2. so	3. finally

Practice Exercise No. 178

1. to be	6. to have thought	10. to be going to hope	15. to wish, want
2. to have been	7. to carry back, report	11. to be led	16. to be wished, wanted
3. to be about to find out	8. to be about to carry back, report	12. to have led	17. to have been able
4. to be found out	9. to have hoped	13. to have been had	18. to be able
5. to have been thought		14. to have	19. to have fought
			20. to have been fought

Practice Exercise No. 179

1. leading	8. having been found out	15. coming	22. having been sent
2. about to lead	9. carrying back, reporting	16. about to come	23. about to see
3. having, holding	10. about to carry back, report	17. fearing	24. seeing
4. having been had	11. hoping	18. having been frightened	25. about to say
5. having been thought	12. having been hoped	19. about to place, put	26. saying
6. about to think	13. about to move	20. putting, placing	27. warning
7. finding out	14. moving	21. sending	28. having been warned

Practice Exercise No. 180

1. they having been seen	5. the men fearing	9. sleep coming	12. the remaining speaking
2. he, it having been captured	6. the girl walking	10. the prison being big	13. the word having been heard
3. these having been said	7. the leaders being afraid	11. the city having been captured	14. hope having been found
4. the war having been made	8. the number being small		15. the kinds being many

Reading

Quintus Horatius Flaccus

He who is upright of life and free from crime
needs neither Moorish javelins nor a bow
nor a quiver heavy with poisoned arrows, Fuscus,
whether he is going to journey through the hot Quicksands
or through the inhospitable
Caucasus or the places which the storied Hydaspes laps.
  First Book of Odes, 22

Carmina Burana

The sun, pure and clear,
Tempers everything,
A new world resows
The appearance of April;
The sweetheart's spirit
Hurries to love,
And over pleasant things rules
The boyish god, Cupid.
So much newness of nature
In the festive springtime
And the power of the spring
Orders us to rejoice,
Shows us the accustomed ways,
And in your own springtime
There is trust and the right
To cling to your loved one.
Love me faithfully,
Mark my trust,
In my heart completely,
And with my whole mind
I am in your presence,
Even when absent at a distance;
Whoever loves in such a way,
Is turned on a wheel of torture.
Behold, pleasing
And longed for,
The spring brings back our joys;
Clad in purple

The meadow is in flower,
The sun makes all serene,
Now, now, sorrows depart,
Summer returns,
Now retreats
The severity of winter.
Now there melts
And disappears
All hail, snow, and such,
Winter flees,
And now the spring
Sucks in the richness of summer;
His heart is wretched,
Who neither lives,
Nor plays
Under the joys of summer.
They glory
and delight
In the honey of sweetness
Who try
To use
The favor of Cupid;
Let us be, at the command of Venus,
Boasting
And rejoicing
To be the equals of Paris.

Chapter Ten

Practice Exercise No. 181

1. debuerint
2. relinqueret
3. oppugnetis
4. sis
5. essem
6. facias
7. iacta essent
8. debitus sim
9. veniret
10. relinqueremur
11. ventae sitis
12. fuerit
13. rogemini
14. conspiciamur
15. venerim
16. debeas
17. fuisset
18. oppugnarent
19. relicta sit
20. deberetur

Practice Exercise No. 182

1. sunt
2. venimus
3. rogata sunt
4. oppugnabat
5. conspiciebam
6. debeo
7. fuimus
8. conspexerant
9. veniebatur
10. debui
11. debita eras
12. reliquit
13. rogavit
14. venieras
15. eras
16. conspecti eratis
17. fueram
18. oppugnavisti
19. relinquis
20. debebatur

Practice Exercise No. 183

1. Present subjunctive.
2. Pluperfect subjunctive.

3. Perfect subjunctive.
4. Imperfect subjunctive.

Practice Exercise No. 184

1.
Active	Passive
laudem	lauder
laudes	lauderis
laudet	laudetur
laudemus	laudemur
laudetis	laudemini
laudent	laudentur

2.
Active	Passive
viderim	visus, -a, -um sim
videris	visus, -a, -um sis
viderit	visus, -a, -um sit
viderimus	visi, -ae, -a simus
videritis	visi, -ae, -a sitis
viderint	visi, -ae, -a sint

3.
Active	Passive
peterem	peterer
peteres	petereris
peteret	peteretur
peteremus	peteremur
peteretis	peteremini
peterent	peterentur

4.
Active	Passive
dormivissem	dormitus, -a, -um essem
dormivisses	dormitus, -a, -um esses
dormivisset	dormitus, -a, -um esset
dormivissemus	dormi, -ae, -a essemus
dormivissetis	dormi, -ae, -a essetis
dormivissent	dormi, -ae, -a essent

Practice Exercise No. 185

1. possis
2. eant
3. tulerit
4. fieretis
5. voluissemus
6. nolit
7. ieris
8. mallent
9. potuerit
10. nolueritis
11. factus sim
12. ferrentur
13. malim
14. issent
15. potuisses
16. vellet
17. maluerit
18. fiam
19. feratis
20. noluissetis

Practice Exercise No. 186

1. let us allow; let us withdraw
2. let him (her) not go
3. let them fight
4. let them flee
5. let us remain
6. let him (her) not write
7. let them not arm
8. let us not demand
9. let him (her) finish
10. let us sleep

Practice Exercise No. 187

1. They fight in order to seize the city.
2. I was hurrying in order to catch up.
3. Daedalus had prepared wings in order that he himself and his son might fly.
4. You have left the city in order not to fight.
5. He brings these things in order for us to know them.
6. We teach so that you might learn.
7. They listen so that they might learn.
8. The woman ran away so she would not be killed.

Practice Exercise No. 188

1. Cicero spoke so well that Catiline left the city.
2. Catiline was so alarmed that he did not attack the city.
3. Psyche loved Cupid so greatly that she went to Those Below.
4. Cupid loved Psyche so greatly that he did not listen to the words of his mother.
5. You have looked so long that you have found the conspiracy.
6. The men ran so fast that they caught up.
7. The severity of the matter was so great that mercy was not given.
8. Your sister teaches so well that we learn much.

Practice Exercise No. 189

1. He warned you not to come to Rome.
2. You will persuade the Tulingi to surrender.
3. I pray that my father not be killed.
4. Your mother has commanded that you not lose the horses.
5. Caesar forbids his soldiers to turn back.
6. Caesar has forbidden the Allobroges to rebuild the captured city.
7. We fear lest the villages be empty.
8. Cicero fears that Catilina will not depart from Rome.
9. The Helvetii doubt if Caesar will receive their surrender.
10. You do not doubt whether the Germans will pass over their own borders.

Practice Exercise No. 190

1. I do not know who you are.
2. Cicero will tell you why Catilina left Rome.
3. The woman has asked how you learned this.
4. They learned what we wanted.
5. We know whence the soldiers will attack.
6. I understand why you like the woman.
7. You told me how the villages had been restored.
8. You were asking me whom I loved.
9. The man knows what your sister saw.
10. The Helvetii burned the houses in which they lived.

Practice Exercise No. 191

1.

Active	Passive
accipiam	accipiar
accipias	acciparis
accipiat	accipatur
accipiamus	accipamur
accipiatis	accipamini
accipiant	accipantur

2. Active
reversus, -a, -um sim
reversus, -a, -um sis
reversus, -a, -um sit
reversi, -ae, -a simus
reversi, -ae, -a sitis
reversi, -ae, -a sint

There is no passive; **revertor** is a deponent verb.

3. Active
irem
ires
iret
iremus
iretis
irent

The verb **eo** has no passive forms.

4.

Active	Passive
vetavissem	vetatus, -a, -um essem
vetavisses	vetatus, -a, -um esses
vetavisset	vetatus, -a, -um esset
vetavissemus	vetati, -ae, -a essemus
vetavissetis	vetati, -ae, -a essetis
vetavissent	vetati, -ae, -a essent

6. If only they would return!
7. If only you had read my books!
8. May they not ask this!
9. If only he had not been condemned to the games!
10. If only I were not ignorant of fighting!

Practice Exercise No. 192

1. There was no one who thought this.
2. She is a woman whom all believe.
3. Is there anyone who has not been freed?
4. There are those who assert that.
5. If only my father were alive!

Practice Exercise No. 193

1. When (Since) they had surrendered weapons and hostages, Caesar rebuilt the towns.
2. Since he had been condemned, he was wretched.
3. Although the women had been freed, they were not happy.
4. Since (Although) I loved the woman, I left the city.
5. Although it was dangerous, we were not alarmed.
6. Although they had hurried, they did not catch up.
7. Since he had hurried, he caught up.
8. Although Cicero was mistaken, he spoke well.
9. Since the fields had been burned, the Helvetii were not living there.
10. When (Since) it had been granted, Catiline left the city.

Practice Exercise No. 194

1. Active
consequor
consequeris
consequitur
consequimur
consequimini
consequuntur

There are no passive forms.

2.

Active	Passive
errare	errarer
errares	errareris
erraret	erraretur
erraremus	erraremur
erraretis	erraremini
errarent	errarentur

3.

Active	Passive
pertulerim	perlatus, -a, -um sim
pertuleris	perlatus, -a, -um sis
pertulerit	perlatus, -a, -um sit
pertulerimus	perlati, -ae, -a simus
pertuleritis	perlati, -ae, -a sitis
pertulerint	perlati, -ae, -a sint

4.

Active	Passive
flagitaveram	flagitus, -a, -um eram
flagitaveras	flagitus, -a, -um eras
flagitaverat	flagitus, -a, -um erat
flagitaveramus	flagiti, -ae, -a eramus
flagitaveratis	flagiti, -ae, -a eratis
flagitaverant	flagiti, -ae, -a erant

Practice Exercise No. 195

1. If you were to hurt me, I would avoid you.
2. Even if he had not been welcomed, he would have come.
3. If I were not afraid, I would fight.
4. Even if Caesar's soldiers had been afraid, they would have attacked the cities and villages of the Helvetii.
5. Even if Catiline will not leave Rome, Cicero will warn the people of his conspiracy.
6. If I loved you, I would tell you.
7. If she were here, she would believe us.
8. Even if you had been there, you would have done nothing.
9. Even if we were to write letters, they would not read them.
10. If the Allobroges had not surrendered their weapons, Caesar would have burned their houses.

Practice Exercise No. 196

1. Although you mistrust me, nevertheless, I believe you.
2. Although you did not know the woman, you listened to her.
3. Although they may not listen, Cicero will speak.
4. Although Catiline may not be welcomed, nevertheless, he will come into the senate.
5. Although the soldier has been wounded, he is alive.
6. Although the city may be captured, nevertheless, we shall not be afraid.
7. Although your body is present, your mind is absent.

Practice Exercise No. 197

1. Active
   adsim
   adsis
   adsit
   adsimus
   adsitis
   adsint

2.

Active	Passive
exsolvero	exsolutus, -a, -um ero
exsolveris	exsolutus, -a, -um eris
exsolverit	exsolutus, -a, -um erit
exsolverimus	exsoluti, -ae, -a erimus
exsolveritis	exsouti, -ae, -a eritis
exsolverint	exsoluti, -ae, -a erunt

3.

Active	Passive
suspexissem	suspectus, -a, -um essem
suspexisses	suspectus, -a, -um esses
suspexisset	suspectus, -a, -um esset
suspexissemus	suspecti, -ae, -a essemus
suspexissetis	suspecti, -ae, -a essetis
suspexissent	suspecti, -ae, -a essent

4.

Active	Passive
vulnerarem	vulnerarer
vulnerares	vulnerareris
vulneraret	vulneraretur
vulneraremus	vulneraremur
vulneraretis	vulneraremini
vulnerarent	vulnerarentur

5.

Active	Passive
vixi	victus, -a, -um sum
vixisti	victus, -a, -um es
vixit	victus, -a, -um est
viximus	victi, -ae, -a sumus
vixitis	victi, -ae, -a estis
vixerunt	victi, -ae, -a sunt

Practice Exercise No. 198

1. He said that the Helvetii, who lived in the fields, had destroyed the city.
2. They say that the woman, whom I know, is not here.
3. He said that the soldiers whom Caesar had commanded had surrendered weapons and hostages.
4. I say that the girls who promised these things were set free.
5. You will say that the arrow which had killed the boy was lost in the forest.
6. They thought that the legion which had deserted Caesar would return.
7. We think that the conspiracy which Cicero brought to light will hurt Rome.
8. I feel that the words which are spoken by you are believed by all.
9. You thought that the promises which had been made by the crowd of Carnutes would guard against murder.
10. He ordered that the man who fed his sons and daughters be praised.

Practice Exercise No. 199

1. Present active infinitive: recidere
   Present passive infinitive: recidi
   Perfect active infinitive: recepisse
   Perfect passive infinitive: receptus, -a, -um esse
   Future active infinitive: recepturus, -a, -um esse
   Future passive participle: receptum iri

2. Present active participle: recusans, recusantis
   Perfect passive participle: recusatus, -a, -um
   Future active participle: recusaturus, -a, -um
   Future passive participle: recusandus, -a, -um

3. Active
   querebar
   querebaris
   querebatur
   querebamur
   querebamini
   querebantur

4.

Active	Passive
praestaverim	praestatus, -a, -um sim
praestaveris	praestatus, -a, -um sis
praestaverit	praestatus, -a, -um sit
praestaverimus	praestati, -ae, -a simus
praestaveritis	praestati, -ae, -a sitis
praestaverint	praestati, -ae, -a sint

Chapter Ten Review

Vocabulary Review

Nouns

1. Acco
2. Allobroges
3. pension, yearly pay
4. look, sight
5. goodness, kindness, benevolence
6. Carnutes
7. downfall, fate
8. conspiracy, plot
9. mistreatment, outrage, injury
10. surrender
11. longing, loss, need
12. famine, hunger
13. crowd
14. produce, fruit
15. Helvetii
16. beginning, start
17. judgment, sentence
18. right, authority
19. Latobrigi
20. legion
21. mercy, mildness, gentleness
22. greatness, vastness
23. ancestors, forefathers
24. mind
25. service, work
26. sympathy, pity
27. relative, friend
28. no one
29. Nicaea
30. Nicomedia
31. official job, official position
32. hostage
33. hatred
34. way, manner
35. parent
36. parricide, murder, treason
37. promise
38. chief
39. presence, effect
40. manner, fashion, reason
41. republic, common good
42. the Rhine
43. health, safety
44. senate
45. sense, sensation, feeling
46. severity, strictness
47. silence
48. Tulingi
49. evening
50. village, street

Pronouns

1. someone, something; anyone, anything
2. that, that one of yours
3. a certain one; pl., some

Adjectives

1. Aurelian
2. secret, hidden
3. common, public
4. yesterday
5. honored, respected
6. threatening, dangerous, hostile
7. useless, harmful
8. that, that one of yours
9. free, at leisure, not working
10. dangerous, perilous
11. continuous, perpetual, uninterrupted
12. most, the largest part
13. last, finally
14. first, foremost
15. former, earlier
16. public, common
17. how much
18. safe, well
19. old, aged
20. higher, past, preceding

Verbs

1. be absent, be away from
2. take, receive
3. hurry
4. strengthen, affirm, assert
5. gain, obtain, reach
6. be present, be here
7. consider, discuss
8. lose
9. think, judge
10. dare
11. be without, be absent from
12. beware of, guard against
13. consider, think
14. learn, ascertain
15. grant, allow, withdraw
16. look for, collect
17. follow, catch up with
18. believe, trust
19. condemn, find guilty
20. destroy, obliterate
21. descend, come down
22. desert, abandon
23. wound, hurt
24. doubt, hesitate, be uncertain
25. carry forth, bring out
26. quit, surpass, go beyond
27. be mistaken, lose one's way
28. happen, come out
29. avoid, go away, depart
30. think, judge
31. release, free
32. demand
33. perform, do
34. hesitate, be at a loss
35. command, order
36. live in, reside
37. shut off, stop
38. judge, sentence, examine
39. swear
40. read
41. say, speak
42. fear, be afraid
43. pity, feel sorry for
44. not know, be ignorant of
45. think, suppose
46. it is right, it is proper
47. beg, pray
48. feed on, eat
49. throw open, bring to light.
50. allow, grant, suffer
51. report
52. allow, permit
53. stir, move
54. persuade
55. fear, be alarmed at
56. calm, reconcile
57. promise
58. ask, beg, demand
59. be better than, be superior to
60. go forth, depart
61. declare, acknowledge, say
62. run away, flee, escape
63. clean, remove, excuse
64. ask, look for
65. complain about
66. recoil, fall
67. recover, get back
68. refuse, reject
69. return, restore
70. report, bring back
71. learn, find out
72. restore, rebuild
73. keep back, retain
74. turn back, return
75. greet, welcome
76. feel, perceive, realize
77. mistrust, suspect
78. decay, melt away
79. bear, endure
80. pass over, cross, desert

Adverbs

1. perhaps
2. temperately, frugally
3. so
4. moderately, modestly
5. very much, too much
6. a little
7. as much as
8. backward, on the other hand
9. so, thus
10. from where, whence
11. as
12. violently, eagerly

Conjunctions

1. or
2. even if
3. even if, although
4. that not, lest
5. if not, unless
6. whether
7. before
8. although
9. because, now that
10. if
11. even if
12. that, so that
13. if only, would that
14. either . . . or

Interjections

1. by Hercules!

Practice Exercise No. 200

1. Present
   loquar
   loquaris
   loquatur
   loquamur
   loquamini
   loquantur

   Perfect
   locutus, -a, -um sim
   locutus, -a, -um sis
   locutus, -a, -um sit
   locuti, -ae, -a simus
   locuti, -ae, -a sitis
   locuti, -ae, -a sint

   Imperfect
   loquerer
   loquereris
   loqueretur
   loqueremur
   loqueremini
   loquerentur

   Pluperfect
   locutus, -a, -um esssem
   locutus, -a, -um esses
   locutus, -a, -um esset
   locuti, -ae, -a essemus
   locuti, -ae, -a essetis
   locuti, -ae, -a essent

2. Present active infinitive: **orare**
   Present passive infinitive: **orari**
   Perfect active infinitive: **oravisse**
   Perfect passive infinitive: **oratus, -a, -um esse**
   Future active infinitive: **oraturus, -a, -um esse**
   Future passive infinitive: **oratum iri**

3. Present active participle: **concedens, concedentis**
   Perfect passive participle: **concessus, -a, -um**
   Future active participle: **concessurus, -a, -um**
   Future passive participle: **concendus, -a, -um**

4. Note that **possum** has no passive forms.
   Present
   possim
   possis
   possit
   possimus
   possitis
   possunt

   Perfect
   potuerim
   potueris
   potuerit
   potuerimus
   potueritis
   potuerint

   Imperfect
   possem
   posses
   posset
   possemus
   possetis
   possent

   Pluperfect
   potuissem
   potuisses
   potuisset
   potuissemus
   potuissetis
   potuissent

5. Present

Active	Passive
sentio	sentior
sentis	sentiris
sentit	sentitur
sentimus	sentimur
sentitis	sentimini
sentiunt	sentiuntur

   Imperfect

Active	Passive
sentiebam	sentiebar
sentiebas	sentiebaris
sentiebat	sentiebatur
sentiebamus	sentiebamur
sentiebatis	sentiebamini
sentiebant	sentiebantur

   Future

Active	Passive
sentiam	sentiar
senties	sentieris
sentiet	sentietur
sentiemus	sentiemur
sentietis	sentiemini
sentient	sentientur

   Perfect

Active	Passive
sensi	sensus, -a, -um sum
sensisti	sensus, -a, -um es
sensit	sensus, -a, -um est
sensimus	sensi, -ae, -a sumus
sensistis	sensi, -ae, -a estis
senserunt	sensi, -ae, -a sunt

   Pluperfect

Active	Passive
senseram	sensus, -a, -um eram
senseras	sensus, -a, -um eras
senserat	sensus, -a, -um erat
senseramus	sensi, -ae, -a eramus
senseratis	sensi, -ae, -a eratis
senserant	sensi, -ae, -a erant

   Future Perfect

Active	Passive
sensero	sensus, -a, -um ero
senseris	sensus, -a, -um eris
senserit	sensus, -a, -um erit
senserimus	sensi, -ae, -a erimus
senseritis	sensi, -ae, -a eritis
senserint	sensi, -ae, -a erunt

Reading

Publius Vergilius Maro

Spare your fear, Cytherea; the Fates remain unmoved
for your children; you will see the city and the promised
walls of Lavinium and you will carry aloft to the starry sky
great Aeneas; nor has intent changed me.
Your son (for indeed, I will speak, since this care troubles you,
and rolling them farther, I will consider the secrets of the Fates)
will wage a great war on Italy and will crush fierce peoples
and will establish customs for the people, and walls,
until the third summer will have seen him ruling at Latium
and three winters will have passed since the Rutulians were subdued.
But the boy Ascanius, to whom now the cognomen Iulus
is added (He was Iulus, while the matter stood with Ilian ruling),
For thirty great circles with rolling months
will fulfill his rule from the seat of Lavinium,
and, with great force, he will fortify Alba Longa.
Here now for three hundred entire years, it will be ruled
by the race of Hector, until a royal priestess
will give to Mars, heavy in birth, twins, the offspring of Ilian.
Then with the yellow skin of the nurturing she-wolf, happy
Romulus will take up the race, and will establish
the walls of Mars, and he will call the Romans by his own name.

For these, I place neither limits of space nor time;
I have given them rule without end. Even harsh Juno,
who now wearies the sea and the shores and the sky with her dread,
will turn to better plans, and with me, she will cherish
the Romans, lords of the world and the toga-clad race.
So it has pleased me. There will come a time, as the seasons glide by,
when the house of Assaracus will repress Phthia
and the famous Mycenas and will rule over the conquered Argos.
A Trojan Caesar will be born, of beautiful origin,
Who will limit his rule with the ocean, his fame with the stars,
Julius, a name descended from great Iulus.
Him, at some time, laden with the spoils of the East,
You, untroubled, will receive in heaven; he also will be called in prayers.
Then the harsh ages will become mild when wars have ceased;
Hoary Faith and Vesta, Romulus with his brother Remus
will give justice; the awful doors of war will be closed
with iron and close-fitting seams; impious Fury within
sitting over fierce weapons and with a hundred bonds of bronze
knotted behind his back shall roar horrible with his bloody mouth.
    Aeneid, 1, 257–296

A

a, ab from, away from; by

abeo, abire, abii, abitus go away

absum, abesse, abfui be absent, be away from

accedo, accedere, accessi, accessurus approach, be added, to agree, support

accido, accidere, accidi happen

accelero, accelerare, acceleravi, acceleratus hurry

accipio, accipere, accepi, acceptus take, receive

acer, acris, acre sharp, active, keen

acies, aciei, f. battle line

Acco, Acconis, m. Acco

ad to, towards

addo, addere, addidi, additus put on, add

adfero, adferre, attuli, adlatus bring

adfirmo, adfirmare, adfirmavi, adfirmatus strengthen, affirm, assert

administro, administrare, administravi, administratus manage, control, rule

adoro, adorare, adoravi, adoratus worship, adore

adsequor, adsequi, adsecutus sum gain, obtain, reach

adsum, adesse, adfui be present, be here

adulescens, adulescentis, m. youth

advenio, advenire, adveni, adventus come to, reach, arrive at

adventus, adventus, m. arrival, approach

aedificium, aedificii or aedifici, n. building

aedifico, aedificare, aedificavi, aedificatus build

aeger, aegra, aegrum sick, ill

aenus, aena, aenum bronze

aequus, aequa, aequum equal, level, fair

aestas, aestatis, f. summer

Africa, Africae, f. Africa

ager, agri, m. field

aggredior, aggredi, aggressus sum approach, attack

agito, agitare, agitavi, agitatus consider, discuss

agricola, agricolae, m. farmer

ala, alae, f. wing

aliquis, aliquid someone, something; anyone, anything

alius, alia, aliud other, another

Allobroges, Allobrogum, m. pl. Allobroges

alter, altera, alterum the one, the other

altus, alta, altum high, deep

ambulo, ambulare, ambulavi, ambulatus walk

amicus, amica, amicum friendly

amicus, amici, m. friend

amitto, amittere, amisi, amissus lose, send away

amo, amare, amavi, amatus like, love

amor, amoris, m. love

amphitheatrum, amphitheatri, n. amphitheater

an or

angustus, angusta, angustum narrow

animal, animalis, n. animal

animus, animi, m. mind, spirit

annua, annuorum, n. pl. pension, yearly pay

annus, anni, m. year

ante before, in front of

antea before

antequam before

antiquus, antiqua, antiquum ancient, old

antrum, antri, n. cave

apertus, aperta, apertum open

Apollo, Apollonis, m. Apollo

appello, appellare, apellavi, appellatus address, call, name

Aprilis, Aprile of April

apud among, in the presence of

aqua, aquae, f. water

arbitror, arbitrari, arbitratus sum think, judge

arbor, arboris, f. tree

arca, arcae, f. chest, box

ardeo, ardere, arsi, arsus burn, be on fire

arena, arenae, f. sand, arena

Ariadne, Ariadnes, f. Ariadne

arma, armae, n. pl. arms, weapons

armo, armare, armavi, armatus arm

aro, arare, aravi, aratus plow

aspectus, aspectus, m. look, sight

at but

Atalanta, Atalantae, f. Atalanta

Athenae, Athenarum, f. pl. Athens

Atlas, Atlantis, m. Atlas

atque, ac and also, also

auctoritas, auctoritatis, f. power, prestige, authority

audacia, audaciae, f. boldness, daring

audeo, audere, ausus dare

audax, audacis bold

augeo, augere, auxi, auctus increase, enlarge

Augustus, Augusta, Augustum of August

Aurelius, Aurelia, Aurelium Aurelian

aureus, aurea, aureum golden

aurum, auri, n. gold

aut or

aut . . aut either . . or

autem but, however

auxilium, auxilii or auxili, n. aid, help

avunculus, avunculi, m. uncle

B

Bacchus, Bacchi, m. Bacchus

barbarus, barbara, barbarum savage, uncivilized, barbarian

barbarus, barbari, m. barbarian

belle prettily, neatly, well

bellum, belli, n. war

bene well

bis twice

bonitas, bonitatis, f. goodness, kindness, benevolence

bonus, bona, bonum good

brevis, breve short, brief

Britannia, Britanniae, f. Britain

C

cado, cadere, cecidi, casus fall

caedes, caedis, f. slaughter, murder

caelum, caeli, n. sky, heaven

canis, canis, m. and f. dog

capio, capere, cepi, captus take, seize, capture

captivus, captivi, m. captive

caput, capitis, n. head

carcer, carceris, n. prison

careo, carere, carui, caritus be without, be absent from

Carnutes, Carnutum, m. pl. Carnutes

casa, casae, f. house, cottage

casus, casus, m. downfall, fate

castra, castrorum, n. pl. camp

causa, causae, f. cause, reason

caveo, cavere, cavi, cautus beware of, guard against

cedo, cedere, cessi, cessus go away, withdraw, yield

celer, celeris, celere quick, swift

celeritas, celeritatis, f. speed, swiftness

cera, cerae, f. wax

Cerberus, Cerberi, m. Cerberus

Ceres, Cereris, f. Ceres

certe surely, indeed

certus, certa, certum certain, sure

Charon, Charontis, m. Charon

cibus, cibi, m. food

Cincinnatus, Cincinnati, m. Cincinnatus

circiter about

circum around, about

civis, civis, m. and f. citizen

civitas, civitatis, f. state

clamito, clamitare, clamitavi, clamitatus proclaim, cry aloud

clamo, clamare, clamavi, clamatus shout, cry

clandestinus, clandestina, clandestinum secret, hidden

clarus, clara, clarum clear, famous, bright

classis, classis, f. fleet

cogito, cogitare, cogitavi, cogatatus consider, think

cognosco, cognoscere, cognovi, cognitus learn, recognize, know

cogo, cogere, coegi, coactus collect, drive, compel

collis, collis, m. hill

colloquor, colloqui, collocutus sum speak with

Colosseum, Colossei, n. the Colosseum

commoror, commorari, commoratus sum linger, stay, remain, abide

communis, commune common, public

comparo, comparare, comparavi, comparatus bring together, compare

comperio, comperire, comperi, compertus learn, ascertain

comprehendo, comprehendere, comprehendi, comprehensus seize, discover, apprehend

concedo, concedere, concessi, concessum grant, allow, withdraw

concilio, conciliare, conciliavi, conciliatus reconcile, win, win over

concilium, concilii or concili, n. council

confero, conferre, contuli, conlatus bring to-

gether, collect

conficio, conficere, confeci, confectus finish, complete, carry out

confirmo, confirmare, confirmavi, confirmatus establish, strengthen, confirm

congrego, congregare, congregavi, congregatus assemble, gather together

coniurati, coniurationis, f. conspiracy, plot

conloco, conlocare, conlocavi, conlocatus place, station

conor, conari, conatus sum try

conquiro, conquirere, conquisivi, conquisitus look for, collect

consensus, consensus, m. agreement

consequor, consequi, consecutus sum follow, catch up with

conservo, conservare, conservavi, conservatus keep safe, preserve

consilium, consilii or consili, n. plan, advice

conspectus, conspectus, m. sight, view

conspicio, conspicere, conspexi, conspectus observe

constituo, constituere, constitui, constitutus decide, establish

consumo, consumere, consumpsi, consumptus use up, consume, spend

contendo, contendere, contendi, contentus hold together, limit, enclose, keep, repress

contra against

contumelia, contumeliae, f. mistreatment, outrage, injury

convenio, convenire, conveni, conventus come together, assemble

copia, coipiae, f. supply, abundance

copiae, copiarum, f. pl. troops

cornu, cornus, n. horn

corpus, corporis, n. body

cotidianus, cotidiana, cotidianum daily, usual

cras tomorrow

credo, credere, credidi, creditus believe, trust

Creta, Cretae, f. Crete

Creusa, Creusae, f. Creusa

cum with; when, while, since, although

cupiditas, cupiditatis, f. desire

Cupido, Cupidinis, m. Cupid

cupidus, cupida, cupidum desirous, eager

cupio, cupere, cupivi, cupitus desire, wish, want

cur why

cura, curae, f. care

curo, curare, curavi, curatus care for, cure

curro, currere, cucurri, cursus run

Cyclops, Cyclopis, m. Cyclops

D

Daedalus, Daedali, m. Dedalus

damno, damnare, damnavi, damnatus condemn, find guilty

de about, concerning, down from

dea, deae, f. goddess

debeo, debere, debui, debitus owe, ought

decem ten

December, Decembris, Decembre of December

deditio, deditionis, f. surrender

dedo, dedere, dedidi, deditus give up, surrender

defendo, defendere, defendi, defensus ward off, repel, defend

defero, deferre, detui, delatus carry off, bring away, report, offer

deinde then, next

deleo, delere, delevi, deletus destroy, obliterate

deligo, deligere, delegi, delectus choose, select

demonstro, demonstrare, demonstravi, demonstratus point out, show

denique finally, at last

desceno, descendere, descendi, descensus descend, come down

desero, deserere, deserui, deseritus desert, aban-

don

desiderium, desiderii or desideri, n. longing, loss, need

desisto, desistere, destiti, destitus cease, desist, stop

deterreo, deterrere, deterrui, deterritus frighten off, deter, prevent, hinder

deus, dei, m. god

dico, dicere, dixi, dictus say, speak

dictator, dictatoris, m. dictator

dies, diei, m. and f. day

difficilis, difficile difficult, hard

difficultas, difficultatis, f. difficulty

diligenter carefully

diligentia, diligentiae, f. diligence, care

diligo, diligere, dilexi, delectus value, love

discedo, discedere, discessi, discessus withdraw, go away, leave

disco, discere, didici learn

diu long, for a long time

dives, divitis rich

do, dare, dedi, datus give

doceo, docere, docui, doctus teach, show

doleo, dolere, dolui, dolitus grieve, be sorry

domi at home

domina, dominae, f. mistress

dominus, domini, m. master

domus, domus, f. house, home

donec until

donum, doni, n. gift, present

dormio, dormire, dormivi, dormitus sleep

dubito, dubitare, dubitavi, dubitatus doubt, hesitate, be uncertain

dubius, dubia, dubium doubtful, uncertain

duco, ducere, duxi, ductus lead

dulcis, dulce sweet

dum while

duodecim twelve

dux, ducis, m. leader

E

e, ex from, out from

educo, educere, eduxi, eductus lead out

effero, efferre, extuli, elatus carry forth, bring out

effugio, effugere, effugi flee away, escape

ego, mei I

egredior, egredi, egressus sum quit, surpass, go beyond

egregius, egregia, egregium excellent, outstanding

emo, emere, emi, emptus buy

enim for

enuntio, enuntiare, enuntiavi, enuntiatus speak out, reveal, make known

eo, ire, ii or ivi, itus go

epistola, epistolae, f. letter

eques, equitis, m. horseman, knight

equus, equi, m. horse

erro, errare, erravi, erratus be mistaken, lose one's way

et and

et . . . et both . . . and

etiam even, also

etiamsi even if

etsi even if, although

Europa, Europae, f. Europe

Eurydice, Eurydices, f. Eurydice

Eurystheus, Eurysthei, m. Eurystheus

evenio, evenire, eveni, evenitus happen, come out

ex, e out, out from

excito, excitare, excitavi, excitatus arouse, stir up

exeo, exire, exii, exitus avoid, go away, depart

exercitus, exercitus, m. army

existimo, existimare, existimavi, exisimatus think, judge

experior, experiri, experitus sum test, try

expono, exponere, exposui, expositus set forth, exhibit, explain

exsolvo, exsolvere, exsolvi, exsolutus release, free

exspecto, exspectare, exspectavi, exspectatus await, expect, wait for

F

fabula, fabulae, f. story

facilis, facile easy

facio, facere, feci, factus make, do

fama, famae, f. rumor, renown, report

familiaris, familiaris, m. or f. friend

fames, famis, f. famine, hunger

febris, febris, f. fever

Februarius, Februaria, Februarium of February

femina, feminae, f. woman

fero, ferre, tuli, latus carry, bear

fides, fidei, f. faith, plege

filia, filiae, f. daughter

filius, filii or fili, m. son

finis, finis, m. end, border

fines, finium, m. pl. territory

finitimus, finitima, finitimum neighboring

finitimus, finitimi, m. neighbor

fio, fieri, factus sum become, be done, be made

firmo, firmare, firmavi, firmatus strengthen, make firm

firmus, firma, firmum firm, strong

flagito, flagitare, flagitavi, flagitatus demand

flumen, flumenis, n. river

fons, fontis, m. fountain, spring

formica, formicae, f. ant

fortasse perhaps

fortis, forte brave, strong

fortuna, fortunae, f. fortune, fate, luck

forum, fori, n. forum, market place

fossa, fossae, f. ditch

frater, fratris, m. brother

frequentia, frequentiae, f. crowd

fructus, fructus, m. produce, fruit

frugaliter temperately, frugally

frumentum, frumenti, n. grain

fuga, fugae, f. flight, escape

fugio, fugere, fugi, fugitus flee, run away, escape

fungor, fungi, functus sum perform, do

furor, furoris, m. rage, fury, passion

G

Gallia, Galliae, f. Gaul

Gallus, Galli, m. a Gaul

gaudium, gaudii or gaudi, n. joy

genus, generis, n. kind, class

Germania, Germaniae, f. Germany

Germanus, Germani, m. a German

gero, gerere, gessi, gestus carry on, wage

gladiator, gladiatoris, m. gladiator

gladius, gladii or gladi, m. sword

gloria, gloriae, f. glory

Graecia, Graeciae, f. Greece

Graecus, Graeca, Graecum Greek

gratus, grata, gratum pleasing

gravis, grave heavy, severe, serious

H

habeo, habere, habui, habitus have, hold

habito, habitare, habitavi, habitatus dwell, live

haesito, haesitare, haesitavi, haesitatus hesitate, be at a loss

Hannibal, Hannibalis, m. Hannibal

Hellespontus, Hellesponti, m. The Hellespont

Helvetii, Helvetiorum, m. pl. the Helvetii

Hercules, Herculis, m. Hercules

Hero, Herus, f. Hero

Hesperides, Hesperidium, f. pl. the Hesperides

hesternus, hesterna, hesternum yesterday

hic here, in this place

hic, haec, hoc this; he, she, it

hiems, hiemis, f. winter

Hippomenes, Hippominis, m. Hippomenes

Hispania, Hispaniae, f. Spain

hodie today

Homerus, Homeri, m. Homer

homo, hominis, m. man

honestus, honesta, honestum honored, respected

hora, horae, f. hour

Horatius, Horati, m. Horatius

hortor, hortari, hortatus sum urge, encourage

hortus, horti, m. garden

hospes, hospitis, m. host, guest, friend

hostis, hostis, m. enemy

huc to this place, hither

I

iacio, iacere, ieci, iactus throw

iam now, already

Ianuarius, Ianuaria, Ianuarium of January

ibi there, in that place

Icarus, Icari, m. Icarus

idem, eadem, idem the same; he, she, it

idoneus, idonea, idoneum fit, suitable

Idus, Iduum, f. the Ides

ignis, ignis, m. fire

ignoro, ignorare, ignoravi, ignoratus not know, be ignorant

ille, illa, illud that; he, she, it

illustro, illustrare, illustravi, illustratus make clear, reveal

immortalis, immortale immortal

impedimentum, impedimenti, n. hindrance

impedio, impedire, impedivi, impeditus hinder

imperator, imperatoris, m. commander, general, emperor

imperium, imperii or imperi, n. command

impero, imperare, imperavi, imperatus command, order

impetus, impetus, m. attack

in in, on; into, onte

incendo, incendere, incendi,

incensus set fire to, burn

incito, incitare, incitavi, incitatus arouse, stir up, incite

incola, incolae, m. or f. inhabitant

incolo, incolere, incolui live in, reside

Inferi, Inferorum, m. pl. Those Below, the dead

infestus, infesta, infestum threatening, dangerous, hostile

inimicus, inimica, inimicum unfriendly

inimicus, inimici, m. personal enemy

initium, initii or initi, n. beginning, start

iniuria, iniuriae, f. injury, harm

in libertatem vindicare set free

inopia, inopiae, f. want, scarcity

insequor, insequi, insecutus sum follow after, pursue

instruo, instruere, instruxi, instructus draw up, form, train

insula, insulae, f. island

intelligo, intelligere, intellexi, intellectus understand

inter among, between

intercludo, intercludere, interclusi, interclusus shut off, stop

interea meanwhile

interficio, interficere, interfeci, interfectus kill

inutilis, inutile useless, harmful

invenio, invenire, inveni, inventus find, come upon

ipse, ipsa, ipsum himself, herself, itself; very

is, ea, id he, she, it; that

iste, ista, istud that, that one of yours.

ita thus, so; yes

Italia, Italiae, f. Italy

itaque and so, therefore

item moreover, also

iter, intineris, n. journey, march, way

iterum again

iubeo, iubere, iussi, iussus order, command

iudicium, iudicii, or iudici, n. judgment, sentence

iudico, iudicare, iudicavi, iudicatus judge, sentence, examine

Iulia, Iuliae, f. Julia

Iulius, Iulia, Iulium, m. of Julius

Iunius, Iunia, Iunium of June

Iuno, Iunonis, f. Juno

Iuppiter, Iovis, m. Jupiter

iureiuro, iureiurare, iureiuravi, iureiuratus swear

ius, iuris, n. right, authority

iuvo, iuvare, iuvi, iutus help, aid

K

Kalendae, Kalendarum, f. the Kalends

L

labor, laboris, m. work, toil, labor

laboro, laborare, laboravi, laboratus work

labyrinthus, labyrinthi, m. labyrinth

laetus, laeta, laetum happy

lana, lanae, f. wool

latinus, latina, latinum Latin

Latinus, Latini, m. Latinus

Latium, Lati, n. Latium

Latobrigi, Latobrigorum, m. pl. Latobrigi

latus, lata, latum wide

laudo, laudare, laudavi, laudatus praise

Leander, Leandri, m. Leander

legatus, legati, m. lieutenant, legate

legio, legionis, f. legion

lego, legere, legi, lectus read

lenitas, lenitatis, f. mercy, mildness, gentleness

lex, legis, f. law

libenter gladly, with pleasure

liber, libera, liberum free

liber, libri, m. book

libero, liberare, liberavi, liberatus free, set free

lingua, linguae, f. language

littera, litterae, f. letter

loco, locare, locavi, locatus place, put

locus, loci, m. place

longus, longa, longum long

loquor, loqui, locutus sum say, speak

ludus, ludi, m. game

luna, lunae, f. moon

lupa, lupae, f. wolf

lux, lucis, f. light

M

magis more

magnitudo, magnitudinis, f. greatness, vastness

magnopere greatly

maior, maius larger

maiores, maiorum, m. pl. ancestors, forefathers

Maius, Maia, Maium of May

male badly

malo, malle, malui prefer

malus, mala, malum bad, evil

mane in the morning

maneo, manere, mansi, mansus remain

manus, manus, f. hand; group

Marathonius, Marathonia, Marathonium of Marathon

mare, maris, n. sea

maritus, mariti, m. husband

Martius, Martia, Martium of Mars, of March

mater, matris, f. mother

matrimonium, matrimonii or matrimoni, n. marriage

maxime most, especially

maximus, maxima, maximum largest

medius, media, medium middle, middle of

mehercule by Hercules!

melior, melius better

memoria, memoriae, f. memory

mens, mentis, f. mind

Mercurius, Mercuri, m. Mercury

metuo, metuere, metui fear, be afraid

meus, mea, meum my, mine

Midas, Midae, m. Midas

miles, milites, m. soldier

mille a thousand

mille passus mile

milia passuum miles

minime by no means, not at all

minimus, minima, minimum smallest

ministerium, ministerii or ministeri, n. service, work

minor, minus smaller

Minos, Minois, m. Minos

Minotaurus, Minotauri, m. the Minotaur

miser, misera, miserum wretched, unhappy

misercordia, misercordiae, f. sympathy, pity

misereor, misereri, miseritus sum pity, feel sorry for

mitto, mittere, misi, missus send

modeste moderately, modestly

modus, modi, m. manner, way

moneo, monere, monui, monitus warn, advise

mons, montis, m. mountain, mount

monstro, monstrare, monstravi, monstratus point out, show

mora, morae, f. delay

morior, mori, moritus sum die

mors, mortis, f. death

mortalis, mortale mortal

mortuus, mortua, mortuum dead

moveo, movere, movi, motus move

mox soon, presently

mulier, mulieris, f. woman

multitudo, multitudinis, f. great number, multitude

multo much, by much

multus, multa, multum much

murus, muri, m. wall

N

nam for

narro, narrare, narravi, narratus tell, relate

nascor, nasci, natus sum be born

natio, nationis, f. nation

nato, natare, natavi, natatus swim

natura, naturae, f. nature

nauta, nautae, m. sailor

navigo, navigare, navigavi, navigatus sail, cruise

navis, navis, f. ship

-ne indicates a question

ne that not, lest

necessaria, necessariae, f. relative, friend

necessarius, necessarii or necessari, m.   relative, friend

neco, necare, necavi, necatus   kill

nemo, neminis, m.   no one

neque   and not

neque . . . neque   neither . . . nor

nescio, nescire, nescivi, nescitus   not know, be ignorant of

Nicaea, Nicaeae, f.   Nicaea

Nicomedia, Nicomediae, f.   Nicomedia

nihil, nil, n.   nothing

nimis   very much, too much

nisi   if not, unless

noctu   at night

nolo, nolle, nolui   wish not, be unwilling

nomen, nomenis, n.   name

non   not

Nonae, Nonarum, f.   the Nones

nonne   indicates a question expecting the answer "yes"

nos, nostrum   we

noster, nostra, nostrum   our, ours

novem   nine

November, Novembris, Novembre   of November

novus, nova, novum   new

nox, noctis, f.   night

nullus, nulla, nullum   no, none

num   whether; indicates a question expecting the answer "no"

numerus, numeri, m.   number

numquam   never

nunc   now

nuntio, nuntiare, nuntiavi, nuntiatus   announce, report

nuntius, nuntii or nunti, m.   message, messenger

O

ob   on account of, because

obses, obsidis, m.   hostage

obtineo, obtinere, obtinui, obtentus   secure, obtain

occupo, occupare, occupavi, occupatus   seize, take possession of

oceanus, oceani, m.   ocean

October, Octobris, Octobre   of October

oculus, oculi, m.   eye

odium, odii or odi, n.   hatred

offendo, offendere, offendi, offensus   wound, offend

officium, officii or offici, n.   official job, official position

olim   formerly, once

omnis, omne   all, every

onus, oneris, n.   weight, burden

opera, operae, f.   service, pains, work

opinor, opinari, opinatus sum   think, suppose

oportet, oportere, oportuit (Impersonal verb)   it is right, it is proper

oppidum, oppidi, n.   town

opprimo, opprimere, oppressi, oppressus   overcome, crush

oppugno, oppugnare, oppugnavi, oppugnatus   attack

optimus, optima, optimum   best

opus, operis, n.   work

oraculum, oraculi, n.   oracle

ordo, ordinis, m.   rank, order

oro, orare, oravi, oratus   beg, pray

Orpheus, Orphei, m.   Orpheus

otiosus, otiosa, otiosum   free, at leisure, not working

ovis, ovis, f.   sheep

P

pactum, pacti, n.   way, manner

paene   almost, nearly

paeninsula, paeninsulae, f.   peninsula

parens, parentis, m. or f.   parent

paro, parare, paravi, paratus   prepare, get ready

parricidium, parricidii or parricidi, n.   parricide, murder, treason

pars, partis, f.   part

parum   too little, not enough

parvus, parva, parvum   small

pascor, pasci, pastus sum   feed on, eat

passus, passus, m.   pace

patefacio, patefacere, patefeci, patefactus   throw open, bring to light

pater, patris, m.   father

patior, pati, passus sum   allow, grant, suffer

patria, patriae, f.   native country

paulo   a little

pax, pacix, f.   peace

pecunia, pecuniae, f.   money

pedes, peditis, m.   foot soldier

peior, peius   worse

per   through

perfero, perferre, pertuli, perlatus   report

periculosus, periculosa, periculosum   dangerous, perilous

periculum, periculi, n.   danger

permitto, permittere, permisi, permissus   allow, permit

permoveo, permovere, permovi   stir, move

perpetuus, perpetus, perpetuum   continuous, perpetual, uninterrupted

Persae, Persarum, m. pl.   the Persians

persuadeo, persuadere, persuasi, persuasus   persuade

pertimesco, pertimescere, pertimui   fear, be alarmed at

pervenio, pervenire, perveni, perventus   arrive

pes, pedis, m.   foot

pessimus, pessima, pessimum   worst

peto, petere, petivi or petii, petitus   seek

piscis, piscis, m.   fish

placo, placare, placavi, placatus   calm, reconcile

plerusque, pleraque, plerumque   most

plurimum posse   be most powerful

plurimus, plurima, plurimum   most

plus, pluris   more

plus posse   be more powerful

Pluto, Plutonis, m.   Pluto

poena, poenae, f.   punishment, fine

poeta, poetae, m.   poet

polliceor, polliceri, pollicatus sum   promise

pollicitatio, pollicitationis, f.   promise

Polyphemus, Polyphemi, m.   Polyphemus

pomum, pomi, n.   apple

pono, ponere, posui, positus   put, place

pons, pontis, m.   bridge

populus, populi, m.   people

porta, portae, f.   gate, door, entrance

porto, portare, portavi, portatus   carry

portus, portus, m.   harbor, port

posco, poscere, poposci   ask, beg, demand

possum, posse, posui   be able

post   behind, at the back of

postea   afterwards

posterus, postera, posterum   next, following

postquam   after, when

postremus, postrema, postremum   last, finally

postridie   on the next day

postumus, postuma, postumum   next, following

praeda, praedae, f.   booty, plunder

praemium, praemii or praemi, n.   reward

praesentia, praesentiae, f.   presence, effect

praesidium, praesidii or praesidi, n.   guard, garrison

praesto, praestare, praestavi, praestatus   be better than, be superior to

pretium, pretii or preti, n.   price

primum, primo   first, at first

primus, prima, primum   first

princeps, princepis   chief; first, foremost

pristinus, pristina, pristinum   former, earlier

prius   before, previously

priusquam   before

pro   in front of; for, instead of; for, in behalf of

proelium, proelii or proeli, n.   battle

proficiscor, profisci, profectus sum   go forth, depart

profiteor, profiteri, professus sum declare, acknowledge, say

profugio, profugere, profugi run away, flee, escape

prohibeo, prohibere, prohibui, prohibitus keep off, hinder, prohibit, prevent

propero, properare, properavi, properatus hurry, hasten

propinquus, propinqua, propinquum near

propter because, on account of

propterea therefore, on that account

Proserpina, Proserpinae, f. Proserpina

provincia, provinciae, f. province

proximus, proxima, proximum next, nearest, most recent

Psyche, Psyches, f. Psyche

publicus, publica, publicum public, common

puella, puellae, f. girl

puer, pueri, m. boy

pugna, pugnae, f. fight

pugno, pugnare, pugnavi, pugnatus fight

pulcher, pulchra, pulchrum pretty, beautiful

pulchritudo, pulchritudinis, f. beauty

purgo, purgare, purgavi, purgatus clean, remove, excuse

puto, putare, putavi, putatus think, believe

Pythia, Pythiae, f. Pythia

Q

quaero, quaerere, quaesivi, quaesitus ask, look for

quam as possible; than

quam diu how long

quamquam although

quamvis although

quantum as much as

quantus, quanta, quantum how much

quare by what means, how, wherefore, therefore

-que and

queror, queri, questus sum complain about

qui, quae, quod who, which, that; which, what

quia because

quidam, quaedam, quiddam a certain one; pl., some

quin but that

quis, quid who, what

quod because

quoniam because, now that

quoque also

R

ratio, rationis, f. manner, fashion, reason

recido, recidere, recepi, receptus recoil, fall

recipio, recipere, recepi, receptus take back, receive

recupero, recuperare, recuperavi, recuperatus recover, get back

recuso, recusare, recusavi, recusatus refuse, reject

reddeo, reddere, reddidi, reditus return, restore

reduco, reducere, reduxi, reductus lead back

refero, referre, retuli, relatus report, bring back

regina, reginae, f. queen

regio, regionis, f. region, boundary

regno, regnare, regnavi, regnatus rule

regnum, regni, n. kingdom

rego, regere, rexi, rectus rule

relinquo, relinquere, reliqui, relictus leave, leave behind

reliquus, reliqua, reliquum remaining, the rest of

reperio, reperire, repperi, repertus find, discover

reporto, reportare, reportavi, reportatus carry back, bring back

res, rei, f. thing, matter, affair

res publica, rei publicae, f. republic, common good

rescisco, resciscere, rescii, rescitus learn, find out

restituo, restituere, restitui, restitutus restore, rebuild

retineo, retinere, retinui, retentus keep back, retain

revertor, reverti, reversus sum turn back, return

rex, regis, m. king

Rhenus, Rheni, m. the Rhine

ripa, ripae, f. river bank

robustus, robusta, robustum strong, robust

Roma, Romae, f. Rome

Romanus, Romana, Romanum Roman

Romanus, Romani, m. a Roman

ruri in the country

rursus backward, on the other hand

S

Sabini, Sabinorum, m. pl. the Sabines

saepe often

sagitta, sagittae, f. arrow

sagittarius, sagittarii or sagittari, m. archer

salus, salutis, f. health, safety

saluto, salutare, salutavi, salutatus greet, welcome

salvus, salva, salvum safe, well

sapientia, sapientiae, f. wisdom

satis enough

saxum, saxi, n. stone, rock

scio, scire, scivi, scitus know

scribo, scribere, scripsi, scriptus write

se him, her, it (reflexive)

sed but

semper always

senatus, senatus, m. senate

senex, senix old, aged

sensus, sensus, m. sense, sensation, feeling

sentio, sentire, sensi, sensum feel, perceive, realize

septem seven

September, Septembris, Septembre of September

septimus, septima, septimum seventh

sequor, sequi, secutus sum follow

serpens, serpentis, f. snake, serpent

servo, servare, servavi, servatus save, preserve

servus, servi, m. slave, servant

severitas, severitatis, f. severity, strictness

sex six

si if

Sibyllinus, Sibyllina, Sibyllinum Sibylline

sic so, thus

signum, signi, n. signal, standard

Silenus, Sileni, m. Silenus

silva, silvae, f. forest, woods

similis like, similar

simulo, simulare, simulavi, simulatus pretend

sine without

socius, socii or soci, m. comrade, ally

sol, solis, m. sun

solum alone, only

solus, sola, solum alone, only

somnus, somni, m. sleep

soror, sororis, f. sister

Sparta, Spartae, f. Sparta

specto, spectare, spectavi, spectatus hope

spes, spei, f. hope

stella, stellae, f. star

sto, stare, steti, status stand

studium, studii or studi, n. zeal, eagerness

sub under

sum, esse, fui, futurus be

summus, summa, summum greatest, highest, top of

superbus, superba, superbum proud, haughty

supero, superare, superavi, superatus surpass, overcome, conquer

superior, superius higher, past, preceding

supra over, above

suscipio, suscipere, suscepi, susceptus take up, undertake

suspicio, suspicere, suspexi, suspectus mistrust, suspect

suus, sua, suum his, her, its, their

T

tabesco, tabescere, tabescui decay, melt away

taciturnitas, taciturnitatis, f. silence

tam so

tamen however, nevertheless

tametsi even if

tandem finally

tango, tangere, tetigi, tactus   touch

tantus, tanta, tantum   so great

Tarquinius, Tarquini, m.   Tarquinius

telum, teli, n.   weapon

tempestas, tempestatis, f.   storm, bad weather

templum, templi, n.   temple

tempus, temporis, n.   time

teneo, tenere, tenui, tentus   hold, keep, have

terra, terrae, f.   land, earth

terreo, terrere, terrui, territus   frighten, scare, terrify

Thermopylae, Thermopylarum, f. pl.   Thermopylae

Theseus, Thesei, m.   Theseus

timeo, timere, timui   fear, be afraid of

timidus, timida, timidum   timid

timor, timoris, m.   fear, dread

tolero, tolerare, toleravi, toleratus   bear, endure

tot   so many

totus, tota, totum   all, whole

trado, tradere, tradidi,

traditus   give up, surrender

traho, trahere, traxi, tractus   drag, draw

trans   across

transeo, transire, transivi, transitus   pass over, cross, desert

Troia, Troiae, f.   Troy

tu, tui   you

Tulingi, Tulingorum, m. pl.   the Tulingi

tum   then, at that time

turris, turris, f.   tower

tuus, tua, tuum   your, yours

U

ubi   where, when

Ulixes, Ulixis, m.   Ulysses

ultimus, ultima, ultimum   last, farthest

umerus, umeri, m.   shoulder

umquam   ever

unde   from where, whence

unus, una, unum   one

urbs, urbis, f.   city

ut, uti   as; that, so that

uterque, utraque, utrumque   each, every

utilis, utile   useful

utinam   if only, would that

uxor, uxoris, f.   wife

V

vaco, vacare, vacavi, vacatus   be empty

vehementer   violently, eagerly

vel   or

vel . . . vel   either . . . or

venio, venire, veni, venitus   come

ventus, venti, m.   word

Venus, Veneris, f.   Venus

verbum, verbi, n.   word

vereor, vereri, veritus sum   fear

vero   truly, in truth

verto, vertere, verti, versus   turn

vespera, vesperae, f.   evening

vester, vestra, vestrum   your, yours

veto, vetare, vetavi, vetatus   forbid

vetus, veteris   old, aged

via, viae, f.   road, way, street

victoria, victoriae, f.   victory

vicus, vici, m.   village, street

video, videre, vidi, visus sum   see

vinco, vincere, vici, victus

conquer

vindico, vindicare, vindicavi, vindicatus   defend, protect

vir, viri, m.   man

virtus, virtutis, f.   courage, virtue

vis, vis, f.   force

vita, vitae, f.   life

vito, vitare, vitavi, vitatus   avoid

vivo, vivere, vixi, victus   live

voco, vocare, vocavi, vocatus   call

volo, velle, volui   wish, be willing

volo, volare, volavi, volatus   fly

vos, vestrum   you

vox, vocix, f.   voice

vulnero, vulnerare, vulneravi, vulneratus   wound, hurt

vulnus, vulneris, n.   wound

Z

Zephyrus, Zephyri, m.   Zephyr, west wind

Nouns

First Declension:

aqua, water

	Singular	Plural
Nom.	aqua	aquae
Gen.	aquae	aquarum
Dat.	aquae	aquis
Acc.	aquam	aquas
Abl.	aqua	aquis
Voc.	aqua	aquae

Second Declension:
Masculine:

servus, slave

Nom.	servus	servi
Gen.	servi	servorum
Dat.	servo	servis
Acc.	servum	servos
Abl.	servo	servis
Voc.	serve	servi

puer, boy

Nom.	puer	pueri
Gen.	pueri	puerorum
Dat.	puero	pueris
Acc.	puerum	pueros
Abl.	puero	pueris
Voc.	puer	pueri

Neuter

periculum, danger

Nom.	periculum	pericula
Gen.	periculi	periculorum
Dat.	periculo	periculis
Acc.	periculum	pericula
Abl.	periculo	periculis
Voc.	periculum	pericula

Third Declension:
Masculine:

miles, soldier

Nom.	miles	milites
Gen.	militis	militum
Dat.	militi	militibus
Acc.	militem	milites
Abl.	milite	militibus
Voc.	miles	milites

Feminine:

urbs, city

Nom.	urbs	urbes
Gen.	urbis	urbium
Dat.	urbi	urbibus
Acc.	urbem	urbes
Abl.	urbe	urbibus
Voc.	urbs	urbes

Neuter:

caput, head

Nom.	caput	capita
Gen.	capitis	capitum
Dat.	capiti	capitibus
Acc.	caput	capita
Abl.	capite	capitibus
Voc.	caput	capita

Irregular Noun:

vis, force

Nom.	vis	vires
Gen.	vis	virium
Dat.	vi	viribus
Acc.	vim	vires
Abl.	vi	viribus

Fourth Declension:
Masculine:

passus, pace

Nom.	passus	passus
Gen.	passus	passuum
Dat.	passui	passibus
Acc.	passum	passus
Abl.	passu	passibus
Voc.	passus	passus

Neuter:

cornu, horn

Nom.	cornu	cornua
Gen.	cornus	cornuum
Dat.	cornu	cornibus
Acc.	cornu	cornua
Abl.	cornu	cornibus
Voc.	cornu	cornua

Fifth Declension:

spes, hope

Nom.	spes	spes
Gen.	spei	sperum
Dat.	spei	spebus
Acc.	spem	spes
Abl.	spe	spebus
Voc.	spes	spes

Adjectives

First and Second Declension:

bonus, good

Singular

	Masc.	Fem.	Neut.
Nom.	bonus	bona	bonum
Gen.	boni	bonae	boni
Dat.	bono	bonae	bono
Acc.	bonum	bonam	bonum
Abl.	bono	bona	bono
Voc.	bone	bona	bonum

Plural

	Masc.	Fem.	Neut.
Nom.	boni	bonae	bona
Gen.	bonorum	bonarum	bonorum
Dat.	bonis	bonis	bonis
Acc.	bonos	bonas	bona
Abl.	bonis	bonis	bonis
Voc.	boni	bonae	bona

liber, free

Singular

	Masc.	Fem.	Neut.
Nom.	liber	libera	liberum
Gen.	liberi	liberae	liberi
Dat.	libero	liberae	libero
	etc.	etc.	etc.

pulcher, pretty

Singular

	Masc.	Fem.	Neut.
Nom.	pulcher	pulchra	pulchrum
Gen.	pulchri	pulchrae	pulchri
Dat.	pulchro	pulchrae	pulchro
	etc.	etc.	etc.

Third Declension:

One ending: **audax**, bold

Singular

	Masc. & Fem.	Neut.
Nom.	audax	audax
Gen.	audacis	audacis
Dat.	audaci	audaci
Acc.	audacem	audax
Abl.	audaci	audaci
Voc.	audax	audax

Plural

	Masc. & Fem.	Neut.
Nom.	audaces	audacia
Gen.	audacium	audacium
Dat.	audacibus	audacibus
Acc.	audaces	audacia
Abl.	audacibus	audacibus
Voc.	audaces	audacia

Two endings: **brevis, breve**, short

Singular

	Masc. & Fem.	Neut.
Nom.	brevis	breve
Gen.	brevis	brevis
Dat.	brevi	brevi
Acc.	brevem	breve
Abl.	brevi	brevi
Voc.	brevis	breve

Plural

	Masc. & Fem.	Neut.
Nom.	breves	brevia
Gen.	brevium	brevium
Dat.	brevibus	brevibus
Acc.	breves	brevia
Abl.	brevibus	brevibus
Voc.	breves	brevia

Three endings: **celer, celeris, celere**, quick

Singular

	Masc.	Fem.	Neut.
Nom.	celer	celeris	celere
Gen.	celeris	celeris	celeris
Dat.	celeri	celeri	celeri
Acc.	celerem	celerem	celere
Abl.	celeri	celeri	celeri
Voc.	celer	celeris	celere

Plural

	Masc. & Fem.	Neut.
Nom.	celeres	celeria
Gen.	celerium	celerium
Dat.	celeribus	celeribus
Acc.	celeres	celeria
Abl.	celeribus	celeribus
Voc.	celeres	celeria

Comparative Adjectives: Singular

facilior, facilius, easier

	Masc. & Fem.	Neut.
Nom.	facilior	facilius
Gen.	facilioris	facilioris
Dat.	faciliori	faciliori
Acc.	faciliorem	faciliorus
Abl.	faciliore	faciliore
Voc.	facilior	facilius

Plural

	Masc. & Fem.	Neut.
Nom.	faciliores	faciliora
Gen.	faciliorum	faciliorum
Dat.	facilioribus	facilioribus
Acc.	faciliores	faciliora
Abl.	facilioribus	facilioribus
Voc.	faciliores	faciliora

Pronouns

Personal Pronouns:

First Person:

	Singular:	Plural:
Nom.	ego	nos
Gen.	mei	nostrum, nostri
Dat.	mihi	nobis
Acc.	me	nos
Abl.	me	nobis

Second Person:

	Singular:	Plural:
Nom.	tu	vos
Gen.	tui	vestrum, vestri
Dat.	tibi	vobis
Acc.	te	vos
Abl.	te	vobis

Third Person (Reflexive):

	Singular:	Plural:
Nom.	—-	—-
Gen.	sui	sui
Dat.	sibi	sibi
Acc.	se	se
Abl.	se	se

Demonstrative Pronouns:

1. hic

Singular

	Masc.	Fem.	Neut.
Nom.	hic	haec	hoc
Gen.	huius	huius	huius
Dat.	huic	huic	huic
Acc.	hunc	hanc	hoc
Abl.	hoc	hac	hoc

Plural

	Masc.	Fem.	Neut.
Nom.	hi	hae	haec
Gen.	horum	harum	horum
Dat.	his	his	his
Acc.	hos	has	haec
Abl.	his	his	his

2. ille

Singular

	Masc.	Fem.	Neut.
Nom.	ille	illa	illud
Gen.	illius	illius	illius
Dat.	illi	illi	illi
Acc.	illum	illam	illum
Abl.	illo	illa	illo

Plural

	Masc.	Fem.	Neut.
Nom.	illi	illae	illa
Gen.	illorum	illarum	illorum
Dat.	illis	illis	illis
Acc.	illos	illas	illos
Abl.	illis	illis	illis

Intensive Pronoun: **ipse**

Singular

	Masc.	Fem.	Neut.
Nom.	ipse	ipsa	ipsum
Gen.	ipsius	ipsius	ipsius
Dat.	ipsi	ipsi	ipsi
Acc.	ipsum	ipsam	ipsum
Abl.	ipso	ipsa	ipso

Plural

	Masc.	Fem.	Neut.
Nom.	ipsi	ipsae	ipsa
Gen.	ipsorum	ipsarum	ipsorum
Dat.	ipsis	ipsis	ipsis
Acc.	ipsos	ipsas	ipsa
Abl.	ipsis	ipsis	ipsis

Remember that **ipse** is also an adjective.

Relative Pronoun: **qui**

Singular

	Masc.	Fem.	Neut.
Nom.	qui	quae	quod
Gen.	cuius	cuius	cuius
Dat.	cui	cui	cui
Acc.	quem	quam	quod
Abl.	quo	qua	quo

Plural

	Masc.	Fem.	Neut.
Nom.	qui	quae	quae
Gen.	quorum	quarum	quorum
Dat.	quibus	quibus	quibus
Acc.	quos	quas	quos
Abl.	quibus	quibus	quibus

Remember that **qui** is also the interrogative adjective.

Interrogative Pronoun: **quis**

Singular

	Masc. & Fem.	Neut.
Nom.	quis	quid
Gen.	cuius	cuius
Dat.	cui	cui
Acc.	quem	quid
Abl.	quo	quo

Plural

The plural of the interrogative pronoun is the same as the plural of the relative pronoun.

Verbs

Regular Verbs:

	Principal Parts:
First Conjugation: **amo**	amo, amare, amavi, amatus
Second Conjugation: **habeo**	habeo, habere, habui, habitus
Third Conjugation: **duco**	duco, ducere, duxi, ductus
Third Conjugation "io" verb: **capio**	capio, capere, cepi, captus
Fourth Conjugation: **audio**	audio, audire, audivi, auditus

Indicative Mood:

Active Voice:
Present:

amo	habeo	duco	capio	audio
amas	habes	ducis	capis	audis
amat	habet	ducit	capit	audit
amamus	habemus	ducimus	capimus	audimus
amatis	habetis	ducitis	capitis	auditis
amant	habent	ducunt	capiunt	audiunt

Imperfect:

amabam	habebam	ducebam	capiebam	audiebam
amabas	habebas	ducebas	capiebas	audiebas
amabat	habebat	ducebat	capiebat	audiebat
amabamus	habebamus	ducebamus	capiebamus	audiebamus
amabatis	habebatis	ducebatis	capiebatis	audiebatis
amabant	habebant	ducebant	capiebant	audiebant

Future:

amabo	habebo	ducam	capiam	audiam
amabis	habebis	duces	capies	audies
amabit	habebit	ducet	capiet	audiet
amabimus	habebimus	ducemus	capiemus	audiemus
amabitis	habebitis	ducetis	capietis	audietis
amabunt	habebunt	ducent	capient	audient

Perfect:

amavi	habui	duxi	cepi	audivi
amavisti	habuisti	duxisti	cepisti	audivisti
amavit	habuit	duxit	cepit	audivit
amavimus	habuimus	duximus	cepimus	audivimus
amavistis	habuistis	duxistis	cepistis	audivistis
amaverunt	habuerunt	duxerunt	ceperunt	audiverunt

Pluperfect:

amaveram	habueram	duxeram	ceperam	audiveram
amaveras	habueras	duxeras	ceperas	audiveras
amaverat	habuerat	duxerat	ceperat	audiverat
amaveramus	habueramus	duxeramus	ceperamus	audiveramus
amaveratis	habueratis	duxeratis	ceperatis	audiveratis
amaverant	habuerant	duxerant	ceperant	audiverant

Future Perfect:

amavero	habuero	duxero	cepero	audivero
amaveris	habueris	duxeris	ceperis	audiveris
amaverit	habuerit	duxerit	ceperit	audiverit
amaverimus	habuerimus	duxerimus	ceperimus	audiverimus
amaveritis	habueritis	duxeritis	ceperitis	audiveritis
amaverint	habuerint	duxerint	ceperint	audiverint

Passive Voice:

Present:

amor	habeor	ducor	capior	audior
amaris	haberis	duceris	caperis	audiris
amatur	habetur	ducitur	capitur	auditur
amamur	habemur	ducimur	capimur	audimur
amamini	habemini	ducimini	capimini	audimini
amantur	habentur	ducuntur	capiuntur	audiuntur

Imperfect:

amabar	habebar	ducebar	capiebar	audiebar
amabaris	habebaris	ducebaris	capiebaris	audiebaris
amabatur	habebatur	ducebatur	capiebatur	audiebatur
amabamur	habebamur	ducebamur	capiebamur	audiebamur
amabamini	habebamini	ducebamini	capiebamini	audiebamini
amabantur	habebantur	ducebantur	capiebantur	audiebantur

Future:

amabor	habebor	ducar	capiar	audiar
amaberis	habeberis	duceris	capieris	audieris
amabitur	habebitur	ducetur	capietur	audietur
amabimur	habebimur	ducemur	capiemur	audiemur
amabimini	habebimini	ducemini	capiemini	audiemini
amabuntur	habebuntur	ducentur	capientur	audientur

Perfect:

amatus, -a, -um sum	habitus, -a, -um sum	ductus, -a, -um sum
amatus es	habitus es	ductus es
amatus est	habitus est	ductus est
amati, -ae, -a sumus	habiti, -ae, -a sumus	ducti, ae, -a sumus
amati estis	habiti estis	ducti estis
amati sunt	habiti sunt	ducti sunt

captus, -a, -um sum	auditus, -a, -um sum
captus es	auditus es
captus est	auditus est
capti, -ae, -a sumus	auditi, -ae, -um sumus
capti estis	auditi estis
capti sunt	auditi sunt

Pluperfect:

amatus, -a, -um eram	habitus eram	ductus eram	captus eram	auditus eram
amatus eras	habitus eras	ductus eras	captus eras	auditus eras
amatus erat	habitus erat	ductus erat	captus erat	auditus erat
amati, -ae, -a eramus	habiti eramus	ducti eramus	capti eramus	auditi eramus
amati eratis	habiti eratis	ducti eratis	capti eratis	auditi eratis
amati erant	habiti erant	ducti erant	capti erant	auditi erant

Future Perfect:

amatus, -a, -um ero	habitus ero	ductus ero	captus ero	auditus ero
amatus eris	habitus eris	ductus eris	captus eris	auditus eris
amatus erit	habitus erit	ductus erit	captus erit	auditus erit
amati, -ae, -a erimus	habiti erimus	ducti erimus	capti erimus	auditi erimus
amati eritis	habiti eritis	ducti eritis	capti eritis	auditi eritis
amati erunt	habiti erunt	ducti erunt	capti erunt	auditi erunt

Subjunctive Mood:

Active Voice:
Present:

amem	habeam	ducam	capiam	audiam
ames	habeas	ducas	capias	audias
amet	habeat	ducat	capiat	audiat
amemus	habeamus	ducamus	capiamus	audiamus
ametis	habetis	ducatis	capiatis	audiatis
ament	habeant	ducant	capiant	audiant

Perfect:

amaverim	habuerim	duxerim	ceperim	audiverim
amaveris	habueris	duxeris	ceperis	audiveris
amaverit	habuerit	duxerit	ceperit	audiverit
amaverimus	habuerimus	duxerimus	ceperimus	audiverimus
amaveritis	habueritis	duxeritis	ceperitis	audiveritis
amaverint	habuerint	duxerint	ceperint	audiverint

Imperfect:

amarem	haberem	ducerem	caperem	audirem
amares	haberes	duceres	caperes	audires
amaret	haberet	duceret	caperet	audiret
amaremus	haberemus	duceremus	caperemus	audiremus
amaretis	haberetis	duceretis	caperetis	audiretis
amarent	haberent	ducerent	caperent	audirent

Pluperfect:

amavissem	habuissem	duxissem	cepissem	audivissem
amavisses	habuisses	duxisses	cepisses	audivisses
amavisset	habuisset	duxisset	cepisset	audivisset
amavissemus	habuissemus	duxissemus	cepissemus	audivissemus
amavissetis	habuissetis	duxissetis	cepissetis	audivissetis
amavissent	habuissent	duxissent	cepissent	audivissent

Passive Voice:
Present:

amer	habear	ducar	capiar	audiar
ameris	habearis	ducaris	capiaris	audiaris
ametur	habeatur	ducatur	capiatur	audiatur
amemur	habeamur	ducamur	capiamur	audiamur
amemini	habeamini	ducamini	capiamini	audiamini
amentur	habeantur	ducantur	capiantur	audiantur

Perfect:

amatus, -a, -um sim	habitus, -a, -um sim	ductus, -a, -um sim
amatus sis	habitus sis	ductus sis
amatus sit	habitus sit	ductus sit
amati, -ae, -a simus	habiti, -ae, -a simus	ducti, -ae, -a simus
amati sitis	habiti sitis	ducti sitis
amati sint	habiti sint	ducti sint

captus, -a, -um sim	auditus, -a, -um sim
captus sis	auditus sis
captus sit	auditus sit
capti, -ae, -a simus	auditi, -ae, -a simus
capti sitis	auditi sitis
capti sint	auditi sint

Imperfect:

amarer	haberer	ducerer	caperer	audirer
amareris	habereris	ducereris	capereris	audireris
amaretur	haberetur	duceretur	caperetur	audiretur
amaremur	haberemur	duceremur	caperemur	audiremur
amaremini	haberemini	duceremini	caperemini	audiremini
amarentur	haberentur	ducerentur	caperentur	audirentur

Pluperfect:

amatus, -a, -um essem	habitus essem	ductus essem	captus essem	auditus essem
amatus esses	habitus esses	ductus esses	captus esses	auditus esses
amatus esset	habitus esset	ductus esset	captus esset	auditus esset
amati, -ae, -a essemus	habiti essemus	ducti essemus	capti essemus	auditi essemus
amati essetis	habiti essetis	ducti essetis	capti essetis	auditi essetis
amati essent	habiti essent	ducti essent	capti essent	auditi essent

Imperative Mood:

Singular: **ama**   habe   duc   cape   audi

Note that **duc** is irregular. Most third conjugation verbs end in -e in the imperative singular.

Plural: **amate**   habete   ducite   capite   audite

Infinitives:
Active Voice:
Present: **amare**   habere   ducere   capere   audire
Perfect: **amavisse**   habuisse   duxisse   cepisse   audivisse
Future: **amaturus esse**   habiturus esse   ducturus esse   capturus esse   auditurus esse

Passive Voice:
Present: **amari**   haberi   duci   capi   audiri
Perfect: **amatus esse**   habitus esse   ductus esse   captus esse   auditus esse
Future: **amatum iri**   habitum iri   ductum iri   captum iri   auditum iri

Participles:
Active Voice:
Present: **amans**   habens   ducens   capiens   audiens
Future: **amaturus**   habiturus   ducturus   capturus   auditurus

Passive Voice:
Perfect: **amatus**   habitus   ductus   captus   auditus
Future: **amandus**   habendus   ducendus   capiendus   audiendus

Irregular Verbs: **Sum, possum, and eo.**   None of these verbs has a passive voice.
Principal parts: **sum, esse, fui, futurus   possum, posse, potui   eo, ire, ii or ivi, itum**

Indicative Mood:
Present:

sum	possum	eo
es	potes	is
est	potest	it
sumus	possumus	imus
estis	potestis	itis
sunt	possunt	eunt

Imperfect:

eram	poteram	ibam
eras	poteras	ibas
erat	poterat	ibat
eramus	poteramus	ibamus
eratis	poteratis	ibatis
erant	poterant	ibant

Future:

ero	potero	ibo
eris	poteris	ibis
erit	poterit	ibit
erimus	poterimus	ibimus
eritis	poteritis	ibitis
erunt	poterunt	ibunt

Perfect:

fui	potui	ii or ivi
fuisti	potuis	isti
fuit	potuit	iit
fuimus	potuimus	iimus
fuistis	potuistis	istis
fuerunt	potuerunt	ierunt

Pluperfect:

fueram	potueram	ieram
fueras	potueras	ieras
fuerat	potuerat	ierat
fueramus	potueramus	ieramus
fueratis	potueratis	ieratis
fuerant	potuerant	ierant

Future Perfect:

fuero	potuero	iero
fueris	potueris	ieris
fuerit	potuerit	ierit
fuerimus	potuerimus	ierimus
fueritis	potueritis	ieritis
fuerint	potuerint	ierint

Subjunctive Mood:
Present:

sim	possim	eam
sis	possis	eas
sit	possit	eat
simus	possimus	eamus
sitis	possitis	eatis
sint	possint	eant

Perfect:

fuerim	potuerim	ierim
fueris	potueris	ieris
fuerit	potuerit	ierit
fuerimus	potuerimus	ierimus
fueritis	potueritis	ieritis
fuerint	potuerint	ierint

Imperfect:

essem	possem	irem
esses	posses	ires
esset	posset	iret
essemus	possemus	iremus
essetis	possetis	iretis
essent	possent	irent

Pluperfect:

fuissem	potuissem	issem
fuisses	potuisses	isses
fuisset	potuisset	isset
fuissemus	potuissemus	issemus
fuissetis	potuissetis	issetis
fuissent	potuissent	issent

Imperative Mood:
Only **sum** has the imperative mood.
Singular: **es**
Plural: **este**

Infinitives:
Present:

esse	posse	ire

Perfect:

fuisse	potuisse	isse

Future:

futurus esse	——-	iturus esse

Participles:
Present:

—— potens iens

Note that the genitive of **iens** is **euntis**.

Future:

futurus —— **iturus**

Volo, nolo, and **malo.**
Note that none of these verbs has a passive voice.
Principal parts:
volo, velle, volui
nolo, nolle, nolui
malo, malle, malui

Indicative Mood:
Present:

volo	nolo	malo
vis	non vis	mavis
vult	non vult	malvult
volumus	nolumus	malumus
vultis	non vultis	mavultis
volunt	nolunt	malunt

Imperfect:

volebam	nolebam	malebam
volebas	nolebas	malebas
volebat	nolebat	malebat
volebamus	nolebamus	malebamus
volebatis	nolebatis	malebatis
volebant	nolebant	malebant

Future:

volam	nolam	malam
voles	noles	males
volet	nolet	malet
volemus	nolemus	malemus
voletis	noletis	maletis
volent	nolent	malent

Perfect:

volui	nolui	malui
voluisti	noluisti	maluisti
voluit	noluit	maluit
voluimus	noluimus	maluimus
voluistis	noluistis	maluistis
voluerunt	noluerunt	maluerunt

Pluperfect:

volueram	nolueram	malueram
volueras	nolueras	malueras
voluerat	noluerat	maluerat
volueramus	nolueramus	malueramus
volueratis	nolueratis	malueratis
voluerant	noluerant	maluerant

Future Perfect:

voluero	noluero	maluero
volueris	nolueris	malueris
voluerit	noluerit	maluerit
voluerimus	noluerimus	maluerimus
volueritis	nolueritis	malueritis
voluerint	noluerint	maluerint

Subjunctive Mood:
Present:

velim	nolim	malim
velis	nolis	malis
velit	nolit	malit
velimus	nolimus	malimus
velitis	nolitis	malitis
velint	nolint	malint

Perfect:

voluerim	noluerim	maluerim
volueris	nolueris	malueris
voluerit	noluerit	maluerit
voluerimus	noluerimus	maluerimus
volueritis	nolueritis	malueritis
voluerint	noluerint	maluerint

Imperfect:

vellem	nollem	mallem
velles	nolles	malles
vellet	nollet	mallet
vellemus	nollemus	mallemus
velletis	nolletis	malletis
vellent	nollent	mallent

Pluperfect:

voluissem	noluissem	maluissem
voluisses	noluisses	maluisses
voluisset	noluisset	maluisset
voluissemus	noluissemus	maluissemus
voluissetis	noluissetis	maluissetis
voluissent	noluissent	maluissent

Imperative Mood:
Only **nolo** has the imperative mood.
Singular: **noli**
Plural: **nolite**

Infinitives:
Present:

| velle | nolle | malle |

Perfect:

| voluisse | noluisse | maluisse |

Participles;
Present:

| volens | nolens | ——- |

Fio.
Note that the verb **fio** has no active voice.
Principal parts: **fio, fieri, factus sum**
Indicative Mood:

Present:	Imperfect:	Future:
fio	fiebam	fiam
fis	fiebas	fies
fit	fiebat	fiet
—	fiebamus	fiemus
—	fiebatis	fietis
fiunt	fiebat	fient

Perfect:	Pluperfect:	Future Perfect:
factus sum	factus eram	factus ero
factus es	factus eras	factus eris
factus est	factus erat	factus erit
facti sumus	facti eramus	facti erimus
facti estis	facti eratis	facti eritis
facti sunt	facti erant	facti erunt

Subjunctive Mood:

Present:	Perfect:
fiam	factus sim
fias	factus sis
fiat	factus sit
fiamus	facti simus
fiatis	facti sitis
fiant	facti sint

Imperfect:	Pluperfect:
fierem	factus essem
fieres	factus esses
fieret	factus esset
fieremus	facti essemus
fieretis	facti essetis
fierent	facti essent

Imperative Mood:
Singular: **fi**
Plural: **fite**

	Infinitives:	Participles:
Present:	fieri	
Perfect:	factus esse	factus
Future:	factum iri	faciendus

Fero.

Principal Parts:
fero, ferre, tuli, latus

Indicative Mood:
Present:

Active:	Passive:
fero	feror
fers	feris
fert	fertur
ferimus	ferimur
fertis	ferimini
ferunt	feruntur

Imperfect:

Active:	Passive:
ferebam	ferebar
ferebas	ferebaris
ferebat	ferebatur
ferebamus	ferebamur
ferebatis	ferebamini
ferebant	ferebantur

Future:

Active:	Passive:
feram	ferar
feres	fereris
feret	feretur
feremus	feremur
feretis	feremini
ferent	ferentur

Perfect:

Active:	Passive:
tuli	latus sum
tulis	latus es
tulit	latus est
tulimus	lati sumus
tulistis	lati estis
tulerunt	lati sunt

Pluperfect:

Active:	Passive:
tuleram	latus eram
tuleras	latus eras
tulierat	latus erat
tuleramus	lati eramus
tuleratis	lati eratis
tulerant	lati erant

Future Perfect:

Active:	Passive:
tulero	latus ero
tuleris	latus eris
tulerit	latus erit
tulerimus	lati erimus
tuleritis	lati eritis
tulerint	lati erunt

Subjunctive Mood:

Present

Active	Passive
feram	ferar
feras	feraris
ferat	feratur
feramus	feramur
feratis	feramini
ferant	ferantur

Perfect:

Active:	Passive:
tulerim	latus sim
tuleris	latus sis
tulerit	latus sit
tulerimus	lati simus
tuleritis	lati sitis
tulerint	lati sint

Imperfect:

Active	Passive
ferrem	ferrer
ferres	ferreris
ferret	ferretur
ferremus	ferremur
ferretis	ferremini
ferrent	ferrentur

Pluperfect:

Active	Passive
tulissem	latus essem
tulisses	latus esses
tulisset	latus esset
tulissemus	lati essemus
tulissetis	lati essetis
tulissent	lati essent

Imperative Mood:

Singular: **fer**   Plural: **ferte**

Infinitives:

	Active:	Passive:
Present:	ferre	ferri
Perfect:	tulisse	latus esse
Future:	laturus esse	latum iri

Participles:

	Active:	Passive:
Present:	ferens	
Perfect:		latus
Future:	laturus	ferendus

Numbers

CARDINAL	ORDINAL	ARABIC	ROMAN
unus, una, unum	primus, -a, -um	1	I
duo, duae, duo	secundus, -a, um	2	II
tres, tria, tria	tertius, -a, um	3	III
quattuor	quartus	4	IIII, IV
quinque	quintus	5	V
sex	sextus	6	VI
septem	septimus	7	VII
octo	octavus	8	VIII
novem	nonus	9	VIIII, IX
decem	decimus	10	X
undecim	undecimus	11	XI
duodecim	duodecimus	12	XII
tredecim	tertius decimus	13	XIII
quattuordecim	quartus decimus	14	XIIII, XIV
quindecim	quintus decimus	15	XV
sedecim	sextus decimus	16	XVI
septendecim	septimus decimus	17	XVII
duodeviginti	duodevicesimus	18	XVIII
undeviginti	undevicesimus	19	XVIIII, XIX
viginti unus, unus et	vicesimus	20	XX
viginti	unus et vicesimus	21	XXI
triginta	tricesimus	30	XXX
quadraginta	quadragesimus	40	XXXX, XL
quinquaginta	quinquagesimus	50	L
sexaginta	sexagesimus	60	LX
septuaginta	septuagesimus	70	LXX
octoginta	octogesimus	80	LXXX
nonaginta	nonagesimus	90	LXXXX, XC
centum	centesimus	100	C

BIBLIOGRAPHY

The following list is by no means exhaustive. Many other Latin books have been translated into English, most of them by several different translators.

Metamorphoses, by Apuleius. Based on the story *Lucius, or the Ass,* by Lucian, this book is also known as *The Golden Ass.* It is one of the only two surviving Roman novels, and tells the story of a man transformed into an ass.

Satyricon, by Petronius Arbiter. This is the other surviving Roman novel. though only fragments of the full work remain. The longest of these is called *Cena Trimalchionis,* or *The Feast of Trimalchio.*

Commentarii de Bello Gallico, by Gaius Julius Caesar.

Poems, by Gaius Valerius Catullus.

Narrationes, by Odo de Cerinton.

In Catilinam I - IV, by Marcus Tullius Cicero.

Brevarium, by Eutropius. This is a history of Rome from 753 B.C. to A.D. 364.

Odes, by Quintus Horatius Flaccus.

Lucius, or the Ass, by Lucian. This was Apuleius' source for *The Golden Ass.*

De Rerum Natura, by Titus Lucretius Carus (Lucretius). As the title suggests, this is a poem discussing *The Nature of Things.*

Epigrams, by Marcus Valerius Martialis.

Metamorphoses, by Publius Ovidius Naso (Ovid). Don't confuse this with Apuleius' work of the same name. This is not a novel, but a long poem which tells the stories of people tranformed into something else.

Fables, by Phaedrus.

Menaechmi, by Titus Maccius Plautus (Plautus). This play is a comedy about twin brothers.

The Letters of Pliny the Younger, by Gaius Plinius Caecilius Secundus.

The Aeneid, by Publius Vergilius Maro.

Sermons, by Jacques de Vitry.

The Vulgate Bible, translated into Latin by St. Jerome